Intelligent Data Analysis: Challenges and Solutions

Intelligent Data Analysis: Challenges and Solutions

Editor: Mana Dixon

New York

Published by NY Research Press
118-35 Queens Blvd., Suite 400,
Forest Hills, NY 11375, USA
www.nyresearchpress.com

Intelligent Data Analysis: Challenges and Solutions
Edited by Mana Dixon

International Standard Book Number: 978-1-64725-372-1 (Hardback)

Cataloging-in-publication Data

Intelligent data analysis : challenges and solutions / edited by Mana Dixon.
    p. cm.
Includes bibliographical references and index.
ISBN 978-1-64725-372-1
1. Data mining. 2. Computational intelligence. 3. Database management. I. Dixon, Mana.
QA76.9.D343 I58 2023
006.312--dc23

Contents

Preface..VII

Chapter 1   **Vouw: Geometric Pattern Mining using the MDL Principle**............................1
Micky Faas and Matthijs van Leeuwen

Chapter 2   **Discriminative Bias for Learning Probabilistic Sentential Decision Diagrams**..14
Laura Isabel Galindez Olascoaga, Wannes Meert, Nimish Shah, Guy Van den Broeck and Marian Verhelst

Chapter 3   **Widening for MDL-Based Retail Signature Discovery**............................27
Clément Gautrais, Peggy Cellier, Matthijs van Leeuwen and Alexandre Termier

Chapter 4   **Estimating Uncertainty in Deep Learning for Reporting Confidence: An Application on Cell Type Prediction in Testes Based on Proteomics**..40
Biraja Ghoshal, Cecilia Lindskog and Allan Tucker

Chapter 5   **Digital Footprints of International Migration on Twitter**............................52
Jisu Kim, Alina Sîrbu, Fosca Giannotti and Lorenzo Gabrielli

Chapter 6   **A Late-Fusion Approach to Community Detection in Attributed Networks**..65
Chang Liu, Christine Largeron, Osmar R. Zaïane and Shiva Zamani Gharaghooshi

Chapter 7   **Actionable Subgroup Discovery and Urban Farm Optimization**............................78
Alexandre Millot, Romain Mathonat, Rémy Cazabet and Jean-François Boulicaut

Chapter 8   **Detection of Derivative Discontinuities in Observational Data**............................91
Dimitar Ninevski and Paul O'Leary

Chapter 9   **Aleatoric and Epistemic Uncertainty with Random Forests**............................104
Mohammad Hossein Shaker and Eyke Hüllermeier

Chapter 10   **Orometric Methods in Bounded Metric Data**............................116
Maximilian Stubbemann, Tom Hanika and Gerd Stumme

Chapter 11   **Making Learners (More) Monotone**............................129
Tom Julian Viering, Alexander Mey and Marco Loog

Chapter 12   **Dual Sequential Variational Autoencoders for Fraud Detection**..............................141
Ayman Alazizi, Amaury Habrard, François Jacquenet,
Liyun He-Guelton and Frédéric Oblé

Chapter 13   **AVATAR - Machine Learning Pipeline Evaluation using
Surrogate Model**...154
Tien-Dung Nguyen, Tomasz Maszczyk, Katarzyna Musial,
Marc-André Zöller and Bogdan Gabrys

Chapter 14   **Multivariate Time Series as Images: Imputation using
Convolutional Denoising Autoencoder**...167
Abdullah Al Safi, Christian Beyer, Vishnu Unnikrishnan and
Myra Spiliopoulou

Chapter 15   **GraphMDL: Graph Pattern Selection Based on Minimum
Description Length**...179
Francesco Bariatti, Peggy Cellier and Sébastien Ferré

Chapter 16   **Gibbs Sampling Subjectively Interesting Tiles**.......................................192
Anes Bendimerad, Jefrey Lijffijt, Marc Plantevit, Céline Robardet
and Tijl De Bie

Chapter 17   **Evaluation of CNN Performance in Semantically Relevant Latent
Spaces**..205
Jeroen van Doorenmalen and Vlado Menkovski

Chapter 18   **Addressing the Resolution Limit and the Field of View Limit in
Community Mining**...218
Shiva Zamani Gharaghooshi, Osmar R. Zaïane, Christine Largeron,
Mohammadmahdi Zafarmand and Chang Liu

Chapter 19   **Overlapping Hierarchical Clustering (OHC)**..230
Ian Jeantet, Zoltán Miklós and David Gross-Amblard

Permissions

List of Contributors

Index

Preface

This book aims to highlight the current researches and provides a platform to further the scope of innovations in this area. This book is a product of the combined efforts of many researchers and scientists, after going through thorough studies and analysis from different parts of the world. The objective of this book is to provide the readers with the latest information of the field.

Intelligent data analysis (IDA) is a method for discovering useful and intriguing information from data to aid in decision making. An IDA task comprises prediction, knowledge discovery, process or system modeling, and constructing knowledge based systems. There are numerous applications of IDA methods in various fields, including finance, marketing, agriculture, and medicine. The demand and availability of more advanced IDA methods has grown in response to the rapidly increasing volume of real-time data that is generated due to an increase in the usage of electronic commerce, web, and multimedia technologies. There are a number of challenges in the application of IDA methods in real-world, such as lack of tools suitable for large data, and lack of user friendly and effective post processing tools. The other challenges include lack of a truly integrated data analysis environment and lack of efficient and automatic preprocessing tools. This book elucidates the challenges and solutions with respect to intelligent data analysis. The topics covered herein offer the readers new insights on this subject.

I would like to express my sincere thanks to the authors for their dedicated efforts in the completion of this book. I acknowledge the efforts of the publisher for providing constant support. Lastly, I would like to thank my family for their support in all academic endeavors.

Editor

Vouw: Geometric Pattern Mining using the MDL Principle

Micky Faas[✉] and Matthijs van Leeuwen

LIACS, Leiden University, Leiden, The Netherlands
micky@edukitty.org, m.van.leeuwen@liacs.leidenuniv.nl

Abstract. We introduce geometric pattern mining, the problem of finding recurring local structure in discrete, geometric matrices. It differs from existing pattern mining problems by identifying complex spatial relations between elements, resulting in arbitrarily shaped patterns. After we formalise this new type of pattern mining, we propose an approach to selecting a set of patterns using the Minimum Description Length principle. We demonstrate the potential of our approach by introducing Vouw, a heuristic algorithm for mining exact geometric patterns. We show that Vouw delivers high-quality results with a synthetic benchmark.

1 Introduction

Frequent pattern mining [1] is the well-known subfield of data mining that aims to find and extract recurring substructures from data, as a form of knowledge discovery. The generic concept of pattern mining has been instantiated for many different types of patterns, e.g., for item sets (in Boolean transaction data) and subgraphs (in graphs/networks). Little research, however, has been done on pattern mining for raster-based data, i.e., geometric matrices in which the row and column orders are fixed. The exception is geometric tiling [4, 11], but that problem only considers tiles, i.e., rectangular-shaped patterns, in Boolean data.

In this paper we generalise this setting in two important ways. First, we consider geometric patterns *of any shape* that are geometrically connected, i.e., it must be possible to reach any element from any other element in a pattern by only traversing elements in that pattern. Second, we consider *discrete geometric data* with any number of possible values (which includes the Boolean case). We call the resulting problem *geometric pattern mining*.

Figure 1 illustrates an example of geometric pattern mining. Figure 1a shows a 32×24 grayscale 'geometric matrix', with each element in $[0, 255]$, apparently filled with noise. If we take a closer look at all horizontal pairs of elements, however, we find that the pair $(146, 11)$ is, amongst others, more prevalent than expected from 'random noise' (Fig. 1b). If we would continue to try all combinations of elements that 'stand out' from the background noise, we would eventually find four copies of the letter 'I' set in 16 point Garamond Italic (Fig. 1c).

(a) 32 × 24 'geometric matrix'.   (b) Pair (146, 11).   (c) Pattern 'I' occurs four times.

Fig. 1. Geometric pattern mining example. Each element is in $[0, 255]$.

The 35 elements that make up a single 'I' in the example form what we call a *geometric pattern*. Since its four occurrences jointly cover a substantial part of the matrix, we could use this pattern to describe the matrix more succinctly than by 768 independent values. That is, we could describe it as the pattern 'I' at locations $(5, 4), (11, 11), (20, 3), (25, 10)$ plus 628 independent values, hereby separating structure from accidental (noise) data. Since the latter description is shorter, we have compressed the data. At the same time we have learned something about the data, namely that it contains four I's. This suggests that we can use compression as a criterion to find patterns that describe the data.

Approach and Contributions. Our first contribution is that we introduce and formally define *geometric pattern mining*, i.e., the problem of finding recurring local structure in geometric, discrete matrices. Although we restrict the scope of this paper to two-dimensional data, the generic concept applies to higher dimensions. Potential applications include the analysis of satellite imagery, texture recognition, and (pattern-based) clustering.

We distinguish three types of geometric patterns: (1) *exact* patterns, which must appear exactly identical in the data to match; (2) *fault-tolerant* patterns, which may have noisy occurrences and are therefore better suited to noisy data; and (3) *transformation-equivalent* patterns, which are identical after some transformation (such as mirror, inverse, rotate, etc.). Each consecutive type makes the problem more expressive and hence more complex. In this initial paper we therefore restrict the scope to the first, exact type.

As many geometric patterns can be found in a typical matrix, it is crucial to find a compact set of patterns that together describe the structure in the data well. We regard this as a model selection problem, where a model is defined by a set of patterns. Following our observation above, that geometric patterns can be used to compress the data, our second contribution is the formalisation of the model selection problem by using the *Minimum Description Length (MDL) principle* [5,8]. Central to MDL is the notion that 'learning' can be thought of as 'finding regularity' and that regularity itself is a property of data that is exploited by *compressing* said data. This matches very well with the goals of pattern mining, as a result of which the MDL principle has proven very successful for MDL-based pattern mining [7,12].

Finally, our third contribution is Vouw, a heuristic algorithm for MDL-based geometric pattern mining that (1) finds compact yet descriptive sets of patterns, (2) requires no parameters, and (3) is tolerant to noise in the data (but not in the occurrences of the patterns). We empirically evaluate Vouw on synthetic data and demonstrate that it is able to accurately recover planted patterns.

2 Related Work

As the first pattern mining approach using the MDL principle, Krimp [12] was one of the main sources of inspiration for this paper. Many papers on pattern-based modelling using MDL have appeared since, both improving search, e.g., Slim [10], and extensions to other problems, e.g., Classy [7] for rule-based classification.

The problem closest to ours is probably that of geometric tiling, as introduced by Gionis et al. [4] and later also combined with the MDL principle by Tatti and Vreeken [11]. Geometric tiling, however, is limited to Boolean data and rectangularly shaped patterns (tiles); we strongly relax both these limitations (but as of yet do not support patterns based on densities or noisy occurrences).

Campana et al. [2] also use matrix-like data (textures) in a compression-based similarity measure. Their method, however, has less value for *explanatory* analysis as it relies on generic compression algorithms that are essentially a black box.

Geometric pattern mining is different from graph mining, although the concept of a matrix can be redefined as a grid-like graph where each node has a fixed degree. This is the approach taken by Deville et al. [3], solving a problem similar to ours but using an approach akin to bag-of-words instead of the MDL principle.

3 Geometric Pattern Mining Using MDL

We define geometric pattern mining on bounded, discrete and two-dimensional raster-based data. We represent this data as an $M \times N$ matrix A whose rows and columns are finite and in a fixed ordering (i.e., reordering rows and columns semantically alters the matrix). Each element $a_{i,j} \in S$, where row $i \in [0; N)$, column $j \in [0; M)$, and S is a finite set of symbols, i.e., the alphabet of A.

According to the MDL principle, the shortest (optimal) description of A reveals all structure of A in the most succinct way possible. This optimal description is only optimal if we can unambiguously reconstruct A from it and nothing more—the compression is both minimal and lossless. Figure 2 illustrates how an example matrix could be succinctly described using patterns: matrix A is decomposed into patterns X and Y. A set of such patterns constitutes the **model** for a matrix A, denoted H_A (or H for short when A is clear from the context). In order to reconstruct A from this model, we also need a mapping from the H_A back to A. This mapping represents what (two-part) MDL calls **the data given the model** H_A. In this context we can think of this as a set of all instructions required to rebuild A from H_A, which we call the **instantiation** of H_A and is denoted by I in the example. These concepts allow us to express matrix A as a decomposition into sets of local and global spatial information, which we will next describe in more detail.

$$A = \begin{bmatrix} 1 & \cdot & \cdot & \cdot & 1 & 1 \\ \cdot & 1 & 1 & 1 & 1 & \cdot \\ 1 & 1 & \cdot & \cdot & \cdot & 1 \end{bmatrix}, \ I = \begin{bmatrix} X & \cdot & \cdot & \cdot & Y & \cdot \\ \cdot & \cdot & Y & \cdot & X & \cdot \\ Y & \cdot & \cdot & \cdot & \cdot & \cdot \end{bmatrix}, \ H = \left\{ X = \begin{bmatrix} 1 & \cdot \\ \cdot & 1 \end{bmatrix}, Y = \begin{bmatrix} 1 & 1 \end{bmatrix} \right\}$$

Fig. 2. Example decomposition of A into instantiation I and patterns X, Y.

3.1 Patterns and Instances

▷ *We define a **pattern** as an $M_X \times N_X$ submatrix X of the original matrix A. Elements of this submatrix may be $\cdot$, the empty element, which gives us the ability to cut-out any irregular-shaped part of A. We additionally require the elements of X to be adjacent (horizontal, vertical or diagonal) to at least one non-empty element and that no rows and columns are empty.*

From this definition, the dimensions $M_X \times N_X$ give the smallest rectangle around X (the *bounding box*). We also define the cardinality $|X|$ of X as the number of non-empty elements. We call a pattern X with $|X| = 1$ a **singleton pattern**, i.e., a pattern containing exactly one element of A.

Each pattern contains a special **pivot** element: $pivot(X)$ is the first non-empty element of X. A pivot can be thought of as a fixed point in X which we can use to position its elements in relation to A. This translation, or **offset**, is a tuple $q = (i, j)$ that is on the same domain as an index in A. We realise this translation by placing all elements of X in an empty $M \times X$ size matrix such that the pivot element is at (i, j). We formalise this in the **instantiation operator** $\otimes$:

▷ *We define the **instance** $X \otimes (i, j)$ as the $M \times N$ matrix containing all elements of X such that $\mathrm{pivot}(X)$ is at index (i, j) and the distances between all elements are preserved. The resulting matrix contains no additional non-empty elements.*

Since this does not yield valid results for arbitrary offsets (i, j), we enforce two constraints: (1) an instance must be **well-defined**: placing $\mathrm{pivot}(X)$ at index (i, j) must result in an instance that contains all elements of X, and (2) elements of instances cannot *overlap*, i.e., each element of A can be described only once.

▷ *Two pattern instances $X \otimes q$ and $Y \otimes r$, with $q \neq r$ are **non-overlapping** if $|(X \otimes q) + (Y \otimes r)| = |X| + |Y|$.*

From here on we will use the same letter in lower case to denote an arbitrary instance of a pattern, e.g., $x = X \otimes q$ when the exact value of q is unimportant. Since instances are simply patterns projected onto an $M \times N$ matrix, we can reverse $\otimes$ by removing all completely empty rows and columns:

▷ *Let $X \otimes q$ be an instance of X, then by definition we say that $\oslash(X \otimes q) = X$.*

We briefly introduced the instantiation I as a set of 'instructions' of where instances of each pattern should be positioned in order to obtain A. As Fig. 2 suggests, this mapping has the shape of an $M \times N$ matrix.

▷ *Given a set of patterns H, the **instantiation (matrix)** I is an $M \times N$ matrix such that $I_{i,j} \in H \cup \{\cdot\}$ for all (i,j), where $\cdot$ denotes the empty element. For all non-empty $I_{i,j}$ it holds that $I_{i,j} \otimes (i,j)$ is a non-overlapping instance of $I_{i,j}$ in A.*

3.2 The Problem and Its Solution Space

Larger patterns can be naturally constructed by joining (or merging) smaller patterns in a bottom-up fashion. To limit the considered patterns to those relevant to A, instances can be used as an intermediate step. As Fig. 3 demonstrates, we can use a simple element-wise matrix addition to sum two instances and use $\oslash$ to obtain a joined pattern. Here we start by instantiating X and Y with offsets $(1,0)$ and $(1,1)$, respectively. We add the resulting x and y to obtain $\oslash z$, the union of X and Y with relative offset $(1,1) - (1,0) = (0,1)$.

$$x = X \otimes (1,0) = \begin{bmatrix} \cdot & \cdot \\ 1 & \cdot \\ \cdot & 1 \end{bmatrix}, \; y = Y \otimes (1,1) = \begin{bmatrix} \cdot & \cdot \\ \cdot & 1 \\ \cdot & \cdot \end{bmatrix}, x + y = \begin{bmatrix} \cdot & \cdot \\ 1 & 1 \\ \cdot & 1 \end{bmatrix}, \; Z = \oslash(x+y) = \begin{bmatrix} 1 & 1 \\ \cdot & 1 \end{bmatrix}$$

Fig. 3. Example of joining patterns X and Y to construct a new pattern Z.

The Sets $\mathcal{H}_A$ and $\mathcal{I}_A$. We define the **model class** $\mathcal{H}$ as the set of all possible models for all possible inputs. Without any prior knowledge, this would be the search space. To simplify the search, however, we only consider the more bounded subset $\mathcal{H}_A$ of all possible models for A, and $\mathcal{I}_A$, the set of all possible instantiations for these models. To this end we first define H_A^0 to be the model with only singleton patterns, i.e., $H_A^0 = S$, and denote its corresponding instantiation matrix by I_A^0. Given that each element of I_A^0 must correspond to exactly one element of A in H_A^0, we see that each $I_{i,j} = a_{i,j}$ and so we have $I_A^0 = A$.

Using H_A^0 and I_A^0 as base cases we can now inductively define $\mathcal{I}_A$:

Base case $I_A^0 \in \mathcal{I}_A$

By induction If I is in $\mathcal{I}_A$ then take any pair $I_{i,j}, I_{k,l} \in I$ such that $(i,j) \leq (k,l)$ in lexicographical order. Then the set I' is also in $\mathcal{I}_A$, providing I' equals I except:

$$I'_{i,j} := \oslash\left(I_{i,j} \otimes (i,j) + I_{k,l} \otimes (k,l)\right)$$
$$I'_{k,l} := \cdot$$

This shows we can add any two instances together, in any order, as they are by definition always non-overlapping and thus valid in A, and hereby obtain another element of $\mathcal{I}_A$. Eventually this results in just one big instance that is equal to A. Note that when we take two elements $I_{i,j}, I_{k,l} \in I$ we force $(i,j) \leq (k,l)$, not only to eliminate different routes to the same instance matrix, but also so that the pivot of the new pattern coincides with $I_{i,j}$. We can then leave $I_{k,l}$ empty.

The construction of $\mathcal{I}_A$ also implicitly defines $\mathcal{H}_A$. While this may seem odd—defining models for instantiations instead of the other way around—note that there is no unambiguous way to find one instantiation for a given model. Instead we find the following definition by applying the inductive construction:

$$\mathcal{H}_A = \{\{\oslash(x) \mid x \in I\} \mid I \in \mathcal{I}_A\}. \tag{1}$$

So for any instantiation $I \in \mathcal{I}_A$ there is a corresponding set in $\mathcal{H}_A$ of all patterns that occur in I. This results in an interesting symbiosis between model and instantiation: increasing the complexity of one decreases that of the other. This construction gives a tightly connected lattice as shown in Fig. 4.

3.3 Encoding Models and Instances

From all models in $\mathcal{H}_A$ we want to select the model that describes A best. Two-part MDL [5] tells us to choose that model that minimises the sum of $L_1(H_A) + L_2(A|H_A)$, where L_1 and L_2 are two functions that give the length of the model and the length of 'the data given the model', respectively. In this context, the data given the model is given by I_A, which represents the accidental information needed to reconstruct the data A from H_A.

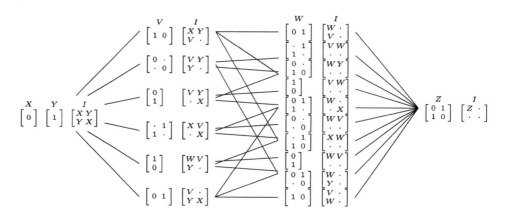

Fig. 4. Model space lattice for a 2×2 Boolean matrix. The V, W, and Z columns show which pattern is added in each step, while I depicts the current instantiation.

In order to compute their lengths, we need to decide how to encode H_A and I. As this encoding is of great influence on the outcome, we should adhere to the conditions that follow from MDL theory: (1) the model and data must be encoded losslessly; and (2) the encoding should be as concise as possible, i.e., it should be optimal. Note that for the purpose of model selection we only need the length functions; we do not need to actually encode the patterns or data.

Code Length Functions. Although the patterns in H and instantiation matrix I are all matrices, they have different characteristics and thus require different encodings. For example, the size of I is constant and can be ignored, while the

Table 1. Code length definitions. Each row specifies the code length given by the first column as the sum of the remaining terms.

	Matrix	Bounds	# Elements	Positions	Symbols
$L_p(X)$	Pattern	$\log(MN)$	$L_N\binom{M_X N_X}{\|X\|}$		$\|X\|\log(\|S\|)$
$L_1(H)$	Model	N/A	$L_N(\|H\|)$	N/A	$\sum_{X \in H} L_p(X)$
$L_2(I)$	Instantiation	$Constant$	$\log(MN)$	$Implicit$	$L_{pp}(I)$

sizes of the patterns vary and should be encoded. Hence we construct different length functions[1] for the different components of H and I, as listed in Table 1.

When encoding I, we observe that it contains each pattern $X \in H$ multiple times, given by the **usage** of X. Using the **prequential plug-in code** [5] to encode I enables us to omit encoding these usages separately, which would create unwanted bias. The prequential plug-in code gives us the following length function for I. We use $\epsilon = 0.5$ and elaborate on its derivation in the Appendix[2].

$$L_{pp}(I \mid P_{plugin}) = - \sum_{X_i \in h}^{|H|} \left[\log \frac{\Gamma(\text{usage}(X_i) + \epsilon)}{\Gamma(\epsilon)} \right] + \log \frac{\Gamma(|I| + \epsilon|H|)}{\Gamma(\epsilon|H|)} \quad (2)$$

Each length function has four terms. First we encode the total size of the matrix. Since we assume MN to be known/constant, we can use this constant to define the uniform distribution $\frac{1}{MN}$, so that $\log MN$ encodes an arbitrary index of A. Next we encode the number of elements that are non-empty. For patterns this value is encoded together with the third term, namely the positions of the non-empty elements. We use the previously encoded $M_X N_X$ in the binominal function to enumerate the ways we can place the $|X|$ elements onto a grid of $M_X N_X$. This gives us both *how many* non-empties there are as well as *where* they are. Finally the fourth term is the length of the actual symbols that encode the elements of the matrix. In case we encode single elements of A, we assume that each unique value in A occurs with equal probability; without other prior knowledge, using the uniform distribution has minimax regret and is therefore optimal. For the instance matrix, which encodes symbols to patterns, the prequential code is used as demonstrated before. Note that L_N is the universal prior for the integers [9], which can be used for arbitrary integers and penalises larger integers.

4 The Vouw Algorithm

Pattern mining often yields vast search spaces and geometric pattern mining is no exception. We therefore use a heuristic approach, as is common in MDL-based approaches [7,10,12]. We devise a greedy algorithm that exploits the inductive

---

[1] We calculate code lengths in bits and therefore all logarithms have base 2.
[2] The appendix is available on https://arxiv.org/abs/1911.09587.

definition of the search space as shown by the lattice in Fig. 4. We start with a completely underfit model (leftmost in the lattice), where there is one instance for each matrix element. Next, in each iteration we combine two patterns, resulting in one or more pairs of instances to be merged (i.e., we move one step right in the lattice). In each step we merge the pair of patterns that improves compression most, and we repeat this until no improvement is possible.

4.1 Finding Candidates

The first step is to find the 'best' **candidate** pair of patterns for merging (Algorithm 1). A candidate is denoted as a tuple (X, Y, δ), where X and Y are patterns and δ is the relative offset of X and Y as they occur in the data. Since we only need to consider pairs of patterns and offsets that actually occur in the instance matrix, we can directly enumerate candidates from the instantiation matrix and never even need to consider the original data.

Algorithm 1 FindCandidates	**Algorithm 2** Vouw
Input: I	**Input:** H, I
Output: C	1: $C \leftarrow$ FindCandidates(I)
1: **for all** $x \in I$ **do**	2: $(X, Y, \delta) \in C : \forall_{c \in C} \Delta L((X, Y, \delta)) \leq \Delta L(c)$
2: **for all** $y \in \text{POST}(x)$ **do**	3: $\Delta L_{best} = \Delta L((X, Y, \delta))$
3: $X \leftarrow \oslash(x), \ Y \leftarrow \oslash(y)$	4: **if** $\Delta L_{best} > 0$ **then**
4: $\delta \leftarrow \text{dist}(X, Y)$	5: $Z \leftarrow \oslash(X \otimes (0,0) + (Y \otimes \delta))$
5: **if** $X = Y$ **then**	6: $H \leftarrow H \cup \{Z\}$
6: **if** $V(x)[e] = 1$ **continue**	7: **for all** $x_i \in I \mid \oslash(x_i) = X$ **do**
7: $V(y)[e] \leftarrow 1$	8: **for all** $y \in \text{POST}(x_i) \mid \oslash(y) = Y$ **do**
8: **end if**	9: $x_i \leftarrow Z, y \leftarrow \cdot$
9: $C \leftarrow C \cup (X, Y, \delta)$	10: **end for**
10: $\sup(X, Y, \delta) \mathrel{+}= 1$	11: **end for**
11: **end for**	12: **end if**
12: **end for**	13: **repeat until** $\Delta L_{best} < 0$

The **support** of a candidate, written $\sup(X, Y, \delta)$, tells how often it is found in the instance matrix. Computing support is not completely trivial, as one candidate occurs multiple times in 'mirrored' configurations, such as (X, Y, δ) and $(Y, X, -\delta)$, which are equivalent but can still be found separately. Furthermore, due to the definition of a pattern, many potential candidates cannot be considered by the simple fact that their elements are not adjacent.

Peripheries. For each instance x we define its *periphery*: the set of instances which are positioned such that their union with x produces a valid pattern. This set is split into *anterior* $\text{ANT}(X)$ and *posterior* $\text{POST}(X)$ peripheries, containing instances that come before and after x in lexicographical order, respectively. This enables us to scan the instance matrix once, in lexicographical order. For each instance x, we only consider the instances $\text{POST}(x)$ as candidates, thereby eliminating any (mirrored) duplicates.

Self-overlap. Self-overlap happens for candidates of the form (X, X, δ). In this case, too many or too few copies may be counted. Take for example a straight line of five instances of X. There are four unique pairs of two X's, but only two can be merged at a time, in three different ways. Therefore, when considering candidates of the form (X, X, δ), we also compute an *overlap coefficient*. This coefficient e is given by $e = (2N_X + 1)\delta_i + \delta_j + N_X$, which essentially transforms δ into a one-dimensional coordinate space of all possible ways that X could be arranged *after* and *adjacent* to itself. For each instance x_1 a vector of bits $V(x)$ is used to remember if we have already encountered a combination x_1, x_2 with coefficient e, such that we do not count a combination x_2, x_3 with an equal e. This eliminates the problem of incorrect counting due to self-overlap.

4.2 Gain Computation

After candidate search we have a set of candidates C and their respective supports. The next step is to select the candidate that gives the best *gain*: the improvement in compression by merging the candidate pair of patterns. For each candidate $c = (X, Y, \delta)$ the gain $\Delta L(A', c)$ is comprised of two parts: (1) the negative gain of adding the union pattern Z to the model H, resulting in H', and (2) the gain of replacing all instances x, y with relative offset δ by Z in I, resulting in I'. We use length functions L_1, L_2 to derive an equation for gain:

$$\Delta L(A', c) = \Big(L_1(H') + L_2(I') \Big) - \Big(L_1(H) + L_2(I) \Big)$$
$$= L_N(|H|) - L_N(|H| + 1) - L_p(Z) + \Big(L_2(I') - L_2(I) \Big) \tag{3}$$

As we can see, the terms with L_1 are simplified to $-L_p(Z)$ and the model's length because L_1 is simply a summation of individual pattern lengths. The equation of L_2 requires the recomputation of the entire instance matrix' length, which is expensive considering we need to perform it for *every candidate, every iteration*. However, we can rework the function L_{pp} in Eq. (2) by observing that we can isolate the logarithms and generalise them into

$$\log_G(a, b) = \log \frac{\Gamma(a + b\epsilon)}{\Gamma(b\epsilon)} = \log \Gamma(a + b\epsilon) - \log \Gamma(b\epsilon), \tag{4}$$

which can be used to rework the second part of Eq. (3) in such way that the gain equation can be computed in constant time complexity.

$$L_2(I') - L_2(I) = \log_G(U(X), 1) + \log_G(U(Y), 1)$$
$$- \log_G(U(X) - U(Z), 1) - \log_G(U(Y) - U(Z), 1) \tag{5}$$
$$- \log_G(U(Z), 1) + \log_G(|I|, |H|) - \log_G(|I'|, |H'|)$$

Notice that in some cases the usages of X and Y are equal to that of Z, which means additional gain is created by removing X and Y from the model.

4.3 Mining a Set of Patterns

In the second part of the algorithm, listed in Algorithm 2, we select the candidate (X, Y, δ) with the largest gain and merge X and Y to form Z, as explained in Sect. 3.2. We linearly traverse I to replace all instances x and y with relative offset δ by instances of Z. (X, Y, δ) was constructed by looking in the posterior periphery of all x to find Y and δ, which means that Y always comes after X in lexicographical order. The pivot of a pattern is the first element in lexicographical order, therefore $\text{pivot}(Z) = \text{pivot}(X)$. This means that we can replace all matching x with an instance of Z and all matching y with $\cdot$.

4.4 Improvements

Local Search. To improve the efficiency of finding large patterns without sacrificing the underlying idea of the original heuristics, we add an optional local search. Observe that without local search, Vouw generates a large pattern X

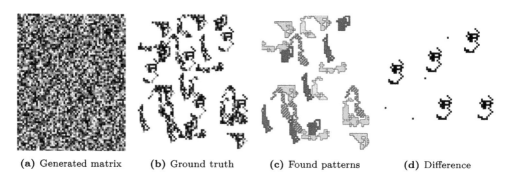

(a) Generated matrix   (b) Ground truth   (c) Found patterns   (d) Difference

Fig. 5. Synthetic patterns are added to a matrix filled with noise. The difference between the ground truth and the matrix reconstructed by the algorithm is used to compute precision and recall.

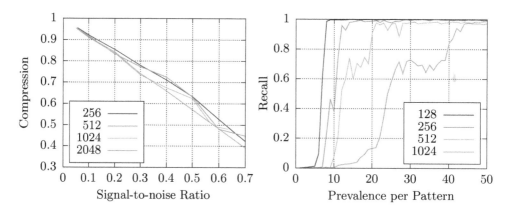

Fig. 6. The influence of SNR in the ground truth (left) and prevalence on recall (right)

by adding small elements to an incrementally growing pattern, resulting in a behaviour that requires up to $|X| - 1$ steps. To speed this up, we can try to 'predict' which elements will be added to X and add them immediately. After selecting candidate (X, Y, δ) and merging X and Y into Z, for all m resulting instances $z_i \in z_0, \dots, z_{m-1}$ we try to find pattern W and offset δ such that

$$\forall_{i \in 0 \dots m} \exists_w \in \text{ANT}(z_i) \cup \text{POST}(z_i) \ \cdot \ \oslash(w) = W \wedge dist(z_i, w) = \delta. \quad (6)$$

This yields zero or more candidates (Z, W, δ), which are then treated as any set of candidates: candidates with the highest gain are iteratively merged until no candidates with positive gain exist. This essentially means that we run the baseline algorithm only on the peripheries of all z_i, with the condition that the support of the candidates is equal to that of Z.

Reusing Candidates. We can improve performance by reusing the candidate set and slightly changing the search heuristic of the algorithm. The **Best-*** heuristic selects multiple candidates on each iteration, as opposed to the baseline **Best-1** heuristic that only selects a single candidate with the highest gain. Best-* selects candidates in descending order of gain until no candidates with positive gain are left. Furthermore we only consider candidates that are all *disjoint*, because when we merge candidate (X, Y, δ), remaining candidates with X and/or Y have unknown support and therefore unknown gain.

5 Experiments

To asses Vouw's practical performance we primarily use Ril, a synthetic dataset generator developed for this purpose. Ril utilises random walks to populate a matrix with patterns of a given size and prevalence, up to a specified density, while filling the remainder of the matrix with noise. Both the pattern elements and the noise are picked from the same uniform random distribution on the interval $[0, 255]$. The *signal-to-noise ratio* (SNR) of the data is defined as the number of pattern elements over the matrix size MN. The objective of the experiment is to assess whether Vouw recovers all of the signal (the patterns) and none of the noise. Figure 5 gives an example of the generated data and how it is evaluated. A more extensive description can be found in the Appendix (see footnote 2).

Implementation. The implementation[3] used consists of the Vouw algorithm (written in vanilla C/C++), a GUI, and the synthetic benchmark Ril. Experiments were performed on an Intel Xeon-E2630v3 with 512 GB RAM.

Evaluation. Completely random data (noise) is unlikely to be compressed. The SNR tells us how much of the data is noise and thus conveniently gives us an upper bound of how much compression could be achieved. We use the ground truth SNR versus the resulting compression ratio as a benchmark to tell us how close we are to finding all the structure in the ground truth.

---

[3] https://github.com/mickymuis/libvouw.

In addition, we also compare the ground truth matrix to the obtained model and instantiation. As singleton patterns do not yield any compression over the baseline model, we reconstruct the matrix omitting any singleton patterns. Ignoring the actual values, this gives us a Boolean matrix with 'positives' (pattern occurrence = signal) and 'negatives' (no pattern = noise). By comparing each element in this matrix with the corresponding element in the ground truth matrix, *precision* and *recall* can be calculated and evaluated.

Figure 6 (left) shows the influence of ground truth SNR on compression ratio for different matrix sizes. Compression ratio and SNR are clearly strongly correlated. Figure 6 (right) shows that patterns with a low prevalence (i.e., number of planted occurrences) have a lower probability of being 'detected' by the algorithm as they are more likely to be accidental/noise. Increasing the matrix size also increases this threshold. In Table 2 we look at the influence of the two improvements upon the baseline algorithm as described in Sect. 4.4. In terms of quality, local search can improve the results quite substantially while Best-* notably *lowers* precision. Both improve speed by an order of magnitude.

Table 2. Performance measurements for the baseline algorithm and its optimisations.

Size	SNR	Precision/Recall				Average time			
		None	Local	Best-*	Both	None	Local	Best-*	Both
256	.05	.98/.98	.99/.99	.93/.98	.95/.99	29 s	1 s	2 s	1 s
	.3	.99/.8	.99/.88	.96/.82	.99/.89	2 m 32 s	9 s	5 s	5 s
512	.05	.98/.97	.99/.99	.87/.97	.93/.98	5 m 26 s	8 s	20 s	6 s
	.3	.97/.93	.99/.99	.94/.91	.97/.90	26 m 52 s	2 m 32 s	24 s	65 s
1024	.05	.97/.98	.99/.99	.84/.98	.92/.96	21 m 34 s	44 s	37 s	34 s
	.3	.98/.98	.99/.99	.93/.96	.98/.97	116 m 4s	7m 31 s	1 m 49 s	3 m 31 s

6   Conclusions

We introduced geometric pattern mining, the problem of finding recurring structures in discrete, geometric matrices, or raster-based data. Further, we presented Vouw, a heuristic algorithm for finding sets of geometric patterns that are good descriptions according to the MDL principle. It is capable of accurately recovering patterns from synthetic data, and the resulting compression ratios are on par with the expectations based on the density of the data. For the future, we think that extensions to fault-tolerant patterns and clustering have large potential.

References

1. Aggarwal, C.C., Han, J.: Frequent Pattern Mining. Springer, Cham (2014). https://doi.org/10.1007/978-3-319-07821-2
2. Bilson, J.L.C., Keogh, E.J.: A compression-based distance measure for texture. Statistical Analysis and Data Mining **3**(6), 381–398 (2010)

3. Deville, R., Fromont, E., Jeudy, B., Solnon, C.: GriMa: a grid mining algorithm for bag-of-grid-based classification. In: Robles-Kelly, A., Loog, M., Biggio, B., Escolano, F., Wilson, R. (eds.) S+SSPR 2016. LNCS, vol. 10029, pp. 132–142. Springer, Cham (2016). https://doi.org/10.1007/978-3-319-49055-7_12
4. Gionis, A., Mannila, H., Seppänen, J.K.: Geometric and combinatorial tiles in 0–1 data. In: Boulicaut, J.-F., Esposito, F., Giannotti, F., Pedreschi, D. (eds.) PKDD 2004. LNCS (LNAI), vol. 3202, pp. 173–184. Springer, Heidelberg (2004). https://doi.org/10.1007/978-3-540-30116-5_18
5. Grünwald, P.D.: The Minimum Description Length Principle. MIT press, Cambridge (2007)
6. Li, M., Vitányi, P.: An Introduction to Kolmogorov Complexity and Its Applications. TCS, vol. 3. Springer, New York (2008). https://doi.org/10.1007/978-0-387-49820-1
7. Proença, H.M., van Leeuwen, M.: Interpretable multiclass classification by MDL-based rule lists. Inf. Sci. 12, 1372–1393 (2020)
8. Rissanen, J.: Modeling by shortest data description. Automatica 14(5), 465–471 (1978)
9. Rissanen, J.: A universal prior for integers and estimation by minimum description length. Ann. Stat. 11, 416–431 (1983)
10. Smets, K., Vreeken, J.: Slim: directly mining descriptive patterns. In: Proceedings of the 2012 SIAM International Conference on Data Mining, SIAM, pp. 236–247 (2012)
11. Tatti, N., Vreeken, J.: Discovering descriptive tile trees - by mining optimal geometric subtiles. In: Proceedings of ECML PKDD 2012, pp. 9–24 (2012)
12. Vreeken, J., van Leeuwen, M., Siebes, A.: KRIMP: mining itemsets that compress. Data Min. Knowl. Disc. 23(1), 169–214 (2011)

Discriminative Bias for Learning Probabilistic Sentential Decision Diagrams

Laura Isabel Galindez Olascoaga[1]([✉]), Wannes Meert[2], Nimish Shah[1], Guy Van den Broeck[3], and Marian Verhelst[1]

[1] Electrical Engineering Department, KU Leuven, Leuven, Belgium
{laura.galindez,nimish.shah,marian.verhelst}@esat.kuleuven.be
[2] Computer Science Department, KU Leuven, Leuven, Belgium
wannes.meert@cs.kuleuven.be
[3] Computer Science Department, University of California, Los Angeles, USA
guyvdb@cs.ucla.edu

Abstract. Methods that learn the structure of Probabilistic Sentential Decision Diagrams (PSDD) from data have achieved state-of-the-art performance in tractable learning tasks. These methods learn PSDDs incrementally by optimizing the likelihood of the induced probability distribution given available data and are thus robust against missing values, a relevant trait to address the challenges of embedded applications, such as failing sensors and resource constraints. However PSDDs are outperformed by discriminatively trained models in classification tasks. In this work, we introduce D-LEARNPSDD, a learner that improves the classification performance of the LEARNPSDD algorithm by introducing a discriminative bias that encodes the conditional relation between the class and feature variables.

Keywords: Probabilistic models · Tractable inference · PSDD

1 Introduction

Probabilistic machine learning models have shown to be a well suited approach to address the challenges inherent to embedded applications, such as the need to handle uncertainty and missing data [11]. Moreover, current efforts in the field of Tractable Probabilistic Modeling have been making great strides towards successfully balancing the trade-offs between model performance and inference efficiency: probabilistic circuits, such as Probabilistic Sentential Decision Diagrams (PSDDs), Sum-Product Networks (SPNs), Arithmetic Circuits (ACs) and Cutset Networks, posses myriad desirable properties [4] that make them amenable to application scenarios where strict resource budget constraints must be met [12]. But these models' robustness against missing data—from learning them generatively—is often at odds with their discriminative capabilities.

We address such a conflict by proposing a discriminative-generative probabilistic circuit learning strategy, which aims to improve the models' discriminative capabilities, while maintaining their robustness against missing features.

We focus in particular on the PSDD [17], a state-of-the-art tractable representation that encodes a joint probability distribution over a set of random variables. Previous work [12] has shown how to learn hardware-efficient PSDDs that remain robust to missing data and noise. This approach relies largely on the LEARNPSDD algorithm [20], a generative algorithm that incrementally learns the structure of a PSDD from data. Moreover, it has been shown how to exploit such robustness to trade off resource usage with accuracy. And while the achieved accuracy is competitive when compared to Bayesian Network classifiers, discriminatively learned models perform consistently better than purely generative models [21] since the latter remain agnostic to the discriminative task they ought to perform. This begs the question of whether the discriminative performance of the PSDD could be improved while remaining robust and tractable.

In this work, we propose a hybrid discriminative-generative PSDD learning strategy, D-LEARNPSDD, that enforces the discriminative relationship between class and feature variables by capitalizing on the model's ability to encode domain knowledge as a logic formula. We show that this approach consistently outperforms the purely generative PSDD and is competitive compared to other classifiers, while remaining robust to missing values at test time.

2 Background

Notation. Variables are denoted by upper case letters X and their instantiations by lower case letters x. Sets of variables are denoted in bold upper case $\mathbf{X}$ and their joint instantiations in bold lower case $\mathbf{x}$. For the classification task, the feature set is denoted by $\mathbf{F}$ while the class variable is denoted by C.

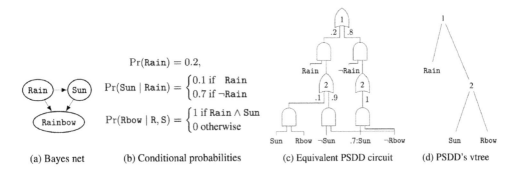

Fig. 1. A Bayesian network and its equivalent PSDD (taken from [20]).

PSDD. Probabilistic Sentential Decision Diagrams (PSDDs) are circuit representations of joint probability distributions over binary random variables [17]. They were introduced as probabilistic extensions to Sentential Decision Diagrams (SDDs) [7], which represent Boolean functions as logical circuits. The inner nodes of a PSDD alternate between AND gates with two inputs and OR gates with arbitrary number of inputs; the root must be an OR node; and each leaf node encodes a distribution over a variable X (see Fig. 1c). The combination of an OR gate with its AND gate inputs is referred to as *decision* node, where the left input of the AND gate is called *prime* (p), and the right is called *sub* (s). Each of the n edges of a decision node are annotated with a normalized probability distribution $\theta_1, ..., \theta_n$.

PSDDs possess two important syntactic restrictions: (1) Each AND node must be *decomposable*, meaning that its input variables must be disjoint. This property is enforced by a *vtree*, a binary tree whose leaves are the random variables and which determines how will variables be arranged in primes and subs in the PSDD (see Fig. 1d): each internal vtree node is associated with the PSDD nodes at the same level, variables appearing in the left subtree $\mathbf{X}$ are the primes and the ones appearing in the right subtree $\mathbf{Y}$ are the subs. (2) Each decision node must be *deterministic*, thus only one of its inputs can be true.

Each PSDD node q represents a probability distribution. Terminal nodes encode a univariate distributions. Decision nodes, when normalized for a vtree node with $\mathbf{X}$ in its left subtree and $\mathbf{Y}$ in its right subtree, encode the following distribution over $\mathbf{XY}$ (see also Fig. 1a and c):

$$Pr_q(\mathbf{XY}) = \sum_i \theta_i Pr_{p_i}(\mathbf{X}) Pr_{s_i}(\mathbf{Y}) \tag{1}$$

Thus, each decision node decomposes the distribution into independent distributions over $\mathbf{X}$ and $\mathbf{Y}$. In general, prime and sub variables are independent at PSDD node q given the prime *base* $[q]$ [17]. This base is the support of the node's distribution, over which it defines a non-zero probability and it is written as a logical sentence using the recursion $[q] = \bigvee_i [p_i] \wedge [s_i]$. Kisa et al. [17] show that prime and sub variables are independent in PSDD node q given a prime base:

$$\begin{aligned} Pr_q(\mathbf{XY}|[p_i]) &= Pr_{p_i}(\mathbf{X}|[p_i]) Pr_{s_i}(\mathbf{Y}|[p_i]) \\ &= Pr_{p_i}(\mathbf{X}) Pr_{s_i}(\mathbf{Y}) \end{aligned} \tag{2}$$

This equation encodes *context specific independence* [2], where variables (or sets of variables) are independent given a logical sentence. The structural constraints of the PSDD are meant to exploit such independencies, leading to a representation that can answer a number of complex queries in polynomial time [1], which is not guaranteed when performing inference on Bayesian Networks, as they don't encode and therefore can't exploit such local structures.

LearnPSDD. The LEARNPSDD algorithm [20] generatively learns a PSDD by maximizing log-likelihood given available data. The algorithm starts by learning a *vtree* that minimizes the mutual information among all possible sets of variables. This vtree is then used to guide the PSDD structure learning stage, which relies on the iterative application of the Split and Clone operations [20]. These operations keep the PSDD syntactically sound while improving likelihood of the distribution represented by the PSDD. A problem with LEARNPSDD when using the resulting model for classification is that when the class variable is only weakly dependent on the features, the learner may choose to ignore that dependency, potentially rendering the model unfit for classification tasks.

3 A Discriminative Bias for PSDD Learning

Generative learners such as LEARNPSDD optimize the likelihood of the distribution given available data rather than the conditional likelihood of the class variable C given a full set of feature variables $\mathbf{F}$. As a result, their accuracy is often worse than that of simple models such as Naive Bayes (NB), and its close relative Tree Augmented Naive Bayes (TANB) [12], which perform surprisingly well on classification tasks even though they encode a simple—or naive—structure [10]. One of the main reasons for their performance, despite being generative, is that (TA)NB models have a discriminative bias that directly encodes the conditional dependence of all the features on the class variable.

We introduce D-LEARNPSDD, an extension to LEARNPSDD based on the insight that the learned model should satisfy the "class conditional constraint" present in Bayesian Network classifiers. That is, all feature variables must be conditioned on the class variable. This enforces a structure that is beneficial for classification while still allowing to generatively learn a PSDD that encodes the distribution over all variables using a state-of-the-art learning strategy [20].

3.1 Discriminative Bias

The classification task can be stated as a probabilistic query:

$$\Pr(C|\mathbf{F}) \sim \Pr(\mathbf{F}|C) \cdot \Pr(C). \tag{3}$$

Our goal is to learn a PSDD whose root decision node directly represents the conditional probability distribution $\Pr(\mathbf{F}|C)$. This can be achieved by forcing the primes of the first line in Eq. 2 to be $[p_0] = [\neg c]$ and $[p_1] = [c]$, where $[c]$ states that the propositional variable c representing the class variable is true (i.e. $C = 1$), and similarly $[\neg c]$ represents $C = 0$. For now we assume the class is binary and will show later how to generalize to a multi-valued class variable. For the feature variables we can assume they are binary without loss of generality since a multi-valued variable can be converted to a set of binary variables via a one-hot encoding (see, for example [20]). To achieve our goal we first need the following proposition:

Proposition 1. *Given (i) a vtree with a single variable C as the prime and variables $\mathbf{F}$ as the sub of the root node, and (ii) an initial PSDD where the root decision node decomposes the distribution as $[root] = ([p_0] \wedge [s_0]) \vee ([p_1] \wedge [s_1])$; applying the Split and Clone operators will never change the root decision decomposition $[root] = ([p_0] \wedge [s_0]) \vee ([p_1] \wedge [s_1])$.*

Proof. The D-LEARNPSDD algorithm iteratively applies two operations: Clone and Split (following the algorithm in [20]). First, the Clone operator requires a parent node, which is not available for the root node. Since the initial PSDD follows the logical formula described above, whose only restriction is on the root node, there is no parent available to clone and the root's base thus remains intact when applying the Clone operator. Second, the Split operator splits one of the subs to extend the sentence that is used to mutually exclusively and exhaustively define all children. Since the given vtree has only one variable, C, as the prime of the root node, there are no other variables available to add to the sub. The Split operator cant thus not be applied anymore and the root's base stays intact (see Figs. 1c and d).

We can now show that the resulting PSDD contains nodes that directly represent the distribution $\Pr(\mathbf{F}|C)$.

Proposition 2. *A PSDD of the form* $[root] = ([\neg c] \wedge [s_0]) \vee ([c] \wedge [s_1])$ *with c the propositional variable stating that the class variable is true, and s_0 and s_1 any formula with propositional feature variables $f_0, \ldots, f_n$, directly expresses the distribution* $\Pr(\mathbf{F}|C)$.

Proof. Applying this to Eq. 1 results in:

$$\Pr_q(C\mathbf{F}) = \Pr_{\neg c}(C)\Pr_{s_0}(\mathbf{F}) + \Pr_c(C)\Pr_{s_1}(\mathbf{F})$$
$$= \Pr_{\neg c}(C|[\neg c]) \cdot \Pr_{s_0}(\mathbf{F}|[\neg c]) + \Pr_c(C|[c]) \cdot \Pr_{s_1}(\mathbf{F}|[c])$$
$$= \Pr_{\neg c}(C = 0) \cdot \Pr_{s_0}(\mathbf{F}|C = 0) + \Pr_c(C = 1) \cdot \Pr_{s_1}(\mathbf{F}|C = 1)$$

The learned PSDD thus contains a node s_0 with distribution $\Pr_{s_0}$ that directly represents $\Pr(\mathbf{F}|C = 0)$ and a node s_1 with distribution $\Pr_{s_1}$ that represents $\Pr(\mathbf{F}|C = 1)$. The PSDD thus encodes $\Pr(\mathbf{F}|C)$ directly because the two possible value assignments of C are $C = 0$ and $C = 1$.

The following examples illustrate why both the specific vtree and initial PSDD are required.

Example 1. Figure 2b shows a PSDD that encodes a fully factorized probability distribution normalized for the vtree in Fig. 2a. The PSDD shown in this example initializes the incremental learning procedure of LEARNPSDD [20]. Note that the vtree does not connect the class variable C to all feature variables (e.g. F_1). Therefore, when initializing the algorithm on this vtree-PSDD combination, there are no guarantees that the conditional relations between certain features and the class will be learned.

Example 2. Figure 2e shows a PSDD that explicitly conditions the feature variables on the class variables by normalizing for the vtree in Fig. 2c and by following the logical formula from Proposition 2. This biased PSDD is then used to initialize the D-LEARNPSDD learner. Note that the vtree in Fig. 2c forces the prime of the root node to be the class variable C.

Example 3. Figure 2d shows, however, that only setting the vtree in Fig. 2c is not sufficient for the learner to condition the features on the class. When initializing on a PSDD that encodes a fully factorized formula, and then applying the Split and Clone operators, the relationship between the class variable and the features are not guaranteed to be learned. In this worst case scenario, the learned model could have an even worse performance than the case from Example 1. By applying Eq. 1 on the top split, we can give intuition why this is the case:

$$\Pr_q(C\mathbf{F}) = \Pr_{p_0}(C|[c \vee \neg c]) \cdot \Pr_{s_0}(\mathbf{F}|[c \vee \neg c])$$
$$= (\Pr_{p_1}(C|[c]) + \Pr_{p_2}(C|[\neg c])) \cdot \Pr_{s_0}(\mathbf{F}|[c \vee \neg c])$$
$$= (\Pr_{p_1}(C = 1) + \Pr_{p_2}(C = 0)) \cdot \Pr_{s_0}(\mathbf{F})$$

The PSDD thus encodes a distribution that assumes that the class variable is independent from all feature variables. While this model might still have a high likelihood, its classification accuracy will be low.

We have so far introduced the D-LEARNPSDD for a binary classification task. However, it can be easily generalized to an n-valued classification scenario: (1) The class variable C will be represented by multiple propositional variables $c_0, c_1, \ldots, c_n$ that represent the set $C = 0, C = 1, \ldots, C = n$, of which exactly one will be true at all times. (2) The vtree in Proposition 1 now starts as a right-linear tree over $c_0, \ldots, c_n$. The $\mathbf{F}$ variables are the sub of the node that has c_n as prime. (3) The initial PSDD in Proposition 2 now has a root the form $[root] = \bigvee_{i=0\ldots n}([c_i \bigwedge_{j:0\ldots n \wedge i \neq j} \neg c_j] \wedge [s_i])$, which remains the same after applying Split and Clone. The root decision node now represents the distribution $\Pr_q(C\mathbf{F}) = \sum_{i:0\ldots n} \Pr_{c_i \bigwedge_{j \neq i} \neg c_j}(C = i) \cdot \Pr_{s_i}(\mathbf{F}|C = i)$ and therefore has nodes at the top of the tree that directly represent the discriminative bias.

3.2 Generative Bias

Learning the distribution over the feature variables is a generative learning process and we can achieve this by applying the Split and Clone operators in the same way as the original LEARNPSDD algorithm. In the previous section we had not yet defined how should $\Pr(\mathbf{F}|C)$ from Proposition 2 be represented in the initial PSDD, we only explained how our constraint enforces it. So the question is how do we exactly define the nodes corresponding to s_0 and s_1 with distributions $\Pr(\mathbf{F}|C = 0)$ and $\Pr(\mathbf{F}|C = 1)$? We follow the intuition behind (TA)NB and start with a PSDD that encodes a distribution where all feature variables are independent given the class variable (see Fig. 2e). Next, the LEARNPSDD algorithm will incrementally learn the relations between the feature variables by applying the Split and Clone operations following the approach in [20].

3.3 Obtaining the Vtree

In LEARNPSDD, the decision nodes decompose the distribution into independent distributions. Thus, the vtree is learned from data by maximizing the approximate pairwise mutual information, as this metric quantifies the level of independence between two sets of variables. For D-LEARNPSDD we are interested in the level of conditional independence between sets of feature variables given the class variable. We thus obtain the vtree by optimizing for Conditional Mutual Information instead and replace mutual information in the approach in [20] with:

$$CMI(\mathbf{X}, \mathbf{Y}|\mathbf{Z}) = \sum_{\mathbf{x}} \sum_{\mathbf{y}} \sum_{\mathbf{z}} \Pr(\mathbf{xy}) \log \frac{\Pr(\mathbf{z}) \Pr(\mathbf{xyz})}{\Pr(\mathbf{xz}) \Pr(\mathbf{yz})}.$$

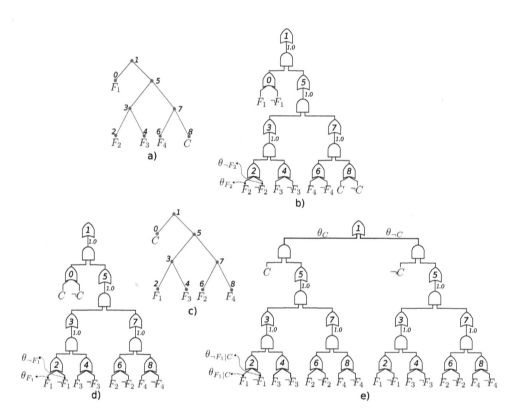

Fig. 2. Examples of vtrees and initial PSDDs.

4   Experiments

We compare the performance of D-LEARNPSDD, LEARNPSDD, two generative Bayesian classifiers (NB and TANB) and a discriminative classifier (logistic regression). In particular, we discuss the following research queries: (1) Sect. 4.2 examines whether the introduced discriminative bias improves classification performance on PSDDs. (2) Sect. 4.3 analyzes the impact of the vtree and the imposed structural constraints on model tractability and performance. (3) Finally, Sect. 4.4 compares the robustness to missing values for all classification approaches.

Table 1. Datasets

Dataset	$|\mathbf{F}|$	$|C|$	$|N|$
Australian	40	2	690
Breast	28	2	683
Chess	39	2	3196
Cleve	25	2	303
Corral	6	2	160
Credit	42	2	653
Diabetes	11	2	768
German	54	2	1000
Glass	17	6	214
Heart	9	2	270
Iris	12	3	150
Mofn	10	2	1324
Pima	11	2	768
Vehicle	57	2	846
Waveform	109	3	5000

4.1 Setup

We ran our experiments on the suite of 15 standard machine learning benchmarks listed in Table 1. All of the datasets come from the UCI machine learning repository [8], with exception of "Mofn" and "Corral" [18]. As pre-processing steps, we applied the discretization method described in [9], and we binarized all variables using a one-hot encoding. Moreover, we removed instances with missing values and features whose value was always equal to 0. Table 1 summarizes the number of binary features $|\mathbf{F}|$, the number of classes $|C|$ and the available number of training samples $|\mathrm{N}|$ per dataset.

4.2 Evaluation of DG-LearnPSDD

Table 2 compares D-LEARNPSDD, LEARNPSDD, Naive Bayes (NB), Tree Augmented Naive Bayes (TANB) and logistic regression (LogReg)[1] in terms of accuracy via five fold cross validation[2]. For LEARNPSDD, we incrementally learned a model on each fold until convergence on validation-data log-likelihood, following the methodology in [20].

For D-LEARNPSDD, we incrementally learned a model on each fold until likelihood converged but then selected the incremental model with the highest training set accuracy. For NB and TANB, we learned a model per fold and compiled them to Arithmetic Circuits[3], a more general form of PSDDs [6], which allows us to compare the size of these Bayes net classifiers and the PSDDs. Finally, we compare all probabilistic models with a discriminative classifier, a multinomial logistic regression model with a ridge estimator.

Table 2 shows that the proposed D-LEARNPSDD clearly benefits from the introduced discriminative bias, outperforming LEARNPSDD in all but two datasets, as the latter method is not guaranteed to learn significant relations between feature and class variables. Moreover, it outperforms Bayesian classifiers in most benchmarks, as the learned PSDDs are more expressive and allow to encode complex relationships among sets of variables or local dependencies such as context specific independence, while remaining tractable. Finally, note that the D-LEARNPSDD is competitive in terms of accuracy with respect to logistic regression (LogReg) a purely discriminative classification approach.

4.3 Impact of the Vtree on Discriminative Performance

The structure and size of the learned PSDD is largely determined by the vtree it is normalized for. Naturally, the vtree also has an important role in determining the quality (in terms of log-likelihood) of the probability distribution encoded by the learned PSDD [20]. In this section, we study the impact that the choice of vtree and learning strategy has on the trade-offs between model tractability, quality and discriminative performance.

---

[1] NB, TANB and LogReg are learned using Weka with default settings.
[2] In each fold, we hold 10% of the data for validation.
[3] Using the ACE tool Available at http://reasoning.cs.ucla.edu/ace/.

Table 2. Five cross fold accuracy and size in number of parameters

Dataset	D-LearnPSDD		LearnPSDD		NB		TANB		LogReg
	Accuracy	Size	Accuracy	Size	Accuracy	Size	Accuracy	Size	Accuracy
Australian	**86.2 ± 3.6**	367	84.9 ± 2.7	386	85.1 ± 3.1	161	85.8 ± 3.4	312	84.1 ± 3.4
Breast	97.1 ± 0.9	291	94.9 ± 0.5	491	**97.7 ± 1.2**	114	97.7 ± 1.2	219	96.5 ± 1.6
Chess	**97.3 ± 1.4**	2178	94.9 ± 1.6	2186	87.7 ± 1.4	158	91.7 ± 2.2	309	96.9 ± 0.7
Cleve	82.2 ± 2.5	292	81.9 ± 3.2	184	**84.9 ± 3.3**	102	79.9 ± 2.2	196	81.5 ± 2.9
Corral 6	**99.4 ± 1.4**	39	98.1 ± 2.8	58	89.4 ± 5.2	26	98.8 ± 1.7	45	86.3 ± 6.7
Credit	85.6 ± 3.1	693	86.1 ± 3.6	611	**86.8 ± 4.4**	170	86.1 ± 3.9	326	84.7 ± 4.9
Diabetes	**78.7 ± 2.9**	124	77.2 ± 3.3	144	77.4 ± 2.56	46	75.8 ± 3.5	86	78.4 ± 2.6
German	72.3 ± 3.2	1185	69.9 ± 2.3	645	73.5 ± 2.7	218	**74.5 ± 1.9**	429	74.4 ± 2.3
Glass	**79.1 ± 1.9**	214	72.4 ± 6.2	321	70.0 ± 4.9	203	69.5 ± 5.2	318	73.0 ± 5.7
Heart	**84.1 ± 4.3**	51	78.5 ± 5.3	75	84.0 ± 3.8	38	83.0 ± 5.1	70	84.0 ± 4.7
Iris	90.0 ± 0.1	76	94.0 ± 3.7	158	**94.7 ± 1.8**	75	94.7 ± 1.8	131	94.7 ± 2.9
Mofn	98.9 ± 0.9	260	97.1 ± 2.4	260	85.0 ± 5.7	42	92.8 ± 2.6	78	**100.0 ± 0**
Pima	**80.2 ± 0.3**	108	74.7 ± 3.2	110	77.6 ± 3.0	46	76.3 ± 2.9	86	77.7 ± 2.9
Vehicle	**95.0 ± 1.7**	1186	93.9 ± 1.69	1560	86.3 ± 2.00	228	93.0 ± 0.8	442	94.5 ± 2.4
Waveform	85.0 ± 1.0	3441	78.7 ± 5.6	2585	80.7 ± 1.9	657	83.1 ± 1.1	1296	**85.5 ± 0.7**

Figure 3a shows test-set log-likelihood and Fig. 3b classification accuracy as a function of model size (in number of parameters) for the "Chess" dataset. We display average log-likelihood and accuracy over logarithmically distributed ranges of model size. This figure contrasts the results of three learning approaches: D-LEARNPSDD when the vtree learning stage optimizes mutual information (MI, shown in light blue); when it optimizes conditional mutual information (CMI, shown in dark blue); and the traditional LEARNPSDD (in orange).

Figure 3a shows that likelihood improves at a faster rate during the first iterations of LEARNPSDD, but eventually settles to the same values as D-LEARNPSDD because both optimize for log-likelihood. However, the discriminative bias guarantees that classification accuracy on the initial model will be at least as high as that of a Naive Bayes classifier (see Fig. 3b). Moreover, this results in consistently superior accuracy (for the CMI case) compared to the purely generative LEARNPSDD approach as shown also in Table 2. The dip in accuracy during the second and third intervals are a consequence of the generative learning, which optimizes for log-likelihood and can therefore initially yield feature-value correlations that decrease the model's performance as a classifier.

Finally, Fig. 3b demonstrates that optimizing the vtree for conditional mutual information results in an overall better performance vs. accuracy trade-off when compared to optimizing for mutual information. Such a conditional mutual information objective function is consistent with the conditional independence constraint we impose on the structure of the PSDD and allows the model to consider the special status of the class variable in the discriminative task.

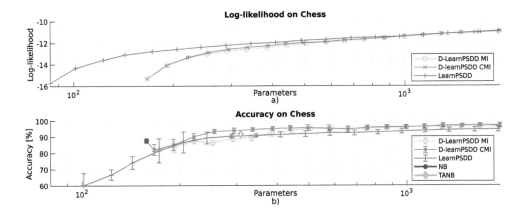

Fig. 3. Log-likelihood and accuracy vs. model size trade-off of the incremental PSDD learning approaches. MI and CMI denote mutual information and conditional mutual information vtree learning, respectively. (Color figure online)

4.4 Robustness to Missing Features

The generative models in this paper encode a joint probability distribution over all variables and therefore tend to be more robust against missing features than discriminative models, which only learn relations relevant to their discriminative task. In this experiment, we assessed this robustness aspect by simulating the random failure of 10% of the original feature set per benchmark and per fold in five-fold cross-validation. Figure 4 shows the average accuracy over 10 such feature failure trials in each of the 5 folds (flat markers) in relation to their full feature set accuracy reported in Table 2 (shaped markers). As expected, the performance of the discriminative classifier (LogReg) suffers the most during feature failure, while D-LEARNPSDD and LEARNPSDD are notably more robust than any other approach, with accuracy losses of no more than 8%. Note from the flat markers that the performance of D-LEARNPSDD under feature failure is the best in all datasets but one.

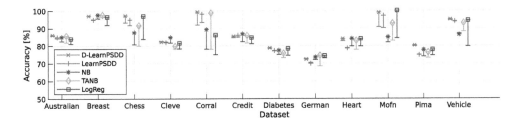

Fig. 4. Classification robustness per method.

5   Related Work

A number of works have dealt with the conflict between generative and discriminative model learning, some dating back decades [14]. There are multiple techniques that support learning of parameters [13,23] and structure [21,24] of probabilistic circuits. Typically, different approaches are followed to either learn generative or discriminative tasks, but some methods exploit discriminative models' properties to deal with missing variables [22]. Other works that also constraint the structure of PSDDs have been proposed before, such as Choi et al. [3]. However, they only do parameter learning, not structure learning: their approach to improve accuracy is to learn separate structured PSDDs for each distribution of features given the class and feed them to a NB classifier. In [5], Correira and de Campos propose a constrained SPN architecture that shows both computational efficiency and classification performance improvements. However, it focuses on decision robustness rather than robustness against missing values, essential to the application range discussed in this paper. There are also a number of methods that focus specifically on the interaction between discriminative and generative learning. In [15], Khosravi et al. provide a method to compute expected predictions of a discriminative model with respect to a probability distribution defined by an arbitrary generative model in a tractable manner. This combination allows to handle missing values using discriminative couterparts of generative classifiers [16]. More distant to this work is the line of hybrid discriminative and generative models [19], their focus is on semisupervised learning and deals with missing labels.

6   Conclusion

This paper introduces a PSDD learning technique that improves classification performance by introducing a discriminative bias. Meanwhile, robustness against missing data is kept by exploiting generative learning. The method capitalizes on PSDDs' domain knowledge encoding capabilities to enforce the conditional relation between the class and the features. We prove that this constraint is guaranteed to be enforced throughout the learning process and we show how not encoding such a relation might lead to poor classification performance. Evaluation on a suite of benchmarking datasets shows that the proposed technique outperforms purely generative PSDDs in terms of classification accuracy and the other baseline classifiers in terms of robustness.

Acknowledgements. This work was supported by the EU-ERC Project Re-SENSE grant ERC-2016-STG-71503; NSF grants IIS-1943641, IIS-1633857, CCF-1837129, DARPA XAI grant N66001-17-2-4032, gifts from Intel and Facebook Research, and the "Onderzoeksprogramma Artificiële Intelligentie Vlaanderen" programme from the Flemish Government.

References

1. Bekker, J., Davis, J., Choi, A., Darwiche, A., Van den Broeck, G.: Tractable learning for complex probability queries. In: Advances in Neural Information Processing Systems (2015)
2. Boutilier, C., Friedman, N., Goldszmidt, M., Koller, D.: Context-specific independence in Bayesian networks. In: Proceedings of the International Conference on Uncertainty in Artificial Intelligence (1996)
3. Choi, A., Tavabi, N., Darwiche, A.: Structured features in naive bayes classification. In: Thirtieth AAAI Conference on Artificial Intelligence (2016)
4. Choi, Y., Vergari, A., Van den Broeck, G.: Lecture Notes: Probabilistic Circuits: Representation and Inference (2020). http://starai.cs.ucla.edu/papers/LecNoAAAI20.pdf
5. Correia, A.H.C., de Campos, C.P.: Towards scalable and robust sum-product networks. In: Ben Amor, N., Quost, B., Theobald, M. (eds.) SUM 2019. LNCS (LNAI), vol. 11940, pp. 409–422. Springer, Cham (2019). https://doi.org/10.1007/978-3-030-35514-2_31
6. Darwiche, A.: Modeling and Reasoning with Bayesian Networks. Cambridge University Press, Cambridge (2009)
7. Darwiche, A.: SDD: a new canonical representation of propositional knowledge bases. In: International Joint Conference on Artificial Intelligence (2011)
8. Dua, D., Graff, C.: UCI machine learning repository (2017). http://archive.ics.uci.edu/ml
9. Fayyad, U., Irani, K.: Multi-interval discretization of continuous-valued attributes for classification learning. In: Proceedings of the International Joint Conference on Artificial Intelligence (IJCAI) (1993)
10. Friedman, N., Geiger, D., Goldszmidt, M.: Bayesian network classifiers. J. Mach. Learn. **29**(2), 131–163 (1997)
11. Galindez, L., Badami, K., Vlasselaer, J., Meert, W., Verhelst, M.: Dynamic sensor-frontend tuning for resource efficient embedded classification. IEEE J. Emerg. Sel. Top. Circuits Syst. **8**(4), 858–872 (2018)
12. Galindez Olascoaga, L., Meert, W., Shah, N., Verhelst, M., Van den Broeck, G.: Towards hardware-aware tractable learning of probabilistic models. In: Advances in Neural Information Processing Systems, pp. 13726–13736 (2019)
13. Gens, R., Domingos, P.: Discriminative learning of sum-product networks. In: Advances in Neural Information Processing Systems (2012)
14. Jaakkola, T., Haussler, D.: Exploiting generative models in discriminative classifiers. In: Advances in Neural Information Processing Systems (1999)
15. Khosravi, P., Choi, Y., Liang, Y., Vergari, A., Van den Broeck, G.: On tractable computation of expected predictions. In: Advances in Neural Information Processing Systems, pp. 11167–11178 (2019)
16. Khosravi, P., Liang, Y., Choi, Y., Van den Broeck, G.: What to expect of classifiers? Reasoning about logistic regression with missing features. In: Proceedings of the 28th International Joint Conference on Artificial Intelligence (IJCAI), (2019)
17. Kisa, D., den Broeck, G.V., Choi, A., Darwiche, A.: Probabilistic sentential decision diagrams. In: International Conference on the Principles of Knowledge Representation and Reasoning (2014)
18. Kohavi, R., John, G.H.: Wrappers for feature subset selection. Artif. Intell. **97**(1–2), 273–324 (1997)

19. Lasserre, J.A., Bishop, C.M., Minka, T.P.: Principled hybrids of generative and discriminative models. In: IEEE Computer Society Conference on Computer Vision and Pattern Recognition (CVPR) (2006)
20. Liang, Y., Bekker, J., Van den Broeck, G.: Learning the structure of probabilistic sentential decision diagrams. In: Proceedings of the Conference on Uncertainty in Artificial Intelligence (UAI) (2017)
21. Liang, Y., Van den Broeck, G.: Learning logistic circuits. In: Proceedings of the Conference on Artificial Intelligence (AAAI) (2019)
22. Peharz, R., et al.: Random sum-product networks: a simple and effective approach to probabilistic deep learning. In: Conference on Uncertainty in Artificial Intelligence (UAI) (2019)
23. Poon, H., Domingos, P.: Sum-product networks: a new deep architecture. In: IEEE International Conference on Computer Vision Workshops (2011)
24. Rooshenas, A., Lowd, D.: Discriminative structure learning of arithmetic circuits. In: Artificial Intelligence and Statistics, pp. 1506–1514 (2016)

Widening for MDL-Based Retail Signature Discovery

Clément Gautrais[1]([⊠])[iD], Peggy Cellier[2], Matthijs van Leeuwen[3], and Alexandre Termier[2]

[1] Department of Computer Science, KU Leuven, Leuven, Belgium
`clement.gautrais@cs.kuleuven.be`
[2] Univ Rennes, Inria, INSA, CNRS, IRISA, Rennes, France
[3] LIACS, Leiden University, Leiden, The Netherlands

Abstract. *Signature patterns* have been introduced to model repetitive behavior, e.g., of customers repeatedly buying the same set of products in consecutive time periods. A disadvantage of existing approaches to signature discovery, however, is that the required number of occurrences of a signature needs to be manually chosen. To address this limitation, we formalize the problem of selecting the best signature using the minimum description length (MDL) principle. To this end, we propose an encoding for signature models and for any data stream given such a signature model. As finding the MDL-optimal solution is unfeasible, we propose a novel algorithm that is an instance of *widening*, i.e., a diversified beam search that heuristically explores promising parts of the search space. Finally, we demonstrate the effectiveness of the problem formalization and the algorithm on a real-world retail dataset, and show that our approach yields relevant signatures.

Keywords: Signature discovery · Minimum description length · Widening

1 Introduction

When analyzing (human) activity logs, it is especially important to discover recurrent behavior. Recurrent behavior can indicate, for example, personal preferences or habits, and can be useful in contexts such as personalized marketing. Some types of behavior are elusive to traditional data mining methods: for example, behavior that has some temporal regularity but not strong enough to be periodic, and which does not form simple itemsets or sequences in the log. A prime example is the set of products that is essential to a retail customer: all of these products are bought regularly, but often not periodically due to different

C. Gautrais—This work has received funding from the European Research Council (ERC) under the European Union's Horizon 2020 research and innovation programme (grant agreement No [694980] SYNTH: Synthesising Inductive Data Models).

depletion rates, and they are typically bought over several transactions—in any arbitrary order—rather than all at the same time.

To model and detect such behavior, we have proposed *signature patterns* [3]: patterns that identify irregular recurrences in an event sequence by segmenting the sequence (see Fig. 1). We have shown the relevance of signature patterns in the retail context, and demonstrated that they are general enough to be used in other domains, such as political speeches [2]. As a disadvantage, however, signature patterns require the analyst to provide the number of recurrences, i.e., the number of segments in the segmentation. This number of segments influences the signature: fewer segments give a more detailed signature, while more segments result in a simpler signature. Although in some cases domain experts may have some intuition on how to choose the number of segments, it is often difficult to decide on a good trade-off between the number of segments and the complexity of the signature. The main problem that we study in this paper is therefore how to automatically set this parameter in a principled way, based on the data.

Our first main contribution is a problem formalization that defines the best signature for a given dataset, so that the analyst no longer needs to choose the number of segments. By considering the signature corresponding to each possible number of segments as a model, we can naturally formulate the problem of selecting the best signature as a model selection problem. We formalize this problem using the minimum description length (MDL) principle [4], which, informally, states that the best model is the one that compresses the data best. The MDL principle perfectly fits our purposes because (1) it allows to select the simplest model that adequately explains the data, and (2) it has been previously shown to be very effective for the selection of pattern-based models (e.g., [7,11]).

After defining the problem using the MDL principle, the remaining question is how to solve it. As the search space of signatures is extremely large and the MDL-based problem formulation does not offer any properties that could be used to substantially prune the search space, we resort to heuristic search. Also here, the properties of signature patterns lead to technical challenges. In particular, we empirically show that a naïve beam search often gets stuck in suboptimal solutions. Our second main contribution is therefore to propose a diverse beam search algorithm, i.e., an instance of *widening* [9], that ensures that a diverse set of candidate solutions is maintained on each level of the beam search. For this, we define a distance measure for signatures based on their segmentations.

2 Preliminaries

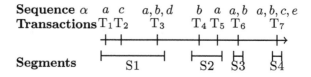

Fig. 1. A sequence of transactions and a 4-segmentation. We have the signature items $\mathcal{R} = \{a, b\}$, the remaining items $\mathcal{E} = \{c, d, e\}$, the set of items $\mathcal{I} = \{a, b, c, d, e\}$, the segmentation $S = \langle [T_1, T_2, T_3], [T_4, T_5], [T_6], [T_7] \rangle$.

Signatures. Let us first recall the definition of a *signature* as presented in [3]. Let $\mathcal{I}$ be the set of all items, and let $\alpha = \langle T_1 \ldots T_n \rangle$, $T_i \subseteq \mathcal{I}$ be a sequence of itemsets. A *k-segmentation* of α, denoted $S(\alpha, k) = \langle S_1 \ldots S_k \rangle$, is a sequence of k non-overlapping consecutive sub-sequences of α, denoted S_i and called *segments*, each consisting of consecutive transactions. An example of a 4-segmentation is given in Fig. 1. Given $S(\alpha, k) = \langle S_1 \ldots S_k \rangle$, a k-segmentation of α, we have $Rec(S(\alpha, k)) = \bigcap_{S_i \in S(\alpha, k)} (\bigcup_{T_j \in S_i} T_j)$: the set of all recurrent items that are present in each segment of $S(\alpha, k)$. For example in Fig. 1, the segmentation $S(\alpha, 4) = \langle S_1, S_2, S_3, S_4 \rangle$ gives $Rec(S(\alpha, 4)) = \{a, b\}$. Given k and α, one can compute $S_{max}(\alpha, k)$, the set of k-segmentation of α yielding the largest sets of recurrent items: $S_{max}(\alpha, k) = \text{argmax}_{S(\alpha, k)} |Rec(S(\alpha, k))|$. For example, in Fig. 4, $\langle S_1, S_2, S_3, S_4 \rangle$ is the only 4-segmentation yielding two recurrent items. As all other 4-segmentations either yield zero or one recurrent item, $S_{max}(\alpha, 4) = \{\langle S_1, S_2, S_3, S_4 \rangle\}$. A k-signature (also named signature when k is clear from context) is then defined as a maximal set of recurrent items in a k-segmentation S, with $S \in S_{max}(\alpha, k)$. As $S_{max}(\alpha, k)$ can contain several segmentations, we define the k-signature set $Sig(\alpha, k)$, which contains all k-signatures: $Sig(\alpha, k) = \{Rec(S_m(\alpha, k)) \mid S_m \in S_{max}(\alpha, k)\}$. k gives the number of recurrences of the recurrent items in sequence α. Given a number of recurrences k, finding a k-*signature* relies on finding a k-segmentation that maximizes the size of the itemset that occurs in each segment of that segmentation. For example, in Fig. 1, given segmentation $S = \langle S_1, S_2, S_3, S_4 \rangle$ and given that $S_{max}(\alpha, 4) = \{S\}$, we have $Sig(\alpha, 4) = \{Rec(S)\} = \{\{a, b\}\}$. For simplicity, the segmentation associated with a k-signature in $Sig(\alpha, k)$ is denoted $S = \langle S_1 \ldots S_k \rangle$, and the signature items are denoted $\mathcal{R} \subseteq \mathcal{I}$. The remaining items are denoted $\mathcal{E}$, i.e., $\mathcal{E} = \mathcal{I} \backslash \mathcal{R}$.

Minimum Description Length (MDL). Let us now briefly introduce the basic notions of the minimum description length (MDL) principle [4] as it is commonly used in compression-based pattern mining [7]. Given a set of models $\mathcal{M}$ and a dataset $\mathcal{D}$, the best model $M \in \mathcal{M}$ is the one that minimizes $L(\mathcal{D}, M) = L(M) + L(\mathcal{D}|M)$, with $L(M)$ the length, in bits, of the encoding of M, and $L(\mathcal{D}|M)$ the length, in bits, of the encoding of the data given M. This is called *two-part MDL* because it separately encodes the model and the data given the model, which results in a natural trade-off between model complexity and data complexity. To fairly compare all models, the encoding has to be *lossless*. To use the MDL principle for model selection, the model class $\mathcal{M}$ has to be defined (in our case, the set of all signatures), as well as how to compute the length of the model and the length of the data given the model. It should be noted that only the *encoded length* of the data is of interest, not the encoded data itself.

3   Problem Definition

To extract recurrent items from a sequence using signatures, one must define the number of segments k. Providing meaningful values for k usually requires expert knowledge and/or many tryouts, as there is no general rule to automatically set

k. Our problem is therefore to devise a method that adjusts k, depending on the data at hand. As this is a typical model selection problem, our approach relies on the minimum description length principle (MDL) to find the best model from a set of candidate models. However, the signature model must be refined into a probabilistic model to use the MDL principle for model selection. Especially, the occurrences of items in α should be defined according to a probability distribution. With no information about these occurrences, the uniform distribution is the most natural choice. Indeed, without information on the transaction in which an item occurs, the best is to assume it can occur uniformly at random in any transaction of the sequence α. Moreover, the choice of the uniform distribution has been shown to minimize the worst case description length [4].

To make the signature model probabilistic, we assume that it generates three different types of occurrences independently and uniformly. As the signature gives the information that there is at least one occurrence of every signature item in every segment, the first type of occurrences correspond to this one occurrence of signature items in every segment. These are generated uniformly over all the transactions of every segment. The second type of occurrences are the remaining signature items occurrences. Here, the information is that these items already have occurrences generated by the previous type of occurrences. As α is a sequence of itemsets, an item can occur at most once in a transaction. Hence, for a given signature item, the second type of occurrences for this item are distributed uniformly over the transactions where this item does not already occur for the first type of occurrences. Finally, the third type are the occurrences of the remaining items: the items that are not part of the signature. There is no information about these items occurrences, hence we assume them to be generated uniformly over all transactions of α.

With these three types of occurrences, the signature model is probabilistic: all occurrences in α are generated according to a probability distribution that takes into account the information provided by the signature specification. Hence, we can now define the problem we are tackling:

Problem 1. Let $\mathbb{S}$ denote the set of signatures for all values of k, $\mathbb{S} = \bigcup_{k=1}^{|\alpha|} Sig(\alpha, k)$. Given a sequence α, it follows from the MDL principle that the best signature $S \in \mathbb{S}$ is the one that minimizes the two-part encoded length of S and α, i.e.,

$$S_{MDL} = \mathrm{argmin}_{S \in \mathbb{S}} L(\alpha, S),$$

where $L(\alpha, S)$ is the two-part encoded length that we present in the next section.

4   An Encoding for Signatures

As typically done in compression-based pattern mining [7], we use a two-part MDL code that leads to decomposing the total encoded length $L(\alpha, S)$ into two parts: $L(S)$ and $L(\alpha|S)$, with the relation $L(\alpha, S) = L(S) + L(\alpha|S)$. In the upcoming subsection we define $L(S)$, i.e., the encoded length of a signature, after which Subsect. 4.2 introduces $L(\alpha|S)$, i.e., the length of the sequence α given a signature S. In the remainder of this paper, all logarithms are in base 2.

4.1 Model Encoding: $L(S)$

A signature is composed of two parts: (1) the signature items, and (2) the signature segmentation. The two parts are detailed below.

Signature Items Encoding. The encoding of the signature items consists of three parts. The signature items are a subset of $\mathcal{I}$, hence we first encode the number of items in $\mathcal{I}$. A common way to encode non-negative integer numbers is to use the universal code for integers [4,8], denoted $L_{\mathbb{N}}$[1]. This yields a code of size $L_{\mathbb{N}}(|\mathcal{I}|)$. Next, we encode the number of items in the signature, using again the universal code for integers, with length $L_{\mathbb{N}}(|\mathcal{R}|)$. Finally, we encode the items of the signature. As the order of signature items is irrelevant, we can use an $|\mathcal{R}|$-combination of $|\mathcal{I}|$ elements without replacement. This yields a length of $\log(\binom{|\mathcal{I}|}{|\mathcal{R}|})$. From $\mathcal{R}$ and $\mathcal{I}$, we can deduce $\mathcal{E}$.

Segmentation Encoding. We now present the encoding of the second part of the signature: the signature segmentation. To encode the segmentation, we encode the segment boundaries. These boundaries are indexed on the size of the sequence, hence we first need to encode the number of transactions n. This can be done using again the universal code for integers, which is of size $L_{\mathbb{N}}(n)$. Then, we need to encode the number of segments $|S|$, which is of length $L_{\mathbb{N}}(|S|)$. To encode the segments, we only have to encode the boundaries between two consecutive segments. As there are $|S|-1$ such boundaries, a naive encoded length would be $(|S|-1)*\log(n)$. An improved encoding takes into account the previous segments. For example, when encoding the second boundary, we know that its value will not be higher than $n - |S_1|$. Hence, we can encode it in $\log(n - |S_1|)$ instead of $\log(n)$ bits. This principle can be applied to encode all boundaries. Another way to further reduce the encoded length is to use the fact that we know that each signature segment contains at least one transaction. We can therefore subtract the number of remaining segments to encode the boundary of the segment we are encoding. This yields an encoded length of $\sum_{i=1}^{|S|-1} \log(n - (|S| - i) - \sum_{j=1}^{i-1} |S_j|)$.

Putting Everything Together. The total encoded length of a signature S is

$$L(S) = L_{\mathbb{N}}(|\mathcal{I}|) + L_{\mathbb{N}}(|\mathcal{R}|) + \log\left(\binom{|\mathcal{I}|}{|\mathcal{R}|}\right) +$$

$$L_{\mathbb{N}}(n) + L_{\mathbb{N}}(|S|) + \sum_{i=1}^{|S|-1} \log(n - (|S| - i) - \sum_{j=1}^{i-1} |S_j|).$$

---

[1] $L_{\mathbb{N}} = \log^*(n) + \log(2.865064)$, with $\log^*(n) = \log(n) + \log(\log(n)) + \ldots$

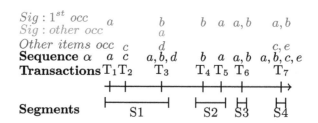

Fig. 2. A sequence of transactions and its encoding scheme. We have $\mathcal{R} = \{a,b\}$, $\mathcal{E} = \{c,d,e\}$ and $\mathcal{I} = \{a,b,c,d,e\}$. The first occurrence of each signature item in each segment is encoded in the red stream, the remaining signature items occurrences in the orange stream, and the items from $\mathcal{E}$ in the blue stream. (Color figure online)

4.2 Data Encoding: $L(\alpha|S)$

We now present the encoding of the sequence given the model: $L(\alpha|S)$. This encoding relies on the refinement of the signature model into a probabilistic model presented in Sect. 3. To summarize, we have three separate encoding streams that encode the three different types of occurrences presented in Sect. 3: (1) one that encodes one occurrence of every signature item in every segment, (2) one that encodes the rest of the signature items occurrences, and (3) one that encodes the remaining items occurrences. An example illustrating the three different encoding streams is presented in Fig. 2.

Encoding One Occurrence of Each Signature Item in Each Segment. As stated in Sect. 3, the signature says that in each segment, there is at least one occurrence of each signature item. The size of each segment is known (from the encoding of the model, in Subsect. 4.1), hence we encode one occurrence of each signature item in segment S_i by encoding the index of the transaction, within segment S_i, that contains this occurrence. From Sect. 3, this occurrence is uniformly distributed over the transactions in S_i. As encoding an index over $|S_i|$ equiprobable possibilities costs $\log(|S_i|)$ bits and as in each segment, $|\mathcal{R}|$ occurrences are encoded this way, we encode each segment in $|\mathcal{R}| * \log(|S_i|)$ bits.

Encoding the Remaining Signature Items' Occurrences. As presented in Fig. 2, we now encode remaining signature items occurrences to guarantee a lossless encoding. Again, this encoding relies on encoding transactions where signature items occur. For each item a, we encode its occurrences $occ(a) = \sum_{T_i \in \alpha} \sum_{p \in T_i} \mathbb{1}_{a=p}$ by encoding to which transaction it belongs. As S occurrences have already been encoded using the previous stream, there are $occ(a) - |S|$ remaining occurrences to encode. These occurrences can be in any of the $n - |S|$ remaining transactions. From Sect. 3, we use a uniform distribution to encode them. More precisely, the first occurrence of item a can belong to any of the $n - |S|$ transactions where a does not already occur. For the second occurrence of a, there are now only $n - |S| - 1$ transactions where a can occur. By applying this principle, we encode all the remaining occurrences of a as $\sum_{i=0}^{occ(a) - |S| - 1} \log(n - |S| - i)$. For each item, we also use $L_{\mathbb{N}}(occ(a) - |S|)$ bits to encode the number of occurrences. This yields a total length of $\sum_{a \in \mathcal{R}} L_{\mathbb{N}}(occ(a) - |S|) + \sum_{i=0}^{occ(a)-|S|-1} \log(n - |S| - i)$.

Remaining Items Occurrences Encoding. Finally, we encode the remaining items occurrences, i.e., the occurrences of items in $\mathcal{E}$. The encoding technique is identical to the one used to encode additional signature items occurrences, with the exception that the remaining items occurrences can initially be present in any of the n transactions. This yields a total code of $\sum_{a \in \mathcal{E}} L_{\mathbb{N}}(occ(a)) + \sum_{i=0}^{occ(a)} \log(n - i)$.

Putting Everything Together. The total encoded length of the data given the model is given by: $L(\alpha|S) = \sum_{S_i \in S} |\mathcal{R}| * \log(|S_i|) + \sum_{a \in \mathcal{R}} L_{\mathbb{N}}(occ(a) - |S|) + \sum_{i=0}^{occ(a)-|S|-1} \log(n - |S| - i) + \sum_{a \in \mathcal{E}} L_{\mathbb{N}}(occ(a)) + \sum_{i=0}^{occ(a)} \log(n - i)$.

5   Algorithms

The previous section presented how a sequence is encoded, completing our problem formalization. The remaining problem is to find the signature minimizing the code length, that is, finding S_{MDL} such that $S_{MDL} = \text{argmin}_{S \in \mathbb{S}} L(\alpha, S)$.

Naive Algorithm. A naive approach would be to directly mine the whole set of signatures $\mathbb{S}$ and find the signature that minimizes the code length. However, mining a signature with k segments has time complexity $O(n^2 k)$. Mining the whole set of signatures requires k to vary from 1 to n, resulting in a total complexity of $O(n^4)$. The quartic complexity does not allow us to quickly mine the complete set of possible signatures on large datasets, hence we have to rely on heuristic approaches.

To quickly search for the signature in $\mathbb{S}$ that minimizes the code length, we initially rely on a top-down greedy algorithm. We start with one segment containing the whole sequence, and then search for the segment boundary that minimizes the encoded length. Then, we recursively search for a new single segment boundary that minimizes the encoded length. We stop when no segment can be added, i.e., when the number of segments is equal to the number of transactions. During this process, we record the signature with the best encoded length. However, this algorithm can perform early segment splits that seem promising initially, but that eventually impair the search for the best signature.

5.1   Widening for Signatures

To solve this issue, a solution is to keep the w signatures with the lowest code length at each step instead of keeping only the best one. This technique is called *beam search* and has been used to tackle optimization problems in pattern mining [6]. The beam width w is the number of solutions to keep at each step of the algorithm. However, the beam search technique suffers from having many of the best w signatures that tend to be similar and correspond to slight variations of one signature. Here, this means that most signatures in the beam would

---

Algorithm 1. Widening algorithm for signature code length minimization.

1: **function** SIGNATURE MINING($\alpha = \langle T_1, \ldots, T_n \rangle$, β, w)
2:     BestKSign $= \emptyset$, BestSign $= \emptyset$
3:     **for** $k = 1 \rightarrow n$ **do**
4:         AllKSign = Split1Segment(BestKSign)
5:         $S_{opt} = \text{argmin}_{S \in AllKSign} L(\alpha, S)$
6:         BestSign = BestSign $\bigcup \{S_{opt}\}$
7:         BestKSign $= \{S_{opt}\}$
8:         $\theta = threshold(\beta, w, \text{AllKSign})$
9:         **while** $S_{opt} \neq \emptyset$ and $|\text{BestKSign}| < w$ **do**
10:            $S_{opt} = \text{argmin}_{S \in AllKSign} L(\alpha, S), \nexists S_i \in BestKSign, d(S_i, S) \leq \theta$
11:            BestKSign = BestKSign $\bigcup \{S_{opt}\}$
12:     **return** $\text{argmin}_{S \in BestSign} L(\alpha, S)$

Algorithm 2. Distance threshold computation.

1: **function** THRESHOLD(β, w, $AllSign$)
2:     KBest $= \beta * |AllSign|$
3:     BestS = GetBestSign(AllSign, KBest)
4:     **return** $\text{argmin}_\theta \{N(\theta), N(\theta) = |\{S \in BestS, d(S, BestS[0]) < \theta\}|, N(\theta) \geq |BestS|/w\}$

---

have segmentations that are very similar. The widening technique [9] solves this issue by adding a diversity constraint into the beam. Different constraints exist [5,6,9], but a common solution is to add a distance constraint between each pair of elements in the beam: all pairwise distances between the signatures in the beam have to be larger than a given threshold θ. As this threshold is dependent on the data and the beam width, we propose a method to automatically set its value.

Algorithm 1 presents the proposed widening algorithm. Line 3 iterates over the number of segments. Line 4 computes all signatures having k segments that are considered to enter the beam. More specifically, function *Split1Segment* computes the direct refinements of each of all signatures in *BestKSign*. A direct refinement of a signature corresponds to splitting one segment in the segmentation associated with that signature. Line 5 selects the refinement having the smallest code length. If several refinements yield the smallest code length, one of these refinements is chosen at random. Lines 8 to 11 perform the widening step by adding new signatures to the beam while respecting the pairwise distance constraint. Line 8 computes the distance threshold (θ) depending on the diversity parameter (β), the beam width (w), and the current refinements. Algorithm 2 presents the details of the threshold computation. With this threshold, we recursively add a new element in the beam, until either the beam is full or no new element can be added (line 9). Lines 10 and 11 add the signature having the smallest code length and being at a distance of at least θ to any current element of the beam. Line 12 returns the best overall signature we have encountered.

Distance Between Signatures. We now define the distance measure for signatures (used in line 10 of Algorithm 1). As the purpose of the signature distance is to ensure diversity in the beam, we will use the segmentation to define the distance between two elements of the beam, i.e., between two signatures. Terzi et al. [10] presented several distance measures for segmentations. The *disagreement distance* is particularly appealing for our purposes as it compares how transactions belonging to the same segment in one segmentation are allocated to the other segmentation. Let $S_a = \langle S_{a1} \ldots S_{ak} \rangle$ and $S_b = \langle S_{b1} \ldots S_{bk} \rangle$ be two k-segmentations of a sequence α. We denote by $d(S_a, S_b)$ the disagreement distance between segmentation a and segmentation b. The disagreement distance corresponds to the number of transaction pairs that belong to the same segment in one segmentation, but that are not in the same segment in the other segmentation. Techniques on how to efficiently compute this distance are presented in [10].

Defining a Distance Threshold. Algorithm 1 uses a distance threshold θ between two signatures, that controls the diversity constraint in the beam. If θ is equal to 0, there is no diversity constraint, as any distance between two different signatures is greater than 0. Higher values of θ enforce more diversity in the beam: good signatures will not be included in the beam if they are too close to signatures already in the beam. However, setting the θ threshold is not easy. For example θ depends on the beam width w. Indeed, with large beam widths, θ should be low enough to allow many good signatures to enter the beam.

To this end, we introduce a method that automatically sets the θ parameter, depending on the beam width and on a new parameter β that is easier to interpret. The β parameter ranges from 0 to 1 and controls the strength of the diversity constraint. The intuition behind β is that its value will approximately correspond to the relative rank of the worst signature in the beam. For example, if β is set to 0.2, it means that signatures in the beam are in the top-20% in ascending order of code length. Algorithm 2 details how θ is derived from β and w; this algorithm is called by the *threshold* function in line 8 of Algorithm 1.

Knowing the set of all candidate signatures that are considered to enter the beam, we retain only the proportion β of the best signatures (line 3 of Algorithm 2). Then, in line 4 we extract the best signature. Finally, we look for the distance threshold θ such that the number of signatures within a distance of θ from the best signature is equal to the number of considered signatures divided by the beam width w (line 5). The rationale behind this threshold is that since we are adding w signatures to the beam and we want to use the proportion β of the best signatures, the distance threshold should approximately discard $1/w$ of the proportion β of the best signatures around each signature of the beam.

6   Experiments

This section, analyzes runtimes and code lengths of variants of our algorithm on a real retail dataset[2]. We show that our method runs significantly faster than the naive baseline, and give advice on how to choose the w and β parameters. Next, we illustrate the usefulness of the encoding to analyze retail customers.

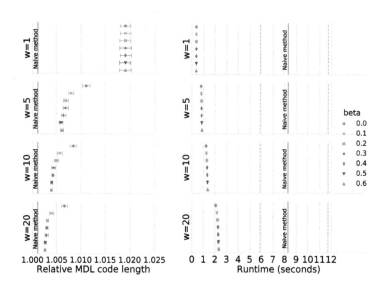

Fig. 3. Left: Mean relative code length for different instances of the widening algorithm. For each customer, the relative code length is computed with regard to the smallest code length found for this customer. Averaging these lengths across all customers gives the mean relative code length. The β parameter sets the diversity constraint and w the beam width. The solid black line shows the mean code length of the naive algorithm. Bootstrapped 95% confidence intervals [1] are displayed. **Right**: Mean runtime in seconds for different instances of the widening algorithm. The dotted black lines shows a bootstrapped 95% confidence interval of the naive algorithm's mean runtime.

6.1   Algorithm Runtime and Code Length Analysis

We here analyze the runtimes and code lengths obtained by variants of Algorithm 1. 3000 customers having more than 40 baskets in the Instacart 2017 dataset are randomly selected[3]. Customers having few purchases are less relevant, as we are looking for purchase regularities. These 3000 customers are analyzed individually, hence the algorithm is evaluated on different sequences.

---

[2] Code is available at https://bitbucket.org/clement_gautrais/mdl_signature_ida 2020/.

[3] The Instacart Online Grocery Shopping Dataset 2017, Accessed from https://www.instacart.com/datasets/grocery-shopping-2017on05/04/2018.

Code Length Analysis. To assess the performance of the different algorithms, we analyze the code length yielded by each algorithm on each of these 3000 customers. We evaluate different instances of the widening algorithm with different beam widths w and diversity constraints β. The resulting relative mean code lengths per algorithm instance are presented in Fig. 3 left. When increasing the beam width, the code length always decreases for a fixed β value. This is expected, as increasing the beam size allows the widening algorithm to explore more solutions. As increasing the beam size improves the search, we recommend setting it as high as your computational budget allows you to do.

Increasing the β parameter usually leads to better code lengths. However, for $w = 5$, higher β values give slightly worse results. Indeed, if β is too high, good signatures might not be included in the beam, if they are too close to existing solutions. Therefore, we recommend setting the β value to a moderate value, for example between 0.3 and 0.5. A strong point of our method is that it is not too sensitive to different β values. Hence, setting this parameter to its optimal value is not critical. The enforced diversity is highly relevant, as a fixed beam size with some diversity finds code lengths that are similar to the ones found by a larger beam size with no diversity. For example, with $w = 5$ and $\beta = 0.3$, the code lengths are better than with $w = 10$ and $\beta = 0$. As using a beam size of 5 with $\beta = 0.3$ is faster than using a beam size of 10 with $\beta = 0$, it shows that using diversity is highly suited to decrease runtime while yielding smaller code lengths.

Runtime Analysis. We now present runtimes of different widening instances in Fig. 3 right. The beam width mostly influences the runtime, whereas the β value has a smaller influence. Overall, increasing β slightly increases computation time, while yielding a noticeable improvement in the resulting code length, especially for small beam sizes. Our method also runs 5 to 10 times faster than the naive method. In this experiment, customers have a limited number of baskets (at most 100), thus the $O(n^4)$ complexity of the naive approach exhibits reasonable runtimes. However in settings with more transactions (retail data over a longer period for example), the naive approach will require hours to run, and the performance gain of our widening approach will be a necessity. Another important thing is that the naive method has a high variability in runtimes. Confidence intervals are narrow for the widening algorithm (they are barely noticeable on the plot), whereas it spans over 5 s for the naive algorithm.

6.2   Qualitative Analysis

Figure 4 presents two signatures of a customer, to illustrate that signatures are of practical use to analyze retail customers, and that finding signatures with smaller code lengths is of interest. We use the widening algorithm to get a variety of good signatures according to our MDL encoding. The top signature in Fig. 4 is the best signature found: it has the smallest code length. This signature seems to correctly capture the regular behavior of this customer, as it contains 7 products that are regularly bought throughout the whole purchase sequence.

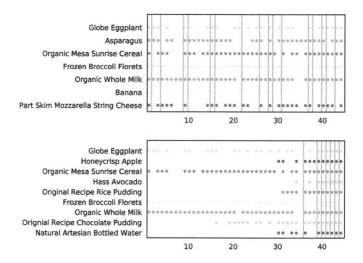

Fig. 4. Example of two signatures found by our algorithms. Gray vertical lines are segments boundaries and each dot represents an item occurrence in a purchase sequence. **Top**: best signature (code length of 5221.33 bits) found by the widening algorithm, with $w = 20$ and $\beta = 0.5$. **Bottom**: signature found by the beam search algorithm: $w = 1$ and $\beta = 0$, with a code length of 5338.46 bits (the worst code length).

Knowing these 7 favorite products, a retailer could target its offers. The segments also give some information regarding the temporal behavior of this customer. For example, because segments tend to be smaller and more frequent towards the end of the sequence, one could guess that this customer is becoming a regular.

On the other hand, the bottom signature is significantly worse than the top one. It is clear that it mostly contains products that are bought only at the end of the purchase sequence of this customer. This phenomenon occurs because the beam search algorithm, with $w = 1$, only picks the best solution at each step of the algorithm. Hence, it can quickly get stuck in a local minimum. This example shows that considering larger beams and adding diversity is an effective approach to optimize code length. Indeed, having a large and diverse beam is necessary to have the algorithm explore different segmentations, yielding better signatures.

7   Conclusions

We tackled the problem of automatically finding the best number of segments for signature patterns. To this end, we defined a model selection problem for signatures based on the minimum description length principle. Then, we introduced a novel algorithm that is an instance of widening. We evaluated the relevance and effectiveness of both the problem formalization and the algorithm on a retail dataset. We have shown that the widening-based algorithm outperforms the beam search approach as well as a naive baseline. Finally, we illustrated the practical usefulness of the signature on a retail use case. As part of future work, we would like to study our optimization techniques on larger databases (thousands of transactions), like online news feeds. We would also like to work on model selection for *sets* of interesting signatures, to highlight diverse recurrences.

References

1. Davison, A.C., Hinkley, D.V., et al.: Bootstrap Methods and Their Application, vol. 1. Cambridge University Press, Cambridge (1997)
2. Gautrais, C., Cellier, P., Quiniou, R., Termier, A.: Topic signatures in political campaign speeches. In: Proceedings of EMNLP 2017, pp. 2342–2347 (2017)
3. Gautrais, C., Quiniou, R., Cellier, P., Guyet, T., Termier, A.: Purchase signatures of retail customers. In: Kim, J., Shim, K., Cao, L., Lee, J.-G., Lin, X., Moon, Y.-S. (eds.) PAKDD 2017. LNCS (LNAI), vol. 10234, pp. 110–121. Springer, Cham (2017). https://doi.org/10.1007/978-3-319-57454-7_9
4. Grünwald, P.D.: The Minimum Description Length Principle. MIT Press, Cambridge (2007)
5. Ivanova, V.N., Berthold, M.R.: Diversity-driven widening. In: Tucker, A., Höppner, F., Siebes, A., Swift, S. (eds.) IDA 2013. LNCS, vol. 8207, pp. 223–236. Springer, Heidelberg (2013). https://doi.org/10.1007/978-3-642-41398-8_20
6. van Leeuwen, M., Knobbe, A.: Diverse subgroup set discovery. Data Min. Knowl. Disc. **25**(2), 208–242 (2012)
7. van Leeuwen, M., Vreeken, J.: Mining and using sets of patterns through compression. In: Aggarwal, C., Han, J. (eds.) Frequent Pattern Mining, pp. 165–198. Springer, Cham (2014). https://doi.org/10.1007/978-3-319-07821-2_8
8. Rissanen, J.: A universal prior for integers and estimation by minimum description length. Ann. Stat. **11**, 416–431 (1983)
9. Shell, P., Rubio, J.A.H., Barro, G.Q.: Improving search through diversity. In: Proceedings of the AAAI National Conference on Artificial Intelligence, pp. 1323–1328. AAAI Press (1994)
10. Terzi, E.: Problems and algorithms for sequence segmentations. Ph.D. thesis (2006)
11. Vreeken, J., van Leeuwen, M., Siebes, A.: KRIMP: mining itemsets that compress. Data Min. Knowl. Disc. **23**(1), 169–214 (2011). https://doi.org/10.1007/s10618-010-0202-x

4

Estimating Uncertainty in Deep Learning for Reporting Confidence: An Application on Cell Type Prediction in Testes Based on Proteomics

Biraja Ghoshal[1](✉), Cecilia Lindskog[2], and Allan Tucker[1]

[1] Brunel University London, Uxbridge UB8 3PH, UK
biraja.ghoshal@brunel.ac.uk
[2] Department of Immunology, Genetics and Pathology, Rudbeck Laboratory, Uppsala University, 75185 Uppsala, Sweden

Abstract. Multi-label classification in deep learning is a practical yet challenging task, because class overlaps in the feature space means that each instance is associated with multiple class labels. This requires a prediction of more than one class category for each input instance. To the best of our knowledge, this is the first deep learning study which quantifies uncertainty and model interpretability in multi-label classification; as well as applying it to the problem of recognising proteins expressed in cell types in testes based on immunohistochemically stained images. Multi-label classification is achieved by thresholding the class probabilities, with the optimal thresholds adaptively determined by a grid search scheme based on Matthews correlation coefficients. We adopt MC-Dropweights to approximate Bayesian Inference in multi-label classification to evaluate the usefulness of estimating uncertainty with predictive score to avoid overconfident, incorrect predictions in decision making. Our experimental results show that the MC-Dropweights visibly improve the performance to estimate uncertainty compared to state of the art approaches.

Keywords: Uncertainty estimation · Multi-label classification · Cell type prediction · Human Protein Atlas · Proteomics

1 Introduction

Proteins are the essential building blocks of life, and resolving the spatial distribution of all human proteins at an organ, tissue, cellular, and subcellular level greatly improves our understanding of human biology in health and disease. The testes is one of the most complex organs in the human body [15]. The spermatogenesis process results in the testes containing the most tissue-specific genes than elsewhere in the human body. Based on an integrated 'omics' approach using transcriptomics and antibody-based proteomics, more than 500 proteins with distinct testicular protein expression patterns have previously been identified [10], and transcriptomics data suggests that over 2,000 genes are elevated in testes compared to other organs. The function of a large proportion of these proteins are however largely unknown, and all genes involved in the complex process of spermatogenesis are yet to be characterized. Manual annotation provides the standard for scoring immunohistochemical staining pattern in different cell types. However, it is tedious, time-consuming and expensive as well as subject to human error as it is sometimes challenging to separate cell types by the human eye. It would be extremely valuable to develop an automated algorithm that can recognise the various cell types in testes based on antibody-based proteomics images while providing information on which proteins are expressed by that cell type [10]. This is, therefore, a multi-label image classification problem.

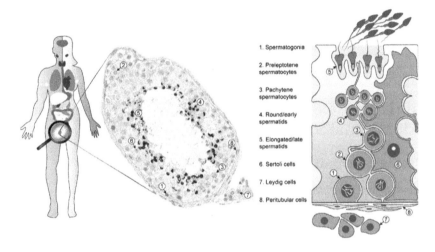

Fig. 1. Schematic overview: cell type-specific expression of testis elevated genes [10]

Exact Bayesian inference with deep neural networks is computationally intractable. There are many methods proposed for quantifying uncertainty or confidence estimates. Recently Gal [5] proved that a dropout neural network, a well-known regularisation technique [13], is equivalent to a specific variational approximation in Bayesian neural networks. Uncertainty estimates can be obtained by training a network with dropout and then taking Monte Carlo (MC) samples of the prediction using dropout during test time. Following Gal [5], Ghoshal et al. [7] also showed similar results for neural networks with Dropweights and Teye [14] with batch normalisation layers in training (Fig. 1).

In this paper, we aim to:

1. Present the first approach in multi-label pattern recognition that can recognise various cell types-specific protein expression patterns in testes based on antibody-based proteomics images and provide information on which cell types express the protein with estimated uncertainty.
2. Show Multi-Label Classification (MLC) is achieved by thresholding the class probabilities, with the Optimal Thresholds adaptively determined by a grid search scheme based on Matthews correlation coefficient.

3. Demonstrate through extensive experimental results that a Deep Learning Model with MC-Dropweights [7] is significantly better than a wide spectrum of MLC algorithms such as Binary Relevance (BR), Classifier Chain (CC), Probabilistic Classifier Chain (PCC) and Condensed Filter Tree (CFT), Cost-sensitive Label Embedding with Multidimensional Scaling (CLEMS) and state-of-the-art MC-Dropout [5] algorithms across various cell types.
4. Develop Saliency Maps in order to increase model interpretability visualizing descriptive regions and highlighting pixels from different areas in the input image. Deep learning models are often accused of being "black boxes", so they need to be precise, interpretable, and uncertainty in predictions must be well understood.

Our objective is not to achieve state-of-the-art performance on these problems, but rather to evaluate the usefulness of estimating uncertainty leveraging MC-Dropweights with predictive score in multi-label classification to avoid over-confident, incorrect predictions for decision making.

2   Multi-label Cell-Type Recognition and Localization with Estimated Uncertainty

2.1   Problem Definition

Given a set of training data D, where $X = \{x_1, x_2 \ldots x_N\}$ is the set of N images and the corresponding labels $Y = \{y_1, y_2 \ldots y_N\}$ is the cell-type information. The vector $y_i = \{y_{i,1}, y_{i,2} \ldots y_{i,M}\}$ is a binary vector, where $y_{i,j} = 1$ indicates that the ith image belongs to the jth cell-type. Note that an image may belong to multiple cell-types, i.e., $1 <= \sum_j y_{i,j} <= M$. Based on $D(X, Y)$, we constructed a Bayesian Deep Learning model giving an output of the predictive probability with estimated uncertainty of a given image x_i belonging to each cell category. That is, the constructed model acts as a function such that $f : X \to Y$ using weights of neural net parameters ω where $(0 <= \hat{y}_{x,j} <= 1)$ as close as possible to the original function that has generated the outputs Y, output the estimated value $(\hat{y}_{i,1}, \hat{y}_{i,2}, \ldots, \hat{y}_{i,M})$ as close to the actual value $(y_{i,1}, y_{i,2}, \ldots, y_{i,M})$.

2.2   Solution Approach

We tailored Deep Convolutional Neural Network (DCNN) architectures for cell type detection and localisation by considering a large image capacity, binary-cross entropy loss, sigmoid activation, along with Dropweights in the fully connected layer and Batch Normalization formulation of propagating uncertainty in deep learning to estimate meaningful model uncertainty.

Multi-label Setup: There are multiple approaches to transform the multi-label classification into multiple single-label problems with the associated loss function [8]. In this study, we used immunohistochemically stained testes tissue consisting of 8 cell types corresponding to 512 testis elevated genes.

Therefore, we define a 8-dimensional class label vector $Y = \{y_1, y_2 \ldots y_N\}$; $Y \in \{0, 1\}$, given 8 cell types. y_c indicates the presence with respect to according cell type expressing the protein in the image while an all-zero vector [0; 0; 0; 0; 0; 0; 0; 0] represents the "Absence" (no cell type expresses the protein in the scope of any of 8 categories).

Multi-label Classification Cost Function: The cost function for Multi-label Classification has to be different considering the fact that a prediction for a class is not mutually exclusive. So we selected the sigmoid function with the addition of binary cross-entropy.

Data Augmentation: We used Keras' image pre-processing package to apply affine transformations to the images, such as rotation, scaling, shearing, and translation during training and inference. This reduces the epistemic uncertainty during training, captures heteroscedastic aleatoric uncertainty during inference and overall improves the performance of models.

Multi-label Classification Algorithm: In Bayesian classification, the mean of the predictive posterior corresponds to the parameter point estimates, and the width of the posterior reflects the confidence of the predictions. The output of the network is an M-dimensional probability vector, where each dimension indicates how likely each cell type in a given image expresses the protein. The number of cell types that simultaneously express the protein in an image varies. One method to solve this multi-label classification problem is placing thresholds on each dimension. However different dimensions may be associated with different thresholds. If the value of the ith dimension of $\hat{y}$ is greater than a threshold, we can say that the i-th cell-type is expressed in the given tissue. The main problem is defining the threshold for each class label.

A threshold based on Matthews Correlation Coefficient (MCC) is used on the model outcome to determine the predicted class to improve the accuracy of the models.

We adopted a grid search scheme based on Matthews Correlation Coefficients (MCC) to estimate the optimal thresholds for each cell type-specific protein expression [2]. Details of the optimal threshold finding algorithm is shown in Algorithm 1.

The idea is to estimate the threshold for each cell category in an image separately. We convert the predicted probability vector with the estimated threshold into binary and calculate the Matthews correlation coefficient (MCC) between the threshold value and the actual value. The Matthews correlation coefficient for all thresholds are stored in the vector ω, from which we find the index of threshold that causes the largest correlation. The Optimal Threshold for the ith dimension is then determined by the corresponding value. We then leveraged Bias-Corrected Uncertainty quantification method [6] using Deep Convolutional Neural Network (DCNN) architectures with Dropweights [7].

Input: Ground Truth Vector: $\{y_{i,1}, y_{i,2}, \ldots, y_{i,M}\}$;
Estimated Probability Vector: $\{\hat{y}_{i,1}, \hat{y}_{i,2}, \ldots, \hat{y}_{i,M}\}$;
Upper Bound for threshold $= \Omega$, and Threshold Stride $=$ S
Result: The Optimal Thresholds T $= (ot_1, ot_2, \ldots, ot_M)$
Initialization: The set of threshold T $= (ot_1 = 0, ot_2 = 0, \ldots, ot_M = 0)$;
for $i \leftarrow 1$ **to** M **do**
    $j \leftarrow 0$;
    $\omega \leftarrow 0$;
    $\pi \leftarrow 0$;
    for $j < \Omega$ **do**
        Initialize M-dimensional binary vector $\mathbf{v} \leftarrow (v_1 = 0, v_2 = 0, \ldots, v_M = 0)$
        ;
        if $\hat{y}_i > j$ **then**
            $v_i \leftarrow 1$;
        end
        else
            $v_i \leftarrow 0$;
        end
        $\omega \leftarrow \omega.append(MCC(\mathbf{y}[1:i], v))$;
        $\pi = \pi.append(j)$;
        $j = j + S$
    end
    $\hat{m} \leftarrow argmax_m \omega = (\omega_1, \omega_2, \ldots, \omega_m, \ldots)$;
    $ot_i = \pi[\hat{m}]$
end

Algorithm 1. Find Optimal Threshold

Network Architecture: Our models are trained and evaluated using Keras with Tensorflow backend. For the DNN architecture, we used a generic building block containing the following model structure: Conv-Relu-BatchNorm-MaxPool-Conv-Relu-BatchNorm-MaxPool-Dense-Relu-Dropweights and Dense-Relu-Dropweights-Dense-Sigmoid, with 32 convolution kernels, 3×3 kernel size, 2×2 pooling, dense layer with 512 units, 128 units, and 8 feed-forward Dropweights probabilities 0.3. We optimised the model using Adam optimizer with the default learning rate of 0.001. The training process was conducted in 1000 epochs, with mini-batch size 32. We repeated our experiments three times for an algorithm and calculated a mean of the results.

3 Estimating Bias-Corrected Uncertainty Using Jackknife Resampling Method

3.1 Bayesian Deep Learning and Estimating Uncertainty

There are many measures to estimate uncertainty such as softmax variance, expected entropy, mutual information, predictive entropy and averaging predictions over multiple models. In supervised learning, information gain, i.e. mutual information between the input data and the model parameters is considered as the most relevant measure of the epistemic uncertainty [4,12]. Estimation of entropy from the finite set of data suffers from a severe downward bias when the data is under-sampled. Even small biases can result in significant inaccuracies when estimating entropy [9]. We leveraged Jackknife resampling method to calculate bias-corrected entropy [11].

Given a set of training data D, where $\mathbf{X} = \{x_1, x_2 \ldots x_N\}$ is the set of N images and the corresponding labels $\mathbf{Y} = \{y_1, y_2 \ldots y_N\}$, a BNN is defined in terms of a prior $p(\omega)$ on the weights, as well as the likelihood $p(D|\omega)$. Consider class probabilities $p(y_{x_i} = c \mid x_i, \omega_t, D)$ with $\omega_t \sim q(\omega \mid D)$ with $\mathcal{W} = (\omega_t)_{t=1}^T$, a set of independent and identically distributed (i.i.d.) samples draws from $q(\omega \mid, D)$. The below procedure computes the Monte Carlo (MC) estimate of the posterior predictive distribution, its Entropy and Mutual Information(MI):

$$\sum_{i=1}^N \mathbb{I}_{\mathrm{MC}}(y_i; \omega \mid x_i, D) = \mathbb{H}\big(\hat{p}(y_i \mid x_i, D)\big) - \frac{1}{|\mathcal{W}|} \sum_{\omega \in \mathcal{W}} \mathbb{H}\big(p(y_i \mid x_i, \omega, D)\big). \quad (1)$$

where

$$\hat{p}(y_i \mid x_i, D) = \frac{1}{|\mathcal{W}|} \sum_{\omega \in \mathcal{W}} p(y_i \mid x_i, \omega, D). \quad (2)$$

The stochastic predictive entropy is $H[y \mid x, \omega] = \mathbb{H}(\hat{p}) = -\sum_c \hat{p}_c \log(\hat{p}_c)$, where $\hat{p}_c = \frac{1}{T} \sum_t p_{tc}$ is the entire sample maximum likelihood estimator of probabilities.

The first term in the MC estimate of the mutual information is called the plug-in estimator of the entropy. It has long been known that the plug-in estimator underestimates the true entropy and plug-in estimate is biased [11,17].

A classic method for correcting the bias is the Jackknife resampling method [3]. In order to solve the bias problem, we propose a Jackknife estimator to estimate the epistemic uncertainty to improve an entropy-based estimation model. Unlike MC-Dropout, it does not assume constant variance. If $\mathcal{D}(X, Y)$ is the observed random sample, the ith Jackknife sample, x_i, is the subset of the sample that leaves-one-out observation $x_i : x_{(i)} = (x_1, \ldots x_{i-1}, x_{i+1} \ldots x_n)$. For sample size N, the Jackknife standard error $\hat{\sigma}$ is defined as: $\sqrt{\frac{(N-1)}{N} \sum_{i=1}^N (\hat{\sigma}_i - \hat{\sigma}_{(\odot)})^2}$, where $\hat{\sigma}_{(\odot)}$ is the empirical average of the Jackknife replicates: $\frac{1}{N} \sum_{i=1}^N \hat{\sigma}_{(i)}$. Here, the Jackknife estimator is an unbiased estimator of the variance of the sample mean. The Jackknife correction of a plug-in estimator $\mathbb{H}(\cdot)$ is computed according to the method below [3]:

Given a sample $(p_t)_{t=1}^T$ with p_t discrete distribution on $1 \ldots C$ classes, T corresponds to the total number of MC-Dropweights forward passes during the test.

1. for each $t = 1 \ldots T$
   - calculate the leave-one-out estimator: $\hat{p}_c^{-t} = \frac{1}{T-1} \sum_{j \neq i} p_{jc}$
   - calculate the plug-in entropy estimate: $\hat{H}_{-t} = \mathbb{H}(\hat{p}^{-t})$
2. calculate the bias-corrected entropy $\hat{H}_J = T\hat{H} + \frac{(T-1)}{T} \sum_{t=1}^T \hat{H}_{(-i)}$, where $\hat{H}_{(-i)}$ is the observed entropy based on a sub-sample in which the ith individual is removed.

We leveraged the following relation:

$$\mu_{-i} = \frac{1}{T-1} \sum_{j \neq i} x_j = \mu + \frac{\mu - x_i}{T-1}.$$

while resolving the i-th data point out of the sample mean $\mu = \frac{1}{T} \sum_i x_i$ and recompute the mean μ_{-i}. This makes it possible to quickly calculate leave-one-out estimators of a discrete probability distribution.

The epistemic uncertainty can be obtained as the difference between the approximate predictive posterior entropy (or total entropy) and the average uncertainty in predictions (i.e: aleatoric entropy):

$$I(\mathbf{y} : \omega) = H_e(\mathbf{y}|\mathbf{x}) = \hat{H}_J(\mathbf{y}|\mathbf{x}) - H_a(\mathbf{y}|\mathbf{x}) = \hat{H}_J(\mathbf{y}|\mathbf{x}) - \mathbb{E}_{q(\omega|\mathbf{D})}[\hat{H}_J(\mathbf{y}|\mathbf{x}, \omega)]$$

Therefore, the mutual information $I(\mathbf{y} : \omega)$ i.e. as a measure of bias-corrected epistemic uncertainty, represents the variability in the predictions made by the neural network weight configurations drawn from approximate posteriors. It derives an estimate of the finite sample bias from the leave-one-out estimators of the entropy and reduces bias considerably down to $O(n^{-2})$ [3].

The bias-corrected uncertainty estimation model explains regions of ambiguous data space or difficult to classify, as data distribution with noise in the inputs or model, which was trained with different domain data. Consequently, these inputs should be assigned a higher aleatoric uncertainty. As a result, we can expect high model uncertainty in these regions.

Following Gal [5], we define the stochastic versions of Bayesian uncertainty using MC-Dropweights, where the class probabilities $p(y_{x_i} = c \mid x_i, \omega_t, D)$ with $\omega_t \sim q(\omega \mid D)$ and $\mathcal{W} = (\omega_t)_{t=1}^T$ along with a set of independent and identically distributed (i.i.d.) samples drawn from $q(\omega \mid, D)$, can be approximated by the average over the MC-Dropweights forward pass.

We trained the multi-label classification network with all eight classes. We dichotomised the network outputs using optimal threshold with Algorithm 1 for each cell type, with a 1000 MC-Dropweights forward passes at test time. In these detection tasks, $p(y_{x_i} >= 0; OptimalThreshold_i \mid x_i, \omega_t, D)$, where 1 marks the presence of cell type, is sufficient to indicate the most likely decision along with estimated uncertainty.

3.2   Dataset

Our main dataset is taken from The Human Protein Atlas project, that maps the distribution of all human proteins in human tissues and organs [15]. Here, we used high-resolution digital images of immunohistochemically stained testes tissue consisting of 8 cell types: spermatogonia, preleptotene spermatocytes, pachytene spermatocytes, round/early spermatids, elongated/late spermatids, sertoli cells, leydig cells, and peritubular cells, publicly available on the Human Protein Atlas version 18 (v18.proteinatlas.org), as shown in Fig. 2:

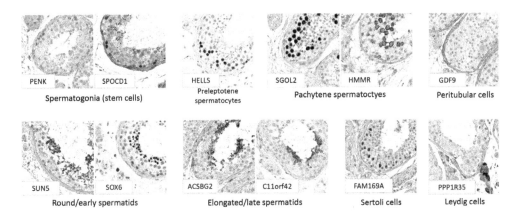

Fig. 2. Examples of proteins expressed only in one cell-type [10]

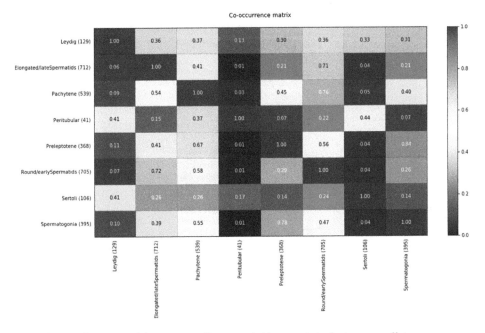

Fig. 3. Annotated heatmap of a correlation matrix between cell types

A relationship was observed between spermatogonia and preleptotene spermatocytes cell types and between round/early spermatids and elongated/late spermatids cell types along with Pachytene spermatocytes cells. Figure 3 illustrates the correlation coefficients between cell types. The observable pattern is that very few cell types are strongly correlated with each other.

3.3   Results and Discussions

We conducted the experiments on Human Protein Atlas datasets to validate the proposed algorithm, MC-Dropweights in Multi-Label Classification.

Multi-label Classification Model Performance: Model evaluation metrics for multi-label classification are different from those used in multi-class (or binary) classification. The performance metrics of multi-label classifiers can be classified as label-based (i.e.: it is assumed that labels are mutually exclusive) and example-based [16]. In this work, example-based measures (Accuracy score, Hamming-loss, F1-Score) and Rank-Loss are used to evaluate the performance of the classifiers.

Table 1. Performance metrics

%Metrics	BR	CC	PCC	CFT	CLEMS	MC-Dropout	MC-Dropweights
Hamming loss	0.2445	0.2420	0.2420	0.2375	0.2370	0.207	0.1925
Rank loss	3.6700	3.5740	3.1580	3.2920	3.1120	2.862	2.626
F1 score	0.5038	0.5184	0.5733	0.5373	0.5902	0.6306	0.6627
Avg. accuracy score	0.4236	0.4389	0.4643	0.4573	0.5052	0.6150	0.7067

In the first experiment, we compared the MC-Dropweights neural network-based method with five machine learning MLC algorithms introduced in Sect. 1: binary relevance (BR), Classifier Chain (CC), Probabilistic Classifier Chain (PCC) and Condensed Filter Tree (CFT), Cost-Sensitive Label Embedding with Multi-dimensional Scaling (CLEMS) and the MC-Dropout neural network model. Table 1 shows that MC-Dropweights exhibits considerably better performance overall the algorithms, which demonstrates the importance of considering the Dropweights in the neural network.

Cell Type-Specific Predictive Uncertainty: The relationship between uncertainty and predictive accuracy grouped by correct and incorrect predictions is shown in Fig. 4. It is interesting to note that, on average, the highest uncertainty is associated with Elongated/late Spermatids and Round/early Spermatids. This indicates that there is some feature which contributes greater uncertainty to the Spermatids class types than to the other cell types.

Cell Type Localization: Estimated uncertainty with Saliency Mapping is a simple technique to uncover discriminative image regions that strongly influence the network prediction in identifying a specific class label in the image. It highlights the most influential features in the image space that affect the predictions of the model [1] and visualises the contributions of individual pixels to epistemic and aleatoric uncertainties separately. We calculated the class activation maps (CAM) [18] using the activations of the fully connected layer and the weights from the prediction layer as shown in Fig. 5.

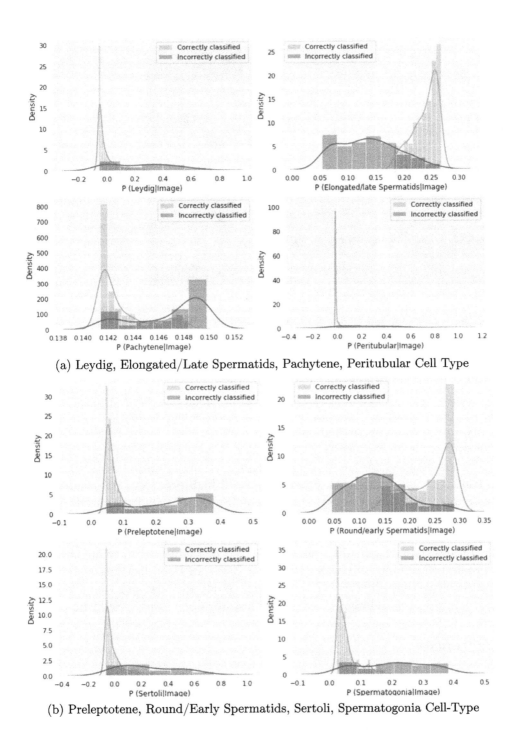

(a) Leydig, Elongated/Late Spermatids, Pachytene, Peritubular Cell Type

(b) Preleptotene, Round/Early Spermatids, Sertoli, Spermatogonia Cell-Type

Fig. 4. Distribution of uncertainty values for all protein images, grouped by correct and incorrect predictions. Label assignment was based on optimal thresholding (Algorithm 1). For an incorrect prediction, there is a strong likelihood that the predictive uncertainty is also high in all cases except for Spermatids.

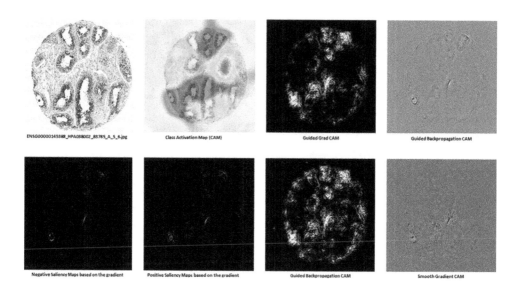

Fig. 5. Saliency maps for some common methods towards model explanation

4   Conclusion and Discussion

In this study, a multi-label classification method was developed using deep learning architecture with Dropweights for the purposes of predicting cell types-specific protein expression with estimated uncertainty, which can increase the ability to interpret, with confidence and make models based on deep learning more applicable in practice. The results show that a Deep Learning Model with MC-Dropweights yields the best performance among all popular classifiers.

Building truly large-scale, fully-automated, high precision, very high dimensional, image analysis system that can recognise various cell type-specific protein expression, specifically for Elongated/Late Spermatids and Round/early Spermatids remains a strenuous task. The properties in the dataset such as label correlations, label cardinality can strongly affect the uncertainty quantification in predictive probability performance of a Bayesian Deep learning algorithm in multi-label settings. There is no systematic study on how and why the performance varies over different data properties; any such study would be of great benefit in progressing multi-label algorithms.

References

1. Adebayo, J., Gilmer, J., Muelly, M., Goodfellow, I., Hardt, M., Kim, B.: Sanity checks for saliency maps. In: Advances in Neural Information Processing Systems, pp. 9505–9515 (2018)
2. Chu, W.T., Guo, H.J.: Movie genre classification based on poster images with deep neural networks. In: Proceedings of the Workshop on Multimodal Understanding of Social, Affective and Subjective Attributes, pp. 39–45. ACM (2017)
3. DasGupta, A.: Asymptotic Theory of Statistics and Probability. Springer, New York (2008). https://doi.org/10.1007/978-0-387-75971-5
4. Depeweg, S., Hernández-Lobato, J.M., Doshi-Velez, F., Udluft, S.: Decomposition of uncertainty in Bayesian deep learning for efficient and risk-sensitive learning. arXiv preprint arXiv:1710.07283 (2017)

5. Gal, Y.: Uncertainty in deep learning. Ph.D. thesis, University of Cambridge (2016)
6. Ghoshal, B., Tucker, A., Sanghera, B., Wong, W.: Estimating uncertainty in deep learning for reporting confidence to clinicians in medical image segmentation and diseases detection. In: Computational Intelligence - Special Issue on Foundations of Biomedical (Big) Data Science, vol. 1 (2019)
7. Ghoshal, B., Tucker, A., Sanghera, B., Wong, W.: Estimating uncertainty in deep learning for reporting confidence to clinicians when segmenting nuclei image data. 2019 IEEE 32nd International Symposium on Computer-Based Medical Systems (CBMS), vol. 1, pp. 318–324, June 2019. https://doi.org/10.1109/CBMS.2019.00072
8. Huang, K.H., Lin, H.T.: Cost-sensitive label embedding for multi-label classification. Mach. Learn. **106**(9–10), 1725–1746 (2017)
9. Macke, J., Murray, I., Latham, P.: Estimation bias in maximum entropy models. Entropy **15**(8), 3109–3129 (2013)
10. Pineau, C., et al.: Cell type-specific expression of testis elevated genes based on transcriptomics and antibody-based proteomics. J. Proteome Res. **18**, 4215–4230 (2019)
11. Quenouille, M.H.: Notes on bias in estimation. Biometrika **43**(3/4), 353–360 (1956)
12. Shannon, C.E.: A mathematical theory of communication. Bell Syst. Tech. J. **27**(3), 379–423 (1948)
13. Srivastava, N., Hinton, G., Krizhevsky, A., Sutskever, I., Salakhutdinov, R.: Dropout: a simple way to prevent neural networks from overfitting. Journal Mach. Learn. Res. **15**(1), 1929–1958 (2014)
14. Teye, M., Azizpour, H., Smith, K.: Bayesian uncertainty estimation for batch normalized deep networks. arXiv preprint arXiv:1802.06455 (2018)
15. Uhlén, M., et al.: Tissue-based map of the human proteome. Science **347**(6220), 1260419 (2015)
16. Wu, X.Z., Zhou, Z.H.: A unified view of multi-label performance measures. In: Proceedings of the 34th International Conference on Machine Learning, vol. 70, pp. 3780–3788. JMLR. org (2017)
17. Yeung, R.W.: A new outlook on Shannon's information measures. IEEE Trans. Inf. Theory **37**(3), 466–474 (1991)
18. Zhou, B., Khosla, A., Lapedriza, A., Oliva, A., Torralba, A.: Learning deep features for discriminative localization. In: CVPR (2016)

5

Digital Footprints of International Migration on Twitter

Jisu Kim[1]([✉])[iD], Alina Sîrbu[2]([✉])[iD], Fosca Giannotti[3]([✉])[iD],
and Lorenzo Gabrielli[3]([✉])

[1] Scuola Normale Superiore, Pisa, Italy
jisu.kim@sns.it
[2] University of Pisa, Pisa, Italy
alina.sirbu@unipi.it
[3] Istituto di Scienza e Tecnologie dell'Informazione,
National Research Council of Italy, Pisa, Italy
{fosca.giannotti,lorenzo.gabrielli}@isti.cnr.it

Abstract. Studying migration using traditional data has some limitations. To date, there have been several studies proposing innovative methodologies to measure migration stocks and flows from social big data. Nevertheless, a uniform definition of a migrant is difficult to find as it varies from one work to another depending on the purpose of the study and nature of the dataset used. In this work, a generic methodology is developed to identify migrants within the Twitter population. This describes a migrant as a person who has the current residence different from the nationality. The residence is defined as the location where a user spends most of his/her time in a certain year. The nationality is inferred from linguistic and social connections to a migrant's country of origin. This methodology is validated first with an internal gold standard dataset and second with two official statistics, and shows strong performance scores and correlation coefficients. Our method has the advantage that it can identify both immigrants and emigrants, regardless of the origin/destination countries. The new methodology can be used to study various aspects of migration, including opinions, integration, attachment, stocks and flows, motivations for migration, etc. Here, we exemplify how trending topics across and throughout different migrant communities can be observed.

Keywords: International migration · Emigration · Big data · Twitter

This work was supported by the European Commission through the Horizon2020 European project "SoBigData Research Infrastructure—Big Data and Social Mining Ecosystem" (grant agreement no 654024) and partially by the Horizon2020 European project "HumMingBird – Enhanced migration measures from a multidimensional perspective" (grant agreement no 870661).

1 Introduction

Understanding where migrants are is an important topic because it touches upon multidimensional aspects of the sending and receiving countries' society. It is not only the demographic fabric of countries but also labour market conditions, as well as economic conditions that may alter due to demographic adjustment. Understanding their allocation is essential for both policy makers and researchers to bring the best of its effects.

Official data such as census, survey and administrative data have been traditionally the main data source to study migration. However, these data have some limitations [12]. They are inconsistent across different nations because countries employ different definitions of a migrant. Moreover, collecting traditional data is costly and time consuming, thus tracking instantaneous stocks of migrants becomes difficult. This becomes even harder when tracking emigrants because of the lack of motivation from citizens to declare their departure.

In recent years, however, we are provided with other alternative data sources for migration. The availability of social big data allows us to study social behaviours both at large scale and at a granular level, and to peek into real-world phenomena. Although known to suffer from other types of issues, such as selection bias, these data could bring complementary value to standard statistics.

Here, we propose a method to identify migrants based on Twitter data, to be used in further analyses. According to the official definition, a migrant[1] is "a person who moves to a country other than that of his or her usual residence for a period of at least a year". In the context of Twitter, we define a migrant as "*a person who has the current residence different from the nationality*".

Following this definition, we performed a two step analysis. First, we estimated the current residence for users by examining location information from tweets. The residence is defined as the country where the user spends most of the time in a year. Second, we estimated nationality, by considering the social network of users. In the international literature, nationality is defined as a relationship between a state and an individual, with rights and duties on both sides [1,6]. Related concepts are ethnicity - in terms of cultural features - and citizenship - in terms of political life. In this paper, we employ the term nationality to define the ensemble of features that make a person feel like they belong to a certain country [2,5]. This could be the country where a person was born, raised and/or lived most of their lives. By comparing labels of residence and nationality of a user, we were able to understand whether the person has moved from their home country to a host country, and thus if they are a migrant. We validated our estimation internally, from the data itself, and externally, with two official datasets (Italian register and Eurostat data).

One of the advantages of our methodology is that it is generic enough to allow for identification of both immigrants and emigrants. We also overcome one of the limitations of traditional data by setting up a uniform definition of

---

[1] Recommendations on Statistics of International Migration, Revision 1 (p. 113). United Nations, 1998.

a migrant across different countries. Furthermore, our definition of a migrant is very close to the official definition. We establish the fact that a person has spent a significant period at the current location. Also, we eliminate visitors or short-term stays that do not follow the definition of a migrant. This is also validated by the comparison with official datasets. Another advantage of our method is the fact that it uses only very basic features from the Twitter data: location, language and network information. This is useful since the settings of the freely available Twitter API change constantly. Some of the user attributes that the existing literature use to estimate nationality are no longer available. In addition, we make use of unknown locations of tweets by examining whether they intersect with identified locations. By doing so, we do not neglect any information provided by the tweets from unknown locations which later provide useful information on trending topics of Italian emigrants overseas.

One of the issues with our method is that the migrants that we observed are selected from the Twitter population, and not from the general world population, and it is known that some demographic groups are missing. Nevertheless, we believe that studying the Twitter migrant population can provide important insight into migration phenomena, even if some findings may not apply to the other demographic groups that are not represented in the data.

It is important to note that tracking individual migrants is not the objective of our study, but it is only an intermediate stage to enable further analyses. We simply perform user classification to identify migrants among users in our data, and then aggregate the findings. Further studies we envision are aimed at devising new population-level indices useful to evaluate and improve the quality of life of migrants, through targeted evidence-based policy making. No individual personal information nor migration status is released at any stage during the current analysis, nor in any population-level analysis, which is performed following the highest ethical and privacy standards.

The rest of the paper is organised as follows. In the next section we describe related work that studies migration using big data. In Sect. 3, we provide details of the experimental setting for data collection as well as data pre-processing. We then explain our identification strategy for both residence and nationality in Sect. 4. In Sect. 5, we evaluate our estimation using both internal and external data. Section 6 covers a possible application of our method on studying trending topics among Italian emigrants, while Sect. 7 concludes the paper.

2   Related Work

In the past few years, there have been several works on migration studies using social big data. Most of these employed Twitter data but Facebook, Skype, Email as well as Call Detail Record (CDR) data have also been used to study both international and internal migration [3, 9, 10, 14, 16]. Here, we focus on studies that have employed freely available data. The definition of a migrant varied from one work to another depending on the purpose of the study and the nature of the dataset. Thus, the definitions provided fit under different types of migration such as refugees, internal migrants, seasonal migrants or even visitors.

One example of using Twitter to observe migration flows is [15]. They defined residence as the country where the tweets were most frequently sent out for periods of four months. If one's residence changed in the following four months period, it was considered that the person has moved. In a more recent work, [11] measure migration flows from Venezuela to neighbouring countries between 2015 and 2019. They look at the bounding boxes and country labels provided by the tweets and identified the most common country of tweets posted monthly. Their definition of a migrant was "any individual leaving Venezuela during the time window of observation" which was observed when an identified Venezuelan resident appeared for the first time in a different country. Our definition of residence is somewhat similar to these works. However, unlike them, we are measuring stocks of migrants, and not flows. Thus, we take into account the aspect of duration of stay. This naturally eliminates short-term trips and visits.

Apart from geo-tagged tweets, there is other information provided by the Twitter API that can help us infer whether a person is a migrant or not. Although [8] did not directly study migrants, but looked at foreigners present in Qatar, it provides important insights to which of the features provided by Twitter is useful in identifying nationality of users. They gathered features from both profile and tweets of users. For features providing information on profile pictures and name, they performed facial recognition and name ethnicity detection. Their final results showed that ethnicity of name, race, language of tweet, language of mention, location of followers and friends are the first six features that are useful. In this paper, we purely employ data provided by Twitter for the analysis and therefore, we do not have name, ethnicity and race features. Nevertheless, our work also shows that locations of users and friends are the useful features. The difference here is that we propose to use the social network of users as one of the main features in identifying nationality, which is more flexible than having to perform ethnicity detection on names and profile pictures.

3   Experimental Setting for Data Collection

We began with a Twitter dataset collected by the SoBigData.eu Laboratory [4]. We started from a three months period of geo-tagged tweets from August to October 2015. Due to our focus on Italy, we selected from these data the users that tweeted from Italy, obtaining thus 34,160 users. We then crawled the network of geo-enabled friends of these 34,160 users, using the Twitter API. Friends are people that the individual users are following. We focused on friends because we believe that for a user, the information on whom they follow is more informative when it comes to nationality, than who they are followed by. We concentrated on geo-enabled friends because geo-location is necessary for our analysis. By collecting friends, the list of users crossed our initial geographic boundary, i.e., Italy. At this stage, the number of unique users grew to over 250,000. For all users we also scraped the profile information and the 200 most recent tweets using the Twitter API. During this process, we were able to collect all 200 recent tweets for 97% of users and at least 55 tweets for 99% of users. Our final user network consists of 258,455 nodes and 1,205,133 edges which includes both our initial 34,160 users and their geo-tagged friends.

For the process of identifying migration status, we focus on the core users, i.e., 34,160 users. We assign a residence and a nationality to each user, based on the geo-locations included in the data, the language of tweets and profile information. The final dataset includes 237 unique countries from where individuals have sent out their tweets, including 'undefined' location. Even if a user enables geo-tags on their tweets, not all tweets are geo-tagged. As a result, 21% of our tweets are 'undefined'. As for the languages, there are 66 unique languages and 12% of our tweets are in English.

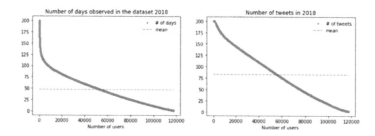

Fig. 1. Distribution of the number of days (left) and the number of tweets (right) observed in the data per user: on average, our users have tweeted 47 days and 82 tweets in 2018.

As for the profile features, we observe that 40% of the users have filled out location description. In addition, most of users have set their profile language to English. The number of unique profile languages detected in our data is 58 which is smaller than the languages used, indicating that some users are using languages different from their profile language when tweeting.

In order to assign a place of residence to users, we needed to restrict the observation time period. We have chosen to look at one year length of tweets from 2018, in order to assign the residence label for the 2018 solar year. We selected users that have tweeted in 2018, identifying 128,305 users. To remove bots, we looked at whether a user is tweeting too many times a day. We considered that tweeting more than 50 tweets on average in a single day was excessive and we have eliminated in this way 39 users. In addition, we removed users that were not very active in 2018. If the number of tweets was less than 20, we checked whether the tweeted days were spread out during the year. If the days were not well spread out, we filtered out the user. On the other hand, if it was well spread out, it meant that the user was regularly tweeting, so the user was kept. During this process, we removed 10,764 users. After removing bots and inactive users, we have 117,502 users. For these, we show the distribution of the number of tweets and number of days in which they tweeted in Fig. 1. On average we see 47 days and 82 tweets.

In addition to the Twitter data, we also collected a list of official and spoken languages for countries identified in our data[2].

4 Identifying Migrants

A migrant is a person that has the residence different from the nationality. We thus consider our core 34,160 Twitter users and assign a residence and nationality based on the information included in our dataset. The difference between the two labels will allow us to detect individuals who have migrated and are currently living in a place different from their home country. The methodology we propose is based on a series of hypotheses: a person that has moved away from their home country stays in contact with their friends back in the home country and may keep using their mother tongue.

4.1 Assigning Residence

In order for a place to be called residence, a person has to spend a considerable amount of time at the location. Our definition of residence is based on the amount of time in which a Twitter user is observed in a country for a given solar year. More precisely, a residence for each user is the country with the longest length of stay which is calculated by taking into account both the number of days in which a user tweets from a country but also the period between consecutive tweets in the same country. In this work we compute residences based on 2018 data.

To compute the residence, we first compute the number of days in which we see tweets for each country for each user. If the top location is not 'undefined', then that is the location chosen as residence. Otherwise, we check whether any tweet sent from 'undefined' country was sent on a same day as tweets sent from the second top country. In case at least one date matched between the two locations, we substitute second country as the user's place of residence. On average, 5 dates matched. This is done under the assumption that a user cannot tweet from two different countries in a day. Although this is not always the case if a user travels, in most of the days of the year this should be true. This approach allowed us to assign a residence in 2018 to 57,180 users.

For the remaining 60,322 users, a slightly different approach was implemented. We computed the length of stay in days by adding together the duration between consecutive tweets in the same country. We selected the country with the largest length of stay. In case the top country was 'undefined', we checked whether 'undefined' locations were in between segments of the second top country, in which case the second country was chosen. In this way, an additional 11,046 users were assigned a place of residence. The remaining 49,276 users were neglected because we considered that we did not have enough information to assign a residence.

---

[2] Retrieved from http://www.geonames.org and https://www.worlddata.info.

4.2   Assigning Nationality

In order to estimate nationalities for Twitter users, we took into account two types of information included in our Twitter data. The first type relates to the users themselves, and includes the countries from which tweets are sent and the languages in which users tweet. For each user u we define two dictionaries loc^u and $lang^u$ where we include, for each country and language the proportion of user tweets in that country/language.

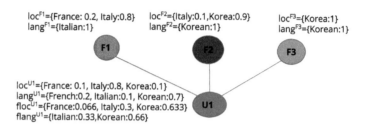

Fig. 2. Example of calculation of the $floc$ and $flang$ values for a user. The calculation of $floc^{U1}$ and $flang^{U1}$ is based of the $floc$ and $flang$ values for the three friends, showing the distribution of tweets in various countries/languages for each.

The second type of information used is related to the user's friends. Again, we look at the languages spoken by friends, and locations from which friends tweet. Specifically, starting from the loc and $lang$ dictionaries of all friends of a user, we define two further dictionaries $floc$ and $flang$. The first stores all countries from where friends tweet, together with the average fraction of tweets in that country, computed over all friends:

$$floc^u[C] = \frac{1}{|F(u)|} \sum_{f \in F(u)} loc^f[C] \tag{1}$$

where $F(u)$ is the set of friends of user u. Similarly, the $flang$ dictionary stores all languages spoken by friends, with the average fraction of tweets in each language l:

$$flang^u[l] = \frac{1}{|F(u)|} \sum_{f \in F(u)} lang^f[l] \tag{2}$$

Figure 2 shows an example of a (fictitious) user with their friends, and the four resulting dictionaries.

The four dictionaries defined above are then used to assign a nationality score to each country C for each user u:

$$N_C^u = w_{loc} loc^u[C] + w_{lang} \sum_{l \in languages(C)} lang^u[l] + \tag{3}$$

$$w_{floc} floc^u[C] + w_{flang} \sum_{l \in languages(C)} flang^u[l] \tag{4}$$

where $languages(C)$ are the set of languages spoken in country C, while w_{loc}, w_{lang}, w_{floc} and w_{flang} are parameters of our model which need to be estimated from the data (one global value estimated for all users). Each of the w value gives a weight to the corresponding user attribute in the calculation of the nationality. To select the nationality for each user we simply select the country C with maximum N_C: $N^u = \text{argmax}_C N_C^u$.

5 Evaluation

To evaluate our strategy for identifying migrants we first propose an internal validation procedure. This defines gold standard datasets for residence and nationality and computes the classification performance of our two strategies to identify the two user attributes. The gold standard datasets are produced using profile information as they are provided by the users themselves. We then perform an external validation where we compare the migrant percentages obtained in our data with those from official statistics.

5.1 Internal Validation: Gold Standards Derived from Our Data

Residence. To devise a gold standard dataset for residence we consider profile locations set by users. We assume that if users declare a location in their profile, then that is most probably their residence. Very few users actually declare a location, and not all of them provide a valid one, thus we only selected profile locations that were identifiable to country level. Among the user accounts for which we could estimate the residence, 3,065 accounts had a valid country in their profile location. Using these accounts as our validation data, we computed the F1 score to measure the performance of our residence calculation. Table 1 shows overall results, and also scores for the most common countries individually. The weighted average of the F1 score is 86%, with individual countries reaching up to 94%, demonstrating the validity of our residence estimation procedure.

Nationality. In order to build a gold standard for nationality, we take into account the profile language declared by the users. The assumption is that profile languages can provide a hint of one's nationality [13]. However, many users might not set their profile language, but use the default English setting. For this reason, we do not include into the gold standard users that have English as their profile language.

Table 1. Average precision, recall and F1 scores, together with scores for the top 7 residences in terms of support size.

	Weighted Avg	Macro avg	Micro avg	IT	KW	US	ID	SG	AU
F1-score	0.858	0.716	0.856	0.928	0.839	0.703	0.945	0.83	0.891
Precision	0.879	0.745	0.856	0.935	0.989	0.572	0.949	0.946	0.883
Recall	0.856	0.727	0.856	0.921	0.728	0.91	0.941	0.739	0.899
Support	3065	3065	3065	343	125	122	119	119	109

Table 2. Average precision, recall and F1 scores for top 8 nationalities in terms of support numbers

	Weighted avg	Macro avg	Micro avg	IT	ES	TR	RU	FR	BR	DE	AR
F1-score	0.99	0.98	0.72	0.99	0.96	0.98	0.95	0.94	0.95	0.92	0.97
Precision	0.99	0.98	0.73	1	0.94	0.98	0.98	0.9	0.96	0.91	0.98
Recall	0.98	0.98	0.75	0.99	0.97	0.99	0.93	0.98	0.94	0.93	0.95
Support	12223	12223	12223	10781	302	173	146	118	113	86	59

The profile language, however, does not immediately translate into nationality. While for some languages the correspondence to a country is immediate, for many others it is not. For instance, Spanish is spoken in Spain and most American countries, so one needs to select the correct one. For this, we look at tweet locations. We consider all countries that match with the profile language and, among these, we select the one with the largest number of tweets, but only if the number of tweets from that country is at least 10% of the total number of tweets of that user. This allows to select the most probable country, also for users who reside outside their native country. If no location satisfies this criterion the user is not included in the gold standard. We were able to identify nationalities of 12,223 users. Due to the fact that during data collection we focused on geo-tags in Italy, the dataset contains a significant number of Italians.

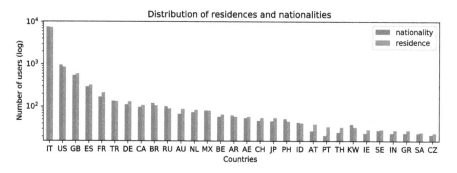

Fig. 3. Distribution of residences and nationalities of top 30 countries, for all users that possess both residence and nationality labels.

We employed this gold standard dataset in two ways. First, we needed to select suitable values for the w weights from Eqs. 3–4. These show the importance of the four components used for nationality computation: own language and location, friends' language and location. We performed a simple grid search and obtained the best accuracy on the gold standard using values 0 for languages and 2 and 1.5 for own and friends' location, respectively. Thus we can conclude that it is the locations that are most important in defining nationality for twitter users, with a slightly stronger weight on the individual's location rather than the friends. The final F1-score, both overall and for top individual nationalities, are included in Table 2, showing a very good performance in all cases.

To assign final residences and nationalities to our core users, we combined the predictions with the gold standards (we predicted only if the gold standard was not present). Figure 3 shows the final distribution of residences and nationalities of top 30 countries for all users that have both the residence and nationality labels. The difference in the residence and nationality can be interpreted as either immigrants or emigrants.

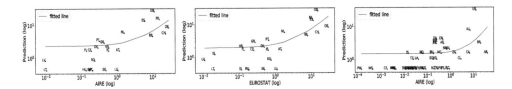

Fig. 4. Comparison between the true and predicted data; the first two plots show predicted versus AIRE/EUROSTAT data on European countries. The last plot shows predicted versus AIRE data on non-European countries.

5.2 External Validations: Validation with Ground Truth Data

In order to validate our results with ground truth data, we study users labelled with Italian nationality and non-Italian residence, i.e. Italian emigrants. We computed the normalised percentage of Italian emigrants resulting from our data for all countries, and compared with two official datasets: AIRE (Anagrafe Italiani residenti all'estero), containing Italian register data, and Eurostat, the European Union statistical office. For comparison we use Spearman correlation coefficients, which allow for quantifying the monotonic relationship between the ground truth data and our estimation by taking ranks of variables into consideration.

Figure 4 displays the various values obtained, compared with official data. A first interesting remark is that even between the official datasets themselves, the numbers do not match completely. The correlation between the two datasets is 0.91. Secondly we observed good agreement between our predictions and the official data for European countries. The correlation with AIRE is 0.753, while with Eurostat it is 0.711 when considering Europe. For non-European countries, however the correlation with AIRE data drops to 0.626. We believe the lower performance is due to several factors related to sampling bias and data quality in the various datasets. This includes bias on Twitter and in our methods, but also errors in the official data, which could be larger in non-EU countries due to less efficient connections in sharing information.

All in all, we believe our method shows good performance and can be successfully used to build population level indices for studying migration. We do not aim to perform nowcasting of immigrant stocks, but rather to identify a population that can be representative enough for further analyses.

6   Case Study: Topics on Twitter

In this section we show that our methodology can be employed to study how trending topics in Italy are also being discussed among Italian emigrants. As an example, we selected one hashtag that has been very popular in the last years: #Salvini. This refers to the Italian politician Matteo Salvini who served as Deputy Prime Minister and Minister of internal affairs in Italy until recently. To this, we added the top nine hashtags that appear frequently with #Salvini in our data: Berlusconi, Conti, Diciott, DiMaio, Facciamorete, Legga, M5S, Migrant, Ottoemezzo. Indeed, they all represent people that are often mentioned together or political parties or other issues that are associated with the hashtag #Salvini.

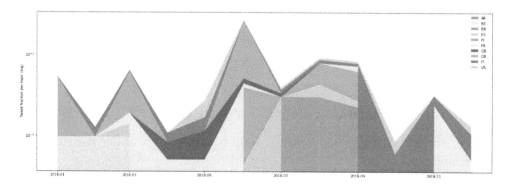

Fig. 5. Stream graph: appearance of hashtags related to #Salvini from Italians across 10 selected residence countries in 2018. The discussion continuously appeared in Italy throughout the year and it became more lively employed by Italians overseas as Salvini gained more political attention.

Figure 5 shows an evolution of the usage of the 10 above mentioned hashtags across different Italian communities both within and abroad Italy. The values shown are the number of tweets from Italian nationals residing in each country that include one of the 10 hashtags, divided by the total number of tweets from Italian nationals from that country. Values are computed monthly. Thus, we show the monthly popularity of the topics in each country. In this way, even the tweets from less represented countries are well shown. As the figure shows, the hashtag was continuously used by Italians in Italy. We observed that the hashtag gradually spread over other residence countries as Salvini received more and more attention. We also observe that most of the attention comes from Italians residing in Europe, with non-European countries less represented.

7   Conclusion and Future Work

We have developed a new methodology to provide a snapshot of migrants within the Twitter population. We considered the length of stay in a country as the key factor to define a user's residence. As for the nationality, connections which migrants maintain with their country of origin provided us with a good indication. In particular, the location of friends seemed to be a strong feature in determining nationality, together with the location of the users themselves. Tweet language, on the other hand, was not considered relevant by our model. This is probably due to the fact that English is the dominating language on Twitter, since a language that is widely understood has to be spoken to get more attention from other users. We have validated our results both with internal and external data. The results show good classification performance scores and good correlation coefficients with official datasets.

The constructed dataset can be applied in different scenarios. We have shown how it can be used to study trending topics on Twitter, and how attention is divided between emigrants and non-migrants of a certain nationality. In the future, we plan to analyse social ties, integration and assimilation of migrants [7]. At the same time, one can investigate the strength of the ties with the community of origin.

References

1. Castillo petruzzi case (1999)
2. Assal, M.A.: Nationality and citizenship questions in Sudan after the Southern Sudan referendum vote. Sudan Report (2011)
3. Blumenstock, J.E.: Inferring patterns of internal migration from mobile phone call records: evidence from Rwanda. Inf. Technol. Dev. **18**(2), 107–125 (2012)
4. Coletto, M., et al.: Perception of social phenomena through the multidimensional analysis of online social networks. Online Soc. Netw. Media **1**, 14–32 (2017)
5. Donner, R.: The Regulation of Nationality in International Law, 2d edn, p. 289. Leiden, Brill Nijhoff (1994). https://brill.com/view/title/14000, ISBN 978-09-41-32077-1
6. Hailbronner, K.: Nationality in public international law and European law. JSTOR (2006)
7. Herdağdelen, et al.: The social ties of immigrant communities in the united states. In: Proceedings of the 8th ACM Conference on Web Science, pp. 78–84. ACM (2016)
8. Huang, W., et al.: Inferring nationalities of Twitter users and studying international linking. In: Proceedings of the 25th ACM Conference on Hypertext and Social Media, pp. 237–242. ACM (2014)
9. Kikas, R., et al.: Explaining international migration in the Skype network: the role of social network features. In: Proceedings of the 1st ACM Workshop on Social Media World Sensors, pp. 17–22. ACM (2015)
10. Lamanna, F., et al.: Immigrant community integration in world cities. PLoS One **13**(3), e0191612 (2018)
11. Mazzoli, M., et al.: Migrant mobility flows characterized with digital data. arXiv preprint arXiv:1908.02540 (2019)
12. Sîrbu, A., et al.: Human migration: the big data perspective. Int. J. Data Sci. Anal. (2020, under review)
13. Stokes, B.: Language: the cornerstone of national identity. Pew Research Center's Global Attitudes Project (2017)

14. Zagheni, E., et al.: Combining social media data and traditional surveys to nowcast migration stocks. In: Annual Meeting of the Population Association of America (2018)
15. Zagheni, E., et al.: Inferring international and internal migration patterns from Twitter data. In: Proceedings of the 23rd International Conference on World Wide Web, pp. 439–444. ACM (2014)
16. Zagheni, E., Weber, I.: You are where you e-mail: using e-mail data to estimate international migration rates. In: Proceedings of the 4th Annual ACM Web Science Conference, pp. 348–351. ACM (2012)

6

A Late-Fusion Approach to Community Detection in Attributed Networks

Chang Liu[1], Christine Largeron[2], Osmar R. Zaïane[1]([✉]),
and Shiva Zamani Gharaghooshi[1]

[1] Alberta Machine Intelligence Institute, University of Alberta, Edmonton, Canada
{chang6,zaiane,zamanigh}@ualberta.ca
[2] Laboratoire Hubert Curien, Université de Lyon, Saint-Etienne, France
christine.largeron@univ-st-etienne.fr

Abstract. The majority of research on community detection in attributed networks follows an "early fusion" approach, in which the structural and attribute information about the network are integrated together as the guide to community detection. In this paper, we propose an approach called *late-fusion*, which looks at this problem from a different perspective. We first exploit the network structure and node attributes separately to produce two different partitionings. Later on, we combine these two sets of communities via a fusion algorithm, where we introduce a parameter for weighting the importance given to each type of information: node connections and attribute values. Extensive experiments on various real and synthetic networks show that our late-fusion approach can improve detection accuracy from using only network structure. Moreover, our approach runs significantly faster than other attributed community detection algorithms including early fusion ones.

Keywords: Community detection · Attributed networks · Late fusion

1 Introduction

In many modern applications, data is represented in the form of relationships between nodes forming a *network*, or interchangeably a *graph*. A typical characteristic of these real networks is the *community structure*, where network nodes can be grouped into densely connected modules called communities. Community identification is an important issue because it can help to understand the network structure and leads to many substantial applications [6]. While traditional community detection methods focus on the network topology where communities can be defined as sets of nodes densely connected internally, recently, increasing attention has been paid to the attributes associated with the nodes in order to take into account homophily effects, and several works have been devoted to community detection in attributed networks. The aim of such process is to obtain a partitioning of the nodes where vertices belonging to the same subgroup are densely connected and homogeneous in terms of attribute values.

In this paper, we propose a new method designed for community detection in attributed networks, called *late fusion*. This is a two-step approach where we first identify two sets of communities based on the network topology and node attributes respectively, then we merge them together to produce the final partitioning of the network that exhibits the homophily effect, according to which linked nodes are more likely to share the same attribute values. The communities based upon the network topology are obtained by simply applying an existing algorithm such like Louvain [2]. For graphs whose node attributes are numeric, we utilize existing clustering algorithms to get the communities (i.e., clusters) based on node attributes. We extend to binary-attributed graphs by generating a virtual graph from the attribute similarities between the nodes, and performing traditional community detection on the virtual graph. Albeit being simple, extensive experiments have shown that our late-fusion method can be competitive in terms of both accuracy and efficiency when compared against other algorithms. We summarize our main contributions in this work are:

1. A new late-fusion approach to community detection in attributed networks, which allows the use of traditional methods as well as the integration of personal preference or prior knowledge.
2. A novel method to identify communities that reflect attribute similarity for networks with binary attributes.
3. Extensive experiments to validate the proposed method in terms of accuracy and efficiency.

The rest of the paper is organized as follows: In Sect. 2, we provide a brief review of community detection algorithms suited for attributed networks, next we present our late fusion approach in Sect. 3. Experiments to illustrate the effectiveness of the proposed method are detailed in Sect. 4. Finally, we summarize our work and point out several future directions in Sect. 5.

2   Related Work

How to incorporate the node attribute information into the process of network community detection has been studied for a long time. One of the early ideas is to transform attribute similarities into edge weights. For example, [13] proposes *matching coefficient* which is the count of shared attributes between two connected nodes in a network; [15] extends the matching coefficient to networks with numeric node attributes; [4] defines edge weights based on self-organizing maps. A drawback of these methods is that new edge weights are only applicable to edges already existed, hence the attribute information is not fully utilized. To overcome this issue, a different approach is to *augment* the original graph by adding virtual edges and/or nodes based on node attribute values. For instance, [14] generates content edges based on the cosine similarity between node attribute vectors, in graphs where nodes are textual documents and the corresponding attribute vector is the TF-IDF vector describing their content. The kNN-enhance algorithm [9] adds directed virtual edges from a node to one of its k-nearest neighbors if their attributes are similar. The SA-Clustering [17] adds both virtual nodes and edges to the original graph, where the virtual nodes represent binary-valued attributes, and the virtual edges connect the real nodes to the virtual nodes representing the attributes that the real nodes own.

Another class of methods is inspired by the modularity measure. These methods incorporate attribute information into an optimization objective like the modularity. [5] injects an attribute based similarity measure into the modularity function; [1] combines the gain in the modularity with multiple common users' attributes as an integrated objective; I-Louvain algorithm [3] proposes inertia-based modularity to describe the similarity between nodes with numeric attributes, and adds the inertia-based modularity to the original modularity formula to form the new optimization objective.

With the wide spreading of deep learning, network representation learning and node embedding (e.g. [8]) motivated new solutions. [12] proposes an embedding based community detection algorithm that applies representation learning of graphs to learn a feature representation of a network structure, which is combined with node attributes to form a cost function. Minimizing it, the optimal community membership matrix is obtained.

Probabilistic models can be used to depict the relationship between node connections, attributes, and community membership. The task of community detection is thus converted to inferring the community assignment of the nodes. A representative of this kind is the CESNA algorithm [16], which builds a generative graphical model for inferring the community memberships.

Whereas the majority of the previous methods exploit simultaneously both types of information, we propose the late-fusion approach that combines two sets of communities obtained separately and independently from the network structure and node attributes via a fusion algorithms.

3   The Late-Fusion Method

Given an attributed network $G = (V, E, A)$, with V being the set of m nodes, E the set of n edges, and A an $m \times r$ attribute matrix describing the attribute values of the nodes with r attributes, the goal is to build a partitioning $\mathcal{P} = \{C_1, ..., C_k\}$ of V into k communities such that nodes in the same community are densely connected and similar in terms of attributes, whereas nodes from distinct communities are loosely connected and different in terms of attribute.

For networks with numeric attributes, we can directly apply a community detection algorithm F_s on G to identify a set of communities based on node connections $\mathcal{P}_s = \{C_1, C_2, ..., C_{k_s}\}$, and a clustering algorithms F_a on A to find a set of clusters based on node attributes $\mathcal{P}_a = \{C_1, C_2, ..., C_{k_a}\}$. When it comes to binary attributed networks, traditional clustering algorithms become inaccessible, we instead build a virtual graph G_a that shares the same node set as G, but there is an edge only when the two nodes are similar enough in terms of attributes. Then we apply F_s on G_a and obtain $\mathcal{P}_a$. Note that we omit categorical attributes since categorical values can be easily converted to the binary case.

The second step is to combine the partitions $\mathcal{P}_s$ and $\mathcal{P}_a$. We first derive the adjacency matrices D_s and D_a from $\mathcal{P}_s$ and $\mathcal{P}_a$ respectively, where $d_{ij} = 1$ when nodes i and j are in the same community in a partitioning $\mathcal{P}$ and $d_{ij} = 0$ otherwise. Next, an integrated adjacency matrix D is given by $D = \alpha D_s + (1 - \alpha)D_a$. Here α is the weighting parameter that leverages the strength between network topology and node attributes. In this way, the information about network topology and node attributes of the original graph G is represented in D. Now G_{int}, derived from the adjacency matrix D, is an integrated, virtual, weighted graph whose edges embody the homophily effect of G. Algorithm 1 shows the steps of our late-fusion approach applied to networks with binary attributes.

Algorithm 1. Late-fusion on networks with binary attributes

    Input: $G = (V, E, A), F_s, \alpha$
    Output: $\mathcal{P} = \{C_1, C_2, ..., C_k\}$
1 $\mathcal{P}_s = F_s(G_s)$
2 $G_a = \text{build\_virtual\_graph}\ (A)$
3 $\mathcal{P}_a = F_s(G_a)$
4 $D_s = \text{get\_adjacency\_matrix}(\mathcal{P}_s)$, $D_a = \text{get\_adjacency\_matrix}(\mathcal{P}_a)$
5 $D = \alpha D_s + (1 - \alpha)D_a$
6 $G_{integrated} = \text{from\_adjacency\_matrix}\ (D)$
7 $\mathcal{P} = F_s(G_{integrated})$
8 **return** $\mathcal{P}$

Here we address an important detail: how to build the virtual graph G_a from the node-attribute matrix A? We compute the inner product as the similarity measure between each node pair, and if the inner product exceeds a predetermined threshold, we regard the nodes as similar and add a virtual edge between them. The threshold can be determined heuristically based on the distribution of the node similarities. However, the threshold should be chosen properly so that the resulted G_a would be neither too dense nor too sparse, where both cases could harm the quality of the final communities. Under this guidance, we put forward two thresholding approaches:

1. **Median thresholding (MT):** Suppose S is the $m \times m$ similarity matrix of all nodes in V, we take all the off-diagonal, upper triangular (or lower triangular) entries of S, find the median of these numbers and set it as the threshold. This approach guarantees that we add virtual edges to half of all node pairs who share a similarity value higher than the other half.
2. **Equal-edge thresholding (EET):** We compute $q = 1 - d(G)$ where $d(G)$ is the density of G. Then the qth quantile of the similarity distribution is the chosen threshold. In this approach, we let the original graph G_s be the proxy that decides how we construct the virtual graph G_a.

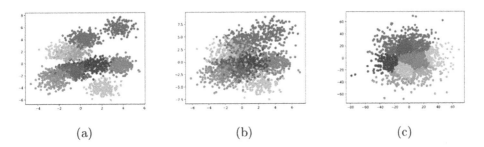

Fig. 1. Node attribute distribution for three groups of experiments. (a) Strong attributes, (b) Medium attributes, (c) Weak attributes. Each color represents a unique community (Color figure online)

4 Experiments

Our proposed method has been evaluated through experiments on multiple synthetic and real networks and results are presented in this section. For networks with numeric attributes, we take advantage of existing clustering algorithms to obtain communities based on attributes (i.e., clusters), and for networks with binary attributes, we employ Algorithm 1 to perform community detection. We have also released our code so that readers can reproduce the results[1].

4.1 Synthetic Networks with Numeric Attributes

Data. We use an attributed graph generator [10] to create three attributed graphs with ground-truth communities, denoted as G_{strong}, G_{medium} and G_{weak}, indicating the corresponding ground-truth partitionings are *strong*, *medium*, and *weak* in terms of modularity Q. To examine the effect of attributes on community detection, for each of G_{strong}, G_{medium} and G_{weak}, we assign three different attribute distributions as shown in Fig. 1, where attributes in Fig. 1a and b are generated from a Gaussian mixture model with a shared standard deviation, and Fig. 1c presents the original attributes generated by [10]. By this way, for each graph having a specific community structure (G_{strong}, G_{medium}, G_{weak}) we have also three types of attributes denoted strong attributes, medium attributes and weak attributes leading in fact to 9 datasets.

Evaluation Measures and Baselines. Normalized Mutual Information (NMI) and Adjusted Rand Index (ARI) and running time are used to evaluate algorithm accuracy and efficiency. Louvain [2] and SIWO [7] have been chosen as baseline algorithms that utilize only the links to identify network communities.

---

[1] https://github.com/changliu94/attributed-community-detection.

Table 1. Properties of synthetic networks

	m	n	k	r	Q
G_{strong}	2000	7430	10	2	0.81
G_{medium}	2000	7445	10	2	0.65
G_{weak}	2000	6988	10	2	0.54

Table 2. Properties of Sina Weibo network

m	n	k	r	Q	I
3490	30282	10	10	0.05	0.04

Note that since the attribute distribution does not affect Louvain and SIWO, the results of Louvain and SIWO are only presented in Table 3. We choose Spectral Clustering (SC) and DBSCAN as two representative clustering algorithms as they both can handle non-flat geometry. We treat the number of clusters as a known input parameter of SC, and the neighborhood size of DBSCAN is set to the average node degree. We adopt default values of the remaining parameters from the *scikit-learn* implementation of these two algorithms. Finally, we take the implementation of the I-Louvain algorithm which exploits links and attribute values as our contender. The code of I-Louvain is available online[2]. Given Louvain, SIWO, SC, and DBSCAN, correspondingly we can have four combinations for our late-fusion method. In all experiments, the α parameter in Algorithm 1 is chosen to be 0.5, i.e., the same weight is allocated to structural and attribute information.

Table 3. Results of strong attributes, time is measured in seconds

	G_{strong}			G_{medium}			G_{weak}		
	NMI	ARI	Time	NMI	ARI	Time	NMI	ARI	Time
Louvain	.795	.797	0.41	.695	.686	0.49	.665	.674	0.64
SIWO	.836	**.850**	0.97	.702	**.705**	1.09	.504	.458	0.98
SC	.802	.713	1.15	.777	.677	0.64	**.768**	.669	0.68
DBSCAN	.469	.103	0.06	.434	.083	0.06	.465	.102	0.24
I-Louvain	.515	.150	39.2	.718	.704	30.0	.608	.503	37.6
Louvain + SC	.824	.704	7.34	.784	.618	5.74	.765	.597	7.14
Louvain + DBSCAN	.818	.813	8.64	.730	.702	8.87	.704	**.690**	10.6
SIWO + SC	**.844**	.738	10.3	**.786**	.636	7.33	.723	.508	6.46
SIWO + DBSCAN	.818	.813	11.7	.730	.702	10.2	.704	**.690**	11.6

---

[2] https://www.dropbox.com/sh/j4aqitujiaifgq4/AAAAH0L3uIPYNWKoLpcAh0TPa.

Table 4. Results of medium attributes, time is measured in seconds

	G_{strong}			G_{medium}			G_{weak}		
	NMI	ARI	Time	NMI	ARI	Time	NMI	ARI	Time
SC	.529	.338	0.83	.522	.322	0.53	.538	.349	0.57
DBSCAN	.096	.012	0.08	.066	.008	0.14	.065	.011	0.09
I-Louvain	.517	.150	36.8	**.707**	**.690**	33.7	.614	.522	33.2
Louvain + SC	.734	.450	5.62	.696	.390	5.96	**.677**	.392	5.66
Louvain + DBSCAN	**.755**	**.726**	9.20	.670	.636	11.9	.641	**.633**	13.6
SIWO + SC	.748	.469	12.7	.699	.402	7.12	.625	.335	7.44
SIWO + DBSCAN	.744	**.726**	8.73	.670	.636	8.98	.641	**.633**	12.4

Results. Table 3, corresponding to strong attributes, shows that late fusion is the best-performing algorithm in terms of NMI on G_{strong} and G_{medium}, and very close to SC on G_{weak} (0.765 against 0.768) whereas it is better in terms of ARI on this last graph. On Tables 4 and 5, corresponding respectively to medium and weak attributes, with the deterioration of the attribute quality, the accuracy of late-fusion degrades, but late fusion still remains at a consistently high level compared to I-Louvain and the clustering algorithms. Moreover, the performance degradation of late-fusion methods is less susceptible to the deterioration of community quality compared to the clustering algorithms, thanks to the complementary structural information. As for the running time, it is expected that classic community detection algorithms Louvain and SIWO are the fastest algorithms, as they do not consider node attributes, but the late-fusion method still outperforms I-Louvain by a remarkable margin.

Table 5. Results of weak attributes, time is measured in seconds

	G_{strong}			G_{medium}			G_{weak}		
	NMI	ARI	Time	NMI	ARI	Time	NMI	ARI	Time
SC	.483	.270	3.31	.514	.307	2.32	.489	.276	2.45
DBSCAN	.000	.000	0.06	.000	.000	0.06	.000	.000	0.14
I-Louvain	.517	.150	35.1	.707	**.690**	34.3	.614	.522	39.5
Louvain + SC	.770	.670	11.8	.705	.613	10.2	**.689**	.564	9.33
Louvain + DBSCAN	.795	**.797**	11.2	.695	.685	10.4	.667	**.674**	12.9
SIWO + SC	**.797**	.703	13.2	**.709**	.635	12.3	.601	.467	11.0
SIWO + DBSCAN	.795	**.797**	11.6	.695	.685	11.3	.667	**.674**	12.6

4.2 Real Network with Numeric Attributes

Data and Baselines. Sina Weibo[3] is the largest online Chinese micro-blog social networking website. Table 2 shows the corresponding properties of the Sina Weibo network built by [9][4]. It includes within-inertia ratio I, a measure of attribute homogeneity of data points that are assigned to the same subgroup. The lower the within-inertia ratio, the more similar the nodes in the same community are. As DBSCAN algorithm performs poorly on the Sina Weibo network and it is costly to infer a good combination of the hyper-parameters of the algorithm, it has been replaced by k-means as a supplement to spectral clustering. The number of clusters required as an input by k-means and SC is inferred from the 'elbow method', which happens to be 10, the actual number of clusters. Moreover, since we have the prior knowledge that the ground truth communities are based on the topics of the forums from which those users are gathered, we reckon that the formation of communities depends more on the attribute values than the structure and set the parameter α at 0.2.

Results. Table 6 presents the results on Sina Weibo network. The two baseline algorithms Louvain and SIWO and the contending algorithm I-Louvain perform poorly on the Sina Weibo network, whereas the clustering algorithms show a high accuracy. Especially, the k-means algorithm together with our four late-fusion methods with the emphasis on attribute information produce results with the best NMI and ARI. This is because modularity of Sina Weibo network is low (0.05 as indicated in Table 2) and the within-inertia ratio is also low (0.04). The results also validate our assumption that communities in this network are mainly determined by the attributes. We will further explore the effect of α in Sect. 4.4.

Table 6. Experimental results on Sina Weibo network

	NMI	ARI	Time
Louvain	.232	.197	1.98
SIWO	.040	.000	3.26
SC	.612	.520	3.16
k-means	**.649**	**.579**	0.25
I-Louvain	.204	.038	261
Louvain+SC	.611	.519	48.9
Louvain+k-means	**.649**	**.579**	42.1
SIWO+SC	.611	.519	37.9
SIWO+k-means	**.649**	**.579**	50.4

Table 7. Properties of Facebook networks

Network ID	m	n	k	r	Q
0	347	5038	24	224	0.179
107	1045	53498	9	576	0.218
348	227	6384	14	161	0.210
414	159	3386	7	105	0.468
686	170	3312	14	63	0.101
698	66	540	13	48	0.239
1684	792	28048	17	319	0.509
1912	755	60050	46	480	0.339
3437	547	9626	32	262	0.026
3980	59	292	17	42	0.242

---

[3] http://www.weibo.com.

[4] This dataset is available online https://github.com/smileyan448/Sinanet.

4.3   Real Network with Binary Attributes

Data. Facebook dataset [11] contains 10 egocentric networks with binary attributes corresponding to anonymous information of the user about the name, work, and education and ground-truth communities. This dataset is available online[5] and Table 7 presents the properties of these networks.

We still treat Louvain and SIWO as our baselines. We use the CESNA algorithm [16], able to handle binary attributes in addition to the links, as our contender[6]. To compare the two thresholding strategies proposed in Section 3, we present experimental results of four late-fusion methods: Louvain + equal-edge thresholding (denoted as Louvain-EET), Louvain + median thresholding (denoted as Louvain-MT), SIWO + equal-edge thresholding (denoted as SIWO-EET), and SIWO + median thresholding (denoted as SIWO-MT). We set α to its default value 0.5.

Table 8. NMI of different community detection results on Facebook network

Network ID	0	107	348	414	686	698	1684	1912	3437	3980	Average
Louvain	.382	.332	.478	**.609**	.284	.281	.047	**.565**	.181	**.729**	.389
SIWO	.390	.363	.375	.586	.215	.259	.053	.557	.174	.605	.358
CESNA	.263	.249	.307	.586	.238	.564	.438	.450	.176	.552	.382
Louvain-EET	**.558**	.355	**.525**	.538	**.463**	**.669**	**.462**	.511	**.310**	.704	**.509**
Louvain-MT	.452	.341	.489	.556	.351	.479	.323	.491	.262	.696	.444
SIWO-EET	.541	**.364**	.452	.531	.406	.630	.460	.509	**.310**	.648	.485
SIWO-MT	.431	.353	.405	.538	.252	.406	.332	.491	.260	.588	.406

Table 9. ARI of different community detection results on Facebook network

Network ID	0	107	348	414	686	698	1684	1912	3437	3980	Average
Louvain	.143	.148	.303	.558	.110	.000	.000	.461	.000	.398	.209
SIWO	.220	.177	.127	.519	.000	.009	.000	.419	.002	.209	.167
CESNA	.073	.097	.156	.480	.001	.202	.310	.361	.014	.067	.176
Louvain-EET	.024	.047	.103	.265	.006	.000	.043	.252	.000	.069	.008
Louvain-MT	.061	.079	.129	.413	.063	.000	.048	.235	.000	.084	.110
SIWO-EET	.043	.045	.124	.252	.003	.000	.057	.235	.000	.095	.009
SIWO-MT	.108	.079	.141	.391	.040	.016	.060	.223	.000	.073	.113

---

[5] http://snap.stanford.edu/data.
[6] The source code of CESNA is available online https://github.com/snap-stanford/snap/tree/master/examples/cesna.

Table 10. Running time of different community detection results on Facebook network, measured in seconds

Network ID	0	107	348	414	686	698	1684	1912	3437	3980	Average
Louvain	0.15	1.83	0.12	0.06	0.09	0.02	0.80	1.28	0.31	0.01	0.47
SIWO	0.34	3.78	0.31	0.16	0.17	0.03	1.46	3.79	0.51	0.02	1.06
CESNA	9.76	103	6.02	2.47	3.12	0.63	38.3	22.9	21.1	0.60	20.8
Louvain-EET	0.72	4.68	0.40	0.25	0.24	0.07	1.95	3.83	0.78	0.03	1.30
Louvain-MT	2.90	20.0	0.82	0.48	0.44	0.08	8.22	9.41	3.28	0.06	4.57
SIWO-EET	1.73	24.4	2.87	0.68	0.76	0.14	5.76	28.5	4.26	0.12	6.92
SIWO-MT	9.45	91.4	5.27	1.73	3.14	0.34	44.9	43.4	13.5	0.17	21.3

Results. Results in terms of NMI, ARI, and running time are respectively presented in Tables 8, 9, and 10. In terms of NMI, results in Table 8 show again that our late-fusion algorithms can significantly improve the community detection accuracy upon Louvain. On average, the late fusion method Louvain+EET outperforms Louvain, SIWO, and CESNA by 30.8%, 42.2%, and 33.2% respectively. The late fusion method Louvain+MT outperforms the three by 14.1%, 24.0%, and 16.2% respectively. However, all of the late-fusion methods perform poorly when evaluated by ARI. This is resulted from the goal of our late-fusion approach. Remember that we aim to find the set of communities such that nodes in the same subgroup are densely connected and similar in terms of attributes, whereas nodes residing in different communities are loosely connected and dissimilar in attributes. This purpose led the late-fusion approach to over-partition communities that are formed by only one of the two sources of information. The over-partitioning greatly hurts the results of ARI. A postprocessing model to resolve the over-partitioning issue with late fusion is left as a future work. The running time results shown in Table 10 again manifests the efficiency advantage of our late-fusion methods over CESNA.

4.4 Effect of Parameter α

In the Sina Weibo experiment, we see the advantage of having a weighting parameter to accordingly leverage the strength of the two sources of information. In this section, we dive deeper into the effect of α on the community detection results. To do so, we devise an experiment where we use the G_{strong} and G_{weak} introduced in Table 1. In reverse, we assign **weak** attributes to G_{strong} and **strong** attributes to G_{weak}. Then we perform our late fusion algorithm on these two graphs with varying α values. In our experiment, we choose SIWO as F_s and k-means as F_a.

Table 11 presents the NMI and ARI of the late fusion with SIWO and k-means when α varies. G_{strong} has communities with a strong structure but weak attributes, so the accuracy score for NMI and ARI goes up as we put more weight on the structure; On the contrary, G_{weak} has weak structural communities but

Table 11. Effect of α

	$\alpha = 0.0$		$\alpha = 0.2$		$\alpha = 0.5$		$\alpha = 0.8$		$\alpha = 1.0$	
	NMI	ARI	NMI	ARI	NMI	ARI	NMI	ARI	NMI	ARI
G_{strong}	0.530	0.359	0.530	0.359	0.756	0.513	0.836	0.850	0.836	0.850
G_{weak}	0.867	0.834	0.867	0.834	0.762	0.470	0.526	0.364	0.526	0.364

strong attributes, hence the accuracy score decreases as α increases. One can also notice that when α is sufficiently high or low, late fusion becomes equivalent to using community detection or clustering only, which is in accordance with our observation done on the Sina Weibo experiment.

In practice, when network communities are mainly determined by the links, α should be greater than 0.5; $\alpha < 0.5$ is recommended if attributes play a more important role in forming the communities; When prior knowledge about network communities is unavailable or both sources of information contribute equally, α should be 0.5.

4.5 Complexity of Late Fusion

It is a known drawback of attributed community detection algorithms that they are very time-consuming due to the need to consider node attributes. Our late-fusion method tries to circumvent this problem by taking advantage of the existing community detection and clustering algorithms that are efficiently optimized, and combining their results by a simple approach. To further show the computational efficiency of our late-fusion method, we compute the running time of the late-fusion method and compare it with other methods.

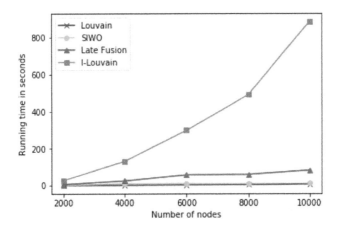

Fig. 2. Running time of Louvain, SIWO, late fusion and I-Louvain on networks of different sizes

We test the running time of four different community detection methods on five graphs with the number of nodes varying from 2000, 4000, 6000, 8000, and 10000. These graphs are also generated by the attributed graph generator [10]. We control the modularity of each graph at the range of 0.64−0.66 and keep other hyperparameters the same. For each size, we randomly sample 10 graphs from the graph generator and plot the average running time of each method. As we can see in Fig. 2, it is expected that our late-fusion method is inevitably slower than the two community detection methods that only utilize node connections. However, our algorithm runs way faster than the I-Louvain algorithm, albeit both being approximately linear in the growth of network sizes.

5 Conclusion and Future Direction

In this paper, we proposed a new approach to the problem of community detection in attributed networks that follows a late-fusion strategy. We showed with extensive experiments that most often, our late-fusion method is not only able to improve the detection accuracy provided by traditional community detection algorithms, but it can also outperform the chosen contenders in terms of both accuracy and efficiency. We learned that combining node connections with attributes to detect communities of a network is not always the best solution, especially when one side of the network properties is strong while the other is weak, using only the best information available can lead to better detection results. It is part of our future work to understand when and how we should use the extra attribute information to help community detection. ARI suffers greatly from over-partitioning issue with our late fusion when applied to networks with binary attributes. A postprocessing model to resolve this issue is desired. We also hope to expand the late-fusion approach to networks with a hybrid of binary and numeric attributes as well as networks with overlapping communities.

References

1. Asim, Y., Ghazal, R., Naeem, W., Majeed, A., Raza, B., Malik, A.K.: Community detection in networks using node attributes and modularity. Int. J. Adv. Comput. Sci. Appl. **8**(1), 382–388 (2017)
2. Blondel, V.D., Guillaume, J.L., Lambiotte, R., Lefebvre, E.: Fast unfolding of communities in large networks. J. Stat. Mech: Theory Exp. **2008**(10), P10008 (2008)
3. Combe, D., Largeron, C., Géry, M., Egyed-Zsigmond, E.: I-Louvain: an attributed graph clustering method. In: Fromont, E., De Bie, T., van Leeuwen, M. (eds.) IDA 2015. LNCS, vol. 9385, pp. 181–192. Springer, Cham (2015). https://doi.org/10. 1007/978-3-319-24465-5_16
4. Cruz, J.D., Bothorel, C., Poulet, F.: Semantic clustering of social networks using points of view. In: CORIA, pp. 175–182 (2011)
5. Dang, T., Viennet, E.: Community detection based on structural and attribute similarities. In: International Conference on Digital Society (ICDS), pp. 7–14 (2012)

6. Fortunato, S., Hric, D.: Community detection in networks: a user guide. Phys. Rep. **659**, 1–44 (2016)
7. Gharaghooshi, S.Z., Zaïane, O., Largeron, C., Zafarmand, M., Liu, C.: Addressing the resolution limit and the field of view limit in community mining. In: Berthold, M.R., et al. (eds.) Symposium on Intelligent Data Analysis, IDA 2020. LNCS, vol. 12080, pp. 1–12. Springer, Cham (2020)
8. Grover, A., Leskovec, J.: node2vec: Scalable feature learning for networks. In: Proceedings of the 22nd ACM SIGKDD Conference, pp. 855–864. ACM (2016)
9. Jia, C., Li, Y., Carson, M.B., Wang, X., Yu, J.: Node attribute-enhanced community detection in complex networks. Sci. Rep. **7**, 1–15 (2017)
10. Largeron, C., Mougel, P., Benyahia, O., Zaïane, O.R.: DANCer: dynamic attributed networks with community structure generation. Knowl. Inf. Syst. **53**(1), 109–151 (2017)
11. Leskovec, J., Mcauley, J.J.: Learning to discover social circles in ego networks. In: Advances in Neural Information Processing Systems, pp. 539–547 (2012)
12. Li, Y., Sha, C., Huang, X., Zhang, Y.: Community detection in attributed graphs: An embedding approach. In: AAAI (2018)
13. Neville, J., Adler, M., Jensen, D.: Clustering relational data using attribute and link information. In: Proceedings of the Text Mining and Link Analysis Workshop, 18th International Joint Conference on Artificial Intelligence, pp. 9–15. Morgan Kaufmann Publishers, San Francisco (2003)
14. Ruan, Y., Fuhry, D., Parthasarathy, S.: Efficient community detection in large networks using content and links. In: Proceedings of the 22nd International Conference on World Wide Web, pp. 1089–1098. ACM (2013)
15. Steinhaeuser, K., Chawla, N.V.: Community detection in a large real-world social network. In: Liu, H., Salerno, J.J., Young, M.J. (eds.) Social Computing, Behavioral Modeling, and Prediction, pp. 168–175. Springer, Boston (2008). https://doi.org/10.1007/978-0-387-77672-9_19
16. Yang, J., McAuley, J., Leskovec, J.: Community detection in networks with node attributes. In: ICDM Conference, pp. 1151–1156. IEEE (2013)
17. Zhou, Y., Cheng, H., Yu, J.X.: Graph clustering based on structural/attribute similarities. Proc. VLDB Endow. **2**(1), 718–729 (2009)

7

Actionable Subgroup Discovery
and Urban Farm Optimization

Alexandre Millot[1], Romain Mathonat[1,2], Rémy Cazabet[3],
and Jean-François Boulicaut[1(✉)]

[1] Univ de Lyon, CNRS, INSA Lyon, LIRIS, UMR5205, 69621 Villeurbanne, France
{alexandre.millot,romain.mathonat,jean-francois.boulicaut}@insa-lyon.fr
[2] Atos, 69100 Villeurbanne, France
[3] Univ de Lyon, CNRS, Université Lyon 1, LIRIS, UMR5205,
69622 Villeurbanne, France
remy.cazabet@univ-lyon1.fr

Abstract. Designing, selling and/or exploiting connected vertical urban farms is now receiving a lot of attention. In such farms, plants grow in controlled environments according to recipes that specify the different growth stages and instructions concerning many parameters (e.g., temperature, humidity, CO_2, light). During the whole process, automated systems collect measures of such parameters and, at the end, we can get some global indicator about the used recipe, e.g., its yield. Looking for innovative ideas to optimize recipes, we investigate the use of a new optimal subgroup discovery method from purely numerical data. It concerns here the computation of subsets of recipes whose labels (e.g., the yield) show an interesting distribution according to a quality measure. When considering optimization, e.g., maximizing the yield, our virtuous circle optimization framework iteratively improves recipes by sampling the discovered optimal subgroup description subspace. We provide our preliminary results about the added-value of this framework thanks to a plant growth simulator that enables inexpensive experiments.

Keywords: Subgroup discovery · Virtuous circle · Urban farms

1 Introduction

Conventional farming methods have to face many challenges like, for instance, soil erosion and/or an overuse of pesticides. The crucial problems related to climate change also stimulate the design of new production systems. The concept of urban farms (see, e.g., AeroFarms, FUL, Infarm[1]) could be part of a solution. It enables the growth of plants in fully controlled environments close to the place where consumers are [8]. Most of the crop protection chemical products can be removed while being able to optimize both the quantity and the quality of plants (e.g., improving the flavor [9] or their chemical proportions [20]).

---

[1] https://aerofarms.com/, http://www.fermeful.com/, https://infarm.com/.

Urban farms can generate large amounts of data that can be pushed towards a cloud environment such that various machine learning and data mining methods can be used. We may then provide new insights about the plant growth process itself (discovering knowledge about not yet identified/understood phenomena) but also offer new services to farm owners. We focus here on services that rely on the optimization of a given target variable, e.g., the yield. The number of parameters influencing plant growth can be relatively large (e.g., temperature, hygrometry, water pH level, nutrient concentration, LED lighting intensity, CO_2 concentration). There are numerous ways of measuring the crop end-product (e.g., energy cost, plant mass and size, flavor and chemical properties). In general, for a given type of plants, expert knowledge exists that concerns the available sub-systems (e.g., to model the impact of nutrient on growth, the effect of LED lighting on photosynthesis, the energy consumption w.r.t. the temperature instruction) but we are far from a global understanding of the interaction between the various underlying phenomena. In other terms, setting the optimal instructions for the diverse set of parameters given an optimization task remains an open problem.

We want to address such an issue by means of data mining techniques. Plant growth recipes are made of instructions in time and space for many numerical attributes. Once a recipe is completed, collections of measures have been collected and we assume that at least one numerical target label value is available, e.g., the yield. Can we learn from available recipe records to suggest new ones that should provide better results w.r.t. the selected target attribute? For that purpose, we investigate the use of subgroup discovery [12,21]. It aims at discovering subsets of objects - called subgroups - with high quality according to a quality measure calculated on the target label. Such a quality measure has to capture deviations in the target label distribution when we consider the overall data set or the considered subset of objects. When addressing only subgroup discovery from numerical data, a few approaches for numerical attributes [6,15] and numerical target labels [14] have been described. To the best of our knowledge, the reference algorithm for subgroup discovery in purely numerical data is SD-Map* [14]. However, like other methods, it uses discretization and leads to loss of information and sub-optimal results.

Our first contribution concerns the proposal of a simple branch and bound algorithm called MinIntChange4SD that exploits the exhaustive enumeration strategy from [11] to achieve a guaranteed optimal subgroup discovery in numerical data without any discretization. Discussing details about this algorithm is out of the scope of this paper and we recently designed a significantly optimized version of MinIntChange4SD in [17]. Our main contribution concerns a new methodology for plant growth recipe optimization that (i) uses MinIntChange4SD to find the optimal subgroup of recipes and (ii) exploits the subgroup description to design better recipes which can in turn be analyzed with subgroup discovery, and so on.

The paper is organized as follows. Section 2 formalizes the problem. In Sect. 3, we discuss related works and their limitations. In Sect. 4, we introduce our new

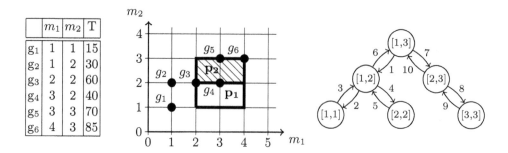

Fig. 1. (left) Purely numerical dataset. **(center)** Non-closed ($p_1 = \langle [2,4], [1,3] \rangle$, non-hatched) and closed ($p_2 = \langle [2,4], [2,3] \rangle$, hatched) interval patterns. **(right)** Depth-first traversal of m_2 using minimal changes.

optimal subgroup discovery algorithm and we detail our framework for plant growth recipe optimization. An empirical evaluation of our method is in Sect. 5. Section 6 briefly concludes.

2 Problem Definition

Numerical Dataset. A numerical dataset (G, M, T) is given by a set of objects G, a set of numerical attributes M and a numerical target label T. In a given dataset, the domain of any attribute $m \in M$ (resp. label T) is a finite ordered set denoted D_m (resp. D_T). Figure 1 (left) provides a numerical dataset made of two attributes $M = \{m_1, m_2\}$ and a target label T. A subgroup p is defined by a pattern, i.e., its intent or description, and the set of objects from the dataset where it appears, i.e., its extent, denoted $ext(p)$. For instance, in Fig. 1, the domain of m_1 is $\{1, 2, 3, 4\}$ and the intent $\langle [2,4], [1,3] \rangle$ (see the definition of interval patterns later) denotes a subgroup whose extent is $\{g_3, g_4, g_5, g_6\}$.

Quality Measure, Optimal Subgroup. The interestingness of a subgroup in a numerical dataset is measured by a numerical value. We consider here the quality measure based on the mean introduced in [14]. Let p be a subgroup. The quality of p is given by: $q^a_{mean}(p) = |ext(p)|^a \times (\mu_{ext(p)} - \mu_{ext(\emptyset)}), a \in [0, 1]$. $|ext(p)|$ denotes the cardinality of $ext(p)$, $\mu_{ext(p)}$ is the mean of the target label in the extent of p, $\mu_{ext(\emptyset)}$ is the mean of the target label in the overall dataset, and a is a parameter that controls the number of objects of the subgroups. Let (G, M, T) be a numerical dataset, q a quality measure and P the set of all subgroups of (G, M, T). A subgroup $p \in P$ is said to be optimal iff $\forall p' \in P : q(p') \le q(p)$.

Plant Growth Recipe and Optimization Measure. A plant growth recipe (M, P, T) is given by a set of numerical parameters M specifying the growing conditions thanks to intervals on numerical values, a numerical value P representing the number of stages of the growth cycle, and a numerical target label T to quantify the recipe quality. In a given recipe, each parameter of M is repeated

P times s.t. we have $|M| \times P$ numerical attributes. Our goal is to optimize recipes and we want to discover actionable patterns in the sense that delivering such patterns will support the design of new growing conditions. An optimization measure f quantifies the quality of an iteration. We are interested in the mean of the target label of the objects of the optimal subgroup after each iteration. The measure is given by $f_{mean} = \frac{\sum_{i \in ext(p)} T(i)}{|ext(p)|}$ where $T(i)$ is the value of the target label for object i.

3 Related Work

Designing recipes that optimize a given target attribute (e.g., the mass, the energy cost) is often tackled by domain experts who exploit the scientific literature. However, in our setting, it has two major drawbacks. First, most of the literature remains oriented towards conventional growing conditions and farming methods. In urban farms, there are more parameters that can be controlled. Secondly, the amount of knowledge about plants is unbalanced from one plant to another. Therefore, relying only on expert knowledge for plant recipe optimization is not sufficient. We have an optimization problem and the need for a limited number of iterations. Indeed, experimenting with plant growth recipes is time consuming (i.e., asking for weeks or months). Therefore, we have to minimize the number of experiments that are needed to optimize a given recipe. There are two main families of methods addressing the problem of optimizing a function over numerical variables: *direct* and *model-based* [18]. For *direct* methods, the common idea is to apply various strategies to sequentially evaluate solutions in the search space of recipes. However such methods do not address the problem of minimizing the number of experiments. For *model-based* methods, the idea is to build a model simulating the ground truth using available data and then to use it to guide the search process. For instance, [9] introduced a solution for recipe optimization using this type of method with the goal of optimizing the flavor of plants. Their framework is based on using a surrogate model, in this case a Symbolic Regression [13]. It considers recipe optimization by means of a promising virtuous circle. However, it suffers from several shortcomings: there is no guarantee on the quality of the generated models (i.e., they may not be able to model correctly the ground truth), the number of tested parameters is small (only 3), and the ratio between the number of objects and the number of parameters in the data needs to be at least ten for Symbolic Regression [10]. Clearly, it would restrict the search to only a few parameters.

Heuristic [2,15] and exhaustive [1,5] solutions have been proposed for subgroup discovery. Usually, these approaches consider a set of nominal attributes with a binary label. To work with numerical data, prior discretization of the attributes is then required (see, e.g., [3]) and it leads to loss of information and suboptimal results. A major issue with exhaustive pattern mining is the size of the search space. Fortunately, optimistic estimates can be used to prune the search space and provide tractability in practice [7,21]. [14] introduces a large panel of quality measures and corresponding optimistic estimates for an exhaustive subgroup mining given numerical target labels. They describe SD-Map*, the reference algorithm for subgroup discovery in numerical data. Notice however that for [14] or others [6,15], discretization techniques over the numerical attributes have to be performed. When looking for an exhaustive search of frequent patterns - not subgroups - in numerical data without discretization, we find the MinIntChange algorithm [11]. Using closure operators (see, e.g., [4]) has become a popular solution to reduce the size of the search space. We indeed exploit most of these ideas to design our optimal subgroup discovery algorithm.

4 Optimization with Subgroup Discovery

4.1 An Efficient Algorithm for Optimal Subgroup Discovery

Let us first introduce MinIntChange4SD, our branch and bound algorithm for the optimal subgroup discovery in purely numerical data. It exploits smart concepts about interval patterns from [11].

Interval Patterns, Extent and Closure. In a numerical dataset (G, M, T), an interval pattern p is a vector of intervals $p = \langle [a_i, b_i] \rangle_{i \in \{1, \ldots, |M|\}}$ with $a_i, b_i \in D_{mi}$, where each interval is a restriction on an attribute of M, and $|M|$ is the number of attributes. Let $g \in G$ be an object. g is in the extent of an interval pattern $p = \langle [a_i, b_i] \rangle_{i \in \{1, \ldots, |M|\}}$ iff $\forall i \in \{1, \ldots, |M|\}, m_i(g) \in [a_i, b_i]$. Let p_1 and p_2 be two interval patterns. $p_1 \subseteq p_2$ means that p_2 encloses p_1, i.e., the hyper-rectangle of p_1 is included in that of p_2. It is said that p_1 is a specialization of p_2. Let p be an interval pattern and $ext(p)$ its extent. p is defined as *closed* if and only if it is the most restrictive pattern (i.e., the smallest hyper-rectangle) that contains $ext(p)$. Figure 1 (center) depicts the dataset of Fig. 1 (left) in a cartesian plane as well as examples of interval patterns that are closed (p_2) or not (p_1).

Traversing the Search Space with Minimal Changes. To guarantee the optimal subgroup discovery, we proceed to the so-called minimal changes introduced in MinIntChange. It enables an exhaustive enumeration within the interval pattern search space. A left minimal change consists in replacing the left bound of an interval by the current value closest higher value in the domain of the corresponding attribute. Similarly, a right minimal change consists in replacing the right bound by the current value closest lower value. The search starts with the computation of the minimal interval pattern that covers all the objects of the dataset. The premise is to apply consecutive right or left minimal changes until obtaining an interval whose left and right bounds have the same value for each interval of the minimal interval pattern. In that case, the algorithm backtracks until it finds a pattern on which a minimal change can be applied. Figure 1 (right) depicts the depth-first traversal of attribute m_2 from the dataset of Fig. 1 (left) using minimal changes.

Compressing and Pruning the Search Space. We leverage the concept of closure to significantly reduce the number of candidate interval patterns. After a minimal change and instead of evaluating the resulting interval pattern, we compute its corresponding closed interval pattern. We exploit advanced pruning techniques to reduce the size of the search space thanks to the use of a tight optimistic estimate. We also exploit a combination of *forward checking* and *branch reordering*. Given an interval pattern, the set of all its direct specializations (application of a right or left minimal change on each interval) are computed - forward checking - and those whose optimistic estimate is higher than the best subgroup quality are stored. Branch reordering by descending order of the optimistic estimate value is then carried out which enables to explore the most promising parts of the search space first. It also enables a more efficient pruning by raising the minimal quality early. In fact, providing details about the algorithm is out of the scope of this paper though its source code is available at https://bit.ly/3bA87NE. The important outcome is that it guarantees the discovery of optimal subgroups for a given quality measure. Indeed, provided that it remains tractable, the runtime efficiency is not here an issue given that we want to use the algorithm at some steps of quite slow vegetable growth processes.

4.2 Leveraging Subgroups to Optimize Recipes

A Virtuous Circle. Our optimization framework can be seen as a virtuous circle, where each new iteration uses information previously gathered to iteratively improve the targeted process. First, a set of recipe experiments - which can be created with or without the use of expert knowledge - is created. With the use of expert knowledge, values or domain of values are defined for each attribute and then recipes are produced using these values. When generating recipes without prior knowledge, we create recipes by randomly sampling the values of each attribute. Secondly, we use subgroup discovery to find the best subgroup of recipes according to the chosen quality measure (e.g., the subgroup of recipes with the best average yield). Then, we exploit the subgroup description - i.e., we apply new restrictions on the range of each parameter according to the description - to generate new, better, recipe experiments. Finally these recipes are in turn processed to find the best subgroup for the new recipes, and so on until recipes cannot be improved anymore. This way, we sample recipes in a space which gets smaller after each iteration and where the ratio between good and bad solutions gets larger and larger. Figure 2 depicts a step-by-step example of the process behind the framework. Our framework makes use of several hyperparameters that affect runtime efficiency, the number of iterations and the quality of the results.

Convergence. The first hyperparameter is the parameter a used in the q_{mean}^a quality measure. In standard subgroup discovery, it controls the number of objects in the returned subgroups. A higher value of a means larger subgroups. For us, a larger subgroup means a larger search space to sample. By extension, a higher value of a means more iterations to be able to reach smaller subspaces of

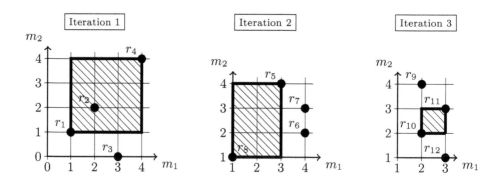

Fig. 2. Example of execution of the optimization framework in 3 iterations. We consider a two-dimensional space (i.e., 2 attributes m_1 and m_2) where 4 recipes are generated during each iteration using our first sampling method. The best subgroup (optimizing the yield) of each iteration (hatched) serves as the next iteration sampling space.

the search space. For that reason, we rename the parameter as the *convergence rate*. The second hyperparameter is called the *minimal improvement (minImp)*. It defines the minimal improvement of the *Optimization measure - f_{mean}* in our setting - needed from one iteration to another for the framework to keep running. After each iteration, we check whether the following statement is true or false.

$$\frac{f_{mean_{it}} - f_{mean_{it-1}}}{f_{mean_{it-1}}} \geq minImp$$

If it is true, then the optimization framework keeps running, else we consider that the recipes cannot be improved any further. This parameter has a direct effect on the number of iterations needed for the algorithm to converge. A higher value for $minImp$ means a lower number of iterations and vice versa. We can also forget $minImp$ and set the number of iterations by means of another parameter that would denote a budget.

Sampling the Subspace. After each iteration, to generate new recipes to experiment with, we need to sample the subspace corresponding to the description of the best subgroup. Three sampling methods are currently available and this defines again a new hyperparameter. The first method consists in sampling recipes using the original set of values of each attribute (i.e., in the first iteration) minus the excluded values due to the new restrictions applied on the subspace. Let D_m^1 be the domain of values of attribute m at Iteration 1 and $[a_m^i, b_m^i]$ be the interval of attribute m at Iteration i according to the description of the best subgroup of Iteration $i-1$. Then, $\forall v \in D_m^1, v \in D_m^i \Leftrightarrow b_m^i \geq v \geq a_m^i$. Using this method, the number of values available for sampling for each attribute gets smaller after each iteration, meaning that each iteration is faster than the previous one. The second consists in discretizing the search space through the discretization of each attribute in k intervals of equal length. Parameter k is set before launching the framework. Recipes are then sampled using the discretized domain of values for each attribute. Finally, we can use *Latin Hypercube*

Sampling [16] as a third method. In *Latin Hypercube Sampling*, each attribute is divided in S equally probable intervals, with S the number of samples (i.e., recipes). Using this method, recipes are sampled such that each recipe is the only one in each hyperspace that contains it. The number of samples generated for each iteration is also a hyperparameter of the framework.

An Explainable Generic Framework. Our optimization framework is explainable contrary to black box optimization algorithms. Each step of the process is easily understandable due to the descriptive nature of subgroup discovery. Although we have been referring to our algorithm `MinIntChange4SD` when introducing the optimization framework, other subgroup discovery algorithms can be used, including [14] and [17]. Notice however that the better the quality of the provided subgroup, the better the results returned by our framework will be. Finally, our method can be applied to quite many application domains where we want to optimize a numerical target given collections of numerical features (e.g., hyperparameter optimization in machine learning).

5 Experiments

We work on urban farm recipe optimization while we do not have access to real farming data yet. One of our partners in the FUI DUF 4.0 project (2018–2021) is designing new types of urban farms. We found a way to support the empirical study of our recipe optimizing framework thanks to inexpensive experiments enabled by a simulator. In an urban farm, plants grow in a controlled environment. In the absence of failure, recipe instructions are followed and we can investigate the optimization of the plant yield at the end of the growth cycle. We simulate recipe experiments by using the PCSE[2] simulation environment by setting the characteristics (e.g., the climate) of the different growth stages. We focus on 3 variables that set the amount of solar irradiation (range $[0, 25000]$), wind (range $[0, 30]$) and rain (range $[0, 40]$). The plant growth is split into 3 stages of equal length such that we finally get 9 attributes. In real life, we can control most of the parameters of an urban farm (e.g., providing more or less light) and a recipe optimization iteration needs for new insights about the promising parameter values. This is what we can emulate using the crop simulator: given the description of the optimal subgroup, we get insights to support the design of the next simulations, say experiments, as if we were controlling the growth environment. At the end of the growth cycle, we retrieve the total mass of plants harvested using a given recipe. Note that in the following experiments, unless stated otherwise, no assumption is made on the values of parameters (i.e., no restriction is applied on the range of values defined above and expert knowledge is not taken into account). Table 1 features examples of plant growth recipes. The source code and datasets used in our evaluation are available at https://bit.ly/3bA87NE.

---

[2] https://pcse.readthedocs.io/en/stable/index.html.

Table 1. Examples of growth recipes split in 3 stages (P1, P2, P3), 3 attributes, and a target label (Yield).

R	Rain^{P1}	Irrad^{P1}	Wind^{P1}	Rain^{P2}	Irrad^{P2}	Wind^{P2}	Rain^{P3}	Irrad^{P3}	Wind^{P3}	Yield
r_1	10	23250	5	10	23250	5	15	21000	10	22000
r_2	35	10000	14	5	25000	10	16	19500	30	20500
r_3	15	17500	26	22	15000	18	30	4000	3	8600
r_4	18	22800	17	38	17000	25	38	12000	19	14200

Table 2. Comparison between descriptions of the overall dataset (DS), the optimal subgroup returned by `MinIntChange4SD` (MIC4SD), the optimal subgroup returned by `SD-Map*`. "–" means no restriction on the attribute compared to DS, Q and S respectively the quality and size of the subgroup.

Subgroup	Rain^{P1}	Irrad^{P1}	Wind^{P1}	Rain^{P2}	Irrad^{P2}	Wind^{P2}	Rain^{P3}	Irrad^{P3}	Wind^{P3}	Q	S
DS	[0, 39]	[1170, 23471]	[2, 29]	[0, 37]	[111, 24111]	[0, 29]	[2, 40]	[964, 24197]	[1, 30]	0	30
MIC4SD	[16, 37]	[1170, 22085]	[2, 24]	[7, 37]	[18309, 23584]	[2, 24]	[15, 37]	[12626, 24197]	[1, 25]	33874	7
SD-Map*	[21, 39]	–	–	–	[14455, 24111]	–	–	[12760, 24197]	–	30662	5

5.1   `MinIntChange4SD` vs `SD-Map*`

We study the description of the best subgroup returned by `MinIntChange4SD` and `SD-Map*`, the state-of-the art algorithm for subgroup discovery in numerical data. Table 2 depicts the descriptions for a dataset comprised of 30 recipes generated randomly with the simulator. Besides the higher quality of the subgroup returned by `MinIntChange4SD`, the optimal subgroup description also enables to extract information that is missing from the description obtained with `SD-Map*`. In fact, where `SD-Map*` only offers a strong restriction on 3 attributes, `MinIntChange4SD` provides actionable information on all the considered attributes, i.e., the 9 attributes. This confirms its qualitative superiority over `SD-Map*` which has to proceed to attribute discretizations.

5.2   Empirical Evaluation of the Model Hyperparameters

Our optimization framework involves several hyperparameters whose values need to be studied to define proper ranges or values that will lead to optimized results with a minimized number of recipe experiments. We choose to apply a random search on discretized hyperparameters. Note that in this setting, grid search is a bad solution due to the combinatorial number of hyperparameter values and the high time cost of the optimization process itself. We discretize each hyperparameter in several values (the convergence rate is split into 10 values ranging from 0.1 to 1, the minimal improvement parameter is split into 12 values between 0 and 0.05, the sampling parameter is split between the 3 available methods, and the number of recipes for each iteration is either 20 or 30). We run 100 iterations of random search, with each iteration - read set of parameter values - being tested 10 times and averaged to account for randomness of the

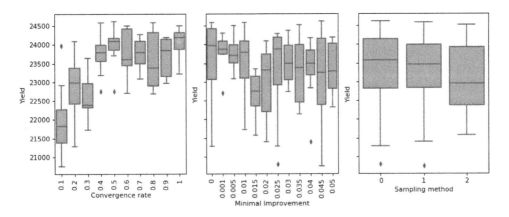

Fig. 3. Yield of the best recipe depending on the value of different hyperparameters using 100 sample recipes for each hyperparameter.

recipes generated. After each iteration of random search, we store the set of hyperparameter values and the corresponding best recipe found. Figure 3 depicts results of the experiments. Optimal values for convergence rate seem to be around 0.5, between 0.001 and 0.01 for minimal improvement, and the best sampling method is tied between the first and second one. Generating 30 recipes for each iteration yields better results than 20 (average yield of 23857 for 30 recipes against 22829 for 20 recipes). To compare our method against other methods, we run our framework with the following parameters: 30 recipes times 5 iterations (for a total of 150 recipes), 0.5 convergence rate, using the second sampling method with $k = 15$. To address the variance in the yield due to randomness in the recipe generation process, we run the framework 10 times, we store the best recipe found at each iteration and then compute the average of the stored recipes. We report the results in Table 3.

5.3 Comparison with Alternative Methods

Good hyperparameter values have been defined for our optimization framework and we can now compare our method with other ones. Let us consider the use of expert knowledge and random search. First, we want to create a model using expert knowledge. With the help of an agricultural engineer, we defined a priori good values for each parameter using expert knowledge and we generated a recipe that can serve as a baseline for our experiments. We then choose to compare our method against a random search model without expert knowledge. We set the number of recipes to 150 for all methods to provide a fair comparison with our own model where the number of recipes is set to 150. To account for randomness in the recipe generation, we run 10 iterations of the random search model, we store the value of the best recipe found in each iteration, and we compute their average yield. Results of the experiments and a description of the best recipe for each method are available in Table 3. Random search and expert knowledge find recipes with almost equal yields, while our framework find recipes with higher

Table 3. Comparison of the description and the yield of the best recipe returned by each method. EK = Expert Knowledge, RS = Random Search, SM = Surrogate Modeling, VC = Virtuous Circle (our framework).

Method	Rain^{P1}	Irrad^{P1}	Wind^{P1}	Rain^{P2}	Irrad^{P2}	Wind^{P2}	Rain^{P3}	Irrad^{P3}	Wind^{P3}	Yield
EK	10	0	5	10	25000	5	10	25000	5	23472
RS	17	23447	8	31	22222	23	39	22385	7	23561
SM	20	44	0	20	24981	0	40	31	30	10170
VC	19	16121	18	25	24052	28	14	21126	7	24336

yield. Note that in industrial settings, an improved yield of 3% to 4% has a significant impact on revenues.

Let us now compare our framework to the Surrogate Modeling method presented in [9]. To be fair, we give the same number of data points to build the Symbolic Regression surrogate model as we used in previous experiments, i.e., 150 for training the model (we evaluated the RMSE of the model on a test set of 38 other samples). We use gplearn [19], with default parameters, except for the number of generations and the number of models evaluated for each generations, which are respectively of 1000 and 2000, as in [9]. Note that the model obtained has a RMSE of 2112, and it is composed of more than 2000 terms (including mathematical operators), therefore the argument of interpretability is questionable. A grid search is finally done on this model and we select the best recipe and obtain their true yield using the PCSE simulation environment. The number of steps for each attribute for the grid search has to be defined. We set it to 5. As we have 9 parameters, it means that the model needs to be evaluated on nearly 9 million potential recipes. Also, the model is composed of hundreds of terms such that experiments are computationally expensive. The best recipe found so far is given in Table 3. The surrogate model predicts a yield value of 21137. Compared to the ground truth of 10170, the model has a strong bias. It illustrates that using a surrogate model for this kind of problem will give good recipes only if it is reliable enough. Interestingly, the RMSE seems to be quite good at first glance, but this does not guarantee that the model will behave correctly on all elements of the search space: on the best recipe found, it largely overestimates the yield, leading to a non-interesting recipe. It seems that this method performs poorly on recipes with more attributes than in [9]. Further studies are here needed.

6   Conclusion

We investigated the optimization of plant growth recipes in controlled environments, a key process in connected urban farms. We motivated the reasons why existing methods fall short of real life constraints, including the necessity to minimize the number of experiments needed to provide good results. We detailed a new optimization framework that leverages subgroup discovery to iteratively find better growth recipes through the use of a virtuous circle. We also introduced an efficient algorithm for the optimal subgroup discovery in purely numerical datasets. It has been recently improved much further in [17]. We avoid discretization and it provides a qualitative added-value (i.e., more interesting optimal subgroups). Future work includes extending our framework to deal with multiple target labels at the same time (e.g., optimizing the yield while keeping the energy cost as low as possible).

Acknowledgment. Our research is partially funded by the French FUI programme (project DUF 4.0, 2018–2021).

References

1. Atzmueller, M., Puppe, F.: SD-Map – a fast algorithm for exhaustive subgroup discovery. In: Fürnkranz, J., Scheffer, T., Spiliopoulou, M. (eds.) PKDD 2006. LNCS (LNAI), vol. 4213, pp. 6–17. Springer, Heidelberg (2006). https://doi.org/10.1007/11871637_6
2. Bosc, G., Boulicaut, J.F., Raïssi, C., Kaytoue, M.: Anytime discovery of a diverse set of patterns with Monte Carlo tree search. Data Min. Knowl. Discov. **32**, 604–650 (2018). https://doi.org/10.1007/s10618-017-0547-5
3. Fayyad, U.M., Irani, K.B.: Multi-interval discretization of continuous-valued attributes for classification learning. In: Proceedings IJCAI, pp. 1022–1029 (1993)
4. Garriga, G.C., Kralj, P., Lavrač, N.: Closed sets for labeled data. J. Mach. Learn. Res. **9**, 559–580 (2008)
5. Grosskreutz, H., Paurat, D.: Fast and memory-efficient discovery of the top-k relevant subgroups in a reduced candidate space. In: Gunopulos, D., Hofmann, T., Malerba, D., Vazirgiannis, M. (eds.) ECML PKDD 2011. LNCS (LNAI), vol. 6911, pp. 533–548. Springer, Heidelberg (2011). https://doi.org/10.1007/978-3-642-23780-5_44
6. Grosskreutz, H., Rüping, S.: On subgroup discovery in numerical domains. Data Min. Knowl. Discov. **19**(2), 210–226 (2009). https://doi.org/10.1007/s10618-009-0136-3
7. Grosskreutz, H., Rüping, S., Wrobel, S.: Tight optimistic estimates for fast subgroup discovery. In: Daelemans, W., Goethals, B., Morik, K. (eds.) ECML PKDD 2008. LNCS (LNAI), vol. 5211, pp. 440–456. Springer, Heidelberg (2008). https://doi.org/10.1007/978-3-540-87479-9_47
8. Harper, C., Siller, M.: OpenAG: a globally distributed network of food computing. IEEE Pervasive Comput. **14**, 24–27 (2015)
9. Johnson, A., Meyerson, E., Parra, J., Savas, T., Miikkulainen, R., Harper, C.: Flavor-cyber-agriculture: optimization of plant metabolites in an open-source control environment through surrogate modeling. PLoS ONE **14**, e0213918 (2019)
10. Jones, D.R., Schonlau, M., Welch, W.J.: Efficient global optimization of expensive black-box functions. J. Global Optim. **13**(4), 455–492 (1998)
11. Kaytoue, M., Kuznetsov, S.O., Napoli, A.: Revisiting numerical pattern mining with formal concept analysis. In: Proceedings IJCAI, pp. 1342–1347 (2011)
12. Klösgen, W.: Explora: a multipattern and multistrategy discovery assistant. In: Advances in Knowledge Discovery and Data Mining, pp. 249–271 (1996)
13. Koza, J.R.: Genetic Programming: On the Programming of Computers by Means of Natural Selection, pp. 162–169. MIT Press, Cambridge (1992)

14. Lemmerich, F., Atzmueller, M., Puppe, F.: Fast exhaustive subgroup discovery with numerical target concepts. Data Min. Knowl. Discov. **30**(3), 711–762 (2015). https://doi.org/10.1007/s10618-015-0436-8

15. Mampaey, M., Nijssen, S., Feelders, A., Knobbe, A.: Efficient algorithms for finding richer subgroup descriptions in numeric and nominal data. In: Proceedings ICDM, pp. 499–508 (2012)

16. McKay, M.D., Beckman, R.J., Conover, W.J.: A comparison of three methods for selecting values of input variables in the analysis of output from a computer code. Technometrics **21**(2), 239–245 (1979)

17. Millot, A., Cazabet, R., Boulicaut, J.F.: Optimal subgroup discovery in purely numerical data. In: Proceedings PaKDD, pp. 1–12 (2020, in press)

18. Rios, L.M., Sahinidis, N.V.: Derivative-free optimization: a review of algorithms and comparison of software implementations. J. Global Optim. **56**(3), 1247–1293 (2013). https://doi.org/10.1007/s10898-012-9951-y

19. Stephens, T.: gplearn (2013). https://github.com/trevorstephens/gplearn

20. Wojciechowska, R., Długosz-Grochowska, O., Kołton, A., Żupnik, M.: Effects of LED supplemental lighting on yield and some quality parameters of lamb's lettuce grown in two winter cycles. Sci. Hortic. **187**, 80–86 (2015)

21. Wrobel, S.: An algorithm for multi-relational discovery of subgroups. In: Komorowski, J., Zytkow, J. (eds.) PKDD 1997. LNCS, vol. 1263, pp. 78–87. Springer, Heidelberg (1997). https://doi.org/10.1007/3-540-63223-9_108

Detection of Derivative Discontinuities
in Observational Data

Dimitar Ninevski$^{(\boxtimes)}$ ⓘ and Paul O'Leary ⓘ

University of Leoben, 8700 Leoben, Austria
`automation@unileoben.ac.at`

Abstract. This paper presents a new approach to the detection of discontinuities in the n-th derivative of observational data. This is achieved by performing two polynomial approximations at each interstitial point. The polynomials are coupled by constraining their coefficients to ensure continuity of the model up to the $(n-1)$-th derivative; while yielding an estimate for the discontinuity of the n-th derivative. The coefficients of the polynomials correspond directly to the derivatives of the approximations at the interstitial points through the prudent selection of a common coordinate system. The approximation residual and extrapolation errors are investigated as measures for detecting discontinuity. This is necessary since discrete observations of continuous systems are discontinuous at every point. It is proven, using matrix algebra, that positive extrema in the combined approximation-extrapolation error correspond exactly to extrema in the difference of the Taylor coefficients. This provides a relative measure for the severity of the discontinuity in the observational data. The matrix algebraic derivations are provided for all aspects of the methods presented here; this includes a solution for the covariance propagation through the computation. The performance of the method is verified with a Monte Carlo simulation using synthetic piecewise polynomial data with known discontinuities. It is also demonstrated that the discontinuities are suitable as knots for B-spline modelling of data. For completeness, the results of applying the method to sensor data acquired during the monitoring of heavy machinery are presented.

Keywords: Data analysis · Discontinuity detection · Free-knot splines

1 Introduction

In the recent past *physics informed data science* has become a focus of research activities, e.g., [9]. It appears under different names e.g., *physics informed* [12]; *hybrid learning* [13]; *physics-based* [17], etc.; but with the same basic idea of embedding physical principles into the data science algorithms. The goal is to ensure that the results obtained obey the laws of physics and/or are based on physically relevant features. Discontinuities in the observations of continuous systems violate some very basic physics and for this reason their detection is of fundamental importance. Consider Newton's second law of motion,

$$F(t) = \frac{\mathrm{d}}{\mathrm{d}t} \left\{ m(t) \, \frac{\mathrm{d}}{\mathrm{d}t} y(t) \right\} = \dot{m}(t) \, \dot{y}(t) + m(t) \, \ddot{y}(t). \tag{1}$$

Any discontinuities in the observations of $m(t)$, $\dot{m}(t)$, $y(t)$, $\dot{y}(t)$ or $\ddot{y}(t)$ indicate a violation of some basic principle: be it that the observation is incorrect or something unexpected is happening in the system. Consequently, detecting discontinuities is of fundamental importance in physics based data science. A function $s(x)$ is said to be C^n discontinuous, if $s \in C^{n-1} \backslash C^n$, that is if $s(x)$ has continuous derivatives up to and including order $n - 1$, but the n-th derivative is discontinuous. Due to the discrete and finite nature of the observational data, only jump discontinuities in the n-th derivative are considered; asymptotic discontinuities are not considered. Furthermore, in more classical data modelling, C^n jump discontinuities form the basis for the locations of knots in B-Spline models of observational data [15].

1.1 State of the Art

There are numerous approaches in the literature dealing with estimating regression functions that are smooth, except at a finite number of points. Based on the methods, these approaches can be classified into four groups: local polynomial methods, spline-based methods, kernel-based methods and wavelet methods. The approaches vary also with respect to the available a priori knowledge about the number of points of discontinuity or the derivative in which these discontinuities appear. For a good literature review of these methods, see [3]. The method used in this paper is relevant both in terms of local polynomials as well as spline-based methods; however, the new approach requires no a priori knowledge about the data.

In the local polynomial literature, namely in [8] and [14], ideas similar to the ones presented here are investigated. In these papers, local polynomial approximations from the left and the right side of the point in question are used. The major difference is that neither of these methods use constraints to ensure that the local polynomial approximations enforce continuity of the lower derivatives, which is done in this paper. As such, they use different residuals to determine the existence of a change point. Using constrained approximation ensures that the underlying physical properties of the system are taken into consideration, which is one of the main advantages of the approach presented here. Additionally, in the aforementioned papers, it is not clear whether only co-locative points are considered as possible change points, or interstitial points are also considered. This distinction between collocative and interstitial is of great importance. Fundamentally, the method presented here can be applied to discontinuities at either locations. However, it has been assumed that discontinuities only make sense between the sampled (co-locative) points, i.e., the discontinuities are interstitial.

In [11] on the other hand, one polynomial instead of two is used, and the focus is mainly on detecting C^0 and C^1 discontinuities. Additionally, the number of change-points must be known a-priori, so only their location is approximated; the required a-priori knowledge make the method unsuitable in real sensor based system observation.

In the spline-based literature there are heuristic methods (top-down and bottom-up) as well as optimization methods. For a more detailed state of the art on splines, see [2]. Most heuristic methods use a discrete geometric measure to calculate whether a point is a knot, such as: discrete curvature, kink angle, etc, and then use some (mostly arbitrary) threshold to improve the initial knot set. In the method presented here, which falls under the category of bottom-up approaches, the selection criterion is based on calculus and statistics, which allows for incorporation of the fundamental physical laws governing the system, in the model, but also ensures mathematical relevance and rigour.

1.2 The New Approach

This paper presents a new approach to detecting C^n discontinuities in observational data. It uses constrained coupled polynomial approximation to obtain two estimates for the nth Taylor coefficients and their uncertainties, at every interstitial point. These correspond approximating the local function by polynomials, once from the left $\mathbf{f}(x, \boldsymbol{\alpha})$ and once from the right $\mathbf{g}(x, \boldsymbol{\beta})$. The constraints couple the polynomials to ensure that $\alpha_i = \beta_i$ for every $i \in [0 \ldots n - 1]$. In this manner the approximations are C^{n-1} continuous at the interstitial points, while delivering an estimate for the difference in the nth Taylor coefficients. All the derivations for the coupled constrained approximations and the numerical implementations are presented. Both the approximation and extrapolation residuals are derived. It is proven that the discontinuities must lie at local positive peaks in the extrapolation error. The new approach is verified with both known synthetic data and on real sensor data obtained from observing the operation of heavy machinery.

2 Detecting C^n Discontinuities

Discrete observations $s(x_i)$ of a continuous system $s(x)$ are, by their very nature, discontinuous at every sample. Consequently, some measure for discontinuity will be required, with uncertainty, which provides the basis for further analysis.

The observations are considered to be the co-locative points, denoted by x_i and collectively by the vector $\boldsymbol{x}$; however, we wish to estimate the discontinuity at the interstitial points, denoted by ζ_i and collectively as $\boldsymbol{\zeta}$. Using interstitial points, one ensures that each data point is used for only one polynomial approximation at a time. Furthermore, in the case of sensor data, one expects the discontinuities to happen between samples. Consequently the data is segmented at the interstitial points, i.e. between the samples. This requires the use of interpolating functions and in this work we have chosen to use polynomials.

Polynomials have been chosen because of their approximating, interpolating and extrapolating properties when modelling continuous systems: The Weierstrass approximation theorem [16] states that if $f(x)$ is a continuous real-valued function defined on the real interval $x \in [a, b]$, then for every $\varepsilon > 0$, there exists a polynomial $p(x)$ such that for all $x \in [a, b]$, the supremum norm $\|f(x) - p(x)\|_\infty < \varepsilon$. That is *any* function $f(x)$ can be approximated by a polynomial to an arbitrary accuracy ε given a sufficiently high degree.

The basic concept (see Fig. 1) to detect a C^n discontinuity is: to approximate the data to the left of an interstitial point by the polynomial $\mathsf{f}(x, \boldsymbol{\alpha})$ of degree d_L and to the right by $\mathsf{g}(x, \boldsymbol{\beta})$ of degree d_R, while constraining these approximations to be C^{n-1} continuous at the interstitial point. This approximation ensures that,

$$\mathsf{f}^{(k-1)}(\zeta_i) = \mathsf{g}^{(k-1)}(\zeta_i), \quad \text{for every } k \in [1 \dots n]. \tag{2}$$

while yielding estimates for $\mathsf{f}^{(n)}(\zeta_i)$ and $\mathsf{g}^{(n)}(\zeta_i)$ together with estimates for their variances $\lambda_{f(\zeta_i)}$ and $\lambda_{g(\zeta_i)}$. This corresponds exactly to estimating the Taylor coefficients of the function twice for each interstitial point, i.e., once from the left and once from the right. It they differ significantly, then the function's n^{th} derivative is discontinuous at this point. The Taylor series of a function $f(x)$ around the point a is defined as,

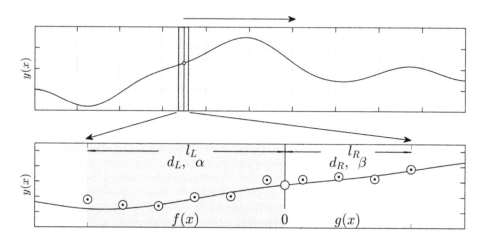

Fig. 1. Schematic of a finite set of discrete observations (dotted circles) of a continuous function. The span of the observation is split into a left and right portion at the interstitial point (circle), with lengths l_L and l_R respectively. The left and right sides are considered to be the functions $f(x)$ and $g(x)$; modelled by the polynomials $\mathsf{f}(x, \boldsymbol{\alpha})$ and $\mathsf{g}(x, \boldsymbol{\beta})$ of degrees d_L and d_R.

$$f(x) = \sum_{k=0}^{\infty} \frac{f^{(k)}(a)}{k!} (x - a)^k \tag{3}$$

for each x for which the infinite series on the right hand side converges. Furthermore, any function which is $n + 1$ times differentiable can be written as

$$f(x) = \tilde{\mathsf{f}}(x) + R(x) \tag{4}$$

where $\tilde{f}(x)$ is an nth degree polynomial approximation of the function $f(x)$,

$$\tilde{f}(x) = \sum_{k=0}^{n} \frac{f^{(k)}(a)}{k!}(x-a)^k \tag{5}$$

and $R(x)$ is the remainder term. The Lagrange form of the remainder $R(x)$ is given by

$$R(x) = \frac{f^{(n+1)}(\xi)}{(n+1)!}(x-a)^{n+1} \tag{6}$$

where ξ is a real number between a and x.

A Taylor expansion around the origin (i.e. $a = 0$ in Eq. 3) is called a Maclaurin expansion; for more details, see [1]. In the rest of this work, the nth Maclaurin coefficient for the function $f(x)$ will be denoted by

$$t_f^{(n)} \triangleq \frac{f^{(n)}(0)}{n!}. \tag{7}$$

The coefficients of a polynomial $f(x, \alpha) = \alpha_n x^n + \ldots + \alpha_1 x + \alpha_0$ are closely related to the coefficients of the Maclaurin expansion of this polynomial. Namely, it's easy to prove that

$$\alpha_k = t_f^{(k)}, \quad \text{for every } k \in [0 \ldots n]. \tag{8}$$

A prudent selection of a common local coordinate system, setting the interstitial point as the origin, ensures that the coefficients of the left and right approximating polynomials correspond to the derivative values at this interstitial point. Namely, one gets a very clear relationship between the coefficients of the left and right polynomial approximations, $\boldsymbol{\alpha}$ and $\boldsymbol{\beta}$, their Maclaurin coefficients, $t_f^{(n)}$ and $t_g^{(n)}$, and the values of the derivatives at the interstitial point

$$t_f^{(n)} = \alpha_n = \frac{f^{(n)}(0)}{n!} \quad \text{and} \quad t_g^{(n)} = \beta_n = \frac{g^{(n)}(0)}{n!}. \tag{9}$$

From Eq. 9 it is clear that performing a left and right polynomial approximation at an interstitial point is sufficient to get the derivative values at that point, as well as their uncertainties.

3 Constrained and Coupled Polynomial Approximation

The goal here is to obtain $\Delta t_{fg}^{(n)} \triangleq t_f^{(n)} - t_g^{(n)}$ via polynomial approximation. To this end two polynomial approximations are required; whereby, the interstitial point is used as the origin in the common coordinate system, see Fig. 1. The approximations are coupled [6] at the interstitial point by constraining the coefficients such that $\alpha_i = \beta_i$, for every $i \in [0 \ldots n-1]$. This ensures that the two polynomials are C^{n-1} continuous at the interstitial points. This also reduces the degrees of freedom during the approximation and with this the variance of the solution is reduced. For more details on constrained polynomial approximation see [4, 7].

To remain fully general, a local polynomial approximation of degree d_L is performed to the left of the interstitial point with the support length l_L creating $f(x, \boldsymbol{\alpha})$; similarly to the right d_R, l_R, $g(x, \boldsymbol{\beta})$. The x coordinates to the left, denoted as $\boldsymbol{x}_L$ are used to form the left Vandermonde matrix $\boldsymbol{V}_L$, similarly $\boldsymbol{x}_R$ form $\boldsymbol{V}_R$ to the right. This leads to the following formulation of the approximation process,

$$\boldsymbol{y}_L = \boldsymbol{V}_L \, \boldsymbol{\alpha} \quad \text{and} \quad \boldsymbol{y}_R = \boldsymbol{V}_R \, \boldsymbol{\beta}. \tag{10}$$

$$\begin{bmatrix} \boldsymbol{V}_L & \mathbf{0} \\ \mathbf{0} & \boldsymbol{V}_R \end{bmatrix} \begin{bmatrix} \boldsymbol{\alpha} \\ \boldsymbol{\beta} \end{bmatrix} = \begin{bmatrix} \boldsymbol{y}_L \\ \boldsymbol{y}_R \end{bmatrix} \tag{11}$$

A C^{n-1} continuity implies $\alpha_i = \beta_i$, for every $i \in [0 \ldots n-1]$ which can be written in matrix form as

$$\begin{bmatrix} \mathbf{0} & \boldsymbol{I}_{n-1} \,\big|\, \mathbf{0} & -\boldsymbol{I}_{n-1} \end{bmatrix} \begin{bmatrix} \boldsymbol{\alpha} \\ \boldsymbol{\beta} \end{bmatrix} = \mathbf{0} \tag{12}$$

Defining

$$\boldsymbol{V} \triangleq \begin{bmatrix} \boldsymbol{V}_L & \mathbf{0} \\ \mathbf{0} & \boldsymbol{V}_R \end{bmatrix}, \gamma \triangleq \begin{bmatrix} \boldsymbol{\alpha} \\ \boldsymbol{\beta} \end{bmatrix}, \boldsymbol{y} \triangleq \begin{bmatrix} \boldsymbol{y}_L \\ \boldsymbol{y}_R \end{bmatrix} \text{ and } \boldsymbol{C} \triangleq \begin{bmatrix} \mathbf{0} & \boldsymbol{I}_{n-1} \,\big|\, \mathbf{0} & -\boldsymbol{I}_{n-1} \end{bmatrix}$$

We obtain the task of least squares minimization with homogeneous linear constraints,

$$\boxed{\begin{array}{c} \min_{\gamma} \quad \|\boldsymbol{y} - \boldsymbol{V} \, \gamma\|_2^2 \\ \text{Given} \quad \boldsymbol{C} \, \gamma = \mathbf{0}. \end{array}} \tag{13}$$

Clearly γ must lie in the null-space of $\boldsymbol{C}$; now, given $\boldsymbol{N}$, an ortho-normal vector basis set for null $\{\boldsymbol{C}\}$, we obtain,

$$\gamma = \boldsymbol{N} \, \boldsymbol{\delta}. \tag{14}$$

Back-substituting into Eq. 13 yields,

$$\min_{\delta} \|\boldsymbol{y} - \boldsymbol{V} \, \boldsymbol{N} \, \boldsymbol{\delta}\|_2^2 \tag{15}$$

The least squares solution to this problem is,

$$\boldsymbol{\delta} = (\boldsymbol{V} \, \boldsymbol{N})^+ \, \boldsymbol{y}, \tag{16}$$

and consequently,

$$\boxed{\gamma = \begin{bmatrix} \boldsymbol{\alpha} \\ \boldsymbol{\beta} \end{bmatrix} = \boldsymbol{N} \, (\boldsymbol{V} \, \boldsymbol{N})^+ \, \boldsymbol{y}} \tag{17}$$

Formulating the approximation in the above manner ensures that the difference in the Taylor coefficients can be simply computed as

$$\Delta t_{\text{fg}}^{(n)} = t_{\text{f}}^{(n)} - t_{\text{g}}^{(n)} = \alpha_n = \beta_n. \tag{18}$$

Now defining $\boldsymbol{d} = [1, \boldsymbol{0}_{d_L-1}, -1, \boldsymbol{0}_{d_R-1}]^{\text{T}}$, $\Delta t_{\text{fg}}^{(n)}$ is obtained from $\boldsymbol{\gamma}$ as

$$\Delta t_{\text{fg}}^{(n)} = \boldsymbol{d}^{\text{T}}\boldsymbol{\gamma} = \boldsymbol{d}^{\text{T}}\boldsymbol{N}\,(\boldsymbol{V}\,\boldsymbol{N})^{+}\,\boldsymbol{y}. \tag{19}$$

3.1   Covariance Propagation

Defining, $\boldsymbol{K} = \boldsymbol{N}\,(\boldsymbol{V}\,\boldsymbol{N})^{+}$, yields, $\boldsymbol{\gamma} = \boldsymbol{K}\,\boldsymbol{y}$. Then given the covariance of $\boldsymbol{y}$, i.e., $\boldsymbol{\Lambda}_y$, one gets that,

$$\boxed{\boldsymbol{\Lambda}_\gamma = \boldsymbol{K}\,\boldsymbol{\Lambda}_y\,\boldsymbol{K}^{\text{T}}.} \tag{20}$$

Additionally, from Eq. 19 one could derive the covariance of the difference in the Taylor coefficients

$$\boldsymbol{\Lambda}_\Delta = \boldsymbol{d}\boldsymbol{\Lambda}_\gamma\boldsymbol{d}^{\text{T}} \tag{22}$$

Keep in mind that, if one uses approximating polynomials of degree n to determine a discontinuity in the nth derivative, as done so far, $\boldsymbol{\Lambda}_\Delta$ is just a scalar and corresponds to the variance of $\Delta t_{\text{fg}}^{(n)}$.

4   Error Analysis

In this paper we consider three measures for error:

1. the norm of the approximation residual;
2. the combined approximation and extrapolation error;
3. the extrapolation error.

4.1   Approximation Error

The residual vector has the form

$$\boldsymbol{r} = \boldsymbol{y} - \boldsymbol{V}\boldsymbol{\gamma} = \begin{bmatrix} \boldsymbol{y}_L - \boldsymbol{V}_L\boldsymbol{\alpha} \\ \boldsymbol{y}_R - \boldsymbol{V}_R\boldsymbol{\beta} \end{bmatrix}.$$

The approximation error is calculated as

$$\begin{aligned}
E_a &= \|\boldsymbol{r}\|_2^2 = \|\boldsymbol{y}_L - \boldsymbol{V}_L\boldsymbol{\alpha}\|_2^2 + \|\boldsymbol{y}_R - \boldsymbol{V}_R\boldsymbol{\beta}\|_2^2 \\
&= (\boldsymbol{y}_L - \boldsymbol{V}_L\boldsymbol{\alpha})^{\text{T}}(\boldsymbol{y}_L - \boldsymbol{V}_L\boldsymbol{\alpha}) + (\boldsymbol{y}_R - \boldsymbol{V}_R\boldsymbol{\beta})^{\text{T}}(\boldsymbol{y}_R - \boldsymbol{V}_R\boldsymbol{\beta}) \\
&= \boldsymbol{y}^{\text{T}}\boldsymbol{y} - 2\boldsymbol{\alpha}^{\text{T}}\boldsymbol{V}_L^{\text{T}}\boldsymbol{y}_L + \boldsymbol{\alpha}^{\text{T}}\boldsymbol{V}_L^{\text{T}}\boldsymbol{V}_L\boldsymbol{\alpha} - 2\boldsymbol{\beta}^{\text{T}}\boldsymbol{V}_R^{\text{T}}\boldsymbol{y}_R + \boldsymbol{\beta}^{\text{T}}\boldsymbol{V}_R^{\text{T}}\boldsymbol{V}_R\boldsymbol{\beta}.
\end{aligned}$$

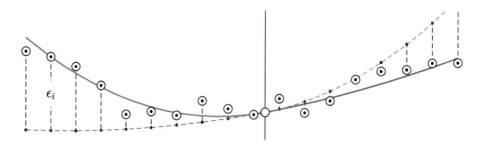

Fig. 2. Schematic of the approximations around the interstitial point. Red: left polynomial approximation $f(x, \boldsymbol{\alpha})$; dotted red: extrapolation of $f(x, \boldsymbol{\alpha})$ to the RHS; blue: right polynomial approximation, $g(x, \boldsymbol{\beta})$; dotted blue: extrapolation of $g(x, \boldsymbol{\beta})$ to the LHS; ε_i is the vertical distance between the extrapolated value and the observation. The approximation is constrained with the conditions: $f(0, \boldsymbol{\alpha}) = g(0, \boldsymbol{\beta})$ and $f'(0, \boldsymbol{\alpha}) = g'(0, \boldsymbol{\beta})$. (Color figure online)

4.2 Combined Error

The basic concept, which can be seen in Fig. 2, is as follows: the left polynomial $f(x, \boldsymbol{\alpha})$, which approximates over the values $\boldsymbol{x}_L$, is extended to the right and evaluated at the points $\boldsymbol{x}_R$. Analogously, the right polynomial $g(x, \boldsymbol{\beta})$ is evaluated at the points $\boldsymbol{x}_L$. If there is no C^n discontinuity in the system, the polynomials f and g must be equal and consequently the extrapolated values won't differ significantly from the approximated values.

Analytical Combined Error. The extrapolation error in a continuous case, i.e. between the two polynomial models, can be computed with the following 2-norm,

$$\varepsilon_x = \int_{x_{min}}^{x_{max}} \{f(x, \boldsymbol{\alpha}) - g(x, \boldsymbol{\beta})\}^2 \ \mathrm{d}x. \tag{23}$$

Given, the constraints which ensure that $\alpha_i = \beta_i \ i \in [0, \dots, n-1]$, we obtain,

$$\varepsilon_x = \int_{x_{min}}^{x_{max}} \{(\alpha_n - \beta_n) \, x^n\}^2 \ \mathrm{d}x. \tag{24}$$

Expanding and performing the integral yields,

$$\varepsilon_x = (\alpha_n - \beta_n)^2 \left\{ \frac{x_{max}^{2n+1} - x_{min}^{2n+1}}{2n+1} \right\} \tag{25}$$

Given fixed values for x_{min} and x_{max} across a single computation implies that the factor,

$$k = \frac{x_{max}^{2n+1} - x_{min}^{2n+1}}{2n+1} \tag{26}$$

is a constant. Consequently, the extrapolation error is directly proportional to the square of the difference in the Taylor coefficients,

$$\varepsilon_x \propto (\alpha_n - \beta_n)^2 \propto \left\{ \Delta t_{\mathrm{fg}}^{(n)} \right\}^2. \tag{27}$$

Numerical Combined Error. In the discrete case, one can write the errors of $\mathsf{f}(x, \boldsymbol{\alpha})$ and $\mathsf{g}(x, \boldsymbol{\beta})$ as

$$e_{\mathsf{f}} = \boldsymbol{y} - \mathsf{f}(\boldsymbol{x}, \boldsymbol{\alpha}) \quad \text{and} \quad e_{\mathsf{g}} = \boldsymbol{y} - \mathsf{g}(\boldsymbol{x}, \boldsymbol{\beta}) \tag{28}$$

respectively. Consequently, one could define an error function as

$$E_{\mathsf{fg}} = \|e_{\mathsf{f}} - e_{\mathsf{g}}\|_2^2 = \|(a_n - b_n)\,\boldsymbol{z}\|_2^2 = (a_n - b_n)^2 \boldsymbol{z}^{\mathsf{T}} \boldsymbol{z}^n = (a_n - b_n)^2 \sum x_i^n \tag{29}$$

where $\boldsymbol{z} \triangleq \boldsymbol{x}.\hat{}\,n$. From these calculations it is clear that in the discrete case the error is also directly proportional to the square of the difference in the Taylor coefficients and that $E_{\mathsf{fg}} \propto \varepsilon_x$. This proves that the numerical computation is consistent with the analytical continuous error.

4.3 Extrapolation Error

One could also define a different kind of error, based just on the extrapolative properties of the polynomials. Namely, using the notation from the beginning of Sect. 3, one defines

$$r_{\mathsf{ef}} = \boldsymbol{y}_L - \mathsf{g}(\boldsymbol{x}_L, \boldsymbol{\beta}) = \boldsymbol{y}_L - \boldsymbol{V}_L \boldsymbol{\beta} \quad \text{and} \quad r_{\mathsf{eg}} = \boldsymbol{y}_R - \mathsf{f}(\boldsymbol{x}_R, \boldsymbol{\alpha}) = \boldsymbol{y}_R - \boldsymbol{V}_R \boldsymbol{\alpha}$$

and then calculates the error as

$$\begin{aligned} E_e &= r_{\mathsf{ef}}^{\mathsf{T}} r_{\mathsf{ef}} + r_{\mathsf{eg}}^{\mathsf{T}} r_{\mathsf{eg}} \\ &= (\boldsymbol{y}_L - \boldsymbol{V}_L \boldsymbol{\beta})^{\mathsf{T}} (\boldsymbol{y}_L - \boldsymbol{V}_L \boldsymbol{\beta}) + (\boldsymbol{y}_R - \boldsymbol{V}_R \boldsymbol{\alpha})^{\mathsf{T}} (\boldsymbol{y}_R - \boldsymbol{V}_R \boldsymbol{\alpha}) \\ &= \boldsymbol{y}^{\mathsf{T}} \boldsymbol{y} - 2\boldsymbol{\beta}^{\mathsf{T}} \boldsymbol{V}_L^{\mathsf{T}} \boldsymbol{y}_L + \boldsymbol{\beta}^{\mathsf{T}} \boldsymbol{V}_L^{\mathsf{T}} \boldsymbol{V}_L \boldsymbol{\beta} - 2\boldsymbol{\alpha}^{\mathsf{T}} \boldsymbol{V}_R^{\mathsf{T}} \boldsymbol{y}_R + \boldsymbol{\alpha}^{\mathsf{T}} \boldsymbol{V}_R^{\mathsf{T}} \boldsymbol{V}_R \boldsymbol{\alpha}. \end{aligned}$$

In the example in Sect. 5, it will be seen that there is no significant numerical difference between these two errors.

5 Numerical Testing

The numerical testing is performed with: synthetic data from a piecewise polynomial, where the locations of the C^n discontinuities are known; and with real sensor data emanating from the monitoring of heavy machinery.

5.1 Synthetic Data

In the literature on splines, functions of the type $y(x) = e^{-x^2}$ are commonly used. However, this function is analytic and C^∞ continuous; consequently it was not considered a suitable function for testing. In Fig. 3 a piecewise polynomial with a similar shape is shown; however, this curve has C^2 discontinuities at known locations. The algorithm was applied to the synthetic data from the piecewise polynomial, with added noise with $\sigma = 0.05$ and the results for a single case can be seen in Fig. 3. Additionally, a Monte Carlo simulation with $m = 10000$ iterations was performed and the results of the algorithm were compared to the true locations of the two known knots. The mean errors in the location of the knots are: $\mu_1 = (5.59 \pm 2.05) \times 10^{-4}$ with 95% confidence, and $\mu_2 = (-4.62 \pm 1.94) \times 10^{-4}$. Errors in the scale of 10^{-4}, in a support with a range $[0, 1]$, and 5% noise amplitude in the curve can be considered a highly satisfactory result.

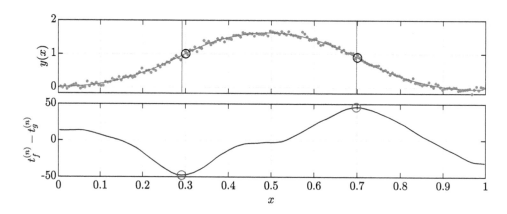

Fig. 3. A piecewise polynomial of degree $d = 2$, created from the knots sequence $x_k = [0, 0.3, 0.7, 1]$ with the corresponding values $y_k = [0, 0.3, 0.7, 1]$. The end points are clamped with $y'(x)_{0,1} = 0$. Gaussian noise is added with $\sigma = 0.05$. Top: the circles mark the known points of C^2 discontinuity; the blue and red lines indicate the detected discontinuities; additionally the data has been approximated by the b-spline (red) using the detected discontinuities as knots. Bottom: shows $\Delta t_{\mathrm{fg}}^{(n)} = t_{\mathrm{f}}^{(n)} - t_{\mathrm{g}}^{(n)}$, together with the two identified peaks. (Color figure online)

5.2 Sensor Data

The algorithm was also applied to a set of real-world sensor data[1] emanating from the monitoring of heavy machinery. The original data set can be seen in Fig. 4 (top). It has many local peaks and periods of little or no change, so the algorithm was used to detect discontinuities in the first derivative, in order to determine the peaks and phases. The peaks in the Taylor differences were used in combination with the peaks of the extrapolation error to determine the points of discontinuity. A peak in the Taylor differences means that the Taylor coefficients are significantly different at that interstitial point, compared to other interstitial points in the neighbourhood. However, if there is no peak in the extrapolation errors at the same location, then the peak found by the Taylor differences is deemed insignificant, since one polynomial could model both the left and right values and as such the peak isn't a discontinuity. Additionally, it can be seen in

---

[1] For confidentiality reasons the data has been anonymized.

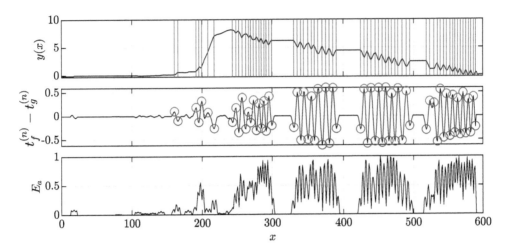

Fig. 4. The top-most graph shows a function $y(x)$, together with the detected C^1 discontinuity points. The middle graph shows the difference in the Taylor polynomials $\Delta t_{\mathrm{fg}}^{(n)}$ calculated at every interstitial point. The red and blue circles mark the relevant local maxima and minima of the difference respectively. According to this, the red and blue lines are drawn in the top-most graph. The bottom graph shows the approximation error evaluated at every interstitial point. (Color figure online)

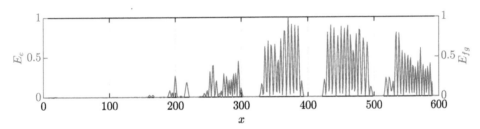

Fig. 5. The two error functions, E_e and E_{fg} as defined in Sect. 4, for the example from Fig. 4. One can see that the location of the peaks doesn't change, and the two errors don't differ significantly.

Fig. 5 that both the extrapolation error and the combined error, as defined in Sect. 4, have peaks at the same locations, and as such the results they provide do not differ significantly.

6 Conclusion and Future Work

It may be concluded, from the results achieved, that the coupled constrained polynomial approximation yield a good method for the detection of C^n discontinuities in discrete observational data of continuous systems. Local peaks in the square of the difference of the Taylor polynomials provide a relative measure as a means of determining the locations of discontinuities.

Current investigations indicate that the method can be implemented directly as a convolutional operator, which will yield a computationally efficient solution.

The use of discrete orthogonal polynomials [5, 10] is being tested as a means of improving the sensitivity of the results to numerical perturbations.

Acknowledgements. This work was partially funded by:

1. The COMET program within the K2 Center "Integrated Computational Material, Process and Product Engineering (IC-MPPE)" (Project No 859480). This program is supported by the Austrian Federal Ministries for Transport, Innovation and Technology (BMVIT) and for Digital and Economic Affairs (BMDW), represented by the Austrian research funding association (FFG), and the federal states of Styria, Upper Austria and Tyrol.
2. The European Institute of Innovation and Technology (EIT), a body of the European Union which receives support from the European Union's Horizon 2020 research and innovation programme. This was carried out under Framework Partnership Agreement No. 17031 (MaMMa - Maintained Mine & Machine).

The authors gratefully acknowledge this financial support.

References

1. Burden, R.L., Faires, J.D.: Numerical Analysis, 9th edn. Pacific Grove, Brooks/-Cole (2010)
2. Dung, V.T., Tjahjowidodo, T.: A direct method to solve optimal knots of B-spline curves: an application for non-uniform B-spline curves fitting. PLoS ONE **12**(3), 1–24 (2017). https://doi.org/10.1371/journal.pone.0173857
3. Gijbels, I., Goderniaux, A.C.: Data-driven discontinuity detection in derivatives of a regression function. Commun. Stat.-Theory Methods **33**(4), 851–871 (2005). https://doi.org/10.1081/STA-120028730
4. Klopfenstein, R.W.: Conditional least squares polynomial approximation. Math. Comput. **18**(88), 659–662 (1964). http://www.jstor.org/stable/2002954
5. O'Leary, P., Harker, M.: Discrete polynomial moments and Savitzky-Golay smoothing. Int. J. Comput. Inf. Eng. **4**(12), 1993–1997 (2010). https://publications.waset.org/vol/48
6. O'Leary, P., Harker, M., Zsombor-Murray, P.: Direct and least square fitting of coupled geometric objects for metric vision. IEE Proc. Vis. Image Sig. Process. **152**, 687–694 (2006). https://doi.org/10.1049/ip-vis:20045206
7. O'Leary, P., Ritt, R., Harker, M.: Constrained polynomial approximation for inverse problems in engineering. In: Abdel Wahab, M. (ed.) NME 2018. LNME, pp. 225–244. Springer, Singapore (2019). https://doi.org/10.1007/978-981-13-2273-0_19
8. Orváth, L., Kokoszka, P.: Change-point detection with non-parametric regression. Statistics **36**(1), 9–31 (2002). https://doi.org/10.1080/02331880210930
9. Owhadi, H.: Bayesian numerical homogenization. Multiscale Model. Simul. **13**(3), 812–828 (2015). https://doi.org/10.1137/140974596
10. Persson, P.O., Strang, G.: Smoothing by Savitzky-Golay and Legendre filters. In: Rosenthal, J., Gilliam, D.S. (eds.) Mathematical Systems Theory in Biology, Communications, Computation, and Finance. IMA, vol. 134, pp. 301–315. Springer, New York (2003). https://doi.org/10.1007/978-0-387-21696-6_11

11. Qiu, P., Yandell, B.: Local polynomial jump-detection algorithm in nonparametric regression. Technometrics **40**(2), 141–152 (1998). https://doi.org/10.1080/00401706.1998.10485196

12. Raissi, M., Perdikaris, P., Karniadakis, G.: Physics-informed neural networks: a deep learning framework for solving forward and inverse problems involving nonlinear partial differential equations. J. Comput. Phys. **378**, 686–707 (2019). https://doi.org/10.1016/j.jcp.2018.10.045. http://www.sciencedirect.com/science/article/pii/S0021999118307125

13. Saxena, H., Aponte, O., McConky, K.T.: A hybrid machine learning model for forecasting a billing period's peak electric load days. Int. J. Forecast. **35**(4), 1288–1303 (2019). https://doi.org/10.1016/j.ijforecast.2019.03.025

14. Spokoiny, V.: Estimation of a function with discontinuities via local polynomial fit with an adaptive window choice. Ann. Stat. **26** (1998). https://doi.org/10.1214/aos/1024691246

15. Wahba, G.: Spline models for observational data. Soc. Ind. Appl. Math. (1990). https://doi.org/10.1137/1.9781611970128

16. Weierstrass, K.: Über die analytische darstellbarkeit sogenannter willkürlicher functionen einer reellen veränderlichen. Sitzungsberichte der Königlich Preußischen Akademie der Wissenschaften zu Berlin, **1885**(II), 633–639, 789–805 (1885)

17. Yaman, B., Hosseini, S.A.H., Moeller, S., Ellermann, J., Uğurbil, K., Akçakaya, M.: Self-supervised physics-based deep learning MRI reconstruction without fully-sampled data (2019)

9

Aleatoric and Epistemic Uncertainty with Random Forests

Mohammad Hossein Shaker$^{(\boxtimes)}$ and Eyke Hüllermeier

Heinz Nixdorf Institute and Department of Computer Science,
Paderborn University, Paderborn, Germany
{mhshaker,eyke}@upb.de

Abstract. Due to the steadily increasing relevance of machine learning for practical applications, many of which are coming with safety requirements, the notion of uncertainty has received increasing attention in machine learning research in the last couple of years. In particular, the idea of distinguishing between two important types of uncertainty, often refereed to as *aleatoric* and *epistemic*, has recently been studied in the setting of supervised learning. In this paper, we propose to quantify these uncertainties, referring, respectively, to inherent randomness and a lack of knowledge, with random forests. More specifically, we show how two general approaches for measuring the learner's aleatoric and epistemic uncertainty in a prediction can be instantiated with decision trees and random forests as learning algorithms in a classification setting. In this regard, we also compare random forests with deep neural networks, which have been used for a similar purpose.

Keywords: Machine learning · Uncertainty · Random forest

1 Introduction

The notion of uncertainty has received increasing attention in machine learning research in the last couple of years, especially due to the steadily increasing relevance of machine learning for practical applications. In fact, a trustworthy representation of uncertainty should be considered as a key feature of any machine learning method, all the more in safety-critical application domains such as medicine [9,22] or socio-technical systems [19,20].

In the general literature on uncertainty, a distinction is made between two inherently different sources of uncertainty, which are often referred to as *aleatoric* and *epistemic* [4]. Roughly speaking, aleatoric (*aka* statistical) uncertainty refers to the notion of randomness, that is, the variability in the outcome of an experiment which is due to inherently random effects. The prototypical example of aleatoric uncertainty is coin flipping. As opposed to this, epistemic (*aka* systematic) uncertainty refers to uncertainty caused by a lack of knowledge, i.e., it relates to the epistemic state of an agent or decision maker. This uncertainty can in principle be reduced on the basis of additional information. In other words, epistemic uncertainty refers to the *reducible* part of the (total) uncertainty, whereas aleatoric uncertainty refers to the *non-reducible* part.

More recently, this distinction has also received attention in machine learning, where the "agent" is a learning algorithm [18]. In particular, a distinction between aleatoric and epistemic uncertainty has been advocated in the literature on deep learning [6], where the limited awareness of neural networks of their own competence has been demonstrated quite nicely. For example, experiments on image classification have shown that a trained model does often fail on specific instances, despite being very confident in its prediction. Moreover, such models are often lacking robustness and can easily be fooled by "adversarial examples" [14]: Drastic changes of a prediction may already be provoked by minor, actually unimportant changes of an object. This problem has not only been observed for images but also for other types of data, such as natural language text [17].

In this paper, we advocate the use of decision trees and random forests, not only as a powerful machine learning method with state-of-the-art predictive performance, but also for measuring and quantifying predictive uncertainty. More specifically, we show how two general approaches for measuring the learner's aleatoric and epistemic uncertainty in a prediction (recalled in Sect. 2) can be instantiated with decision trees and random forests as learning algorithms in a classification setting (Sect. 3). In an experimental study on uncertainty-based abstention (Sect. 4), we compare random forests with deep neural networks, which have been used for a similar purpose.

2 Epistemic and Aleatoric Uncertainty

We consider a standard setting of supervised learning, in which a learner is given access to a set of (i.i.d.) training data $\mathcal{D} := \{(\boldsymbol{x}_i, y_i)\}_{i=1}^{N} \subset \mathcal{X} \times \mathcal{Y}$, where $\mathcal{X}$ is an instance space and $\mathcal{Y}$ the set of outcomes that can be associated with an instance. In particular, we focus on the classification scenario, where $\mathcal{Y} = \{y_1, \ldots, y_K\}$ consists of a finite set of class labels, with binary classification ($\mathcal{Y} = \{0, 1\}$) as an important special case.

Suppose a *hypothesis space* $\mathcal{H}$ to be given, where a hypothesis $h \in \mathcal{H}$ is a mapping $\mathcal{X} \longrightarrow \mathbb{P}(\mathcal{Y})$, i.e., a hypothesis maps instances $\boldsymbol{x} \in \mathcal{X}$ to probability distributions on outcomes. The goal of the learner is to induce a hypothesis $h^* \in \mathcal{H}$ with low risk (expected loss)

$$R(h) := \int_{\mathcal{X} \times \mathcal{Y}} \ell(h(\boldsymbol{x}), y) \, d\, P(\boldsymbol{x}, y), \tag{1}$$

where P is the (unknown) data-generating process (a probability distribution on $\mathcal{X} \times \mathcal{Y}$), and $\ell : \mathcal{Y} \times \mathcal{Y} \longrightarrow \mathbb{R}$ a loss function. This choice of a hypothesis is commonly guided by the empirical risk

$$R_{emp}(h) := \frac{1}{N} \sum_{i=1}^{N} \ell(h(\boldsymbol{x}), y), \tag{2}$$

i.e., the performance of a hypothesis on the training data. However, since $R_{emp}(h)$ is only an estimation of the true risk $R(h)$, the empirical risk minimizer (or any other predictor)

$$\widehat{h} := \underset{h \in \mathcal{H}}{\operatorname{argmin}} R_{emp}(h) \tag{3}$$

favored by the learner will normally not coincide with the true risk minimizer (Bayes predictor)

$$h^* := \underset{h \in \mathcal{H}}{\operatorname{argmin}} R(h). \tag{4}$$

Correspondingly, there remains uncertainty regarding h^* as well as the approximation quality of $\widehat{h}$ (in the sense of its proximity to h^*) and its true risk $R(\widehat{h})$.

Eventually, one is often interested in the *predictive uncertainty*, i.e., the uncertainty related to the prediction $\widehat{y}_q$ for a concrete query instance $\boldsymbol{x}_q \in \mathcal{X}$. In other words, given a partial observation $(\boldsymbol{x}_q, \cdot)$, we are wondering what can be said about the missing outcome, especially about the uncertainty related to a prediction of that outcome. Indeed, estimating and quantifying uncertainty in a transductive way, in the sense of tailoring it to individual instances, is arguably important and practically more relevant than a kind of average accuracy or confidence, which is often reported in machine learning.

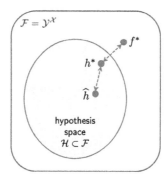

Fig. 1. Different types of uncertainties related to different types of discrepancies and approximation errors: f^* is the pointwise Bayes predictor, h^* is the best predictor within the hypothesis space, and $\widehat{h}$ the predictor produced by the learning algorithm.

As the prediction $\widehat{y}_q$ constitutes the end of a process that consists of different learning and approximation steps, all errors and uncertainties related to these steps may also contribute to the uncertainty about $\widehat{y}_q$ (cf. Fig. 1):

– Since the dependency between $\mathcal{X}$ and $\mathcal{Y}$ is typically non-deterministic, the description of a new prediction problem in the form of an instance $\boldsymbol{x}_q$ gives rise to a conditional probability distribution

$$p(y \mid \boldsymbol{x}_q) = \frac{p(\boldsymbol{x}_q, y)}{p(\boldsymbol{x}_q)} \tag{5}$$

on $\mathcal{Y}$, but it does normally not identify a single outcome y in a unique way. Thus, even given full information in the form of the measure P (and its density p), uncertainty about the actual outcome y remains. This uncertainty is of an *aleatoric* nature. In some cases, the distribution (5) itself (called the predictive posterior distribution in Bayesian inference) might be delivered as a prediction. Yet, when having to commit to a point estimate, the best prediction (in the sense of minimizing the expected loss) is prescribed by the pointwise Bayes predictor f^*, which is defined by

$$f^*(\boldsymbol{x}) := \operatorname*{argmin}_{\widehat{y} \in \mathcal{Y}} \int_{\mathcal{Y}} \ell(y, \widehat{y}) \, dP(y \mid \boldsymbol{x}) \qquad (6)$$

for each $\boldsymbol{x} \in \mathcal{X}$.

- The Bayes predictor (4) does not necessarily coincide with the pointwise Bayes predictor (6). This discrepancy between h^* and f^* is connected to the uncertainty regarding the right type of model to be fit, and hence the choice of the hypothesis space $\mathcal{H}$. We refer to this uncertainty as *model uncertainty*. Thus, due to this uncertainty, one can not guarantee that $h^*(\boldsymbol{x}) = f^*(\boldsymbol{x})$, or, in case the hypothesis h^* delivers probabilistic predictions $p(y \mid h^*, \boldsymbol{x})$ instead of point predictions, that $p(\cdot \mid h^*, \boldsymbol{x}) = p(\cdot \mid \boldsymbol{x})$.
- The hypothesis $\widehat{h}$ produced by the learning algorithm, for example the empirical risk minimizer (3), is only an estimate of h^*, and the quality of this estimate strongly depends on the quality and the amount of training data. We refer to the discrepancy between $\widehat{h}$ and h^*, i.e., the uncertainty about how well the former approximates the latter, as *approximation uncertainty*.

As already said, aleatoric uncertainty is typically understood as uncertainty that is due to influences on the data-generating process that are inherently random, that is, due to the non-deterministic nature of the sought input/output dependency. This part of the uncertainty is irreducible, in the sense that the learner cannot get rid of it. Model uncertainty and approximation uncertainty, on the other hand, are subsumed under the notion of epistemic uncertainty, that is, uncertainty due to a lack of knowledge about the perfect predictor (6). Obviously, this lack of knowledge will strongly depend on the underlying hypothesis space $\mathcal{H}$ as well as the amount of data seen so far: The larger the number $N = |\mathcal{D}|$ of observations, the less ignorant the learner will be when having to make a new prediction. In the limit, when $N \to \infty$, a consistent learner will be able to identify h^*. Moreover, the "larger" the hypothesis pace $\mathcal{H}$, i.e., the weaker the prior knowledge about the sought dependency, the higher the epistemic uncertainty will be, and the more data will be needed to resolve this uncertainty.

How to capture these intuitive notions of aleatoric and epistemic uncertainty in terms of quantitative measures? In the following, we briefly recall two proposals that have recently been made in the literature.

2.1 Entropy Measures

An attempt at measuring and separating aleatoric and epistemic uncertainty on the basis of classical information-theoretic measures of entropy is made in [2].

This approach is developed in the context of neural networks for regression, but the idea as such is more general and can also be applied to other settings. A similar approach was recently adopted in [10].

Given a query instance $\boldsymbol{x}$, the idea is to measure the total uncertainty in a prediction in terms of the (Shannon) entropy of the predictive posterior distribution, which, in the case of discrete $\mathcal{Y}$, is given as

$$H\big[p(y\,|\,\boldsymbol{x})\big] = \mathbf{E}_{p(y\,|\,\boldsymbol{x})}\big\{-\log_2 p(y\,|\,\boldsymbol{x})\big\} = -\sum_{y\in\mathcal{Y}} p(y\,|\,\boldsymbol{x})\log_2 p(y\,|\,\boldsymbol{x}). \qquad (7)$$

Moreover, the epistemic uncertainty is measured in terms of the mutual information between hypotheses and outcomes (i.e., the Kullback-Leibler divergence between the joint distribution of outcomes and hypotheses and the product of their marginals):

$$I(y, h) = \mathbf{E}_{p(y,h)}\left\{\log_2\left(\frac{p(y, h)}{p(y)p(h)}\right)\right\}, \qquad (8)$$

Finally, the aleatoric uncertainty is specified in terms of the difference between (7) and (8), which is given by

$$\mathbf{E}_{p(h\,|\,\mathcal{D})}H\big[p(y\,|\,h,\boldsymbol{x})\big] = -\int_{\mathcal{H}} p(h\,|\,\mathcal{D})\left(\sum_{y\in\mathcal{Y}} p(y\,|\,h,\boldsymbol{x})\log_2 p(y\,|\,h,\boldsymbol{x})\right)d\,h \quad (9)$$

The idea underlying (9) is as follows: By fixing a hypothesis $h \in \mathcal{H}$, the epistemic uncertainty is essentially removed. Thus, the entropy $H[p(y\,|\,h,\boldsymbol{x})]$, i.e., the entropy of the conditional distribution on $\mathcal{Y}$ predicted by h for the query instance $\boldsymbol{x}$, is a natural measure of the aleatoric uncertainty. However, since h is not precisely known, aleatoric uncertainty is measured in terms of the expectation of this entropy with regard to the posterior probability $p(h\,|\,\mathcal{D})$.

The epistemic uncertainty (8) captures the dependency between the probability distribution on $\mathcal{Y}$ and the hypothesis h. Roughly speaking, (8) is high if the distribution $p(y\,|\,h,\boldsymbol{x})$ varies a lot for different hypotheses h with high probability. This is plausible, because the existence of different hypotheses, all considered (more or less) probable but leading to quite different predictions, can indeed be seen as a sign for high epistemic uncertainty.

Obviously, (8) and (9) cannot be computed efficiently, because they involve an integration over the hypothesis space $\mathcal{H}$. One idea, therefore, is to approximate these measures by means of ensemble techniques [10], that is, to represent the posterior distribution $p(h\,|\,\mathcal{D})$ by a finite ensemble of hypotheses $H = \{h_1,\ldots,h_M\}$. An approximation of (9) can then be obtained by

$$u_a(\boldsymbol{x}) := -\frac{1}{M}\sum_{i=1}^{M}\sum_{y\in\mathcal{Y}} p(y\,|\,h_i,\boldsymbol{x})\log_2 p(y\,|\,h_i,\boldsymbol{x}), \qquad (10)$$

an approximation of (7) by

$$u_t(\boldsymbol{x}) := -\sum_{y \in \mathcal{Y}} \left(\frac{1}{M} \sum_{i=1}^{M} p(y \mid h_i, \boldsymbol{x}) \right) \log_2 \left(\frac{1}{M} \sum_{i=1}^{M} p(y \mid h_i, \boldsymbol{x}) \right), \qquad (11)$$

and finally and approximation of (8) by $u_e(\boldsymbol{x}) := u_t(\boldsymbol{x}) - u_a(\boldsymbol{x})$.

2.2   Measures Based on Relative Likelihood

Another approach, put forward in [18], is based on the use of relative likelihoods, historically proposed by [1] and then justified in other settings such as possibility theory [21]. Here, we briefly recall this approach for the case of binary classification, i.e., where $\mathcal{Y} = \{0, 1\}$; see [13] for an extension to the case of multinomial classification.

Given training data $\mathcal{D} = \{(\boldsymbol{x}_i, y_i)\}_{i=1}^{N} \subset \mathcal{X} \times \mathcal{Y}$, the normalized likelihood of $h \in \mathcal{H}$ is defined as

$$\pi_{\mathcal{H}}(h) := \frac{L(h)}{L(h^{ml})} = \frac{L(h)}{\max_{h' \in \mathcal{H}} L(h')}, \qquad (12)$$

where $L(h) = \prod_{i=1}^{N} p(y_i \mid h, \boldsymbol{x}_i)$ is the likelihood of h, and $h^{ml} \in \mathcal{H}$ the maximum likelihood estimation. For a given instance $\boldsymbol{x}$, the degrees of support (plausibility) of the two classes are defined as follows:

$$\pi(1 \mid \boldsymbol{x}) = \sup_{h \in \mathcal{H}} \min \left[\pi_{\mathcal{H}}(h), p(1 \mid h, \boldsymbol{x}) - p(0 \mid h, \boldsymbol{x}) \right], \qquad (13)$$

$$\pi(0 \mid \boldsymbol{x}) = \sup_{h \in \mathcal{H}} \min \left[\pi_{\mathcal{H}}(h), p(0 \mid h, \boldsymbol{x}) - p(1 \mid h, \boldsymbol{x}) \right]. \qquad (14)$$

So, $\pi(1 \mid \boldsymbol{x})$ is high if and only if a highly plausible hypothesis supports the positive class much stronger (in terms of the assigned probability) than the negative class (and $\pi(0 \mid \boldsymbol{x})$ can be interpreted analogously). Given the above degrees of support, the degrees of epistemic and aleatoric uncertainty are defined as follows:

$$u_e(\boldsymbol{x}) = \min \left[\pi(1 \mid \boldsymbol{x}), \pi(0 \mid \boldsymbol{x}) \right], \qquad (15)$$

$$u_a(\boldsymbol{x}) = 1 - \max \left[\pi(1 \mid \boldsymbol{x}), \pi(0 \mid \boldsymbol{x}) \right]. \qquad (16)$$

Thus, epistemic uncertainty refers to the case where both the positive and the negative class appear to be plausible, while the degree of aleatoric uncertainty (16) is the degree to which none of the classes is supported. More specifically, the above measures have the following properties:

- $u_e(\boldsymbol{x})$ will be high if class probabilities strongly vary within the set of plausible hypotheses, i.e., if we are unsure how to compare these probabilities. In particular, it will be 1 if and only if we have $h(\boldsymbol{x}) = 1$ and $h'(\boldsymbol{x}) = 0$ for two totally plausible hypotheses h and h';

– $u_a(\boldsymbol{x})$ will be high if class probabilities are similar for all plausible hypotheses, i.e., if there is strong evidence that $h(\boldsymbol{x}) \approx 0.5$. In particular, it will be close to 1 if all plausible hypotheses allocate their probability mass around $h(\boldsymbol{x}) = 0.5$.

As can be seen, the measures (15) and (16) are actually quite similar in spirit to the measures (8) and (9).

3 Random Forests

Our basic idea is to instantiate the (generic) uncertainty measures presented in the previous section by means of decision trees [15,16], that is, with decision trees as an underlying hypothesis space $\mathcal{H}$. This idea is motivated by the fact that, firstly, decision trees can naturally be seen as probabilistic predictors [7], and secondly, they can easily be used as an ensemble in the form of a random forest—recall that ensembling is needed for the (approximate) computation of the entropy-based measures in Sect. 2.1.

3.1 Entropy Measures

The approach in Sect. 2.1 can be realized with decision forests in a quite straightforward way. Let $H = \{h_1, \ldots, h_M\}$ be a classifier ensemble in the form of a random forest consisting of decision trees h_i. Moreover, recall that a decision tree h_i partitions the instance space $\mathcal{X}$ into (rectangular) regions $R_{i,1}, \ldots, R_{i,L_i}$ (i.e., $\bigcup_{l=1}^{L_i} R_{i,l} = \mathcal{X}$ and $R_{i,k} \cap R_{i,l} = \emptyset$ for $k \neq l$) associated with corresponding leafs of the tree (each leaf node defines a region R). Given a query instance $\boldsymbol{x}$, the probabilistic prediction produced by the tree h_i is specified by the Laplace-corrected relative frequencies of the classes $y \in \mathcal{Y}$ in the region $R_{i,j} \ni \boldsymbol{x}$:

$$p(y \mid h_i, \boldsymbol{x}) = \frac{n_{i,j}(y) + 1}{n_{i,j} + |\mathcal{Y}|},$$

where $n_{i,j}$ is the number of training instances in the leaf node $R_{i,j}$, and $n_{i,j}(y)$ the number of instances with class y. With probabilities estimated in this way, the uncertainty degrees (10) and (11) can directly be derived.

3.2 Measures Based on Relative Likelihood

Instantiating the approach in Sect. 2.2 essentially means computing the degrees of support (13–14), from which everything else can easily be derived.

As already said, a decision tree partitions the instance space into several regions, each of which can be associated with a constant predictor. More specifically, in the case of binary classification, the predictor is of the form h_θ, $\theta \in \Theta = [0, 1]$, where $h_\theta(\boldsymbol{x}) \equiv \theta$ is the (predicted) probability $p(1 \mid \boldsymbol{x} \in R)$ of the positive class in the region. If we restrict inference to a local region, the underlying hypothesis space is hence given by $\mathcal{H} = \{h_\theta \mid 0 \leq \theta \leq 1\}$.

With p and n the number of positive and negative instances, respectively, within a region R, the likelihood and the maximum likelihood estimate of θ are respectively given by

$$L(\theta) = \binom{n+p}{n} \theta^n (1-\theta)^p \text{ and } \theta^{ml} = \frac{n}{n+p}. \tag{17}$$

Therefore, the degrees of support for the positive and negative classes are

$$\pi(1 \mid \boldsymbol{x}) = \sup_{\theta \in [0,1]} \min \left(\frac{\theta^p (1-\theta)^n}{\left(\frac{p}{n+p}\right)^p \left(\frac{n}{n+p}\right)^n}, 2\theta - 1 \right), \tag{18}$$

$$\pi(0 \mid \boldsymbol{x}) = \sup_{\theta \in [0,1]} \min \left(\frac{\theta^p (1-\theta)^n}{\left(\frac{p}{n+p}\right)^p \left(\frac{n}{n+p}\right)^n}, 1 - 2\theta \right). \tag{19}$$

Solving (18) and (19) comes down to maximizing a scalar function over a bounded domain, for which standard solvers can be used. From (18–19), the epistemic and aleatoric uncertainty associated with the region R can be derived according to (15) and (16), respectively. For different combinations of n and p, these uncertainty degrees can be pre-computed.

Note that, for this approach, the uncertainty degrees (15) and (16) can be obtained for a single tree. To leverage the ensemble H, we average both uncertainties over all trees in the random forest.

4   Experiments

The empirical evaluation of methods for quantifying uncertainty is a non-trivial problem. In fact, unlike for the prediction of a target variable, the data does normally not contain information about any sort of "ground truth" uncertainty. What is often done, therefore, is to evaluate predicted uncertainties *indirectly*, that is, by assessing their usefulness for improved prediction and decision making. Adopting an approach of that kind, we produced *accuracy-rejection curves*, which depict the accuracy of a predictor as a function of the percentage of rejections [5]: A classifier, which is allowed to abstain on a certain percentage p of predictions, will predict on those $(1-p)\%$ on which it feels most certain. Being able to quantify its own uncertainty well, it should improve its accuracy with increasing p, hence the accuracy-rejection curve should be monotone increasing (unlike a flat curve obtained for random abstention).

4.1   Implementation Details

For this work, we used the Random Forest Classifier from SKlearn. The number of trees within the forest is set to 50, with the maximum level of tree grows set to 10. We use bootstrapping to create diversity between the trees of the forest.

As a baseline to compare with, we used the DropConnect model for deep neural networks as introduced in [10]. The idea of DropConnect is similar to

Dropout, but here, instead of randomly deleting neurons, we randomly delete the connections between neurons. In this model, the act of dropping the connections is also active in the test phase. In this way, the data passes through a different network on each iteration, and therefore we can compute Monte Carlo samples for each query instance. The DropConnect model is a feed forward neural network consisting of two DropConnect layers with 32 neurons and a final softmax layer for the output. The model is trained for 20 epochs with mini batch size of 32. After the training is done, we take 50 Monte Carlo samples to create an ensemble, from which the uncertainty values can be calculated.

4.2 Results

Due to space limitations, we show results in the form of accuracy-rejection curves for only two exemplary data sets from the UCI repository[1], spect and diabetes— yet, very similar results were obtained for other data sets. The data is randomly split into 70% for training and 30% for testing, and accuracy-rejection curves are computed on the latter (the curves shown are averages over 100 repetitions). In the following, we abbreviate the aleatoric and epistemic uncertainty degrees produced by the entropy-based approach (Sect. 2.1) and the approach based on relative likelihood (Sect. 2.2) by AU-ent, EU-ent, AU-rl, and EU-rl, respectively.

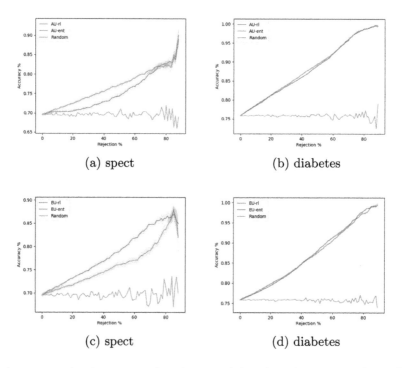

(a) spect   (b) diabetes

(c) spect   (d) diabetes

Fig. 2. Accuracy-rejection curves for aleatoric (above) and epistemic (below) uncertainty using random forests. The curve for random rejection is included as a baseline.

---

[1] https://archive.ics.uci.edu/ml/datasets/.

As can be seen from Figs. 1, 2, 3 and 4, both approaches to measuring uncertainty are effective in the sense of producing monotone increasing accuracy-rejection curves, and on the data sets we analyzed so far, we could not detect any systematic differences in performance. Besides, rejection seems to work well on the basis of both criteria, aleatoric as well as epistemic uncertainty. This is plausible, since both provide reasonable reasons for a learner to abstain from a prediction. Likewise, there are no big differences between random forests and neural networks, showing that the former are indeed a viable alternative to the latter—this was actually a major concern of our study.

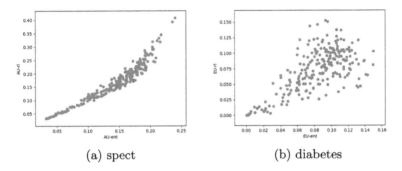

(a) spect   (b) diabetes

Fig. 3. Scatter plot for test set on diabetes data, showing the relationship between the uncertainty degrees (aleatoric left, epistemic right) estimated by the two approaches.

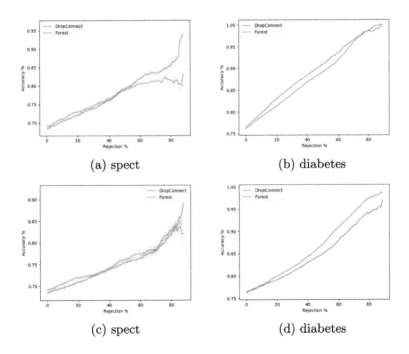

(a) spect   (b) diabetes

(c) spect   (d) diabetes

Fig. 4. Comparison between random forests and neural networks (DropConnect) for aleatoric (above) and epistemic (below) in the entropy-based uncertainty approach.

5   Conclusion

The distinction between aleatoric and epistemic uncertainty has recently received a lot of attention in machine learning, especially in the deep learning community [6]. Roughly speaking, the approaches in deep learning are either based on the idea of equipping networks with a probabilistic component, like in Bayesian deep learning [11], or on using ensemble techniques [8], which can be implemented (indirectly) through techniques such as Dropout [3] or DropConnect. The main purpose of this paper was to show that the use of decision trees and random forests is an interesting alternative to neural networks.

Indeed, as we have shown, the basic ideas underlying the estimation of aleatoric and epistemic uncertainty can be realized with random forests in a very natural way. In a sense, they even appear to be simpler and more flexible than neural networks. For example, while the approach based on relative likelihood (Sect. 2.2) could be realized efficiently for random forests, a neural network implementation is far from obvious (and was therefore not included in the experiments).

There are various directions for future work. For example, since the hyperparameters of random forests have an influence on the hypothesis space we are (indirectly) working with, they also influence the estimation of uncertainty degrees. This relationship calls for a thorough investigation. Besides, going beyond a proof of principle with statistics such as accuracy-rejection curves, it would be interesting to make use of uncertainty quantification with random forests in applications such as active learning, as recently proposed in [12].

References

1. Birnbaum, A.: On the foundations of statistical inference. J. Am. Stat. Assoc. **57**(298), 269–306 (1962)
2. Depeweg, S., Hernandez-Lobato, J., Doshi-Velez, F., Udluft, S.: Decomposition of uncertainty in Bayesian deep learning for efficient and risk-sensitive learning. In: Proceedings of the ICML, 35th International Conference on Machine Learning, Stockholm, Sweden (2018)
3. Gal, Y., Ghahramani, Z.: Bayesian convolutional neural networks with Bernoulli approximate variational inference. In: Proceedings of the ICLR Workshop Track (2016)
4. Hora, S.: Aleatory and epistemic uncertainty in probability elicitation with an example from hazardous waste management. Reliab. Eng. Syst. Saf. **54**(2–3), 217–223 (1996)
5. Hühn, J., Hüllermeier, E.: FR3: a fuzzy rule learner for inducing reliable classifiers. IEEE Trans. Fuzzy Syst. **17**(1), 138–149 (2009)
6. Kendall, A., Gal, Y.: What uncertainties do we need in Bayesian deep learning for computer vision? In: Proceedings of the NIPS, pp. 5574–5584 (2017)
7. Kruppa, J., et al.: Probability estimation with machine learning methods for dichotomous and multi-category outcome: theory. Biometrical J. **56**(4), 534–563 (2014)

8. Lakshminarayanan, B., Pritzel, A., Blundell, C.: Simple and scalable predictive uncertainty estimation using deep ensembles. In: Proceedings of the NeurIPS, 31st Conference on Neural Information Processing Systems, Long Beach, California, USA (2017)
9. Lambrou, A., Papadopoulos, H., Gammerman, A.: Reliable confidence measures for medical diagnosis with evolutionary algorithms. IEEE Trans. Inf. Technol. Biomed. **15**(1), 93–99 (2011)
10. Mobiny, A., Nguyen, H., Moulik, S., Garg, N., Wu, C.: DropConnect is effective in modeling uncertainty of Bayesian networks. CoRR abs/1906.04569 (2017). http://arxiv.org/abs/1906.04569
11. Neal, R.: Bayesian Learning for Neural Networks, vol. 118. Springer, Heidelberg (2012). https://doi.org/10.1007/978-1-4612-0745-0
12. Nguyen, V., Destercke, S., Hüllermeier, E.: Epistemic uncertainty sampling. In: Proceedings of the DS 2019, 22nd International Conference on Discovery Science, Split, Croatia (2019)
13. Nguyen, V.L., Destercke, S., Masson, M.H., Hüllermeier, E.: Reliable multi-class classification based on pairwise epistemic and aleatoric uncertainty. In: Proceedings of the IJCAI, pp. 5089–5095. AAAI Press (2018)
14. Papernot, N., McDaniel, P.: Deep k-nearest neighbors: towards confident, interpretable and robust deep learning. CoRR abs/1803.04765v1 (2018). http://arxiv.org/abs/1803.04765
15. Quinlan, J.R.: Induction of decision trees. Mach. Learn. **1**(1), 81–106 (1986)
16. Safavian, S.R., Landgrebe, D.: A survey of decision tree classifier methodology. IEEE Trans. Syst. Man Cybern. **21**(3), 660–674 (1991)
17. Sato, M., Suzuki, J., Shindo, H., Matsumoto, Y.: Interpretable adversarial perturbation in input embedding space for text. In: Proceedings IJCAI 2018, Stockholm, Sweden, pp. 4323–4330 (2018)
18. Senge, R., et al.: Reliable classification: learning classifiers that distinguish aleatoric and epistemic uncertainty. Inf. Sci. **255**, 16–29 (2014)
19. Varshney, K.: Engineering safety in machine learning. In: Proceedings of the Information Theory and Applications Workshop, La Jolla, CA (2016)
20. Varshney, K., Alemzadeh, H.: On the safety of machine learning: cyber-physical systems, decision sciences, and data products. CoRR abs/1610.01256 (2016). http://arxiv.org/abs/1610.01256
21. Walley, P., Moral, S.: Upper probabilities based only on the likelihood function. J. R. Stat. Soc.: Ser. B (Stat. Methodol.) **61**(4), 831–847 (1999)
22. Yang, F., Wanga, H.Z., Mi, H., de Lin, C., Cai, W.W.: Using random forest for reliable classification and cost-sensitive learning for medical diagnosis. BMC Bioinform. **10**, S22 (2009)

10

Orometric Methods in Bounded Metric Data

Maximilian Stubbemann[1,2](✉) ⓘ, Tom Hanika[2] ⓘ, and Gerd Stumme[1,2] ⓘ

[1] L3S Research Center, Leibniz University of Hannover, Hannover, Germany
{stubbemann,stumme}@l3s.de
[2] Knowledge and Data Engineering Group, University of Kassel, Kassel, Germany
{stubbemann,hanika,stumme}@cs.uni-kassel.de

Abstract. A large amount of data accommodated in knowledge graphs (KG) is metric. For example, the Wikidata KG contains a plenitude of metric facts about geographic entities like cities or celestial objects. In this paper, we propose a novel approach that transfers orometric (topographic) measures to bounded metric spaces. While these methods were originally designed to identify relevant mountain peaks on the surface of the earth, we demonstrate a notion to use them for metric data sets in general. Notably, metric sets of items enclosed in knowledge graphs. Based on this we present a method for identifying outstanding items using the transferred valuations functions isolation and prominence. Building up on this we imagine an item recommendation process. To demonstrate the relevance of the valuations for such processes, we evaluate the usefulness of isolation and prominence empirically in a machine learning setting. In particular, we find structurally relevant items in the geographic population distributions of Germany and France.

Keywords: Metric spaces · Orometry · Knowledge graphs · Classification

1 Introduction

Knowledge graphs (KG), such as DBpedia [15] or Wikidata [24], are the state of the art for storing information and to draw knowledge from. They represent knowledge through graphs and consist essentially of *items* which are related through *properties* and *values*. This enables them to fulfill the task of giving exact answers to exact questions. However, their ability to present a concise overview over collections of items with metric distances is limited. The number of such data sets in Wikidata is tremendous, e.g., the set of all cities of the world, including their geographic coordinates. Further examples are celestial bodies and their trajectories or, more general, feature spaces of data mining tasks.

One approach to understand such metric data is to identify outstanding elements, i.e., outstanding items. Based on such elements it is possible to compose or enhance item recommendations to users. For example, such recommendations could provide a set of the most relevant cities in the world with respect

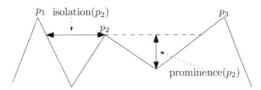

Fig. 1. Isolation: minimal horizontal distance to another point of at least equal height. Prominence: minimal vertical descent to reach a point of at least equal height.

to being outstanding in their local surroundings. However, it is a challenging task to identify outstanding items in metric data sets. In cases where the metric space is equipped with an additional valuation function, this task becomes more feasible. Such functions, often called *scores* or *height* functions, are often naturally provided: cities may be ranked by population; the importance of scientific authors by the h-index [12]. A naïve approach for recommending relevant items in such settings would be: items with higher scores are more relevant items. As this method seems reasonable for many applications, some obstacles arise if the "highest" items concentrate into a specific region of the underlying metric space. For example, representing the cities of the world by the twenty most populated ones would include no western European city.[1] Recommending the 100 highest mountains would not lead to knowledge about the mountains outside of Asia.[2]

Our novel approach shall overcome this problem: we combine the valuation measure (e.g., "height") and distances, to provide new valuation functions on the set of items, called *prominence* and *isolation*. These functions do rate items based on their height in relation to the valuations of the surrounding items. This results in valuation functions on the set of items that reflect the extend to which an item is locally outstanding. The basic idea is the following: the prominence values an item based on the minimal descent (w.r.t. the height function) that is needed to get to another point of at least same height. The isolation, sometimes also called *dominance radius*, values the distance to the next higher point w.r.t. the metric (Fig. 1). These measures are adapted from the field of topography where isolation and prominence are used in order to identify outstanding mountain peaks. We base our approach on [22], where the authors proposed prominence and dominance for networks. We generalize these to the realm of bounded metric space.

We provide insights to the novel valuation functions and demonstrate their ability to identify relevant items for a given topic in metric knowledge graph applications. The contributions of this paper are as follows: ● We propose prominence and isolation for bounded metric spaces. For this we generalize the results in [22] and overcome the limitations to finite, undirected graphs. ● We demonstrate an artificial machine learning task for evaluating our novel valuation functions in metric data. ● We introduce an approach for using prominence and isolation to enrich metric data in knowledge graphs. We show empirically that this information helps to identify a set of representative items.

2   Related Work

Item recommendations for knowledge graphs is a contemporary topic of high interest in research. Investigations cover for example music recommendation using content and collaborative information [17] or movie recommendations using PageRank like methods [5]. The former is based on the common notion of embedding, i.e., embedding of the graph structure into d-dimensional real vector spaces. The latter operates on the relational structure itself. Our approach differs from those as it is based on combining a valuation measure with the metric of the data space. Nonetheless, given an embedding into an finite dimensional real vector space, one could apply isolation and prominence in those as well.

The novel valuation functions prominence and isolation are inspired by topographic measures, which have their origin in the classification of mountain peaks. The idea of ranking peaks solely by their absolute height was already deprecated in 1978 by Fry in his work [8]. The author introduced prominence for geographic mountains, a function still investigated in this realm, e.g., in Torres et al. [23], where the authors used deep learning methods to identify prominent mountain peaks. Another recent step for this was made in [14], where the authors investigated methods for discovering new ultra-prominent mountains. Isolation and more valuations functions motivated in the orometric realm are collected in [11]. A well-known procedure for identifying peaks and saddles in 3D terrain data is described in [6]. However, these approaches rely on data that approximates a continuous terrain surface via a regular square grid or a triangulation. Our data cannot fulfill this requirement. Recently the idea of transferring orometric functions to different realms of research gained attention: The authors of [16] used topographic prominence to identify population areas in several U.S. States. In [22] the authors Schmidt and Stumme transferred prominence and dominance, i.e., isolation, to co-author graphs in order to evaluate their potential of identifying ACM Fellows. We build on this for proposing our valuation functions on bounded metric data. This generalization results in a wide range of applications.

3   Mathematical Modeling

While the Wikidata knowledge graph itself could be analyzed with the prominence and isolation measures for networks, this paper focuses on bounded metric data sets. To analyze such data sets is more sufficient, since real world networks often suffer from a small average shortest path length [26]. This leads to a low amount of outstanding items: an item is outstanding if it is "higher" than the items that have a low distance to it. This leads to a strict measure for many real-world network data when the shortest path length is used as the metric function. Hence, we model our functions for bounded metric data instead of networks.

We consider the following scenario: We have a data set M, consisting of a set of items, in the following called *points*, equipped with a metric d and a valuation function h, in the following called *height function*. The goal of the orometric (topographic) measures prominence and isolation is, to provide measures that reflect the extent to which a point is locally outstanding in its neighborhood.

More precisely, let M be a non-empty set and $d : M \times M \to \mathbb{R}_{\geq 0}$. We call d a *metric* on the set M iff • $\forall x, y \in M : d(x, y) = 0 \iff x = y$, and • $d(x, y) = d(y, x)$ for all $x, y \in M$, called symmetry, and • $\forall x, y, z \in M : d(x, z) \leq d(x, y) + d(y, z)$, called triangle inequality. If d is a metric on M, we call (M, d) a *metric space* and if M is finite we call (M, d) a *finite metric space*. If there exists a $C \in \mathbb{R}_{\geq 0}$ such that we have $d(m, n) \leq C$ for all $m, n \in M$, we call (M, d) *bounded*. For the rest of our work we assume that $|M| > 1$ and (M, d) is a bounded metric space. Additionally, we have that M is equipped with a height function (valuation/score function) $h : M \to \mathbb{R}_{\geq 0}, m \mapsto h(m)$.

Definition 1 (Isolation). *Let (M, d) be a bounded metric space and let $h : M \to \mathbb{R}_{\geq 0}$ be a height function on M. The isolation of a point $x \in M$ is then defined as follows:*

- *If there is no point with at least equal height to m, than $\mathrm{iso}(m) := \sup\{d(m, n) \mid n \in M\}$. The boundedness of M guarantees the existence of this supremum.*
- *If there is at least one other point in M with at least equal height to m, we define its isolation by:*

$$\mathrm{iso}(m) := \inf\{d(m, n) \mid n \in M \setminus \{m\} \wedge h(n) \geq h(m)\}.$$

The isolation of a mountain peek is often called the *dominance radius* or sometimes the *dominance*. Since the term *orometric dominance* of a mountain sometimes refers to the quotient of prominence and height, we will stick to the term *isolation* to avoid confusion. While the isolation can be defined within the given setup, we have to equip our metric space with some more structure in order to transfer the notion of prominence. Informally, the prominence of a point is given by the minimal vertical distance one has to descend to get to a point of at least the same height. To adapt this measure to our given setup in metric spaces with a height function, we have to define what a path is. Structures that provide paths in a natural way are graph structures. For a given graph $G = (V, E)$ with vertex set V and edge set $E \subseteq \binom{V}{2}$, *walks* are defined as sequences of nodes $\{v_i\}_{i=0}^n$ which satisfy $\{v_{i-1}, v_i\} \in E$ for all $i \in \{1, ..., n\}$. If we also have $v_i \neq v_j$ for $i \neq j$, we call such a sequence a *path*. For $v, w \in V$ we say v and w are *connected* iff there exists a path connecting them. Furthermore, we denote by $G(v)$ the *connected component* of G containing v, i.e., $G(v) := \{w \in V \mid v \text{ is connected with } w\}$.

To use the prominence measure as introduced by Schmidt and Stumme in [22], which is indeed defined on graphs, we have to derive an appropriate graph structure from our metric space. The topic of graphs embedded in finite dimensional vector spaces, so called spatial networks [2], is a topic of current interest. These networks appear in real world scenarios frequently, for example in the modeling of urban street networks [13]. Note that our setting, in contrast to the afore mentioned, is not based on a priori given graph structure. In our scenario the graph structure must be derived from the structure of the given metric space.

Our approach is, to construct a *step size graph* or *threshold graph*, where we consider points in the metric space as nodes and connect two points through an edge, iff their distance is smaller then a given threshold δ.

Definition 2 (δ-Step Graph). *Let (M, d) be a metric space and $\delta > 0$. We define the δ-step graph or δ-threshold graph, denoted by G_δ, as the tuple (M, E_δ) via*

$$E_\delta := \left\{ \{m, n\} \in \binom{M}{2} \mid d(m, n) \leq \delta \right\}. \tag{1}$$

This approach is similar to the one found in the realm of random geometric graphs, where it is common sense to define random graphs by placing points uniformly in the plane and connect them via edges if their distance is less than a given threshold [21]. Since we introduced a possibility to derive a graph that just depends on the metric space, we use a slight modification of the definition of prominence compared to [22] for networks.

Definition 3 (Prominence in Networks). *Let $G = (V, E)$ be a graph and let $h : V \to \mathbb{R}_{\geq 0}$ be a height function. The prominence $\mathrm{prom}_G(v)$ of $v \in V$ is defined by*

$$\mathrm{prom}_G(v) := \min\{h(v), \mathrm{mindesc}_G(v)\} \tag{2}$$

where $\mathrm{mindesc}_G(v) := \inf\{\max\{h(v) - h(u) \mid u \in p\} \mid p \in P_v\}$. The set P_v contains of all paths to vertices w with $h(w) \geq h(v)$, i.e., $P_v := \{\{v_i\}_{i=0}^n \in P \mid v_0 = v \wedge v_n \neq v \wedge h(v_n) \geq h(v)\}$, where P denotes the set of all paths of G.

Informally, $\mathrm{mindesc}_G(v)$ reflects on the minimal descent in order to get to a vertex in G which has a height of at least $h(v)$. For this the definition makes use of the fact that $\inf \emptyset = \infty$. This case results in $\mathrm{prom}_G(v)$ being the height of v. A distinction to the definition in [22] is, that we now consider all paths and not just shortest paths. This change better reflects the calculation of the prominence for mountains. Based on this we transfer the notions above to metric spaces.

Definition 4 (δ-Prominence). *Let (M, d) be a bounded metric space and $h : M \to \mathbb{R}_{\geq 0}$ be a height function. We define the δ-prominence $\mathrm{prom}_\delta(m)$ of $m \in M$ as $\mathrm{prom}_{G_\delta}(v)$, i.e., the prominence of m in G_δ from Definition 2.*

We now have a prominence term for all metric spaces that depends on a parameter δ to choose. For all knowledge procedures, choosing such a parameter is a demanding task. Hence, we want to provide in the following a natural choice for δ. We consider only those values for δ such that corresponding G_δ does not exhibit noise, i.e., there is no element without a neighbor.

Definition 5 (Minimal Threshold). *For a bounded metric space (M, d) with $|M| > 1$ we define the* minimal threshold δ_M *of M as*

$$\delta_M := \sup\{\inf\{d(m, n) \mid n \in M \setminus \{m\}\} \mid m \in M\}.$$

Based on this definition a natural notion of prominence for metric spaces (equipped with a height function) emerges via a limit process.

Lemma 1. *Let M be a bounded metric space and δ_M as in Definition 5. For $m \in M$ the following descending limit exists:*

$$\lim_{\delta \searrow \delta_M} \mathrm{prom}_\delta(m). \tag{3}$$

Proof. Fix any $\hat{\delta} > \delta_M$ and consider on the open interval from δ_M to $\hat{\delta}$ the function that maps δ to $\mathrm{prom}_\delta(m)$: $\mathrm{prom}_{(.)}(m) :]\delta_M, \hat{\delta}[\to \mathbb{R}, \delta \mapsto \mathrm{prom}_\delta(m)$. It is known that it is sufficient to show that $\mathrm{prom}_{(.)}(m)$ is monotone decreasing and bounded from above. Since we have for any δ that $\mathrm{prom}_\delta(m) \leq h(m)$ holds, we need to show the monotony. Let δ_1, δ_2 be in $]\delta_M, \hat{\delta}[$ with $\delta_1 \leq \delta_2$. If we consider the corresponding graphs (M, E_{δ_1}) and (M, E_{δ_2}), it easy to see $E_{\delta_1} \subseteq E_{\delta_2}$. Hence, we have to consider more paths in Eq. (2) for E_{δ_2}, resulting in a not larger value for the infimum. We obtain $\mathrm{prom}_{\delta_1}(m) \geq \mathrm{prom}_{\delta_2}(m)$, as required.

Definition 6 (Prominence in Metric Spaces). *If M is a bounded metric space with $|M| > 1$ and a height function h, the* prominence $\mathrm{prom}(m)$ *of m is defined as:*

$$\mathrm{prom}(m) := \lim_{\delta \searrow \delta_M} \mathrm{prom}_\delta(m).$$

Note, if we want to compute prominence on a real world finite metric data set, it is possible to directly compute the prominence values: in that case the supremum in Definition 5 can be replaced by a maximum and the infimum by a minimum, which leads to $\mathrm{prom}(m)$ being equal to $\mathrm{prom}_{\delta_M}(m)$. There are results for efficiently creating such step graphs [3]. However, for our needs in this work, in particular in the experiment section, a quadratic brute force approach for generating all edges is sufficient. We want to show that our prominence definition for bounded metric spaces is a natural generalization of Definition 3.

Lemma 2. *Let $G = (V, E)$ be a finite, connected graph with $|V| \geq 2$. Consider V equipped with the shortest path metric as a metric space. Then the prominence $\mathrm{prom}_G(\cdot)$ from Definition 3 and $\mathrm{prom}(\cdot)$ from Definition 6 coincide.*

Proof. Let $M := V$ be equipped with the shortest path metric d on G. As G is connected and has more than one node, we have $\delta_M = 1$. Hence, (M, E_{δ_M}) from Definition 2 and G are equal. Therefore, the prominence terms coincide.

4 Application

Score Based Item Recommending. As an application we envisage a general approach for a score based item recommending process. The task of item recommending with knowledge graphs is a current research topic [17,18]. However,
most approaches are solely based on knowledge about preferences of the user
and graph structural properties, often accessed through KG embeddings [19].
The idea of the recommendation process we imagine differs from those. We stip-
ulate on a procedure that is based on the information entailed in the connection
of the metric aspects of the data together with some (often naturally present)
height function. We are aware that this limits our approach to metric data in
KGs. Nonetheless, given the large amounts of metric item sets in prominent KGs,
we claim the existence of a plenitude of applications. For example, while considering sets of cities, such a system could recommend a *relevant* subset, based on
a height function, like population, and a metric, like geographical distances. By
doing so, we introduce a source of information for recommending metric data in
relational structures, like KGs. A common approach for analyzing and learning
in KGs is embedding. There is an extensive amount of research about that, see
for example [4,25]. Since our novel methods rely solely on bounded metric spaces
and some valuation function, one may apply those after the embedding step as
well. In particular, one may use isolation and prominence for investigating or
completing KG embeddings. This constitutes our second envisioned application.
Finally, common item recommending scores/ranks can also be used as height
functions in our sense. Hence, computing prominence and isolation for already
setup recommendation systems is another possibility. Here, our valuation functions have the potential to enrich the recommendation process with additional
information. In such a way our measures can provide a novel additional aspect to
existing approaches. The realization and evaluation of our proposed recommendation approach is out of scope of this paper. Nonetheless, we want to provide
some first insights for the applicability of valuation functions for item sets based
on empirical experiments. As a first experiment, we will evaluate if isolation and
prominence help to separate important and unimportant items in specific item
sets in Wikidata. In detail, we evaluate if the valuation functions help to differen-
tiate important and unimportant municipalities in France and Germany, solely
based on their geographic metric properties and their population as height.

4.1 Resulting Questions

Given a bounded metric space M which represents the data set and a given
height h. The following questions shall evaluate if our functions isolation and
prominence provide useful information about the relevance of given points in the
metric space. If (M, d, h) is a metric space equipped with an additional height
function, let $c : M \to \{0, 1\}$ be a binary function that classifies the points in the
data set as relevant (1) or not (0). We connect this to our running example using
a function that classifies municipalities having a university (1) and municipalities
that do not have an university (0). We admit that the underlying classification

is not meaningful in itself. It treats a real geographic case while our model could also handle more abstract scenarios. However, since this setup is essentially a benchmark framework (in which we assume cities with universities to be more relevant) we refrain from employing a more meaningful classification task in favor of a controllable classification scenario. Our research questions are now: **1. Are prominence and isolation alone characteristical for relevance?** We use isolation and/or prominence for a given set of data points as features. To which extend do these features improve learning a classification function for relevance? **2. Do prominence and isolation provide additional information, not catered by the absolute height?** Do prominence and isolation improve the prediction performance of relevance compared to just using the height? Does a classifier that uses prominence and isolation as additional features produce better results than a classifier that just uses the height? We will evaluate the proposed setup in the realm of a KG and take on the questions stated above in the following section and present some experimental evidence.

5   Experiments

We extract information about municipalities in the countries of Germany and France from the Wikidata KG. This KG is a structure that stores knowledge via *statements*, linking *entities* via *properties* to *values*. A detailed description can be found in [24], while [9] gives an explicit mathematical structure to the Wikidata graph and shows how to use the graph for extracting implicational knowledge from Wikidata subsets. We investigate if prominence and isolation of a given municipality can be used as features to predict university locations in a classification setup. We use the query service of Wikidata[3] to extract points in the country maps from Germany and France and to extract all their universities. We report all necessary SPAQRL queries employed on GitHub.[4]

- Wikidata provides different relations for extracting items that are instances of the notion city. The obvious choice is to employ the *instance of* (P31) property for the item *city* (Q515). Using this, including *subclass of* (P279), we find insufficient results. More specific, we find only 102 French cities and 2215 German cities.[5] For Germany, there exists a more commonly used item *urban municipality of Germany* (Q42744322) for extracting all cities, while to the best of our knowledge, a counterpart for France is not provided.
- The preliminary investigation leads us to use *municipality* (Q15284), again including the *subclass of* (P279) property, with more than 5000 inhabitants.
- Since there are multiple french municipalities that are not located in the mainland of France, we encounter problems for constructing the metric space. To cope with that we draw a basic approximating square around the mainland of France and consider only those municipalities inside.

---

[3] https://query.wikidata.org/.
[4] https://github.com/mstubbemann/Orometric-Methods-in-Bounded-Metric-Data.
[5] Queried on 2019-08-07.

– We find the class of every municipality, i.e, university location or non-university location as follows. We use the properties *located in the administrative territorial entity* (P131) and *headquarters location* (P159) on the set of all universities and checked if these are set in Germany or France. An example of a University that has not set P131 is *TU Dortmund* (Q685557).[6]
– We match the municipalities with the university properties. This is necessary because some universities are not related to municipalities through P131, e.g., *Hochschule Niederrhein* (Q1318081) is located in the administrative location *North Rhine-Westphalie* (Q1198) (See footnote 6), which is a federal state containing multiple municipalities. For these cases we check the university locations manually. This results in 2064 municipalities (89 university loc.) in France and 2986 municipalities (160 university loc.) in Germany.
– While constructing the data set we encounter twenty-two universities that are associated to a country having neither *located in the administrative territorial entity* (P131) nor *headquarters location* (P159). We check them manually and are able to discard them all for different reasons.

5.1   Binary Classification Task

Setup. We compute prominence and isolation for all data points and normalize them as well as the height. The data that is used for the classification task consists of the following information for each city: The height, the prominence, the isolation and the binary information whether the city has a university. Since our data set is highly imbalanced, common classifiers tend to simply predict the majority class. To overcome the imbalance, we use inverse penalty weights with respect to the class distribution. We want to stress out again that the goal for the to be introduced classification task is not to identify the best classifier. Rather we want to produce evidence for the applicability of employing isolation and prominence as features for learning a classification function. We decide to use logistic regression with L^2 regularization and Support Vector Machines [7] with a radial kernel. For our experiment we use Scikit-Learn [20]. As penalty factor for the SVC we set $C = 1$, and experiment with $C \in \{0.5, 1, 2, 5, 10, 100\}$. For γ we rely on previous work by [1] and set it to one. For all combinations of population, isolation and prominence we use 100 iterations of 5-fold-cross-validation.

Evaluation. We use the g-mean (i.e., geometric mean) as evaluation function. Consider for this denotations TN (True Negative), FP (False Positive), FN (False Negative), and TP (True Positive). Overall accuracy is highly misleading for heavily imbalanced data. Therefore, we evaluate the classification decisions by using the geometric mean of the accuracy on the positive instances, $acc_+ := \frac{TP}{TP+FN}$ and the accuracy on the negative instances $acc_- := \frac{TN}{TN+FP}$. Hence, the g-mean score is then defined by the formula $g_{mean} := \sqrt{acc_+ \cdot acc_-}$. The evaluation function g-mean is established in the topic of imbalanced data mining. It is mentioned in [10] and used for evaluation in [1]. We compare the values for

---

[6] Last checked on 2019-10-26.

Table 1. Results of the classification task. We do 100 rounds of 5-fold-cross-validation and shuffle the data between the rounds. For all rounds we compute the g-mean value and then compute the average over the 100 rounds.

Country	France				Germany			
Classifier	SVM		LR		SVM		LR	
	Mean	Std	Mean	Std	Mean	Std	Mean	Std
iso	0.7416	0.0059	0.7703	0.0034	0.7463	0.0028	0.7761	0.0035
pro	0.4861	0.0053	0.6362	0.0055	0.3998	0.0068	0.5750	0.0049
pop	0.6940	0.0031	0.7593	0.0086	0.5982	0.0038	0.7134	0.0043
iso+pro	0.7329	0.0067	0.7657	0.0066	0.7320	0.0042	0.7642	0.0041
iso+pop	**0.7668**	0.0086	**0.7812**	0.0039	**0.7971**	0.0041	**0.8068**	0.0038
pro+pop	0.7011	0.0040	0.7496	0.0051	0.6134	0.0050	0.7108	0.0065
iso+pro+pop	0.7653	0.0078	0.7778	0.0052	0.7947	0.0042	0.8006	0.0042

po = population, pr = prominence, is = isolation
SVM = Support Vector Machine, LR = Logistic Regression

g-mean for the following cases. First, we train a classifier function purely on the features population, prominence or isolation. Secondly, we try combinations of them for the training process. We consider the classifier trained using the population feature as baseline. An increase in g-mean while using prominence or isolation together with the population function is evidence for the utility of the introduced valuation functions. Even stronger evidence is a comparison of isolation/prominence trained classifiers versus baseline.

In our experiments, we are not expecting high g-mean values, since the placement of university locations depends on many additional features, including historical evolution of the country and political decisions. Still, the described evaluation setup is sufficient to demonstrate the potential of the novel features.

Results. The results of the computations are depicted in Table 1. ● *Isolation is a good indicator for structural relevance.* For both countries and classifiers isolation outperforms population. ● *Combining absolute height with our valuation functions leads to better results.* ● *Prominence is not useful as a solo indicator.* We draw from our result that prominence solely is not a useful indicator. Prominence is a very strict valuation function: recall that we constructed the graphs by using distance margins as indicators for edges, leading to a dense graph structure in more dense parts of the metric space. Hence, a point in a more dense part has many neighbors and thus many potential paths that may lead to a very low prominence value. From Definition 3 we see that having a higher neighbor always leads to a prominence value of zero. This threshold is about 34 km for Germany and 54 km for France. Thus, a municipality has a not vanishing prominence if it is the most populated point in a radius of over 34 km, respectively 54 km. Only 75 municipalities of France have non zero prominence, with 40 of them being university locations. Germany has 104 municipalities with positive prominence with 72 of them being university locations. Thus, prominence alone as a feature is insufficient for the prediction of university locations. • *Support vector machine and logistic regression lead to similar results.* To the question, whether our valuation functions improve the classification compared with the population feature, support vector machines and logistic regressions provide the same answer: isolation always outperforms population, a combination of all features is always better then using just the plain population feature. • *Support vector machine penalty parameter.* Finally, for our last test we check the different results for support vector machines using the penalty parameters $C \in \{0.5, 1, 2, 5, 10, 100\}$. We observe that increasing the penalty results in better performance using the population feature. However, for lower values of C, i.e., less overfitting models, we see better performance in using the isolation feature. In short, the more the model overfits due to C, the less useful are the novel valuation functions we introduced in this paper.

6   Conclusion and Outlook

In this work, we presented a novel approach to identify outstanding elements in item sets. For this we employed orometric valuation functions, namely prominence and isolation. We investigated a computationally reasonable transfer to the realm of bounded metric spaces. In particular, we generalized previously known results that were researched in the field of finite networks.

The theoretical work was motivated by the observation that KGs, like Wikidata, do contain huge amounts of metric data. These are often equipped with some kind of height functions in a natural way. Based on this we proposed in this work the groundwork for a locally working item recommending scheme.

To evaluate the capabilities for identifying locally outstanding items we selected an artificial classification task. We identified all French and German municipalities from Wikidata and evaluated if a classifier can learn a meaningful connection between our valuation functions and the relevance of a municipality. To gain a binary classification task and to have a benchmark, we assumed that universities are primarily located at relevant municipalities. In consequence, we evaluated if a classifier can use prominence and isolation as features to predict university locations. Our results showed that isolation and prominence are indeed helpful for identifying relevant items.

For future work we propose to develop the conceptualized item recommender system and to investigate its practical usability in an empirical user study. Furthermore, we urge to research the transferability of other orometric based valuation functions.

Acknowledgement. The authors would like to express thanks to Dominik Dürrschnabel for fruitful discussions. This work was funded by the German Federal Ministry of Education and Research (BMBF) in its program "Quantitative Wissenschaftsforschung" as part of the REGIO project under grant 01PU17012.

References

1. Akbani, R., Kwek, S., Japkowicz, N.: Applying support vector machines to imbalanced datasets. In: Boulicaut, J.-F., Esposito, F., Giannotti, F., Pedreschi, D. (eds.) ECML 2004. LNCS (LNAI), vol. 3201, pp. 39–50. Springer, Heidelberg (2004). https://doi.org/10.1007/978-3-540-30115-8_7
2. Barthélemy, M.: Spatial networks. Phys. Rep. **499**(1), 1–101 (2011)
3. Bentley, J.L.: A survey of techniques for fixed radius near neighbor searching. Technical report, SLAC, SCIDOC, Stanford, CA, USA (1975). SLAC-R-0186, SLAC-0186
4. Bordes, A., Weston, J., Collobert, R., Bengio, Y.: Learning structured embeddings of knowledge bases. In: Burgard, W., Roth, D. (eds.) Proceedings of the 25th Conference on Artificial Intelligence, pp. 301–306. AAAI Press, Palo Alto (2011)
5. Catherine, R., Cohen, W.: Personalized recommendations using knowledge graphs: a probabilistic logic programming approach. In: Proceedings of the 10th ACM Conference on Recommender Systems, RecSys, pp. 325–332. ACM, New York (2016)
6. Čomić, L., De Floriani, L., Papaleo, L.: Morse-smale decompositions for modeling terrain knowledge. In: Cohn, A.G., Mark, D.M. (eds.) COSIT 2005. LNCS, vol. 3693, pp. 426–444. Springer, Heidelberg (2005). https://doi.org/10.1007/11556114_27
7. Cortes, C., Vapnik, V.: Support-vector networks. Mach. Learn. **20**(3), 273–297 (1995)
8. Fry, S.: Defining and sizing-up mountains. Summit, pp. 16–21, January-February 1987
9. Hanika, T., Marx, M., Stumme, G.: Discovering implicational knowledge in wikidata. In: Cristea, D., Le Ber, F., Sertkaya, B. (eds.) ICFCA 2019. LNCS (LNAI), vol. 11511, pp. 315–323. Springer, Cham (2019). https://doi.org/10.1007/978-3-030-21462-3_21
10. He, H., Garcia, E.A.: Learning from imbalanced data. IEEE Trans. Knowl. Data Eng. **21**(9), 1263–1284 (2009)
11. Helman, A.: The Finest Peaks-Prominence and Other Mountain Measures. Trafford, Victoria (2005)
12. Hirsch, J.E.: An index to quantify an individual's scientific research output. Proc. Nat. Acad. Sci. **102**(46), 16569–16572 (2005)
13. Jiang, B., Claramunt, C.: Topological analysis of urban street networks. Environ. Plan. B: Plan. Des. **31**(1), 151–162 (2004)
14. Kirmse, A., de Ferranti, J.: Calculating the prominence and isolation of every mountain in the world. Prog. Phys. Geogr.: Earth Environ. **41**(6), 788–802 (2017)
15. Lehmann, J., et al.: DBpedia - a large-scale, multilingual knowledge base extracted from wikipedia. Semant. Web **6**(2), 167–195 (2015)
16. Nelson, G.D., McKeon, R.: Peaks of people: using topographic prominence as a method for determining the ranked significance of population centers. Prof. Geogr. **71**(2), 342–354 (2019)
17. Oramas, S., Ostuni, V.C., Noia, T.D., Serra, X., Sciascio, E.D.: Sound and music recommendation with knowledge graphs. ACM Trans. Intell. Syst. Technol. **8**(2), 21:1–21:21 (2016)
18. Palumbo, E., Rizzo, G., Troncy, R.: Entity2rec: learning user-item relatedness from knowledge graphs for top-n item recommendation. In: Proceedings of the Eleventh ACM Conference on Recommender Systems, pp. 32–36. ACM (2017)

19. Palumbo, E., Rizzo, G., Troncy, R., Baralis, E., Osella, M., Ferro, E.: Knowledge graph embeddings with node2vec for item recommendation. In: Gangemi, A., et al. (eds.) ESWC 2018. LNCS, vol. 11155, pp. 117–120. Springer, Cham (2018). https://doi.org/10.1007/978-3-319-98192-5_22

20. Pedregosa, F., et al.: Scikit-learn: machine learning in Python. JMLR **12**, 2825–2830 (2011)

21. Penrose, M.: Random Geometric Graphs. Oxford Studies in Probability, vol. 5. Oxford University Press, Oxford (2003)

22. Schmidt, A., Stumme, G.: Prominence and dominance in networks. In: Faron Zucker, C., Ghidini, C., Napoli, A., Toussaint, Y. (eds.) EKAW 2018. LNCS (LNAI), vol. 11313, pp. 370–385. Springer, Cham (2018). https://doi.org/10.1007/978-3-030-03667-6_24

23. Torres, R.N., Fraternali, P., Milani, F., Frajberg, D.: A deep learning model for identifying mountain summits in digital elevation model data. In: First IEEE International Conference on Artificial Intelligence and Knowledge Engineering, AIKE 2018, Laguna Hills, CA, USA, 26–28 September 2018, pp. 212–217. IEEE Computer Society (2018)

24. Vrandečić, D., Krötzsch, M.: Wikidata: a free collaborative knowledge base. Commun. ACM **57**, 78–85 (2014)

25. Wang, Z., Zhang, J., Feng, J., Chen, Z.: Knowledge graph embedding by translating on hyperplanes. In: Brodley, C.E., Stone, P. (eds.) Proceedings of the 28th Conference on Artificial Intelligence, pp. 1112–1119. AAAI Press (2014)

26. Watts, D.J.: Six Degrees: The Science of a Connected Age. W. W. Norton, New York (2003)

11

Making Learners (More) Monotone

Tom Julian Viering[1]([⊠])[iD], Alexander Mey[1][iD], and Marco Loog[1,2][iD]

[1] Delft University of Technology, Delft, The Netherlands
{t.j.viering,a.mey,m.loog}@tudelft.nl
[2] University of Copenhagen, Copenhagen, Denmark

Abstract. Learning performance can show non-monotonic behavior. That is, more data does not necessarily lead to better models, even on average. We propose three algorithms that take a supervised learning model and make it perform more monotone. We prove consistency and monotonicity with high probability, and evaluate the algorithms on scenarios where non-monotone behaviour occurs. Our proposed algorithm MT_{HT} makes less than 1% non-monotone decisions on MNIST while staying competitive in terms of error rate compared to several baselines.

Keywords: Learning curve · Model selection · Learning theory

1 Introduction

It is a widely held belief that more training data usually results in better generalizing machine learning models—cf. [11,17] for instance. Several learning problems have illustrated, however, that more training data can lead to worse generalization performance [3,9,12]. For the peaking phenomenon [3], this occurs exactly at the transition from the underparametrized to the overparametrized regime. This double-descent behavior has found regained interest in the context of deep neural networks [1,18], since these models are typically overparametrized. Recently, also several new examples have been found, where in quite simple settings more data results in worse generalization performance [10,19].

It can be difficult to explain to a user that machine learning models can actually perform worse when more, possibly expensive to collect data has been used for training. Besides, it seems generally desirable to have algorithms that guarantee increased performance with more data. How to get such a guarantee? That is the question we investigate in this work and for which we use learning curves. Such curves plot the expected performance of a learning algorithm versus the amount of training data.[1] In other words, we wonder how we can make learning curves monotonic.

The core approach to make learners monotone is that, when more data is gathered and a new model is trained, this newly trained model is compared to

---

[1] Not to be confused with training curves, where the loss versus epochs (optimization iterations) is plotted.

the currently adopted model that was trained on less data. Only if the new model performs better should it be used. We introduce several wrapper algorithms for supervised classification techniques that use the holdout set or cross-validation to make this comparison. Our proposed algorithm MT_{HT} uses a hypothesis test to switch if the new model improves significantly upon the old model. Using guarantees from the hypothesis test we can prove that the resulting learning curve is monotone with high probability. We empirically study the effect of the parameters of the algorithms and benchmark them on several datasets including MNIST [8] to check to what degree the learning curves become monotone.

This work is organized as follows. The notion of monotonicity of learning curves is reviewed in Sect. 2. We introduce our approaches and algorithms in Sect. 3, and prove consistency and monotonicity with high probability in Sect. 4. Section 5 provides the empirical evaluation. We discuss the main findings of our results in Sect. 6 and end with the most important conclusions.

2 The Setting and the Definition of Monotonicity

We consider the setting where we have a learner that now and then receives data and that is evaluated over time. The question is then, how to make sure that the performance of this learner over time is monotone—or with other words, how can we guarantee that this learner over time improves its performance?

We analyze this question in a (frequentist) classification framework. We assume there exists an (unknown) distribution P over $\mathcal{X} \times \mathcal{Y}$, where $\mathcal{X}$ is the input space (features) and $\mathcal{Y}$ is the output space (classification labels). To simplify the setup we operate in rounds indicated by i, where $i \in \{1, \ldots, n\}$. In each round, we receive a batch of samples S^i that is sampled i.i.d. from P. The learner L can use this data in combination with data from previous rounds to come up with a hypothesis h_i in round i. The hypothesis comes from a hypothesis space $\mathcal{H}$. We consider learners L that, as subroutine, use a supervised learner $A : \mathcal{S} \to \mathcal{H}$, where $\mathcal{S}$ is the space of all possible training sets.

We measure performance by the error rate. The true error rate on P equals

$$\epsilon(h_i) = \int_{x \in \mathcal{X}} \sum_{y \in \mathcal{Y}} l_{0\text{-}1}(h_i(x), y) dP(x, y) \tag{1}$$

where $l_{0\text{-}1}$ is the zero-one loss. We indicate the empirical error rate of h on a sample S as $\hat{\epsilon}(h, S)$. We call n rounds a run. The true error of the returned h_i by the learner L in round i is indicated by ϵ_i, all the ϵ_i's of a run form a learning curve. By averaging multiple runs one obtains the expected learning curve, $\bar{\epsilon}_i$.

The goal for the learner L is twofold. The error rates of the returned models ϵ_i's should (1) be as small as possible, and (2) be monotonically decreasing. These goals can be at odds with another. For example, always returning a fixed model ensures monotonicity but incurs large error rates. To measure (1), we summarize performance of a learning curve using the Area Under the Learning Curve (AULC) [6,13,16]. The AULC averages all ϵ_i's of a run. Low AULC indicates that a learner manages to quickly reduce the error rate.

Monotone in round i means that $\epsilon_{i+1} \leq \epsilon_i$. We may care about monotonicity of the expected learning curve *or* individual learning curves. In practice, however, we typically get one chance to gather data and submit models. In that case, we rather want to make sure that then any additional data also leads to better performance. Therefore, we are mainly concerned with monotonicity of *individual* learning curves. We quantify monotonicity of a run by the fraction of non-monotone transitions in an individual curve.

3   Approaches and Algorithms

We introduce three algorithms (learners L) that wrap around supervised learners with the aim of making them monotone. First, we provide some intuition how to achieve this: ideally, during the generation of the learning curve, we would check whether $\epsilon(h_{i+1}) \leq \epsilon(h_i)$. A fix to make a learner monotone would be to output h_i instead of h_{i+1} if the error rate of h_{i+1} is larger. Since learners do not have access to $\epsilon(h_i)$, we have to estimate it using the incoming data. The first two algorithms, $\mathrm{MT_{SIMPLE}}$ and $\mathrm{MT_{HT}}$, use the holdout method to this end; newly arriving data is partitioned into training and validation sets. The third algorithm, $\mathrm{MT_{CV}}$, makes use of cross validation.

$\mathrm{MT_{SIMPLE}}$: Monotone Simple. The pseudo-code for $\mathrm{MT_{SIMPLE}}$ is given by Algorithm 1 in combination with the function UpdateSimple. Batches S^i are split into training (S_t^i) and validation (S_v^i). The training set S_t is enlarged each round with S_t^i and a new model h_i is trained. S_v^i is used to estimate the performance of h_i and h_{best}. We store the previously best performing model, h_{best}, and compare its performance to that of h_i. If the new model h_i is better, it is returned and h_{best} is updated, otherwise h_{best} is returned.

Because h_i and h_{best} are both compared on S_v^i the comparison is more accurate because the comparison is paired. After the comparison S_v^i can safely be added to the training set (line 7 of Algorithm 1).

We call this algorithm $\mathrm{MT_{SIMPLE}}$ because the model selection is a bit naive: for small validation sets, the variance in the performance measure could be quite large, leading to many non-monotone decisions. In the limit of infinitely large S_v^i, however, this algorithm should always be monotone (and very data hungry).

$\mathrm{MT_{HT}}$: Monotone Hypothesis Test. The second algorithm, $\mathrm{MT_{HT}}$, aims to resolve the issues of $\mathrm{MT_{SIMPLE}}$ with small validation set sizes. In addition, for this algorithm, we prove that individual learning curves are monotone with high probability. The same pseudo-code is used as for $\mathrm{MT_{SIMPLE}}$ (Algorithm 1), but with a different update function UpdateHT. Now a hypothesis test *HT* determines if the newly trained model is significantly better than the previous model. The hypothesis test makes sure that the newly trained model is not better due to chance (such as an unlucky sample). The hypothesis test is conservative, and only switches to a new model if we are reasonably sure it is significantly better, to avoid non-monotone decisions. Japkowicz and Shah [7] provide an accessible introduction to understand the frequentist hypothesis testing.

Algorithm 1. M_{SIMPLE} and M_{HT}

---

    input: supervised learner A, rounds n, batches S^i
        $u \in \{\text{updateSimple, updateHT}\}$
        if $u = \text{updateHT}$: confidence level α, hypothesis test HT

1 $S_t = \{\}$
2 **for** $i = 1, \ldots, n$ **do**
3   Split S^i in S_t^i and S_v^i
4   Append to $S_t : S_t = [S_t; S_t^i]$
5 $h_i \leftarrow A(S_t)$
6 $Update_i \leftarrow u(S_v^i, h_i, h_{\text{best}}, \alpha, HT)$ // see below
7   Append to $S_t : S_t = [S_t; S_v^i]$
8   **if** $Update_i$ or $i = 1$ **then**
9 $\mid$ $h_{\text{best}} \leftarrow h_i$
10   **end**
11   Return h_{best} in round i
12 **end**

Function UpdateSimple	**Function** UpdateHT
input: S_v^i, h_i, h_{best}	**input:** S_v^i, h_i, h_{best}, confidence level α, hypothesis test HT
1 $P_{current} \leftarrow \hat{\epsilon}(h_i, S_v^i)$	**1** $p = HT(S_v^i, h_i, h_{\text{best}})$ // p-value
2 $P_{best} \leftarrow \hat{\epsilon}(h_{\text{best}}, S_v^i)$	**2** return $(p \le alpha)$
3 return $(P_{current} \le P_{best})$	

The choice of hypothesis test depends on the performance measure. For the error rate the McNemar test can be used [7,14]. The hypothesis test should use paired data, since we evaluate two models on one sample, and it should be one-tailed. One-tailed, since we only want to know whether h_i is better than h_{best} (a two tailed test would switch to h_i if its performance is significantly different). The test compares two hypotheses: $H_0 : \epsilon(h_i) = \epsilon(h_{\text{best}})$ and $H_1 : \epsilon(h_i) < \epsilon(h_{\text{best}})$.

Several versions of the McNemar test can be used [4,7,14]. We use the McNemar exact conditional test which we briefly review. Let b be the random variable indicating the number of samples classified correctly by h_{best} and incorrectly by h_i of the sample S_v^i, and let N_d be the number of samples where they disagree. The test conditions on N_d. Assuming H_0 is true, $P(b = x | H_0, N_d) = \binom{N_d}{x}(\frac{1}{2})^{N_d}$. Given x b's, the p-value for our one tailed test is $p = \sum_{i=0}^{x} P(b = i | H_0, N_d)$.

The one tailed p-value is the probability of observing a more extreme sample given hypothesis H_0 considering the tail direction of H_1. The smaller the p-value, the more evidence we have for H_1. If the p-value is smaller than α, we accept H_1, and thus we update the model h_{best}. The smaller α, the more conservative the hypothesis test, and thus the smaller the chance that a wrong decision is made due to unlucky sampling. For the McNemar exact conditional test [4] the False Positive Rate (FPR, or the probability to make a Type I error) is bounded by α: $P(p \le \alpha | H_0) \le \alpha$. We need this to prove monotonicity with high probability.

MT$_{CV}$: Monotone Cross Validation. In practice, often K-fold cross validation (CV) is used to estimate model performance instead of the holdout. This is what MT$_{CV}$ does, and is similar to MT$_{SIMPLE}$. As described in Algorithm 2, for each incoming sample an index I maintains to which fold it belongs. These indices are used to generate the folds for the K-fold cross validation.

During CV, K models are trained and evaluated on the validation sets. We now have to memorize K previously best models, one for each fold. We average the performance of the newly trained models over the K-folds, and compare that to the average of the best previous K models. This averaging over folds is essential, as this reduces the variance of the model selection step as compared to selecting the best model overall (like MT$_{SIMPLE}$ does).

In our framework we return a single model in each iteration. We return the model with the optimal training set size that performed best during CV. This can further improve performance.

Algorithm 2. M$_{CV}$

---

input: K folds, learner A, rounds n, batches S^i

1   $b \leftarrow 1$ // keeps track of best round
2   $S = \{\}, I = \{\}$
3   **for** $i = 1, \ldots, n$ **do**
4   $\quad$ Generate stratified CV indices for S^i and put in I^i. Each index i
    $\quad\quad$ indicates to which validation fold the corresponding sample belongs.
5   $\quad$ Append to S: $S \leftarrow [S; S^i]$
6   $\quad$ Append to I: $I \leftarrow [I; I^i]$
7   $\quad$ **for** $k = 1, \ldots, K$ **do**
8   $\quad\quad$ $h_i^k \leftarrow A(S[I \neq k])$ // training set of kth fold
9   $\quad\quad$ $P_i^k \leftarrow \hat{\epsilon}(h_i^k, S[I = k])$ // validation set of kth fold
10 $\quad\quad$ $P_b^k \leftarrow \hat{\epsilon}(h_b^k, S[I = k])$ // update performance of prev. models
11 $\quad$ **end**
12 $\quad$ $Update_i \leftarrow (mean(P_i^k) \leq mean(P_b^k))$ // mean w.r.t. k
13 $\quad$ **if** $Update_i$ or $i = 1$ **then**
14 $\quad\quad$ $b \leftarrow i$
15 $\quad$ **end**
16 $\quad$ $k \leftarrow \arg\min_k P_b^k$ // break ties
17 $\quad$ Return h_b^k in round i
18 **end**

---

4   Theoretical Analysis

We derive the probability of a monotone learning curve for MT$_{SIMPLE}$ and MT$_{HT}$, and we prove our algorithms are consistent if the model updates enough.

Theorem 1. *Assume we use the McNemar exact conditional test (see Sect. 3) with $\alpha \in (0, \frac{1}{2}]$, then the individual learning curve generated by Algorithm MT$_{HT}$ with n rounds is monotone with probability at least $(1 - \alpha)^n$.*

Proof. First we argue that the probability of making a non-monotone decision in round i is at most α. If $H_1 : \epsilon(h_i) < \epsilon(h_{\text{best}})$ or $H_0 : \epsilon(h_i) = \epsilon(h_{\text{best}})$ is true, we are monotone in round i, so we only need to consider a new alternative hypothesis $H_2 : \epsilon(h_i) > \epsilon(h_{\text{best}})$. Under H_0 we have [4]: $P(p \leq \alpha | H_0) \leq \alpha$. Conditioned on H_2, b is binomial with larger mean than in the case of H_0, thus we observe larger p-values if $\alpha \in (0, \frac{1}{2}]$, thus $P(p \leq \alpha | H_2) \leq P(p \leq \alpha | H_0) \leq \alpha$. Therefore the probability of being non-monotone in round i is at most α. This holds for any model h_i, h_{best} and anything that happened before round i. Since S_v^i are independent samples, being non-monotone in each round can be seen as independent events, resulting in $(1 - \alpha)^n$.   □

If the probability of being non-monotone in all rounds is at most β, we can set $\alpha = 1 - \beta^{\frac{1}{n}}$ to fulfill this condition. Note that this analysis also holds for $\text{MT}_{\text{SIMPLE}}$, since running MT_{HT} with $\alpha = \frac{1}{2}$ results in the same algorithm as $\text{MT}_{\text{SIMPLE}}$ for the McNemar exact conditional test.

We now argue that all proposed algorithms are consistent under some conditions. First, let us revisit the definition of consistency [17].

Definition 1 (Consistency [17]). *Let L be a learner that returns a hypothesis $L(S) \in \mathcal{H}$ when evaluated on S. For all $\epsilon_{excess} \in (0, 1)$, for all distributions D over $X \times Y$, for all $\delta \in (0, 1)$, if there exists a $n(\epsilon_{excess}, D, \delta)$, such that for all $m \geq n(\epsilon_{excess}, D, \delta)$, if L uses a sample S of size m, and the following holds with probability (over the choice of S) at least $1 - \delta$,*

$$\epsilon(L(S)) \leq \min_{h \in \mathcal{H}} \epsilon(h) + \epsilon_{excess}, \tag{2}$$

then L is said to be consistent.

Before we can state the main result, we have to introduce a bit of notation. U_i indicates the event that the algorithm updates h_{best} (or in case of M_{CV} it updates the variable b). H_i^{i+z} to indicates the event that $\neg U_i \cap \neg U_{i+1} \cap \ldots \cap \neg U_{i+z}$, or in words, that in round i to $i + z$ there has been no update. To fulfill consistency, we need that when the number of rounds grows to infinity, the probability of updating is large enough. Then consistency of A makes sure that h_{best} has sufficiently low error. For this analysis it is assumed that the number of rounds of the algorithms is not fixed.

Theorem 2. *MT_{SIMPLE}, MT_{HT} and MT_{CV} are consistent, if A is consistent and if for all i there exists a $z_i \in \mathbb{N} \setminus 0$ and $C_i > 0$ such that for all $k \in \mathbb{N} \setminus 0$ it holds that $P(H_i^{i+kz_i}) \leq (1 - C_i)^k$.*

Proof. Let A be consistent with $n_A(\epsilon_{\text{excess}}, D, \delta)$ samples. Let us analyze round i where i is big enough such that[2] $|S_t| > n_A(\epsilon_{\text{excess}}, D, \frac{\delta}{2})$. Assume that

$$\epsilon(h_{\text{best}}) > \min_{h \in \mathcal{H}} \epsilon(h) + \epsilon_{\text{excess}}, \tag{3}$$

---

[2] In case of MT_{CV}, take $|S_t|$ to be the smallest training fold size in round i.

otherwise the proof is trivial. For any round $j \geq i$, since A produces hypothesis h_j with $|S_t| > n_A(\epsilon_{\text{excess}}, D, \frac{\delta}{2})$ samples,

$$\epsilon(h_j) \leq \min_{h \in \mathcal{H}} \epsilon(h) + \epsilon_{\text{excess}} \tag{4}$$

holds with probability of at least $1 - \frac{\delta}{2}$. Now L should update. The probability that in the next kz_i rounds we don't update is, by assumption, bounded by $(1 - C_i)^k$. Since $C_i > 0$, we can choose k big enough so that $(1 - C_i)^k \leq \frac{\delta}{2}$. Thus the probability of not updating after kz_i more rounds is at most $\frac{\delta}{2}$, and we have a probability of $\frac{\delta}{2}$ that the model after updating is not good enough. Applying the union bound we find the probability of failure is at most δ.   □

A few remarks about the assumption. It tells us, that an update is more and more likely if we have more consecutive rounds where there has been no update. It holds if each z_i rounds the update probability is nonzero. A weaker but also sufficient assumption is $\forall_i : \lim_{z \to \infty} P(H_i^{i+z}) \to 0$.

For $\text{MT}_{\text{SIMPLE}}$ and MT_{CV} the assumption is always satisfied, because these algorithms look directly at the mean error rate—and due to fluctuations in the sampling there is always a non-zero probability that $\hat{\epsilon}(h_i) \leq \hat{\epsilon}(h_{\text{best}})$. However, for MT_{HT} this may not always be satisfied. Especially if the validation batches N_v are small, the hypothesis test may not be able to detect small differences in error—the test then has zero power. If N_v stays small, even in future rounds the power may stay zero, in which case the learner is not consistent.

5 Experiments

We evaluate $\text{MT}_{\text{SIMPLE}}$ and MT_{HT} on artificial datasets to understand the influence of their parameters. Afterward we perform a benchmark where we also include MT_{CV} and a baseline that uses validation data to tune the regularization strength. This last experiment is also performed on the MNIST dataset to get an impression of the practicality of the proposed algorithms. First we describe the experimental setup in more detail.

Experimental Setup. The peaking dataset [3] and dipping dataset [9] are artificial datasets that cause non-monotone behaviour. We use stratified sampling to obtain batches S^i for the peaking and dipping dataset, for MNIST we use random sampling. For simplicity all batches have the same size. N indicates batch size, and N_v and N_t indicate the sizes of the validation and training sets.

As model we use least squares classification [5,15]. This is ordinary linear least squares regression on the classification labels $\{-1, +1\}$ with intercept. For MNIST one-versus-all is used to train a multi-class model. In case there are less samples for training than dimensions, the required inverse of the covariance matrix is ill-defined and we resort to the Moore-Penrose Pseudo-Inverse.

Monotonicity is calculated by the fraction of non-monotone iterations per run. AULC is also calculated per run. We do 100 runs with different batches and average to reduce variation from the randomness in the batches. Each run uses a newly sampled test set consisting of 10000 samples. The test set is used to estimate the true error rate and is not accessible by any of the algorithms.

We evaluate M_{SIMPLE}, M_{HT} and M_{CV} and several baselines. The standard learner just trains on all received data. A second baseline, λ_S, splits the data in train and validation like M_{SIMPLE} and uses the validation data to select the optimal L_2 regularization parameter λ for the least square classifier. Regularization is implemented by adding λI to the estimate of the covariance matrix.

In the first experiment we investigate the influence of N_v and α for MT_{SIMPLE} and MT_{HT} on the decisions. A complicating factor is that if N_v changes, not only decisions change, but also training set sizes because S_v is appended to the training set (see line 7 of Algorithm 1). This makes interpretation of the results difficult because decisions are then made in a different context. Therefore, for the first set of experiments, we do not add S_v to the training sets, also not for the standard learner. For this set of experiment We use $N_t = 4$, $n = 150$, $d = 200$ for the peaking dataset, and we vary α and N_v.

For the benchmark, we set $N_t = 10$, $N_v = 40$, $n = 150$ for peaking and dipping, and we set $N_t = 5$, $N_v = 20$, $n = 40$ for MNIST. We fix $\alpha = 0.05$ and use $d = 500$ for the peaking dataset. For MNIST, as preprocessing step we extract 500 random Fourier-features as also done by Belkin et al. [1]. For MT_{CV} we use $K = 5$ folds. For λ_S we try $\lambda \in \{10^{-5}, 10^{-4.5}, \ldots, 10^{4.5}, 10^5\}$ for peaking and dipping, and we try $\lambda \in \{10^{-3}, 10^{-2}, \ldots, 10^3\}$ for MNIST.

Results. We perform a preliminary investigation of the algorithms M_{SIMPLE} and M_{HT} and the influence of the parameters N_v and α. We show several learning curves in Fig. 1a and d. For small N_v and α we observe MT_{HT} gets stuck: it does not switch models anymore, indicating that consistency could be violated.

In Fig. 1b and e we give a more complete picture of all tried hyperparameters in terms of the AULC. In Fig. 1c and f we plot the fraction of non-monotone decisions during a run (note that the legends for the subfigures are different). Observe that the axes are scaled differently (some are logarithmic). In some cases zero non-monotone decisions were observed, resulting in a missing value due to $\log(0)$. This occurs for example if MT_{HT} always sticks to the same model, then no non-monotone decisions are made. The results of the benchmark are shown in Fig. 2. The AULC and fraction of monotone decisions are given in Table 1.

6   Discussion

First Experiment: Tuning α and N_v. As predicted MT_{SIMPLE} typically performs worse than MT_{HT} in terms of AULC and monotonicity unless N_v is very large. The variance in the estimate of the error rates on S_v^i is so large that in most cases the algorithm doesn't switch to the correct model. However, MT_{SIMPLE} seems to be consistently better than the standard learner in terms of monotonicity and AULC, while MT_{HT} can perform worse if badly tuned.

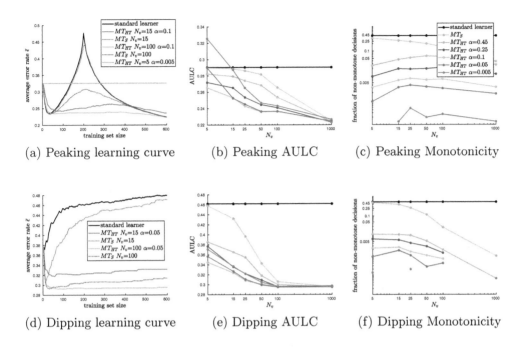

(a) Peaking learning curve (b) Peaking AULC (c) Peaking Monotonicity

(d) Dipping learning curve (e) Dipping AULC (f) Dipping Monotonicity

Fig. 1. Influence of N_v and α for $\mathrm{MT_{SIMPLE}}$ and $\mathrm{MT_{HT}}$ on the Peaking and Dipping dataset. Note that some axes are logarithmic and b, c, e, f have the same legend.

Larger N_v leads typically to improved AULC for both. $\alpha \in [0.05, 0.1]$ seems to work best in terms of AULC for most values of N_v. If α is too small, $\mathrm{MT_{HT}}$ can get stuck, if α is too large, it switches models too often and non-monotone behaviour occurs. If $\alpha \to \frac{1}{2}$, $\mathrm{MT_{HT}}$ becomes increasingly similar to $\mathrm{MT_{SIMPLE}}$ as predicted by the theory.

The fraction of non-monotone decisions of $\mathrm{MT_{HT}}$ is much lower than α. This is in agreement with Theorem 1, but could indicate in addition that the hypothesis test is rather pessimistic. The standard learner and $\mathrm{MT_{SIMPLE}}$ often make non-monotone decisions. In some cases almost 50% of the decisions are not-monotone.

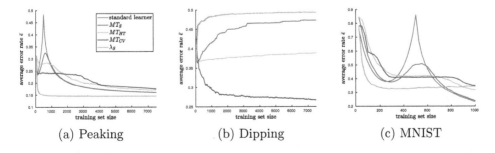

(a) Peaking (b) Dipping (c) MNIST

Fig. 2. Expected learning curves on the benchmark datasets.

Table 1. Results of the benchmark. SL is the Standard Learner. AULC is the Area Under the Learning Curve of the error rate. Fraction indicates the average fraction of non-monotone decisions during a single run. Standard deviation shown in (braces). Best monotonicity result is <u>underlined</u>.

	Peaking		Dipping		MNIST	
	AULC	Fraction	AULC	Fraction	AULC	Fraction
SL	0.198 (0.003)	0.31 (0.02)	0.49 (0.01)	0.50 (0.03)	0.44 (0.01)	0.27 (0.04)
MT_S	0.195 (0.005)	0.23 (0.03)	0.45 (0.06)	0.37 (0.15)	0.42 (0.02)	0.11 (0.04)
MT_{HT}	0.208 (0.009)	<u>0.00</u> (0.00)	0.38 (0.08)	<u>0.00</u> (0.00)	0.45 (0.02)	<u>0.00</u> (0.00)
MT_{CV}	0.208 (0.005)	0.34 (0.03)	0.28 (0.02)	0.19 (0.08)	0.45 (0.01)	0.30 (0.06)
λ_S	0.147 (0.003)	0.43 (0.03)	0.49 (0.01)	0.50 (0.03)	0.36 (0.02)	0.46 (0.05)

Second Experiment: Benchmark on Peaking, Dipping, MNIST. Interestingly, for peaking and MNIST datasets any non-monotonicity (double descent [1]) in the *expected* learning curve almost completely disappears for λ_S, which tunes the regularization parameter using validation data (Fig. 2). We wonder if regularization can also help reducing the severity of double descent in other settings. For the dipping dataset, regularization doesn't help, showing that it cannot prevent non-monotone behaviour. Furthermore, the fraction of non-monotone decisions *per run* is largest for this learner (Table 1).

For the dipping dataset M_{CV} has a large advantage in terms of AULC. We hypothesize that this is largely due to tie breaking and small training set sizes due to the 5-folds. Surprisingly on the peaking dataset it seems to learn quite slowly. The expected learning curves of MT_{HT} look better than that of MT_{SIMPLE}, however, in terms of AULC the difference is quite small.

The fraction of non-monotone decisions for MT_{HT} per run is very small as guaranteed. However, it is interesting to note that this does not always translate to monotonicity in the expected learning curve. For example, for peaking and dipping the expected curve doesn't seem entirely monotone. But MT_{CV}, which makes many non-monotone decisions per run, still seems to have a monotone expected learning curve. While monotonicity of each individual learning curves guarantees monotonicity in the expected curve, this result indicates monotonicity of each individual curve may not be necessary. This raises the question: under what conditions do we have monotonicity of the expected learning curve?

General Remarks. The fraction of non-monotone decisions of MT_{HT} being so much smaller than α could indicate the hypothesis test is too pessimistic. Fagerland et al. [4] note that the asymptotic McNemar test can have more power, which could further improve the AULC. For this test the guarantee $P(p \leq \alpha | H_0) \leq \alpha$ can be violated, but in light of the monotonicity results obtained, practically this may not be an issue.

MT_{HT} is inconsistent at times, but this does not have to be problematic. If one knows the desired error rate, a minimum N_v can be determined that ensures the hypothesis test will not get stuck before reaching that error rate. Another possibility is to make the size N_v dependent on i: if N_v is monotonically increasing this directly leads to consistency of MT_{HT}. It would be ideal if somehow N_v could be automatically tuned to trade off sample size requirements, consistency and monotonicity. Since for CV N_v automatically grows and thus also directly implies consistency, a combination of MT_{HT} and MT_{CV} is another option.

Devroye et al. [2] conjectured that it is impossible to construct a consistent learner that is monotone in terms of the expected learning curve. Since we look at individual curves, our work does not disprove this conjecture, but some of the authors on this paper believe that the conjecture can be disproved. One step to make is to get to an essentially better understanding of the relation between individual learning curves and the expected one.

Currently, our definition judges any decision that increases the error rate, by however small amount, as non-monotone. It would be desirable to have a broader definition of non-monotonicity that allows for small and negligible increases of the error rate. Using a hypothesis test satisfying such a less strict condition could allow us to use less data for validation.

Finally, the user of the learning system should be notified that non-monotonicity has occurred. Then the cause can be investigated and mitigated by regularization, model selection, etc. However, in automated systems our algorithm can prevent any known and unknown causes of non-monotonicity (as long as data is i.i.d.), and thus can be used as a failsafe that requires no human intervention.

7 Conclusion

We have introduced three algorithms to make learners more monotone. We proved under which conditions the algorithms are consistent and we have shown for MT_{HT} that the learning curve is monotone with high probability. If one cares only about monotonicity of the expected learning curve, MT_{SIMPLE} with very large N_v or MT_{CV} may prove sufficient as shown by our experiments. If N_v is small, or one desires that individual learning curves are monotone with high probability (as practically most relevant), MT_{HT} is the right choice. Our algorithms are a first step towards developing learners that, given more data, improve their performance in expectation.

Acknowledgments. We would like to thank the reviewers for their useful feedback for preparing the camera ready version of this paper.

References

1. Belkin, M., Hsu, D., Ma, S., Mandal, S.: Reconciling modern machine-learning practice and the classical bias-variance trade-off. Proc. Nat. Acad. Sci. **116**(32), 15849–15854 (2019)
2. Devroye, L., Györfi, L., Lugosi, G.: A Probabilistic Theory of Pattern Recognition. Stochastic Modelling and Applied Probability. Springer, Heidelberg (1996). https://doi.org/10.1007/978-1-4612-0711-5
3. Duin, R.: Small sample size generalization. In: Proceedings of the Scandinavian Conference on Image Analysis, vol. 2, pp. 957–964 (1995)
4. Fagerland, M.W., Lydersen, S., Laake, P.: The McNemar test for binary matched-pairs data: mid-p and asymptotic are better than exact conditional. BMC Med. Res. Methodol. **13**, 91 (2013). https://doi.org/10.1186/1471-2288-13-91
5. Hastie, T., Tibshirani, R., Friedman, J.: The Elements of Statistical Learning. SSS. Springer, New York (2009). https://doi.org/10.1007/978-0-387-84858-7
6. Huijser, M., van Gemert, J.C.: Active decision boundary annotation with deep generative models. In: ICCV, pp. 5286–5295 (2017)
7. Japkowicz, N., Shah, M.: Evaluating Learning Algorithms: A Classification Perspective. Cambridge University Press, Cambridge (2011)
8. LeCun, Y., Bottou, L., Bengio, Y., Haffner, P.: Gradient-based learning applied to document recognition. Proc. IEEE **86**(11), 2278–2324 (1998)
9. Loog, M., Duin, R.: The dipping phenomenon. In: S+SSPR, Hiroshima, Japan, pp. 310–317 (2012)
10. Loog, M., Viering, T., Mey, A.: Minimizers of the empirical risk and risk monotonicity. In: NeuRIPS, vol. 32, pp. 7476–7485 (2019)
11. Mohri, M., Rostamizadeh, A., Talwalkar, A.: Foundations of Machine Learning. MIT Press, Cambridge (2012)
12. Opper, M., Kinzel, W., Kleinz, J., Nehl, R.: On the ability of the optimal perceptron to generalise. J. Phys. A: Math. General **23**(11), L581 (1990)
13. O'Neill, J., Jane Delany, S., MacNamee, B.: Model-free and model-based active learning for regression. In: Angelov, P., Gegov, A., Jayne, C., Shen, Q. (eds.) Advances in Computational Intelligence Systems. AISC, vol. 513, pp. 375–386. Springer, Cham (2017). https://doi.org/10.1007/978-3-319-46562-3_24
14. Raschka, S.: Model evaluation, model selection, and algorithm selection in machine learning (2018). arXiv preprint arXiv:1811.12808
15. Rifkin, R., Yeo, G., Poggio, T.: Regularized least-squares classification. Nato Sci. Ser. Sub Ser. III Comput. Syst. Sci. **190**, 131–154 (2003)
16. Settles, B., Craven, M.: An analysis of active learning strategies for sequence labeling tasks. In: EMNLP, pp. 1070–1079 (2008)
17. Shalev-Shwartz, S., Ben-David, S.: Understanding Machine Learning: From Theory to Algorithms. Cambridge University Press, Cambridge (2014)
18. Spigler, S., Geiger, M., D'Ascoli, S., Sagun, L., Biroli, G., Wyart, M.: A jamming transition from under- to over-parametrization affects loss landscape and generalization (2018). arXiv preprint arXiv:1810.09665
19. Viering, T., Mey, A., Loog, M.: Open problem: monotonicity of learning. In: Conference on Learning Theory, COLT, pp. 3198–3201 (2019)

12

Dual Sequential Variational Autoencoders for Fraud Detection

Ayman Alazizi[1,2]([✉]), Amaury Habrard[1], François Jacquenet[1],
Liyun He-Guelton[2], and Frédéric Oblé[2]

[1] Univ. Lyon, Univ. St-Etienne, UMR CNRS 5516, Laboratoire Hubert-Curien,
42000 Saint-Etienne, France
{ayman.alazizi,amaury.habrard,francois.jacquenet}@univ-st-etienne.fr
[2] Worldline, 95870 Bezons, France
{ayman.alazizi,liyun.he-guelton,frederic.oble}@worldline.com

Abstract. Fraud detection is an important research area where machine learning has a significant role to play. An important task in that context, on which the quality of the results obtained depends, is feature engineering. Unfortunately, this is very time and human consuming. Thus, in this article, we present the DuSVAE model that consists of a generative model that takes into account the sequential nature of the data. It combines two variational autoencoders that can generate a condensed representation of the input sequential data that can then be processed by a classifier to label each new sequence as fraudulent or genuine. The experiments we carried out on a large real-word dataset, from the Worldline company, demonstrate the ability of our system to better detect frauds in credit card transactions without any feature engineering effort.

Keywords: Anomaly detection · Fraud detection · Sequential data · Variational autoencoder

1 Introduction

An anomaly (also called outlier, change, deviation, surprise, peculiarity, intrusion, etc.) is a pattern, in a dataset, that does not conform to an expected behavior. Thus, anomaly detection is the process of finding anomalies in a dataset [4]. Fraud detection, a subdomain of anomaly detection, is a research area where the use of machine learning can have a significant financial impact for companies suffering from large frauds and it is not surprising that a very large amount of research has been conducted over many years in that field [1].

At the Wordline company, we process billions of electronic transactions per year in our highly secured data centers. It is obvious that detecting frauds in that context is a very difficult task. For many years, the detection of credit card frauds within Wordline has been based on a set of rules manually designed by experts. Nevertheless such rules are difficult to maintain, difficult to transfer to other business lines, and dependent on experts who need a very long training period. The contribution of machine learning in this context seems obvious and Wordline has decided for several years to develop research in this field.

Firstly, Worldline has put a lot of effort in feature engineering [3,9,12] to develop discriminative handcrafted features. This improved drastically supervised learning of classifiers that aim to label card transactions as genuine or fraudulent. Nevertheless, designing such features requires a huge amount of time and human resources which is very costly. Thus developing automatic feature engineering methods becomes a critical issue to improve the efficiency of our models. However, in our industrial setting, we have to face with many issues among which the presence of highly imbalanced data where the fraud ratio is about 0.3%. For this reason, we first focused on classic unsupervised approaches in anomaly detection where the objective is to learn a model from normal data and then isolate non-compliant samples and consider them as anomalies [5,17,19,21,22].

In this context, Deep autoencoder [7] is considered as a powerful data modeling tool in the unsupervised setting. An autoencoder (AE) is made up of two parts: an encoder designed to generate a compressed coding from the training input data and a decoder that reconstructs the original input from the compressed coding. In the context of anomaly detection [6,20,22], an autoencoder is generally trained by minimizing the reconstruction error only on normal data. Afterwards, the reconstruction error is applied as an anomaly score. This assumes that the reconstruction error for a normal data should be small as it is close to the learning data, while the reconstruction error for an abnormal data should be high.

However, this assumption is not always valid. Indeed, it has been observed that sometimes the autoencoder generalizes so well that it can also reconstruct anomalies, which leads to view some anomalies as normal data. This can also be the case when some abnormal data share some characteristics of normal data in the training set or when the decoder is "too powerful" to properly decode abnormal codings. To solve the shortcomings of autoencoders, [13,18] proposed the *negative learning technique* that aims to control the compressing capacity of an autoencoder by optimizing conflicting objectives of normal and abnormal data. Thus, this approach looks for a solution in the gradient direction for the desired normal input and in the opposite direction for the undesired input.

This approach could be very appealing to deal with fraud detection problems but we found that it is sometimes not sufficient in the context of our data. Indeed, it is generally almost impossible to obtain in advance a dataset containing all representative frauds, especially in the context where unknown fraudulent transactions occur on new terminals or via new fraudulent behaviors. This has led us to consider more complex models with variational autoencoders (VAE), a probabilistic generative extension of AE, able to model complex generative distributions that we found more adapted to efficiently model new possible frauds.

Another important point for credit card fraud detection is the sequential aspect of the data. Indeed, to test a card for example, a fraudster may try to make several (small) transactions in a short time interval, or directly perform an abnormally high transaction with respect to existing transactions of the true card holder. In fact this sequential aspect has been addressed either indirectly via aggregated features [3], that we would like to avoid designing, or directly by sequential models such as LSTM, but [9] report nevertheless that the LSTM did not improve much the detection performance for e-commerce transactions. One of the main contribution of this paper is to propose a method to identify fraudulent sequences of credit transactions in the context of highly imbalanced data. For this purpose, we propose a model called DuSVAE, for Dual Sequential Variational Autoencoders, that consists of a combination of two variational autoencoders. The first one is trained from fraudulent sequences of transactions in order to be able to project the input data into another feature space and to assign a fraud score to each sequence thanks to the reconstruction error information. Once this model is trained, we plug a second VAE at the output of the first one. This second VAE is then trained with a negative learning approach with the objective to maximize the reconstruction error of the fraudulent sequences and minimize the reconstruction error of the genuine ones.

Our method has been evaluated on a Wordline dataset for credit card fraud detection. The obtained results show that DuSVAE can extract hidden representations able to provide results close to those obtained after a significant work of feature engineering, therefore saving time and human effort. It is even possible to improve the results when combining engineered features with DuSVAE.

The article is organized as follows: some preliminaries about the techniques used in this work are given in Sect. 2. Then we describe the architecture and the training strategy of the DusVAE method in Sect. 3. Experiments are presented in Sect. 4 after a presentation of the dataset and useful metrics. Finally Sect. 5 concludes this article.

2 Preliminaries

In this section, we briefly describe the main techniques that are used in DuSVAE: vanilla and variational autoencoders, negative learning and mixture of experts.

2.1 Autoencoder (AE)

An AE is a neural network [7], which is optimized in an unsupervised manner, usually used to reduce the dimensionality of the input data. It is made up of two parts linked together: an encoder $E(x)$ and a decoder $\mathcal{D}(z)$. Given an input sample x, the encoder generates z, a condensed representation of x. The decoder is then tuned to reconstruct the original input x from the encoded representation z. The objective function used during the training of the AE is given by:

$$\mathcal{L}_{AE}(x) = \|x - \mathcal{D}(E(x))\| \tag{1}$$

where $\| \cdot \|$ denotes an arbitrary distance function. The ℓ_2 norm is typically applied here. The AE can be optimized for example using stochastic gradient descent (SGD) [10].

2.2   Variational Autoencoder (VAE)

A VAE [11,16] is an attractive probabilistic generative version of the standard autoencoder. It can learn a complex distribution and then use it as a generative model defined by a prior $p(z)$ and conditional distribution $p_\theta(x|z)$. Due to the fact that the true likelihood of the data is generally intractable, a VAE is trained through maximizing the evidence lower bound (ELBO):

$$\mathcal{L}(x; \theta, \phi) = \mathbb{E}_{q_\phi(z|x)} \left[\log p_\theta(x|z)\right] - D_{\mathrm{KL}}\left(q_\phi(z|x) \| p(z)\right) \tag{2}$$

where the first term $\mathbb{E}_{q_\phi(z|x)}\left[\log p_\theta(x|z)\right]$ is a negative reconstruction loss that enforces $q_\phi(z|x)$ (the encoder) to generate a meaningful latent vector z, so that $p_\theta(x|z)$ (the decoder) can reconstruct the input x from z. The second term $D_{\mathrm{KL}}\left(q_\phi(z|x) \| p(z)\right)$ is a KL regularization loss that minimizes the KL divergence between the approximate posterior $q_\phi(z|x)$ and the prior $p(z) = \mathcal{N}(\mathbf{0}, \mathbf{I})$.

2.3   Negative Learning

Negative learning is a technique used for regularizing the training of the AE in the presence of labelled data by limiting reconstruction capability (LRC) [13]. The basic idea is to maximize the reconstruction error for abnormal instances, while minimizing the reconstruction error for normal ones in order to improve the discriminative ability of the AE. Given an input instance $x \in \mathbb{R}^n$ and $y \in \{0, 1\}$ denotes its associated label where $y = 1$ stands for a fraudulent instance and $y = 0$ for a genuine one. The objective function of LRC to be minimized is:

$$(1 - y)\mathcal{L}_{AE}(x) - (y)\mathcal{L}_{AE}(x) \tag{3}$$

Training LRC-based models has the major disadvantage to be generally unstable due to the fact that the anomaly reconstruction error is not upper bounded. The LRC approach tends then to maximize the reconstruction error for known anomalies rather than minimizing the reconstruction error for normal points leading to a bad reconstruction of normal data points. To overcome this problem, [18] has proposed Autoencoding Binary Classifiers (ABC) for supervised anomaly detection that improves LRC by using an objective function based on a bounded reconstruction loss for anomalies, leading to a better training stability. The objective function of the ABC to be minimized is:

$$(1 - y)\mathcal{L}_{AE}(x) - y \log_2(1 - e^{-\mathcal{L}_{AE}(x)}) \tag{4}$$

2.4   Mixture-of-Experts Layer (MoE)

In addition to the previous methods, we now present the notion of MoE layer [8] that will be used in our model.

The MoE layer aims to combine the outputs of a group of n neural networks called experts $EX_1, EX_2, ..., EX_n$. The experts have their specific parameters but work on the same input, their n output are combined linearly with the

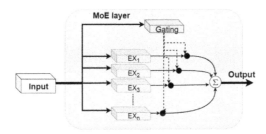

Fig. 1. An illustration of the MoE layer architecture

outputs of the gating network G which weights the experts according to the input x. See Fig. 1 for an illustration. Let $E_i(x)$ be the output of expert EX_i, and $G(x)_i$ be the ith attribute of $G(x)$, then the output y of the MoE is defined as follows:

$$y = \sum_{i=1}^{n} G(x)_i EX_i(x). \qquad (5)$$

The intuition behind MoE layers is to train different network experts that can focus on specific peculiarities of the data and then choose an appropriate combination of experts with respect to the input x. In our industrial context, such a layer would help us to take into account different behaviors from millions of cardholders, which results in a variety of data distributions. The different expert networks can thus model various behaviors observed in the dataset and be combined adequately in function of the input data.

3 The DuSVAE Model

In this section, we present our approach to extract a hidden representation of input sequences to be used for anomaly/fraud detection. We first introduce the model architecture with the loss functions used, then we describe the learning procedure used to train the model.

3.1 Model Architecture

We assume in the following that we are given as input a set of sequences $\mathcal{X} = \{x \mid x = (t^1, t^2, ..., t^m)$ with $t^i \in \mathbb{R}^d\}$, every sequence being composed of m transactions encoded by numerical vectors. Each sequence is associated to a label $y \in \{0, 1\}$ such that $y = 1$ indicates a fraudulent sequence and $y = 0$ a genuine one. We label a sequence as fraudulent if its last transaction is a fraud.

As illustrated in Fig. 2, our approach consists of two sequential variational autoencoders. The first one is trained only on fraudulent sequences of the training data. We use the generative capacity of this autoencoder to generate diverse and representative instances of fraudulent instances with respect to the sequences given as input. This autoencoder has the objective to prepare the data for the

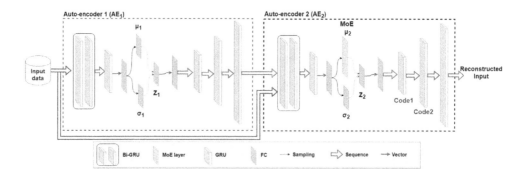

Fig. 2. The DuSVAE model architecture

second autoencoder and to provide also a first anomaly/fraud score with the reconstruction error.

The first layers of the autoencoders are bi-directional GRU layers allowing us to handle sequential data. The remaining parts of the encoder and the decoder contain GRU and fully connected (FC) layers, as shown in Fig. 2. The loss function used to optimize the reconstruction error of the first autoencoder is defined as follows:

$$\mathcal{L}_{rec}(x, \phi_1, \theta_1) = mse(x, \mathcal{D}_{\theta_1}(E_{\phi_1}(x))) + D_{\mathrm{KL}}\left(q_{\phi_1}(z|x) \| p(z)\right), \qquad (6)$$

where mse is the mean square error function and $p(z) = \mathcal{N}(\mathbf{0}, \mathbf{I})$. The encoder $E_{\phi_1}(x)$ generates a latent representation z according to $q_{\phi_1}(z|x) = \mathcal{N}(\mu_1, \sigma_1)$. The decoder $\mathcal{D}_{\theta_1}$ tries to reconstruct the input sequence from z. In order to avoid mode collapse between the reconstructed transactions of the sequence, we add the following loss function to control the reconstruction of individual transactions with respect to relative distances from an input sequence x:

$$\mathcal{L}_{trxAE}(x, \phi_1, \theta_1) = \sum_{i=1}^{m} \sum_{j=i+1}^{m} \frac{1}{d} \|abs(t^i - t^j) - abs(\bar{t}^i - \bar{t}^j)\|_1 \qquad (7)$$

where $\bar{t}^i$ is the reconstruction obtained by the AE for the ith transaction of the sequence and $abs(t)$ returns a vector where the features are the absolute values of the original input vector t.

So, we train the parameters (ϕ_1, θ_1) of the first autoencoder by minimizing the following loss function over all the fraudulent sequences of the training samples:

$$\mathcal{L}_1(x, \phi_1, \theta_1) = \mathcal{L}_{rec}(x, \phi_1, \theta_1) + \lambda \mathcal{L}_{trx}(x, \phi_1, \theta_1), \qquad (8)$$

where λ is a tradeoff parameter.

The second autoencoder is then trained over all the training sequences by negative learning. It takes as input both a sequence x and its reconstructed version from the first autoencoder $AE_1(x)$ that corresponds to the output of its last layer. The loss function considered to optimize the parameters (ϕ_2, θ_2) of the second autoencoder is then defined as follows:

$$\mathcal{L}_2(x, AE_1(x), \phi_2, \theta_2) = (1 - y)\mathcal{L}_1(x, \phi_2, \theta_2)$$
$$-y(\overline{\mathcal{L}_1}(x, \phi_1, \theta_1) + \epsilon)\log_2(1 - e^{-\mathcal{L}_1(x, \phi_2, \theta_2)}), \quad (9)$$

where $\overline{\mathcal{L}_1}(x, \phi_1, \theta_1)$ denotes the reconstruction loss $\mathcal{L}_1$ rescaled in the $[0, 1]$-interval with respect to all fraudulent sequences and ϵ is a small value used to smooth very low anomaly scores. The architecture of this second autoencoder is similar to that of the first one, except that we use a MoE layer to compute the mean of the normal distribution $\mathcal{N}(\mu_2, \sigma_2)$ defined by the encoder. As said previously, the objective is to take into account the variety of the different behavior patterns found in our genuine data. The experts used in that layer are simple one-layer feed-forward neural networks.

3.2 The Training Strategy

The global learning algorithm is presented in Algorithm 1. We have two training phases, the first one focuses on training the first autoencoder AE_1 as a backing model for the second phase. It is trained only on fraudulent sequences by minimizing Eq. 8. Once the model has converged, we freeze its weights and start the second phase. For training the second autoencoder AE_2, we use both genuine and fraudulent sequences and their reconstructed versions given by AE_1. We then optimize the weights of AE_2 by minimizing Eq. 9. To control the imbalance ratio, the training is done at each iteration by sampling n examples from fraudulent sequences and n from genuine sequences. We repeat this step iteratively by increasing the number n of sampled transactions for each novel iteration until the model converges.

Algorithm 1. Dual sequential variational autoencoder (DuSVAE)

1: **Input:** $\mathcal{X}_g$ genuine data, $\mathcal{X}_f$ fraudulent data.
2: **Parameters:** n number of sampled examples; h increment step.
3: **Output:** AE_1 Autoencoder, AE_2 Autoencoder.
4: **repeat**
5:     Train AE_1 on $\mathcal{X}_f$ by minimizing Equation 8
6: **until** convergence
7: Freeze the weights of AE_1
8: **repeat**
9:     $\mathcal{X}_1 \leftarrow Sample(\mathcal{X}_f, n) \cup Sample(\mathcal{X}_g, n)$
10:     $\mathcal{X}_2 \leftarrow AE_1(\mathcal{X}_1)$
11:     Train AE_2 on $(\mathcal{X}_1, \mathcal{X}_2)$ by minimizing Equation 9
12:     **if** $n \leq |\mathcal{X}_f|$ **then**
13:         $n \leftarrow n + h$
14:     **end if**
15: **until** convergence

Table 1. Properties of the Worldline dataset used in the experiments.

	Train (01/01-21/03)	Validation (22/03-31/03)	Test (01/04-30/04)
# of genuine	25,120,194	3,019,078	9,287,673
# of fraud	88,878	9,631	29,614
Total	25,209,072	3,028,709	9,317,287
Imbalance ratio	0.003526	0.00318	0.003178

4 Experiments

In this section, we provide an experimental evaluation of our approach on a real-world dataset of credit card e-payment transactions provided by Worldline. First, we present the dataset, then we present the metrics used to evaluate the models learned by our system and finally, we compare DuSVAE with other state-of-the-art approaches.

4.1 Dataset

The dataset provided by Wordline covers 4 months of credit card e-payment transactions made by European cardholders in e-commerce mode that has been splitted into **Train**, **Validation** and **Test** sets used respectively to train, tune and test the learned models. Its main challenges have been studied in [2], one of them being the imbalance ratio as we can see on Table 1 that presents the main characteristics of this dataset.

Each transaction is described by 12 features. A Boolean value is assigned to each transaction to specify whether it corresponds to a fraud or not. This labeling is handled by a team of human experts.

Since most features have a large number of values, using brute one-hot encoding would generate a huge number of features. For example the "Merchant Category Code" feature has 283 possible values and one-hot encoding would produce 283 new features. That would make our approach inefficient. Thus, before using one-hot encoding, we transform each categorical value of each feature by a score which is its risk to be associated with a fraudulent transaction. Let's consider for example a categorical feature f. We can compute the probability of the jth value of feature f to be associated with a fraudulent transaction, denoted as β_j, as follows: $\beta_j = \frac{N^+_{f=j}}{N_{f=j}}$, where $N^+_{f=j}$ is the number of fraudulent transactions where the value of feature f is equal to j and $N_{f=j}$ is the total number of transactions where the value of feature f is equal to j. In order to take into account the number of transactions related to a particular value of a given feature, we follow [14]. For each value j of a given feature, the fraud score S_j for this value is defined as follows:

$$S_j = \alpha'_j \beta_j + \left(1 - \alpha'_j\right) \text{AFP} \tag{10}$$

This score computes a weighted value of β_j and the probability of having a fraud in a day (Average Fraud Probability: AFP). The weight α'_j is a normalized value of α_j in the range $[0, 1]$, where α_j is defined as the proportion of the number of transactions for that value on the total number N of transactions: $\alpha_j = \frac{N_{f=j}}{N}$.

Having replaced each value for each feature by its score, we can then run one-hot encoding and thus significantly reduce the number of features generated. For example, the "Merchant Category Code" feature has 283 possible values and instead of generating 283 features, this technique produces only 29 features.

Finally, to generate sequences from transactions, we grouped all the transactions by cardholder ID and we ordered each cardholder's transactions by time. Then, with a sliding window over the transactions we obtained a time-ordered sequence of transactions for each cardholder. For each sequence, we have assigned the label *fraudulent* or *genuine* of its last transaction.

4.2 Metrics

In the context of fraud detection, fortunately, the number of fraudulent transactions is significantly lower than the number of normal transactions. This leads to a very imbalanced dataset. In this situation, the traditional performance measures are not appropriate. Indeed, with an overall fraud rate of 0.3%, classifying each transaction as normal leads to an accuracy of 99.7%, despite the fact that the model is absolutely naive. That means we have to choose appropriate performance measures that are robust in the case of imbalanced data. In this work we rely on the area under the precision-recall curve (AUC-PR) as a robust and clear measure of the accuracy of the classifier in an imbalanced setting. Each point of the precision-recall curve corresponds to the precision of the classifier at a specific recall level.

Once an alert is raised after a fraud has been detected, fraud experts can contact the card-holder to check the validity of suspicious transactions. So, within a single day, the fraud experts have to check a large number of transactions provided by the fraud detection system. Consequently, the precision of the transactions highlighted as fraud is an important metric because that can help human experts at Worldline to focus on the most important frauds and leave aside minor frauds due to lack of time to process them. For this purpose, we rely on the $P_{@K}$ as a global metric to compare models. It is the average of the precision of the first K transactions which are calculated according to the following equation.

$$\text{Average} P_{@K} = \frac{1}{K} \sum_{i=1}^{K} P_{@i} \tag{11}$$

4.3 Comparison with the State of the Art

We compare our approach with the following methods: variational autoencoder [11,16] trained on fraudulent or genuine data only (VAE(F) or VAE(G) respectively); limiting reconstruction capability (LRC) [13] and autoencoding binary classifiers for supervised anomaly detection (ABC) [18]. It is important to note

Table 2. AUC-PR achieved by CatBoost using various autoencoder models

Models	Raw		Reconstructed		Reconstruction error	Code1	Code2
	Trx	Seq	Trx	Seq			
VAE (F)	0.19	0.40	0.36	0.38	0.29	0.30	0.27
VAE (G)			0.42	0.43	0.31	0.32	0.33
LRC			0.46	0.46	0.17	0.28	0.13
ABC			0.48	0.50	**0.37**	0.32	0.3
DuSVAE			**0.51**	**0.53**	0.36	**0.50**	**0.49**

that ABC and LRC are not sequential models by nature. So, to make our comparison more fair, we adapted their implementation to allow them to process sequential data. As a classifier, we used CatBoost [15] which is robust in the context of imbalanced data and efficient on GPUs.

First, as we can observe in Table 2, the AUC-PR values obtained by running CatBoost directly on transactions and sequences of transactions are respectively equal to 0.19 and 0.40. If we look at the AUC-PR values obtained by running CatBoost on the reconstructed transactions and sequences of transactions, we can observe that the results are always greater than those obtained by running CatBoost on raw data. Moreover it is interesting to note that DuSVAE achieved the best results (0.51 and 0.53) compared to other state-of-the-art systems.

Now, if we look at the performance obtained by CatBoost on the hidden representation vectors Code1 and Code2, we observe that DuSVAE outperforms the results obtained by other state-of-the-art systems and those results are quite similar to the ones obtained on the reconstructed sequences of transactions. This is interesting because it means that using DuSVAE a condensed representation of the input data can be obtained, which still gives approximately the same results as on the reconstructed sequences of transactions but that are of higher dimensionality (about 10 times more) and can be less efficiently processed by the classifier. Finally, when using the reconstruction error as a score to classify fraudulent data, as done usually in anomaly detection, we can observe that DuSVAE is competitive with the best method. However, the performance level of Code1 and Code2 with CatBoost being significantly better makes the use of the hidden representations a better strategy than using the reconstruction error.

We then evaluated the impact of handcrafted features built by Worldline on the classifier performance. As we can see on the first two lines of Table 3, adding handcrafted features to the original sequential raw dataset leads to much better results both from the point of view of AUC-PR measure and P@K measure.

Now if we consider using DuSVAE (rows 3 and 4 of Table 3), we can also notice a significant improvement of the results obtained on the raw dataset of sequences augmented by handcrafted features compared to the results obtained on the original one without these additional features. This is observed for both the AUC-PR measure and the P@K measure. We see that, for the moment, by using a classifier on the sequences reconstructed by DuSVAE on just the

Table 3. AUC-PR and P@K achieved by CatBoost for sequence classification.

Input	AUC-PR	P@100	P@500
Raw data	0,40	0.43	0.11
Raw data + Handcrafted features	0,60	0.62	0.938
DuSVAE (The input:raw data)	0,53	0.88	0.72
DuSVAE (The input: raw data + Handcrafted features)	0,65	0.85	0.941

raw dataset (AUC-PR = 0.53), we cannot reach the results obtained when we use this classifier on the raw dataset augmented by handcrafted features (AUC-PR = 0.60). This can be explained by the fact that those features are based on history and profiling techniques that embed information covering a period of time larger than the one used for our dataset. Nevertheless we are not so far and the fact that using DuSVAE on the dataset augmented by handcrafted features (AUC-PR = 0.65) leads to better results than using the classifier without DuSVAE (AUC-PR = 0.60) is promising.

Table 3 also shows that the very good P@K values obtained when running the classifier on the sequences of transactions reconstructed by DuSVAE mean that DuSVAE can be a very significant help for experts to focus on real fraudulent transactions and not waste time on fake ones.

5 Conclusion

In this paper, we presented the DuSVAE model which is a new fraud detection technique. Our model combines two sequential variational autoencoders to produce a condensed representation vector of the input sequential data that can then be used by a classifier to label new sequences of transactions as genuine or fraudulent. Our experiments have shown that the DuSVAE model produces much better results, in terms of AUC-PR and $P_{@K}$ measures, than state-of-the-art systems. Moreover, the DuSVAE model produces a condensed representation of the input data which can replace very favorably the handcrafted features. Indeed, running a classifier on the condensed representation of the input data built by the DuSVAE model leads to outperform the results obtained on the raw data, with or without handcrafted features.

We believe that a first interesting way to further improve our results will be to focus on attention mechanisms to better take into account the history of past transactions in the detection of present frauds. A second approach will be to better take into account the temporal aspects in the sequential representation of our data and to reflect it in the core algorithm.

References

1. Abdallah, A., Maarof, M.A., Zainal, A.: Fraud detection system: a survey. J. Netw. Comput. Appl. **68**, 90–113 (2016)
2. Alazizi, A., Habrard, A., Jacquenet, F., He-Guelton, L., Oblé, F., Siblini, W.: Anomaly detection, consider your dataset first, an illustration on fraud detection. In: Proceedings of ICTAI 2019. IEEE (2019)
3. Bahnsen, A.C., Aouada, D., Stojanovic, A., Ottersten, B.: Feature engineering strategies for credit card fraud detection. Expert Syst. Appl. **51**, 134–142 (2016)
4. Chandola, V., Banerjee, A., Kumar, V.: Anomaly detection: a survey. ACM Comput. Surv. **41**(3), 15:1–15:58 (2009)
5. Golan, I., El-Yaniv, R.: Deep anomaly detection using geometric transformations. In: Proceedings of NIPS, pp. 9758–9769 (2018)
6. Hasan, M., Choi, J., Neumann, J., Roy-Chowdhury, A.K., Davis, L.S.: Learning temporal regularity in video sequences. In: Proceedings of CVPR, pp. 733–742 (2016)
7. Hinton, G.E.: Connectionist learning procedures. Artif. Intell. **40**(1–3), 185–234 (1989)
8. Jacobs, R.A., Jordan, M.I., Nowlan, S.J., Hinton, G.E., et al.: Adaptive mixtures of local experts. Neural Comput. **3**(1), 79–87 (1991)
9. Jurgovsky, J., et al.: Sequence classification for credit-card fraud detection. Expert Syst. Appl. **100**, 234–245 (2018)
10. Kingma, D.P., Ba, J.: Adam: a method for stochastic optimization. arXiv:1412.6980 (2014)
11. Kingma, D.P., Welling, M.: Auto-encoding variational bayes. In: Proceedings of ICLR (2014)
12. Lucas, Y., et al.: Towards automated feature engineering for credit card fraud detection using multi-perspective HMMs. Future Gener. Comput. Syst. **102**, 393–402 (2020)
13. Munawar, A., Vinayavekhin, P., De Magistris, G.: Limiting the reconstruction capability of generative neural network using negative learning. In: Proceedings of the International Workshop on Machine Learning for Signal Processing, pp. 1–6 (2017)
14. Pozzolo, A.D.: Adaptive machine learning for credit card fraud detection. Ph.D. thesis, Université libre de Bruxelles (2015)
15. Prokhorenkova, L., Gusev, G., Vorobev, A., Dorogush, A.V., Gulin, A.: Catboost: unbiased boosting with categorical features. In: Proceedings of NIPS, pp. 6638–6648 (2018)
16. Rezende, D.J., Mohamed, S., Wierstra, D.: Stochastic backpropagation and approximate inference in deep generative models. arXiv:1401.4082 (2014)
17. Sabokrou, M., Khalooei, M., Fathy, M., Adeli, E.: Adversarially learned one-class classifier for novelty detection. In: Proceedings of CVPR, pp. 3379–3388 (2018)
18. Yamanaka, Y., Iwata, T., Takahashi, H., Yamada, M., Kanai, S.: Autoencoding binary classifiers for supervised anomaly detection. arXiv:1903.10709 (2019)
19. Zhai, S., Cheng, Y., Lu, W., Zhang, Z.: Deep structured energy based models for anomaly detection. arXiv:1605.07717 (2016)
20. Zhao, Y., Deng, B., Shen, C., Liu, Y., Lu, H., Hua, X.S.: Spatio-temporal autoencoder for video anomaly detection. In: Proceedings of the ACM International Conference on Multimedia, pp. 1933–1941 (2017)

21. Zimek, A., Schubert, E., Kriegel, H.P.: A survey on unsupervised outlier detection in high-dimensional numerical data. Stat. Anal. Data Mining: ASA Data Sci. J. **5**(5), 363–387 (2012)
22. Zong, B., et al.: Deep autoencoding gaussian mixture model for unsupervised anomaly detection. In: Proceedings of ICLR (2018)

13

AVATAR - Machine Learning Pipeline Evaluation using Surrogate Model

Tien-Dung Nguyen[1(✉)], Tomasz Maszczyk[1], Katarzyna Musial[1], Marc-André Zöller[2], and Bogdan Gabrys[1]

[1] University of Technology Sydney, Sydney, Australia
TienDung.Nguyen-2@student.uts.edu.au,
{Tomasz.Maszczyk,Katarzyna.Musial-Gabrys,Bogdan.Gabrys}@uts.edu.au
[2] USU Software AG, Karlsruhe, Germany
m.zoeller@usu.de

Abstract. The evaluation of machine learning (ML) pipelines is essential during automatic ML pipeline composition and optimisation. The previous methods such as Bayesian-based and genetic-based optimisation, which are implemented in Auto-Weka, Auto-sklearn and TPOT, evaluate pipelines by executing them. Therefore, the pipeline composition and optimisation of these methods requires a tremendous amount of time that prevents them from exploring complex pipelines to find better predictive models. To further explore this research challenge, we have conducted experiments showing that many of the generated pipelines are invalid, and it is unnecessary to execute them to find out whether they are good pipelines. To address this issue, we propose a novel method to evaluate the validity of ML pipelines using a surrogate model (AVATAR). The AVATAR enables to accelerate automatic ML pipeline composition and optimisation by quickly ignoring invalid pipelines. Our experiments show that the AVATAR is more efficient in evaluating complex pipelines in comparison with the traditional evaluation approaches requiring their execution.

1 Introduction

Automatic machine learning (AutoML) has been studied to automate the process of data analytics to collect and integrate data, compose and optimise ML pipelines, and deploy and maintain predictive models [1–3]. Although many existing studies proposed methods to tackle the problem of pipeline composition and optimisation [2,4–9], these methods have two main drawbacks. Firstly, the pipelines' structures, which define the executed order of the pipeline components, use fixed templates [2,5]. Although using fixed structures can reduce the number of invalid pipelines during the composition and optimisation, these approaches limit the exploration of promising pipelines which may have a variety of structures. Secondly, while evolutionary algorithms based methods [4] enable the randomness of the pipelines' structure using the concept of evolution, this randomness tends to construct more invalid pipelines than valid ones.

Besides, the search spaces of the pipelines' structures and hyperparameters of the pipelines' components expand significantly. Therefore, the existing approaches tend to be inefficient as they often attempt to evaluate invalid pipelines. There are several attempts to reduce the randomness of pipeline construction by using context-free grammars [8,9] or AI planning to guide the construction of pipelines [6,7]. Nevertheless, all of these methods evaluate the validity of a pipeline by executing them (T-method). After executing a pipeline, if the result is a predictive model, the T-method evaluates the pipeline to be valid; otherwise it is invalid. If a pipeline is complex, the complexity of preprocessing/predictor components within the pipeline is high, or the size of the dataset is large, the evaluation of the pipeline is expensive. Consequently, the optimisation will require a significant time budget to find well-performing pipelines.

To address this issue, we propose the AVATAR to evaluate ML pipelines using their surrogate models. The AVATAR transforms a pipeline to its surrogate model and evaluates it instead of executing the original pipeline. We use the business process model and notation (BPMN) [10] to represent ML pipelines. BPMN was invented for the purposes of a graphical representation of business processes, as well as a description of resources for process execution. In addition, BPMN simplifies the understanding of business activities and interpretation of behaviours of ML pipelines. The ML pipelines' components use the Weka libraries[1] for ML algorithms. The evaluation of the surrogate models requires a knowledge base which is generated from many synthetic datasets. To this end, this paper has two main contributions:

- We conduct experiments on current state-of-the-art AutoML tools to show that the construction of invalid pipelines during the pipeline composition and optimisation may lead to bad performance.
- We propose the AVATAR to accelerate the automatic pipeline composition and optimisation by evaluating pipelines using a surrogate model.

This paper is divided into five sections. After the Introduction, Sect. 2 reviews previous approaches to representing and evaluating ML pipelines in the context of AutoML. Section 3 presents the AVATAR to evaluate ML pipelines. Section 4 presents experiments to motivate our research and prove the efficiency of the proposed method. Finally, Sect. 5 concludes this study.

2   Related Work

Salvador et al. [2] proposed an automatic pipeline composition and optimisation method of multicomponent predictive systems (MCPS) to deal with the problem of combined algorithm selection and hyperparameter optimisation (CASH). This proposed method is implemented in the tool AutoWeka4MCPS [2] developed on top of Auto-Weka 0.5 [11]. The pipelines, which are generated by

---

[1] https://www.cs.waikato.ac.nz/ml/weka/.

AutoWeka4MCPS, are represented using Petri nets [12]. A Petri net is a mathematical modelling language used to represent pipelines [2] as well as data service compositions [13]. The main idea of Petri nets is to represent transitions of states of a system. Although it is not clearly mentioned in these previous works [4–7], directed acyclic graph (DAG) is often used to model sequential pipelines in the methods/tools such as AutoWeka4MCPS [14], ML-Plan [6], P4ML [7], TPOT [4] and Auto-sklearn [5]. DAG is a type of graph that has connected vertexes, and the connections of vertexes have only one direction [15]. In addition, a DAG does not allow any directed loop. It means that it is a topological ordering. ML-Plan generates sequential workflows consisting of ML components. Thus, the workflows are a type of DAG. The final output of P4ML is a pipeline which is constructed by making an ensemble of other pipelines. Auto-sklearn generates fixed-length sequential pipelines consisting of scikit-learn components. TPOT construct pipelines consisting of multiple preprocessing sub-pipelines. The authors claim that the representation of the pipelines is a tree-based structure. However, a tree-based structure always starts with a root node and ends with many leaf nodes, but the output of a TPOT's pipeline is a single predictive model. Therefore, the representation of TPOT pipeline is more like a DAG. P4ML uses a tree-based structure to make a multi-layer ensemble. This tree-based structure can be specialised into a DAG. The reason is that the execution of these pipelines will start from leaf nodes and end at root nodes where the construction of the ensembles are completed. It means that the control flows of these pipelines have one direction, or they are topologically ordered. Using a DAG to model an ML pipeline makes it easy to understand by humans as DAGs facilitate visualisation and interpretation of the control flow. However, DAGs do not model inputs/outputs (i.e. possibly datasets, output predictive models, parameters and hyperparameters of components) between vertexes. Therefore, the existing studies use ad-hoc approaches and make assumptions about data inputs/outputs of the pipelines' components.

Although AutoWeka4MCPS, ML-Plan, P4ML, TPOT and Auto-sklearn evaluate pipelines by executing them, these methods have strategies to limit the generation of invalid pipelines. Auto-sklearn uses a fixed pipeline template including preprocessing, predictor and ensemble components. AutoWeka4MCPS also uses a fixed pipeline template consisting of six components. TPOT, ML-Plan and P4ML use grammars/primitive catalogues, which are designed manually, to guide the construction of pipelines. Although these approaches can reduce the number of invalid pipelines, our experiments showed that the wasted time used to evaluate the invalid pipelines is significant. Moreover, using fixed templates, grammars and primitive catalogues reduce search spaces of potential pipelines, which is a drawback during pipeline composition and optimisation.

3 Evaluation of ML Pipelines Using Surrogate Models

Because the evaluation of ML pipelines is expensive in certain cases (i.e., complex pipelines, high complexity pipeline's components and large datasets) in the context of AutoML, we propose the AVATAR[2] to speed up the process by evaluating their surrogate pipelines. The main idea of the AVATAR is to expand the purpose and representation of MCPS introduced in [12]. The AVATAR uses a surrogate model in the form of a Petri net. This surrogate pipeline keeps the structure of the original pipeline, replaces the datasets in the form of data matrices (i.e., components' input/output simplified mappings) by the matrices of transformed-features, and the ML algorithms by transition functions to calculate the output from the input tokens (i.e., the matrices of transformed-features). Because of the simplicity of the surrogate pipelines in terms of the size of the tokens and the simplicity of the transition functions, the evaluation of these pipelines is substantially less expensive than the original ones.

3.1   The AVATAR Knowledge Base

We define transformed-features as the features, which represent dataset's characteristics. These characteristics can be changed because of the transformations of this dataset by ML algorithms. Table 1 describes the transformed-features used

Table 1. Descriptions of the transformed-features of a dataset.

Transformed-feature	Description
BINARY_CLASS	A dataset has binary classes
NUMERIC_CLASS	A dataset has numeric classes
DATE_CLASS	A dataset has date classes
MISSING_CLASS_VALUES	A dataset has missing values in classes
NOMINAL_CLASS	A dataset has nominal classes
SYMBOLIC_CLASS	A dataset has symbolic data in classes
STRING_CLASS	A dataset has string classes
UNARY_CLASS	A dataset has unary classes
BINARY_ATTRIBUTES	A dataset has binary attributes
DATE_ATTRIBUTES	A dataset has date attributes
EMPTY_NOMINAL_ATTRIBUTES	A dataset has an empty column
MISSING_VALUES	A dataset has missing values in attributes
NOMINAL_ATTRIBUTES	A dataset has nominal attributes
NUMERIC_ATTRIBUTES	A dataset has numeric attributes
UNARY_ATTRIBUTES	A dataset has unary attributes
PREDICTIVE_MODEL	A predictive model generated by a predictor

---

[2] https://github.com/UTS-AAi/AVATAR.

for the knowledge base. We select these transformed-features because the capabilities of a ML algorithm to work with a dataset depend on these transformed-features. These transformed-features are extended from the capabilities of Weka algorithms[3].

The purpose of the AVATAR knowledge base is for describing the logic of transition functions of the surrogate pipelines. The logic includes the capabilities and effects of ML algorithms (i.e., pipeline components).

The capabilities are used to verify whether an algorithm is compatible to work with a dataset or not. For example, whether the linear regression algorithm can work with missing value and numeric attributes or not? The capabilities have a list of transformed-features. The value of each capability-related transformed-feature is either 0 (i.e., the algorithm can not work with the dataset which has this transformed-feature) or 1 (i.e., the algorithm can work with the dataset which has this transformed-feature). Based on the capabilities, we can determine which components of a pipeline (i.e., ML algorithms) are not able to process specific transformed-features of a dataset.

The effects describe data transformations. Similar to the capabilities, the effects have a list of transformed-features. Each effect-related transformed-feature can have three values, 0 (i.e., do not transform this transformed-feature), 1 (i.e., transform one or more attributes/classes to this transformed-feature), or −1 (i.e., disable the effect of this transformed-feature on one or more attributes/classes).

To generate the AVATAR knowledge base[4], we have to use synthetic datasets[5] to minimise the number of active transformed-features in each dataset to evaluate which and how transformed-features impact on the capabilities and effects of ML algorithms[6]. Real-world datasets usually have many active transformed-features that make them not suitable for our purpose. We minimise the number of available transformed-features in each synthetic dataset so that the knowledge base can be applicable in a variety of pipelines and datasets. Figure 1 presents the algorithm to generate the AVATAR knowledge base. This algorithm has four main stages:

1. Initialisation: The first stage initialises all transformed-features in the capabilities and effects to 0.
2. Execution: Run ML algorithms with every synthetic dataset and get outputs (i.e., output datasets or predictive models).
3. Find capabilities: If the execution is successful, we set the active transformed-features of the input dataset for the ones in the capabilities.
4. Find effects: If an algorithm is a predictor/transformed-predictor, we set *PREDICTIVE_MODEL* for its effects. If the algorithm is a filter and its

---

[3] http://weka.sourceforge.net/doc.dev/weka/core/Capabilities.html.

[4] https://github.com/UTS-AAi/AVATAR/blob/master/avatar-knowledge-base/avatar_knowledge_base.json.

[5] https://github.com/UTS-AAi/AVATAR/tree/master/synthetic-datasets.

[6] https://github.com/UTS-AAi/AVATAR/blob/master/supplementary-documents/avatar_algorithms.txt.

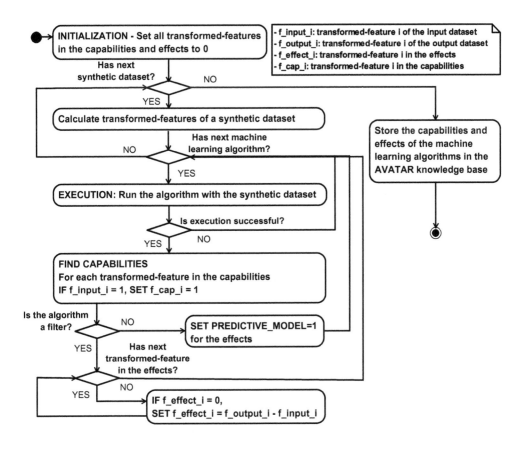

Fig. 1. Algorithm to generate the knowledge base for evaluating surrogate pipelines.

current value is a default value, we set this effect-related transformed-feature equal the difference of the values of this transformed-feature of the output and input dataset.

3.2 Evaluation of ML Pipelines

The AVATAR evaluates a ML pipeline by mapping it to its surrogate pipeline and evaluating this surrogate pipeline. BPMN is the most promising method to represent an ML pipeline. The reasons are that a BPMN-based ML pipeline can be executable, has a better interpretation of the pipeline in terms of control, data flows and resources for execution, as well as integrates into existing business processes as a subprocess. Moreover, we claim that a Petri net is the most promising method to represent a surrogate pipeline. The reason is that it is fast to verify the validity of a Petri net based simplified ML pipeline.

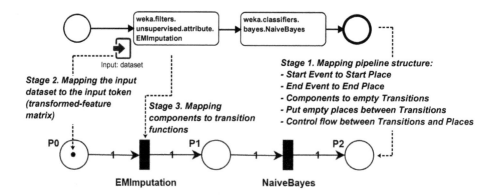

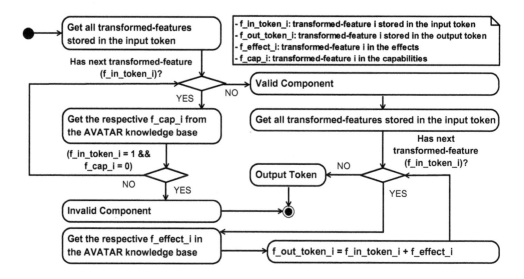

Fig. 2. Mapping a ML pipeline to its surrogate model.

Mapping a ML Pipeline to Its Surrogate Model. The AVATAR maps a BPMN pipeline to a Petri net pipeline via three stages (Fig. 2).

1. The structure of the BPMN-based ML pipeline is mapped to the respective structure of the Petri net surrogate pipeline. The start and end events are mapped to the start and end places respectively. The components are mapped to empty transitions. Empty places are put between all transitions. Finally, all flows are mapped to arcs.
2. The values of transformed-features are calculated from the input dataset to form a transformed-feature matrix which is the input token in the start place of the surrogate pipeline.
3. The transition functions are mapped from the components. In this stage, only the corresponding algorithm information is mapped to the transition function.

Fig. 3. Algorithm for firing a transition of the surrogate model.

Evaluating a Surrogate Model. The evaluation of a surrogate model will execute a Petri net pipeline. This execution starts by firing each transition of the Petri net pipeline and transforming the input token. As shown in Fig. 3, firing a transition consists of two tasks: (i) the evaluation of the capabilities of each component; and (ii) the calculation of the output token. The first task verifies the validity of the component using the following rules. If the value of a transformed-feature stored in the input token ($f\_in\_token\_i$) is 1 and the corresponding transformed-feature in the component's capabilities (f_cap_i) is 0, this component is invalid. Otherwise, this component is always valid. If a component is invalid, the surrogate pipeline is evaluated as invalid. The second task calculates each transformed-feature stored in the output token ($f\_out\_token\_i$) in the next place from the input token by adding the value of a transformed-feature stored in the input token ($f\_in\_token\_i$) and the respective transformed-feature in the component's effects (f_effect_i).

4   Experiments

To investigate the impact of invalid pipelines on ML pipeline composition and optimisation, we have first conducted a series of experiments with current state-of-the-art AutoML tools. After that, we have conducted the experiments to compare the performance of the AVATAR and the existing methods.

4.1   Experimental Settings

Table 2 summarises characteristics of datasets[7] used for experiments. We use these datasets because they were used in previous studies [2,4,5]. The AutoML tools used for the experiments are AutoWeka4MCPS [2] and Auto-sklearn [5]. These tools are selected because their abilities to construct and optimise hyperparameters of complex ML pipelines have been empirically proven to be effective in a number of previous studies [2,5,16]. However, these previous experiments

Table 2. Summary of datasets' characteristics: the number of numeric attributes, nominal attributes, distinct classes, instances in training and testing sets.

Dataset	Numeric	Nominal	No. of distinct classes	Training	Testing
abalone	7	1	26	2,924	1,253
car	0	6	4	1,210	518
convex	784	0	2	8,000	50,000
gcredit	7	13	2	700	300
wineqw	11	0	7	3,429	1,469

---

[7] https://archive.ics.uci.edu.

had not investigated the negative impact of the evaluation of invalid pipelines on the quality of the pipeline composition and optimisation yet. This is the goal of our first set of experiments. In the second set of experiments, we show that the AVATAR can significantly reduce the evaluation time of ML pipelines.

4.2 Experiments to Investigate the Impact of Invalid Pipelines

To investigate the impact of invalid pipelines, we use five iterations (Iter) for the first set of experiments. We run these experiments on AWS EC2 $t3a.small$ virtual machines which have 2 vCPU and 2 GB memory. Each iteration uses a different seed number. We set the time budget to 1 h and the memory to 1 GB. We evaluate the pipelines produced by the AutoML tools using three criteria: (1) the number of invalid/valid pipelines, (2) the total evaluation time of invalid/valid pipelines (seconds), and (3) the wasted evaluation time (%). The wasted evaluation time is calculated by the percentage of the total evaluation time of invalid pipelines over the total runtime of the pipeline composition and optimisation. The wasted evaluation time represents the degree of negative impacts of invalid pipelines.

Tables 3 and 4 present negative impacts of invalid pipelines in ML pipeline composition and optimisation of AutoWeka4MCPS and Auto-sklearn using the above criteria. These tables show that not all of constructed pipelines are valid. Because AutoWeka4MCPS can compose pipelines which have up to six components, it is more likely to generate invalid pipelines and the evaluation time

Table 3. Negative impacts of invalid pipelines in pipeline composition and optimisation of AutoWeka4MCPS. (1): the number of invalid/valid pipelines, (2): the total evaluation time of invalid/valid pipelines (s), (3): the wasted evaluation time (%).

Dataset	Criteria	Iter 1	Iter 2	Iter 3	Iter 4	Iter 5
abalone	(1)	16/26	90/79	69/88	34/29	53/80
	(2)	3607.7/1322.5	2007.1/1236.4	4512.9/2172.3	3615.4/277.6	23.2/3509.0
	(3)	73.18	61.88	67.51	92.87	0.66
car	(1)	205/152	108/70	197/313	139/156	85/64
	(2)	3818.1/291.8	3498.5/113.0	4523.6/532.6	5232.2/251.3	4365.1/90.1
	(3)	92.90	96.87	89.47	95.42	97.98
convex	(1)	18/20	2/0	17/11	crashed	crashed
	(2)	76.3/3588.1	3475.2/0.0	1324.7/2331.8		
	(3)	2.08	100.00	36.23		
gcredit	(1)	112/195	229/364	208/166	12/54	30/54
	(2)	2821.0/2260.1	3829.8/285.6	3933.8/184.0	3667.6/34.1	3634.8/64.7
	(3)	55.52	93.06	95.53	99.08	98.25
wineqw	(1)	203/213	121/139	crashed	201/302	36/54
	(2)	4880.6/1052.9	4183.4/1078.6		2418.5/1132.2	1639.2/862.2
	(3)	82.26	79.50		68.11	65.53

Table 4. Negative impacts of invalid pipelines in pipeline composition and optimisation of Auto-sklearn. (1): the number of invalid/valid pipelines, (2): the total evaluation time of invalid/valid pipelines (s), (3): the wasted evaluation time (%).

Dataset	Criteria	Iter 1	Iter 2	Iter 3	Iter 4	Iter 5
abalone		crashed	crashed	crashed	crashed	crashed
car		crashed	crashed	crashed	crashed	crashed
convex	(1)	2/13	2/6	2/8	2/6	2/8
	(2)	560.8/2981.8	537.7/629.2	584.1/1537.5	558.1/977.1	560.0/1655.9
	(3)	15.76	15.07	16.39	15.66	15.72
gcredit		crashed	crashed	crashed	crashed	crashed
wineqw	(1)	0/42	0/22	0/42	0/32	0/32
	(2)	0.0/3523.4	0.0/909.7	0.0/3197.4	0.0/3054.0	0.0/3163.5
	(3)	0.00	0.00	0.00	0.00	0.00

of these invalid pipelines are significant. For example, the wasted evaluation time is 97.98% in the case of using the dataset car and Iter 5. We can see that changing the different random iterations has a strong impact on the wasted evaluation time in the case of AutoWeka4MCPS. For example, the experiments with the dataset abalone show that the wasted evaluation time is in the range between 0.66% and 92.87%. The reason is that Weka libraries them-self can evaluate the compatibility of a single component pipeline without execution. If the initialisation of the pipeline composition and optimisation with a specific seed number results in pipelines consisting of only one predictor, and these pipelines are well-performing, it tends to exploit similar ML pipelines. As a result, the wasted evaluation time is low. However, this impact is negligible in the case of Auto-sklearn. The reason is that Auto-sklearn uses meta-learning to initialise with promising ML pipelines. The experiments with the datasets abalone, car and gcredit show that Auto-sklearn limits the generation of invalid pipelines by making assumption about cleaned input datasets, because the experiments crash if the input datasets have multiple attribute types. It means that Auto-sklearn can not handle invalid pipelines effectively.

4.3 Experiments to Compare the Performance of AVATAR and the Existing Methods

In order to demonstrate the efficiency of the AVATAR, we have conducted a second set of experiments. We run these experiments on a machine with an Intel core i7-8650U CPU and 16 GB memory. We compare the performance of the AVATAR and the T-method that requires the executions of pipelines. The T-method is used to evaluate the validity of pipelines in the pipeline composition and optimisation of AutoWeka4MCPS and Auto-sklearn. We randomly generate ML pipelines which have up to six components (i.e., these component types are missing value handling, dimensionality reduction, outlier removal, data transformation, data sampling and predictor). The predictor is put at the end

Table 5. Comparison of the performance of the AVATAR and T-method

Dataset		abalone	car	convex	gcredit	winequality
T-method	Invalid/valid pipelines	683/ 1,097	4,387/ 6,817	252/ 428	4,557/ 7,208	1,276/ 1,951
	Total evaluation time of invalid/valid pipelines (s)	27,711.9/ 15,484.1	18,627.9/ 24,459.4	5,818.3/ 37,765.1	19,597.9/ 23,452.5	10,830.1/ 32,326.9
AVATAR	Invalid/valid pipelines	663/ 1,117	4,387/ 6,817	250/ 430	4,552/ 7,213	1,262/ 1,965
	Total evaluation time of invalid/valid pipelines (s)	3.5/4.9	43.1/64.8	19.6/131.1	57.0/89.2	17.1/25.4
Pipelines have different/similar evaluated results		20/1,760	0/11,204	2/678	5/11,760	14/3,213
The percentage of pipelines that the AVATAR can validate accurately (%)		98.88	100.00	99.71	99.96	99.57

of the pipelines because a valid pipeline always has a predictor at the end. Each pipeline is evaluated by the AVATAR and the T-method. We set the time budget to 12 h per dataset. We use the following criteria to compare the performance: the number of invalid/valid pipelines, the total evaluation time of invalid/valid pipelines (seconds), the number of pipelines that have the same evaluated results between the AVATAR and the T-method, and the percentage of the pipelines that the AVATAR can validate accurately (%) in comparison to the T-method.

Table 5 compares the performance of the AVATAR and the T-method using the above criteria. We can see that the total evaluation time of invalid/valid pipelines of the AVATAR is significantly lower than the T-method. While the evaluation time of pipelines of the AVATAR is quite stable, the evaluation time of pipelines of the T-method is much higher and depends on the size of the datasets. It means that the AVATAR is faster than the T-method in evaluating both invalid and valid pipelines regardless of the size of datasets. Moreover, we can see that the accuracy of the AVATAR is approximately 99% in comparison with the T-method. We have carefully reviewed the pipelines which have different evaluated results between the AVATAR and the T-method. Interestingly, the AVATAR evaluates all of these pipelines to be valid and vice versa in the case of the T-method. The reason is that executions of these pipelines cause the out of memory problem. In other words, the AVATAR does not consider the allocated memory as an impact on the validity of a pipeline. A promising solution is to reduce the size of an input dataset by adding a sampling component with appropriate hyperparameters. If the sampling size is too small, we may miss important features. If the sampling size is large, we may continue to run into the problem of out of memory. We cannot conclude that if we allocate more memory, whether the executions of these pipelines would be successful or not. It proves that the validity of a pipeline also depends on its execution environment such as memory. These factors have not been considered yet in the AVATAR. This is an interesting research gap that should be addressed in the future.

Table 6. Five invalid pipelines with the longest evaluation time using the T-method on the gcredit dataset.

Pipeline	#1	#2	#3	#4	#5
T-method (s)	11.092	11.068	11.067	11.067	11.066
AVATAR (s)	0.014	0.012	0.011	0.011	0.011

Finally, we take a detailed look at the invalid pipelines with the longest evaluation time using the T-method on the gcredit dataset, as shown in Table 6. Pipeline #1 (11.092 s) has the structure *ReplaceMissingValues → PeriodicSampling → NumericToNominal → PrincipalComponents → SMOreg*. This pipeline is invalid because *SMOreg* does not work with nominal classes, and there is no component transforming the nominal to numeric data. We can see that the AVATAR is able to evaluate the validity of this pipeline without executing it in just 0.014 s.

5 Conclusion

We empirically demonstrate the problem of generation of invalid pipelines during pipeline composition and optimisation. We propose the AVATAR which is a pipeline evaluation method using a surrogate model. The AVATAR can be used to accelerate pipeline composition and optimisation methods by quickly ignoring invalid pipelines to improve the effectiveness of the AutoML optimisation process. In future, we will improve the AVATAR to evaluate pipelines' quality besides their validity. Moreover, we will investigate how to employ the AVATAR to reduce search spaces dynamically.

Acknowledgment. This research is sponsored by AAi, University of Technology Sydney (UTS).

References

1. Kadlec, P., Gabrys, B.: Architecture for development of adaptive on-line prediction models. Memetic Computing **1** (2009). https://doi.org/10.1007/s12293-009-0017-8. Article number. 241

2. Salvador, M.M., Budka, M., Gabrys, B.: Automatic composition and optimization of multicomponent predictive systems with an extended auto-WEKA. IEEE Trans. Autom. Sci. Eng. **16**(2), 946–959 (2019)
3. Zöller, M.A., Huber, M.F.: Survey on automated machine learning. arXiv preprint arXiv:1904.12054 (2019)
4. Olson, R.S., Moore, J.H.: TPOT: a tree-based pipeline optimization tool for automating machine learning. In: Workshop on Automatic Machine Learning, pp. 66–74 (2016)
5. Feurer, M., Klein, A., Eggensperger, K., Springenberg, J., Blum, M., Hutter, F.: Efficient and robust automated machine learning. In: Advances in Neural Information Processing Systems, pp. 2962–2970 (2015)
6. Mohr, F., Wever, M., Hüllermeier, E.: ML-Plan: automated machine learning via hierarchical planning. Mach. Learn. **107**, 1495–1515 (2018). https://doi.org/10.1007/s10994-018-5735-z
7. Gil, Y., et al.: P4ML: a phased performance-based pipeline planner for automated machine learning. In: AutoML Workshop at ICML (2018)
8. de Sá, A.G.C., Pinto, W.J.G.S., Oliveira, L.O.V.B., Pappa, G.L.: RECIPE: a grammar-based framework for automatically evolving classification pipelines. In: McDermott, J., Castelli, M., Sekanina, L., Haasdijk, E., García-Sánchez, P. (eds.) EuroGP 2017. LNCS, vol. 10196, pp. 246–261. Springer, Cham (2017). https://doi.org/10.1007/978-3-319-55696-3_16
9. Tsakonas, A., Gabrys, B.: GRADIENT: grammar-driven genetic programming framework for building multi-component, hierarchical predictive systems. Expert Syst. Appl. **39**, 13253–13266 (2012)
10. Chinosi, M., Trombetta, A.: Modeling and validating BPMN diagrams. In: 2009 IEEE Conference on Commerce and Enterprise Computing, pp. 353–360. IEEE (2009)
11. Thornton, C., Hutter, F., Hoos, H.H., Leyton-Brown, K.: Auto-WEKA: combined selection and hyperparameter optimization of classification algorithms. In: Proceedings of the 19th ACM SIGKDD International Conference on Knowledge Discovery and Data Mining, pp. 847–855. ACM (2013)
12. Salvador, M.M., Budka, M., Gabrys, B.: Modelling multi-component predictive systems as Petri nets (2017)
13. Tan, W., Fan, Y., Zhou, M., Tian, Z.: Data-driven service composition in enterprise SOA solutions: a Petri net approach. IEEE Trans. Autom. Sci. Eng. **7**, 686–694 (2010)
14. Martin Salvador, M., Budka, M., Gabrys, B.: Towards automatic composition of multicomponent predictive systems. In: Martínez-Álvarez, F., Troncoso, A., Quintián, H., Corchado, E. (eds.) HAIS 2016. LNCS (LNAI), vol. 9648, pp. 27–39. Springer, Cham (2016). https://doi.org/10.1007/978-3-319-32034-2_3
15. Barker, A., van Hemert, J.: Scientific workflow: a survey and research directions. In: Wyrzykowski, R., Dongarra, J., Karczewski, K., Wasniewski, J. (eds.) PPAM 2007. LNCS, vol. 4967, pp. 746–753. Springer, Heidelberg (2008). https://doi.org/10.1007/978-3-540-68111-3_78
16. Balaji, A., Allen, A.: Benchmarking automatic machine learning frameworks. arXiv preprint arXiv:1808.06492 (2018)

Multivariate Time Series as Images: Imputation using Convolutional Denoising Autoencoder

Abdullah Al Safi, Christian Beyer(✉), Vishnu Unnikrishnan, and Myra Spiliopoulou

Fakultät für Informatik, Otto-von-Guericke-Universität, Postfach 4120, 39106 Magdeburg, Germany
abdullah.safi@st.ovgu.de,
{christian.beyer,vishnu.unnikrishnan,myra}@ovgu.de

Abstract. Missing data is a common occurrence in the time series domain, for instance due to faulty sensors, server downtime or patients not attending their scheduled appointments. One of the best methods to impute these missing values is *Multiple Imputations by Chained Equations (MICE)* which has the drawback that it can only model linear relationships among the variables in a multivariate time series. The advancement of deep learning and its ability to model non-linear relationships among variables make it a promising candidate for time series imputation. This work proposes a modified Convolutional Denoising Autoencoder (CDA) based approach to impute multivariate time series data in combination with a preprocessing step that encodes time series data into 2D images using Gramian Angular Summation Field (GASF). We compare our approach against a standard feed-forward Multi Layer Perceptron (MLP) and MICE. All our experiments were performed on 5 UEA MTSC multivariate time series datasets, where 20 to 50% of the data was simulated to be missing completely at random. The CDA model outperforms all the other models in 4 out of 5 datasets and is tied for the best algorithm in the remaining case.

Keywords: Convolutional Denoising Autoencoder · Gramian Angular Summation Field · MICE · MLP. · Imputation · Time series

1 Introduction

Time series data resides in various domains of industries and research fields and is often corrupted with missing data. For further use or analysis, the data often needs to be complete, which gives the rise to the need for imputation techniques with enhanced capabilities of introducing least possible error into the data. One of the most prominent imputation methods is MICE which uses iterative regression and value replacement to achieve state-of-the-art imputation quality but has the drawback that it can only model linear relationships among variables (dimensions).

In past few years, different deep learning architectures were able to break into different problem domains, often exceeding previously achieved performances by other algorithms [7]. Areas like speech recognition, natural language processing, computer vision, etc. were greatly impacted and improved by deep learning architectures. Deep learning models have a robust capability of modelling latent representation of the data and non-linear patterns, given enough training data. Hence, this work presents a deep learning based imputation model called Convolutional Denoising Autoencoder (CDA) with altered convolution and pooling operations in Encoder and Decoder segments. Instead of using the traditional steps of convolution and pooling, we use deconvolution and upsampling which was inspired by [5]. The time series to image transformation mechanisms proposed in [12] and [13] were inherited as a preprocessing step as CDA models are typically designed for images. As rival imputation models, Multiple Imputation by Chained Equations (MICE) and a Multi Layer Perceptron (MLP) based imputation were incorporated.

2 Related Work

Three distinct types of missingness in data were identified in [8]. The first one is *Missing Completely At Random (MCAR)*, where the missingness of the data does not depend on itself or any other variables. In *Missing At Random (MAR)* the missing value depends on other variables but not on the variable where the data is actually missing and in *Missing Not At Random (MNAR)* the missingness of an observation depends on the concerned variable itself. All the experiments in this study were carried out on MCAR missingness as reproducing MAR and MNAR missingness can be challenging and hard to distinguish [5].

Multiple Imputation by Chained Equations (MICE) has secured its place as a principal method for imputing missing data [1]. Costa et al. in [3] experimented and showed that MICE offered the better imputation quality than a Denoising Autoencoder based model for several missing percentages and missing types.

A novel approach was proposed in [14], incorporating General Adversarial Networks (GAN) to perform imputations, thus authors named it Generative Adversarial Imputation Nets (GAIN). The approach imputed significantly well against some state-of-the-art imputation methods including MICE. An Autoencoder based approach was proposed in [4], which was compared against an Artificial Neural Network (NN) model on MCAR missing type and several missing percentages. The proposed model performed well against NN. A novel Denoising Autoencoder based imputation using partial loss (DAPL) approach was presented in [9], where different missing data percentages and MCAR missing type were simulated in a breast cancer dataset. The comparisons incorporated statistical, machine learning based approaches and standard Denoising Autoencoder (DAE) model where DAPL outperformed DAE and all the other models. An MLP based imputation approach was presented for MCAR missingness in [10] and also outperformed other statistical models. A Convolutional Denoising Autoencoder model which did not impute missing data but denoised audio signals was presented in [15]. A Denoising Autoencoder with more units in the encoder layer than input layer was presented in [5] and achieved good imputation results against MICE. Our work was inspired from both of these works which is why we combined the two approaches into a Convolutional Denoising Autoencoder which maps input data into a higher subspace in the Encoder.

3 Methodology

In this section we first describe how we introduce missing data in our datasets, then we show the process used to turn multivariate time series into images which is required by one of our imputation methods and finally we introduce the imputation methods which were compared in this study.

3.1 Simulating Missing Data

Simulating missing data is a mechanism of artificially introducing unobserved data into a complete time series dataset. Our experiment incorporated 20%, 30%, 40% and 50% of missing data and the missing type was MCAR. Introducing MCAR missingness is quite a simple approach as it does not depend on observed or unobserved data. Many studies assume MCAR missing type quite often when there is no concrete evidence of missingness type [6]. In this experimental framework, values at randomly selected indices were erased from randomly selected variables which simulated MCAR missingness of different percentages.

3.2 Translating Time Series into Images

A novel approach of encoding time series data into various types of images using Gramian Angular Field (GAF) was presented in [12] to improve classification and imputation. One of the variants of GAF was Gramian Angular Summation Field (GASF), which comprised of multiple steps to perform the encoding. First, the time series is scaled within $[-1, 1]$ range.

$$x_i' = \frac{(x_i - Max(X)) + (x_i - Min(X))}{Max(X) - Min(X)} \tag{1}$$

Here, x_i is a specific value at timepoint i where x_i' is derived by scaling and X is the time series. The time series is scaled within $[-1, 1]$ range in order to be represented as polar coordinates achieved by applying angular cosine.

$$\theta_i = arccos(x_i')\{-1 <= x_i' <= 1, x_i' \in X\} \tag{2}$$

The polar encoded time series vector is then transformed into a matrix. If the length of the time series vector is n, then the transformed matrix is of shape $(n \times n)$.

$$GASF_{i,j} = cos(\theta_i + \theta_j) \tag{3}$$

The GASF represents the temporal features in the form of an image where the timestamps move along top-left to bottom-right, thereby preserving the time factor in the data. Figure 1 shows the different steps of time series to image transformation.

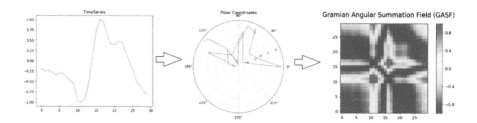

Fig. 1. Time series to image transformation

The methods of encoding time series into images described in [12] were only applicable for univariate time series. The GASF transformation generates one image for one time series dimension and thus it is possible to generate multiple images for multivariate time series. An approach which vertically stacked images transformed from different variables was presented in [13], see Fig. 2. The images were grayscaled and the different orders of vertical stacking (ascending, descending and random) were examined by performing a statistical test. The stacking order did not impact classification accuracy.

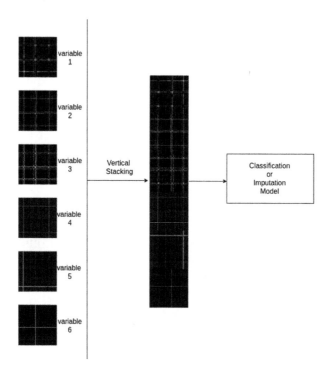

Fig. 2. Vertical stacking of images transformed from different variables

3.3   Convolutional Denoising Autoencoder

Autoencoder is a very popular unsupervised deep learning model frequently found in different application areas. Autoencoder is unsupervised in fashion and reconstructs the original input by discovering robust features in the hidden layer representation. The latent representation of high dimensional data in the hidden layer contributes in reconstructing the original data. The architecture of Autoencoder consists of two principal segments named Encoder and Decoder. The Encoder usually compresses the original representation of the data into lower dimension. The Decoder decodes the low dimensional representation of the input back into its original dimensional representation.

$$Encoder(x^n) = s(x^n W_E + b_E) = x^d \qquad (4)$$

$$Decoder(x^d) = s(x^d W_D + b_D) = x^n \qquad (5)$$

Here, x^n is the original input with n dimensions. s is any non-linear activation function, W is weight and b is bias.

Denoising Autoencoder model is an extension of Autoencoder where the input is reconstructed from a corrupted version of it. There are different ways of adding corruption, such as Gaussian noise, setting some values to zero etc. The noisy input is fed as input and the model minimizes the loss between the clean input and corrupted reconstructed input. The objective function looks as follows

$$RMSE(X, X') \frac{1}{n} \sqrt{|X_{clean} - X'_{reconstructed}|^2} \qquad (6)$$

Convolutional Denoising Autoencoder (CDA) incorporates convolution operation which is ideally performed in Convolutional Neural Networks (CNN). CNN is a methodology, where the layers of perceptrons are replaced by convolution layers and convolution operation is performed on the data. Convolution is defined as multiplication of two function within a finite or infinite range, where two functions refer to input data (e.g. Image) and a fixed size kernel consecutively. The kernel traverses through the input space to generate feature maps. The feature maps consist of important features of the data. The multiple features are pooled, preserving important features.

The combination of convoluted feature maps generation and pooling is performed in the Encoder layer of CDA where the corrupted version of the input is fed into the input layer of the network. The Decoder layer performs Deconvolutiont and Upsampling which decompresses the output coming from Encoder layer back into the shape of input data. The loss between reconstructed data and clean data is minimized. In this work, the default architecture of CDA is tweaked in the favor of imputing multivariate time series data. Deconvolution and Upsampling were performed in the Encoder layer and Convolution and Maxpooling was performed in Decoder layer. The motivation behind this specific tweaking came from [5], where a Denoising Autoencoder was designed with more hidden units in the Encoder layer than input layer. The high dimensional representation in Encoder layer created additional feature which was the contributor of data recovery.

3.4 Competitor Models

Multiple Imputation by Chained Equations (MICE): MICE, which is sometimes addressed as fully conditional specification or sequential regression multiple imputation, has emerged in the statistical literature as the principal method of addressing missing data [1]. MICE creates multiple versions of the imputed datasets through multiple imputation technique.

The steps for performing MICE are the following:

- A simple imputation method is performed across the time series (mean, mode or median). The missing time points are referred as "placeholders".
- If there are total m variables having missing points, then one of the variables are set back to missing state. The variable with "missing state" label is considered as dependent variable and other variables are considered as predictors.
- A regression is performed over these settings and "missing state" variable is imputed. Different regressions are supported in this architecture but since the dataset only contains continuous values, linear, ridge or lasso regression are chosen.
- The remaining $m - 1$ "missing state" are regressed and imputed by the same way. Once all the m variables are imputed, one iteration is completed. More iterations are performed and the imputations are placed in the time series in each iteration.
- The number of iterations can be determined by observing whether coefficients of the regression model are converged or not.

According to the experimental setup of our work, MICE had three different regression supports, namely Linear, Ridge and Lasso regression.

Multi Layer Perceptron (MLP) Based Imputation: The imputation mechanism of MLP is inspired by the MICE algorithm. Nevertheless, MLP based imputation models do not perform the chained or multiple imputations like MICE but improve the quality of imputation over several epochs as stochastic gradient descent optimizes the weights and biases per epoch. A concrete MLP architecture was described in literature [10] which was a three layered MLP with the hyperbolic tangent activation function in the hidden layer and the identity function (linear) as the activation function for the output layer. The train and test split were slightly different, where training set and test set consisted of both observed and unobserved data.

The imputation process of MLP model in our work is similar to MICE but the non-linear activation function of MLP facilitates finding complex non-linear patterns. However, the imputation of a variable is performed only once, in contrast to the multiple iterations in MICE.

4   Experiments

In this section we present the used datasets, the preprocessing steps that were conducted before training, the chosen hyperparameters and our evaluation method. Our complete imputation process for the CDA model is depicted in Fig. 3. The process for the competitors is the same except that corrupting the training data and turning the time series into images is not being done.

Fig. 3. Experiment steps for the CDA model

4.1   Datasets and Data Preprocessing

Our experiments were conducted on 5 time series datasets from the UEA MTSC repository [2]. Each dataset in UEA time series archive has training and test splits and specific number of dimensions. Each training or test split represents a time series. The table below presents all the relevant structural details (Table 1).

Table 1. A structural summary of the 5 UEA MTSC dataset

Dataset name	Number of series	Dimensions	Length	Classes
ArticularyWordRecognition	275	9	144	25
Cricket	108	6	1197	12
Handwriting	150	3	152	26
StandWalkJump	12	4	2500	3
UWaveGestureLibrary	120	3	315	8

The Length column of the table denotes the length of each time series. In our framework, each time series was transformed into images. The number of time series for any of the datasets was not very high in number. As we had selected a deep learning model for imputation, such low number of samples could cause overfitting. Experiments showed us that the default number of time series could not perform well. Therefore, the main idea was to increase the number of time series by splitting them into multiple parts and reducing their corresponding lengths. This modification facilitated us by introducing more patterns for learning which aided in imputation. The final lengths chosen were those that yielded the best results. The table below presents the modified number of time series and lengths for each dataset (Table 2).

Table 2. Modified number of time series and lengths

Dataset name	Number of series	Dimension	Length
ArticularyWordRecognition	6600	9	6
Cricket	6804	6	19
Handwriting	1200	3	19
StandWalkJump	3000	4	10
UWaveGestureLibrary	1800	3	21

The evaluation of the imputation models require a complete dataset and the corresponding incomplete dataset. Therefore, artificial missingness was introduced at different percentages (20%, 30%, 40% and 50%) into all the datasets. After simulating artificial missingness, each dataset has an observed part, which contains all the time series segments where no variables are missing and an unobserved part, where at least one variable is missing. After simulating artificial missingness, each dataset had an observed and unobserved split and the observed data was further processed for training. As CDA models learn denoising from a corrupted version of the input, we introduced noise by discarding a certain amount of values for each observed case from specific variables and replacing them by the mean of the corresponding variables. A higher amount of noise has seen to be contributing more in learning dependencies of different variables, which leads to denoising of good quality [11]. The variables selected for adding noise were the same variables having missing data in unobserved data. Different amount of noise was examined but 90% noise lead to good results. Unobserved data was also mean imputed as the CDA model would apply the denoising technique on the "mean-noise" for imputation. So the CDA learns to deal with "mean-noise" on the observed part and is then applied on mean imputed unobserved part to create the final imputation.

The next step was to perform time series to image transformation where, all the observed and unobserved chunks were rescaled between −1 to 1 using min-max scaling. Rescaled data was further transformed into polar coordinates and then GASF encoded image was achieved for each dimension. Multiple images referring to multiple variables were vertically aggregated. Finally, both observed and unobserved splits consisted their own set of images.

Note that, the following data preprocessing was performed only for CDA based imputation models. The competitor models imputed using the raw format of the data.

4.2 Model Architecture and Hyperparameters

Our Model architecture was different from a general CDA, where the Encoder layer incorporates Deconvolution and Upsampling operations and the Decoder layer incorporates Convolution and Maxpooling operations. The Encoder and Decoder both have 3 layers. The table below demonstrates the structure of the imputation model (Table 3).

Table 3. The architecture of CDA based imputation model

	Operation	Layer name	Kernel size	Number of feature maps
Encoder	Upsampling	up_0	(2, 2)	–
	Deconvolution	deconv_0	(5, 5)	64
	Upsampling	up_1	(2, 2)	–
	Deconvolution	deconv_1	(7, 7)	64
	Upsampling	up_2	(2, 2)	–
	Deconvolution	deconv_2	(5, 6)	128
Decoder	Convolution	conv_0	(5, 6)	128
	Maxpool	pool_0	(2, 2)	–
	Convolution	conv_1	(7, 7)	64
	Maxpool	pool_1	(2, 2)	–
	Convolution	conv_2	(5, 5)	64
	Maxpool	pool_2	(2, 2)	–

Hyperparameter specification was achieved by performing random search on different random combinations of hyperparameter values and the root mean square error (RMSE) was used to decide on the best combination. The random search allowed us to avoid the exhaustive searching unlike grid search. Applying random search, we selected stochastic gradient descent (SGD) as optimizer, which backpropagates the error to optimize the weights and biases. The number of epochs was 100 and the batch size was 16.

4.3   Competitor Model's Architecture and Hyperparameters

As competitor models, MICE and MLP based imputation models were selected. MLP based model had 3 hidden layers and number of hidden units were 2/3 of the number of input units in each layer. The hyperparameters for both of the models were tuned by using random search.

Hyperbolic Tangent Function was selected as activation function with a dropout of 0.3. Stochastic Gradient Descent operated as optimizer for 150 epochs and with a batch size of 20.

MICE based imputation was demonstrated using Linear, Ridge and Lasso regression and 10 iterations were performed for each of them.

4.4   Training

Based on the preprocessed data and model architecture described above, the training is started. L2 regularization was used with weight of 0.01 and stochastic gradient descent was used as the optimizer which outperformed Adam and Adagrad optimizers. The whole training process was about learning to minimize loss between the clean and corrupted data so that it can be applied on the unobserved data (noisy data after mean imputation) to perform imputation. The training and validation split was 70% and 30%. Experiments show that, the training and validation loss was saturated approximately after 10–15 epochs, which was observed for most of the cases.

The training was conducted on a machine with Nvidia RTX 2060 with RAM memory of 16 GB. The programming language for the training and all the steps above was Python 3.7 and the operating system was Ubuntu 16.04 LTS.

4.5   Evaluation Criteria

As all the time series dataset contain continuous numeric values, Root Mean Square Error (RMSE) was selected for evaluation. In out experimental setup, RMSE is not calculated on overall time series but only missing data points are taken into account to be compared with ground truth while calculating RMSE $RMSE = \sqrt{\frac{1}{m}\Sigma_{i=1}^{m}(x_i - x_i')^2}$. Where m is the total number of missing time points and I represents all the indices of missing values across the time series.

5   Results

Our proposed CDA based imputation model was compared with MLP and three different versions of MICE, each using a different type of regression. Figure 4 presents the RMSE values for 20%, 30% 40% and 50% missingness.

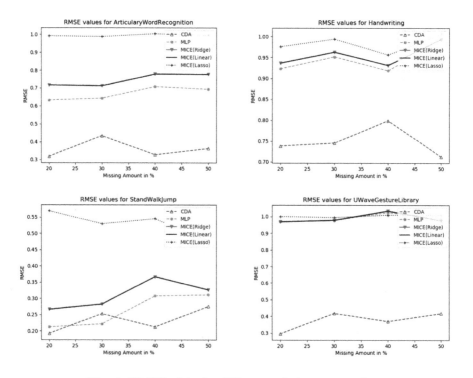

Fig. 4. RMSE plots for different missing proportions

The RMSE values for the CDA based model are the lowest at every percentage of missingness on the *Handwriting, ArticularyWordRecognition, UWaveGestureLibrary and Cricket* dataset. The depiction of the results on the *Cricket* dataset is omitted due to space limitations. Unexpectedly, in *StandWalkJump* dataset the performance of MLP and CDA model are very similar, and MLP is even better at 30% missingness. MICE (Linear) and MICE (Ridge) are identical in imputation for all the datasets. MICE (Lasso) performed worst of all the models, which implies that changing the regression type could potentially cause an impact on the imputation quality. The MLP model beat all the MICE models but was outperformed by the CDA model in at least for 80% of the cases.

6   Conclusion

In this work, we introduce an architecture of a Convolutional Denoising Autoencoder (CDA) adapted for multivariate time series imputation which inflates the size of the hidden layers in the Encoder instead of reducing them. We also employ a preprocessing step that turns the time series into 2D images based on Gramian Angular Summation Fields in order to make the data more suitable for our CDA. We compare our method against a standard Multi Layer Perceptron (MLP) and the state-of-the-art imputation method Multiple Imputations by Chained Equations (MICE) with three different types of regression (Linear, Ridge and Lasso). Our experiments were conducted on five different multivariate time series datasets, for which we simulated 20%, 30%, 40% and 50% missingness with data missing completely at random. Our results show that the CDA based imputation outperforms MICE on all five datasets and also beats the MLP on four datasets. On the fifth dataset CDA and MLP perform very similarly, but CDA is still better on four out of the five degrees of missingness. Additionally we present a preprocessing step on the datasets which manipulates the time series lengths to generate more training samples for our model which led to a better performance. The results show that the CDA model performs strongly against both linear and non-linear regression based imputation models. Deep Learning Networks are usually computationally more intensive than MICE but the imputation quality of CDA was convincing enough to be chosen over MICE or MLP based imputation.

In the future we plan to investigate also other types of missing data apart from *Missing Completely At Random (MCAR)* and want to incorporate more datasets as well as other deep learning based approaches for imputation.

Acknowledgments. This work is partially funded by the German Research Foundation, project OSCAR "Opinion Stream Classification with Ensembles and Active Learners". The principal investigators of OSCAR are Myra Spiliopoulou and Eirini Ntoutsi. Additionally, Christian Beyer is also partially funded by a PhD grant from the federal state of Saxony-Anhalt.

References

1. Azur, M.J., Stuart, E.A., Frangakis, C., Leaf, P.J.: Multiple imputation by chained equations: what is it and how does it work? Int. J. Methods Psychiatr. Res. **20**(1), 40–49 (2011)
2. Bagnall, A., et al.: The UEA multivariate time series classification archive, 2018. arXiv preprint arXiv:1811.00075 (2018)
3. Costa, A.F., Santos, M.S., Soares, J.P., Abreu, P.H.: Missing data imputation via denoising autoencoders: the untold story. In: Duivesteijn, W., Siebes, A., Ukkonen, A. (eds.) IDA 2018. LNCS, vol. 11191, pp. 87–98. Springer, Cham (2018). https://doi.org/10.1007/978-3-030-01768-2_8
4. Duan, Y., Lv, Y., Kang, W., Zhao, Y.: A deep learning based approach for traffic data imputation. In: 17th International IEEE Conference on Intelligent Transportation Systems (ITSC), pp. 912–917. IEEE (2014)
5. Gondara, L., Wang, K.: MIDA: multiple imputation using denoising autoencoders. In: Phung, D., Tseng, V.S., Webb, G.I., Ho, B., Ganji, M., Rashidi, L. (eds.) PAKDD 2018, Part III. LNCS (LNAI), vol. 10939, pp. 260–272. Springer, Cham (2018). https://doi.org/10.1007/978-3-319-93040-4_21
6. Kang, H.: The prevention and handling of the missing data. Korean J. Anesthesiol. **64**(5), 402–406 (2013)
7. LeCun, Y., Bengio, Y., Hinton, G.: Deep learning. Nature **521**(7553), 436–444 (2015)
8. Little, R.J., Rubin, D.B.: Statistical Analysis with Missing Data, vol. 793. Wiley, Hoboken (2019)
9. Qiu, Y.L., Zheng, H., Gevaert, O.: A deep learning framework for imputing missing values in genomic data. bioRxiv, p. 406066 (2018)
10. Silva-Ramírez, E.L., Pino-Mejías, R., López-Coello, M., Cubiles-de-la Vega, M.D.: Missing value imputation on missing completely at random data using multilayer perceptrons. Neural Netw. **24**(1), 121–129 (2011)
11. Vincent, P., Larochelle, H., Bengio, Y., Manzagol, P.A.: Extracting and composing robust features with denoising autoencoders. In: Proceedings of the 25th International Conference on Machine Learning, pp. 1096–1103 (2008)
12. Wang, Z., Oates, T.: Imaging time-series to improve classification and imputation. In: Twenty-Fourth International Joint Conference on Artificial Intelligence (2015)
13. Yang, C.L., Yang, C.Y., Chen, Z.X., Lo, N.W.: Multivariate time series data transformation for convolutional neural network. In: 2019 IEEE/SICE International Symposium on System Integration (SII), pp. 188–192. IEEE (2019)
14. Yoon, J., Jordon, J., Van Der Schaar, M.: Gain: missing data imputation using generative adversarial nets. arXiv preprint arXiv:1806.02920 (2018)
15. Zhao, M., Wang, D., Zhang, Z., Zhang, X.: Music removal by convolutional denoising autoencoder in speech recognition. In: 2015 Asia-Pacific Signal and Information Processing Association Annual Summit and Conference (APSIPA), pp. 338–341. IEEE (2015)

15

GraphMDL: Graph Pattern Selection Based on Minimum Description Length

Francesco Bariatti[(✉)], Peggy Cellier, and Sébastien Ferré

Univ Rennes, INSA, CNRS, IRISA,
Campus de Beaulieu, Rennes, France
{francesco.bariatti,peggy.cellier,sebastien.ferre}@irisa.fr

Abstract. Many graph pattern mining algorithms have been designed to identify recurring structures in graphs. The main drawback of these approaches is that they often extract too many patterns for human analysis. Recently, pattern mining methods using the *Minimum Description Length* (MDL) principle have been proposed to select a characteristic subset of patterns from transactional, sequential and relational data. In this paper, we propose an MDL-based approach for selecting a characteristic subset of patterns on labeled graphs. A key notion in this paper is the introduction of *ports* to encode connections between pattern occurrences without any loss of information. Experiments show that the number of patterns is drastically reduced. The selected patterns have complex shapes and are representative of the data.

Keywords: Pattern mining · Graph mining · Minimum Description Length

1 Introduction

Many fields have complex data that need labeled graphs, i.e. graphs where vertices and edges have labels, for an accurate representation. For instance, in chemistry and biology, molecules are represented as atoms and bonds; in linguistics, sentences are represented as words and dependency links; in the semantic web, knowledge graphs are represented as entities and relationships. Depending on the domain, graph datasets can be made of large graphs or large collections of graphs. Graphs are complex to analyze in order to extract knowledge, for instance to identify frequent structures in order to make them more intelligible.

In the field of pattern mining, there has been a number of proposals, namely *graph mining* approaches, to extract frequent subgraphs. Classical approaches to graph mining, e.g. gSpan [12] and Gaston [7], work on collections of graphs, and generate all patterns w.r.t. a frequency threshold. The major drawback of this kind of approach is the huge amount of generated patterns, which renders them difficult to analyze. Some approaches such as CloseGraph [13] reduce the number of patterns by only generating *closed patterns*. However, the set of closed patterns generally remains too large, with a lot of redundancy between patterns. *Constraint-based* approaches, such as gPrune [14], reduce the number of extracted patterns by extracting only the patterns following a certain acceptance rule. These algorithms generally manage to reduce the number of patterns, however they also limit their type. Additionally, if the acceptance rule is user-provided, the user needs some background knowledge on the data.

More effective approaches to reduce the number of patterns are those based on the *Minimum Description Length* (MDL) principle [3]. The MDL principle comes from information theory, and states that the *model* that describes the data the best is the one that compresses the data the best. It has been shown on sets of items [10], sequences [9] and relations [4] that an MDL-based approach can select a small and descriptive subset of patterns. Few MDL-based approaches have been proposed for graphs. SUBDUE [1] iteratively compresses a graph by replacing each occurrence of a pattern by a single vertex. At each step, the chosen pattern is the one that compresses the most. The drawback of SUBDUE is that the replacement of pattern occurrences by vertices entails a loss of information. VoG [5] summarizes graphs as a composition of predefined families of patterns (e.g., paths, stars). Like SUBDUE, VoG aims to only extract "interesting" patterns, but instead of evaluating each pattern individually like SUBDUE, it evaluates the set of extracted patterns as a whole. This allows the algorithm to find a "good set of patterns" instead of a "set of good patterns". One limitation of VoG is that the type of patterns is restricted to predefined ones. Another limitation is that VoG works on unlabeled graphs, (e.g. network graphs), while we are interested in labeled graphs.

The contribution of this paper (Sect. 3) is a novel approach called GRAPH-MDL, leveraging the MDL principle to select graph patterns from labeled graphs. Contrary to SUBDUE, GRAPHMDL ensures that there is no loss of information thanks to the introduction of the notion of *ports* associated to graph patterns. Ports represent how adjacent occurrences of patterns are connected. We evaluate our approach experimentally (Sect. 4) on two datasets with different kinds of graphs: one on AIDS-related molecules (few labels, many cycles), and the other one on dependency trees (many labels, no cycles). Experiments validate our approach by showing that the data can be significantly compressed, and that the number of selected patterns is drastically reduced compared to the number of candidate patterns. More so, we observe that the patterns can have complex and varied shapes, and are representative of the data.

2   Background Knowledge

2.1   The MDL Principle

The *Minimum Description Length* (MDL) principle [3] is a technique from the domain of information theory that allows to select the model, from a family of models, that best describes some data. The MDL principle states that the best model M for describing some data D is the one that minimizes the *description length* $L(M, D) = L(M) + L(D|M)$, where $L(M)$ is the length of the model and $L(D|M)$ the length of the data encoded with the model. The MDL principle does

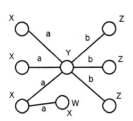
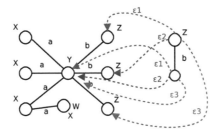
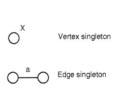

Fig. 1. A labeled undirected simple graph.

Fig. 2. Embeddings of a pattern in the graph of Fig. 1.

Fig. 3. Two singleton patterns.

not define how to compute every possible description length. However, common primitives exist for data and distributions [6]:

- An element $x \in \mathcal{X}$ with uniform distribution has a code of $\log(|\mathcal{X}|)$ bits.
- An element $x \in \mathcal{X}$, appearing $usage(x, D)$ times in some data D has a code of $L_{usage}^{\mathcal{X}}(x, D) = -\log\left(\frac{usage(x,D)}{\sum_{x_i \in \mathcal{X}} usage(x_i,D)}\right)$ bits. This encoding is optimal.
- An integer $n \in \mathbb{N}$ without a known upper bound can be encoded with a *universal integer encoding*, whose size in bits is noted $L_{\mathbb{N}}(n)$[1].

Description lengths of elements that are common to all models are usually ignored, since they do not affect their comparison.

Krimp [10] is a pattern mining algorithm using the MDL principle to select a "characteristic" set of itemset patterns from a transactional database. Because of its good performances, Krimp has been adapted to other types of data, such as sequences [9] and relational databases [4]. In our approach we redefine Krimp's key concepts on graphs, in order to apply a Krimp-like approach to graph mining.

2.2 Graphs and Graph Patterns

Definition 1. *A labeled graph $G = (V, E, l_V, l_E)$ over two label sets $\mathcal{L}_V$ and $\mathcal{L}_E$ is a data structure composed of a set of* vertices V, *a set of* edges $E \subseteq V \times V$, *and two labeling functions $l_V \in V \to 2^{\mathcal{L}_V}$ and $l_E \in E \to \mathcal{L}_E$ that associate a set of labels to vertices, and one label to edges.*

G is said undirected *if E is symmetric, and* simple *if E is irreflexive.*

Although our approach applies to all labeled graphs, in the following we only consider undirected simple graphs, so as to compare ourselves with existing tools and benchmarks. Figure 1 shows an example of graph, with 8 vertices and 7 edges, defined over vertex label set $\{W, X, Y, Z\}$ and edge label set $\{a, b\}$. In our definition vertices can have several or no labels, unlike usual definitions in graph mining, because it makes it applicable to more datasets.

---

[1] In our implementation we use *Elias gamma encoding* [2], shifted by 1 so that it can encode 0. Therefore $L_{\mathbb{N}}(n) = 2\lfloor \log(n+1) \rfloor + 1$.

P	G^P			c_P		v_π		c_π	
	Pattern structure	Pattern usage	Pattern code	Pattern code length (bits)	Port count	Port ID	Port usage	Port code	Port code length (bits)
P1	X—a—Y—b—Z ①—②—③	3	[P1]	1	2	v1 v2	1 3	[v1] [v2]	2 0.42
Pa	①—a—②	1	[Pa]	2.58	2	v1 v2	1 1	[v1] [v2]	1 1
Pw	①^W	1	[Pw]	2.58	1	v1	1		0
Px	①^X	1	[Px]	2.58	1	v1	1		0

Fig. 4. Example of a GRAPHMDL code table over the graph of Fig. 1. Pattern and port usages, and code lengths have been added as illustration and are not part of the table definition. Unused singleton patterns are omitted.

Definition 2. *Let G^P and G^D be graphs. An embedding (or occurrence) of G^P in G^D is an injective function $\varepsilon \in V^P \to V^D$ such that: (1) $l_V^P(v) \subseteq l_V^D(\varepsilon(v))$ for all $v \in V^P$; (2) $(\varepsilon(u), \varepsilon(v)) \in E^D$ for all $(u,v) \in E^P$; and (3) $l_E^P(e) = l_E^D(\varepsilon(e))$ for all $e \in E^P$.*

We define *graph patterns* as graphs G^P having some occurrences in the data graph G^D. Figure 2 shows the three embeddings $\varepsilon_1, \varepsilon_2, \varepsilon_3$ of a two-vertices graph pattern into the graph of Fig. 1. We define *singleton patterns* as the elementary patterns. A *vertex singleton pattern* is a graph with one vertex having one label. An *edge singleton pattern* is a graph with two unlabeled vertices, connected by a single labeled edge. Figure 3 shows examples of singleton patterns.

3   GRAPHMDL: MDL for Graphs

In this section we present our contribution: the GRAPHMDL approach. This approach takes as input a graph—the *original graph* G^o—and a set of patterns extracted from that graph—the *candidate patterns*—and outputs the most descriptive subset of candidate patterns according to the MDL principle. The candidates can be generated with any graph mining algorithm, e.g. gSpan [12].

The intuition behind GRAPHMDL is that since data and patterns are both graphs, the data can be seen as a composition of pattern embeddings. Informally, we want a user analyzing the output of GRAPHMDL to be able to say "the data is composed of one occurrence of pattern A, connected to one occurrence of pattern B, which is itself connected to one occurrence of pattern C". More so, we want the user to be able to tell *how* these structures are connected together: which vertices of each pattern are used to connect it to other patterns.

3.1   Model: A Code Table for Graph Patterns

Similarly to Krimp [10], we define our model as a *Code Table* (CT), i.e. a set $\mathcal{P}$ of patterns with associated coding information. A first difference with Krimp is that the patterns are graph patterns. A second difference is the need for additional coding information: a single code would not suffice since all the information related to connectivity between pattern occurrences would be lost.

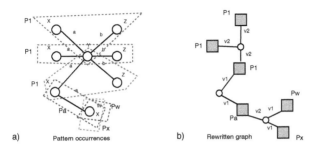

Fig. 5. How the data graph of Fig. 1 is encoded with the code table of Fig. 4. *(a)* Retained occurrences of CT patterns. *(b)* The rewritten graph. Blue squares are pattern embeddings (their label indicates the pattern), white circles are port vertices. Edge labels represent which pattern port correspond to each port vertex. (Color figure online)

We therefore introduce the notion of *ports* in order to represent how pattern embeddings connect to each other to form the original graph. The set of ports of a pattern is a subset of the vertices of the pattern. Intuitively, a pattern vertex is a port if at least one pattern embedding maps this vertex to a vertex in the original graph that is also used by another embedding (be it of the same pattern or a different one). For example, in Fig. 5a the three occurrences of pattern $P1$ are inter-connected through their middle vertex: this vertex is a port. Since port information increases the description length, we expect our approach to select patterns with few ports.

Figure 4 shows an example of CT associated to the graph of Fig. 1. Every row of the CT is composed of three parts, and contains information about a pattern $P \in \mathcal{P}$ (e.g. the first row contains information about pattern $P1$). The first part of a row is the graph G^P, which represents the structure of the pattern (e.g. $P1$ is a pattern with three labeled vertices and two labeled edges). The second part of a row is the code c_P, associated to the pattern. The third part of a row is the description of the port set of the pattern, Π_P, (e.g. $P1$ has two ports, its first two vertices, with codes of 2 and 0.42 bits[2]). We note Π the set of all ports of all patterns. Like Krimp, the length of the code of a pattern or port depends on its usage in the encoding of the data, i.e. how many times it is used to describe the original graph G^o (e.g. $P1$ has a code of 1 bit because it is used 3 times and the sum of pattern usages in the CT is 6, see Sects. 3.2 and 3.3).

3.2   Encoding the Data with a Code Table

The intuition behind GRAPHMDL is that we can represent the original graph G^o (i.e. the data) as a set of pattern occurrences, connected via ports. Encoding the data with a CT consists in creating a structure that explicits which occurrences are used and how they interconnect to form the original graph. We call this structure the *rewritten graph* G^r.

---

[2] MDL approaches deal with *theoretical* code lengths, which may not be integers.

Definition 3. *A rewritten graph* $G^r = (V^r, E^r, l^r_V, l^r_E)$ *is a graph where the set of vertices is* $V^r = V^r_{emb} \cup V^r_{port}$*:* V^r_{emb} *is the set of pattern embedding vertices and* V^r_{port} *is the set of port vertices.* $E^r \subseteq V^r_{emb} \times V^r_{port}$ *is the set of edges from embeddings to ports,* $l^r_V \in V^r_{emb} \to \mathcal{P}$ *and* $l^r_E \in E^r \to \Pi$ *are the labelings.*

In order to compute the encoding of the data graph with a given CT, we start with an empty rewritten graph. One after another, we select patterns from the CT. For each pattern, we compute the occurrences of its graph G^P. Similarly to Krimp, we limit embeddings overlaps: we admit overlap on vertices (since it is the key notion behind ports), but we forbid edge overlaps.

Each retained embedding is represented in the rewritten graph by a *pattern embedding vertex*: a vertex $v_e \in V^r_{emb}$ with a label $P \in \mathcal{P}$ indicating which pattern it instantiates. Vertices that are shared by several embeddings are represented in the rewritten graph by a *port vertex* $v_p \in V^r_{port}$. We add an edge $(v_e, v_p) \in E^r$ between the pattern embedding vertex v_e of a pattern P and the port vertex v_p, when the embedding associated to v_e maps the pattern's port $v_\pi \in \Pi_P$ to v_p. We label this edge v_π.

We make sure that code tables always include all singleton patterns, so that they can always encode any vertex and edge of the original graph.

Figure 5 shows the graph of Fig. 1 encoded with the CT of Fig. 4. Embeddings of CT patterns become pattern embedding vertices in the rewritten graph (blue squares). Vertices that are at the boundary between multiple embeddings become port vertices in the rewritten graph (white circles). When an embedding has a port, its pattern embedding vertex in the rewritten graph is connected to the corresponding port vertex and the edge label indicates which pattern's port it is. For instance, the three retained occurrences of pattern $P1$ all share the same vertex labeled Y (middle of the original graph), thus in the rewritten graph the three corresponding pattern embedding vertices are connected to the same port vertex via port v_2.

3.3   Description Lengths

In this section we define how to compute the description length of the CT and the rewritten graph. Description lengths are used to compare CTs. Formulas are explained below and grouped in Fig. 6.

Code Table. The description length $L(M) = L(CT)$ of a CT is the sum of the description lengths of its rows (skipping rows with unused patterns), and every row is composed of three parts: the pattern graph structure, the pattern code, and the pattern port description.

To describe the structure $G = G^P$ of a pattern ($L(G)$) we start by encoding the number of vertices of the pattern. Then we encode the vertices one after the other. For each vertex v, we encode its labels then its adjacent edges. To encode the vertex labels ($L_V(v, G)$) we specify their number first, then the labels themselves. To encode the adjacent edges ($L_E(v, G)$) we specify their number (between 0 and $|V| - 1$ in a simple graph), then for each edge, its destination

$$L(c_P) = L^{\mathcal{P}}_{usage}(P, G^r) \quad \text{where } usage(P_i, G^r) = |\{v_e \in V^r_{emb} \mid l^r_V(v_e) = P_i\}|$$

$$L(c_\pi, P) = L^{\Pi_P}_{usage}(\pi, G^r) \quad \text{where } usage(\pi_i, G^r) = |\{e \in E^r_{emb} \mid l^r_E(e) = \pi_i\}|$$

$$L(M) = L(CT) = \underbrace{\sum_{\substack{P \in \mathcal{P} \\ usage(P) \neq 0}} L(G)}_{\text{structure}} + \underbrace{L(c_P)}_{\text{code}} + \underbrace{L(\Pi_P)}_{\text{ports}}$$

$$\left| \begin{array}{l}
L(G) = \underbrace{L_{\mathbb{N}}(|V|)}_{\text{vertex count}} + \sum_{v \in V} [\underbrace{L_V(v, G)}_{\text{vertex labels}} + \underbrace{L_E(v, G)}_{\text{edges of vertex}}] \\[2ex]
L_V(v, G) = \underbrace{L_{\mathbb{N}}(|l_V(v)|)}_{\text{label count}} + \sum_{l \in l_V(v)} \underbrace{L^{\mathcal{L}_V}_{usage}(l, G^o)}_{\text{label code}} \\[2ex]
L_E(v, G) = \underbrace{\log(|V|)}_{\text{edge count}} + \sum_{(v,w) \in E | v < w} [\underbrace{\log(|V|)}_{\text{destination}} + \underbrace{L^{\mathcal{L}_E}_{usage}(l_E(v, w), G^o)}_{\text{label}}] \\[2ex]
L(\Pi_P) = \underbrace{\log(|V| + 1)}_{\text{port count } |\Pi_P|} + \underbrace{\log(\binom{|V|}{|\Pi_P|})}_{\text{port ids}} + \sum_{\pi \in \Pi_P} \underbrace{L(c_\pi, P)}_{\text{port code}}
\end{array} \right.$$

$$L(D|M) = L(G^r) = \underbrace{L_{\mathbb{N}}(|V^r_{port}|)}_{\text{port vertex count}} + \sum_{v \in V^r_{emb}} L_{emb}(v, P, G^r) \quad \text{with} \quad P = l^r_V(v)$$

$$\left| \begin{array}{l}
L_{emb}(v, P, G^r) = \underbrace{L(c_P)}_{\text{pattern code}} + \underbrace{\log(|\Pi_P| + 1)}_{\text{edge count}} + \sum_{\substack{(v,w) \in E^r \\ \pi = l^r_E(v,w)}} \underbrace{\log(|V^r_{port}|)}_{\text{port vertex id}} + \underbrace{L(c_\pi, P)}_{\text{port code}}
\end{array} \right.$$

Fig. 6. Formulas used for computing description lengths. The structure $G^P = (V^P, E^P, l^P_V, l^P_E)$ is shortened to $G = (V, E, l_V, l_E)$ for ease of reading.

vertex and its label. To avoid encoding twice the same edge, we decide—in undirected graphs—to encode edges with the vertex with the smallest identifier. Vertex and edge labels are encoded based on their relative usage in the original graph G^o ($L^{\mathcal{L}_V}_{usage}(l, G^o)$ and $L^{\mathcal{L}_E}_{usage}(l_E(v, w), G^o)$). Since this encoding does not change between CTs, it is a meaningful way to compare them.

The second element of a CT row is the code c_P associated to the pattern ($L(c_P)$). This code is based on the usage of the pattern in the rewritten graph.

The last element of a CT row is the description of the pattern's ports ($L(\Pi_P)$). First, we encode the number of pattern's ports (between 0 and $|V|$). Then we specify which vertices are ports: if there are k ports, then there are $\binom{|V|}{k}$ possibilities. Finally, we encode the port codes ($L(c_\pi, P)$): their code is based on the usage of the port in the rewritten graph w.r.t. other ports of the pattern.

Rewritten Graph. The rewritten graph has two types of vertices: port vertices and pattern embedding vertices. Port vertices do not have any associated information, so we just need to encode their number. The description length $L(D|M) = L(G^r)$ of the rewritten graph is the length needed for encoding the number of vertex ports plus the sum of the description lengths $L_{emb}(v, P, G^r)$ of the pattern embedding vertices v. Every pattern embedding vertex has a label $l^r_V(v)$ specifying its pattern P, encoded with the code c_P of the pattern. We then encode the number of edges of the vertex i.e. the number of ports of this embedding in particular (between 0 and $|\Pi_P|$). Then for each edge we encode the port vertex to which it is connected and to which port it corresponds (using the port code c_π).

Table 1. Characteristics of the datasets used in the experiments

Dataset	Graph count	$|V|$	$|E|$	$|\mathcal{L}_V|$	$|\mathcal{L}_E|$
AIDS-CA	423	16714	17854	21	3
AIDS-CM	1082	34387	37033	26	3
UD-PUD-En	1000	21176	20176	17	46

3.4 The GRAPHMDL Algorithm

In previous subsections we presented the different MDL definitions that GRAPH-MDL uses to evaluate pattern sets (CT). A naive algorithm for finding the most descriptive pattern set (in the MDL sense) could be to create a CT for every possible subset of candidates and retain the one yielding the smallest description length. However, such an approach is often infeasible because of the large amount of possible subsets. That is why GRAPHMDL applies a greedy heuristic algorithm, adapting Krimp algorithm [10] to our MDL definitions.

Like Krimp, our algorithm starts with a CT composed of all singletons, which we call CT_0. One after the other, candidates are added to the CT if they allow to lower the description length. Two heuristics guide GRAPHMDL: the candidate order and the order of patterns in the CT. We use the same heuristics as Krimp, with the difference that we define the size of a pattern as its total number of labels (vertices and edges). We also implement Krimp's "post-acceptance pruning": after a pattern is accepted in the CT, GRAPHMDL verifies if the removal of some patterns from the CT allows to lower the description length $L(M, D)$.

4 Experimental Evaluation

In order to evaluate our proposal, we developed a prototype of GRAPHMDL. The prototype was developed in Java 1.8 and is available as a git repository[3].

4.1 Datasets

The first two datasets that we use, AIDS-CA and AIDS-CM, are part of the National Cancer Institute AIDS antiviral screen data[4]. They are collections of graphs often used to compare graph mining algorithms [11]. Graphs of this collection represent molecules: vertices are atoms and edges are bonds. We stripped all hydrogen atoms from the molecules, since their positions can be inferred.

We took our third dataset, UD-PUD-En, from the Universal Dependencies project[5]. This project curates a collection of trees describing dependency

---

[3] https://gitlab.inria.fr/fbariatt/graphmdl.
[4] https://wiki.nci.nih.gov/display/NCIDTPdata/AIDS+Antiviral+Screen+Data.
[5] https://universaldependencies.org/.

Table 2. Experimental results for different candidate sets

Dataset	gSpan support	Candidate count	Runtime	$|CT|$	$\frac{L(CT,D)}{L(CT_0,D)}$	Median label count	Median port count
AIDS-CA	20%	2194	19 m	115	24.42%	9	3
AIDS-CA	15%	7867	1 h 47 m	123	21.64%	10	4
AIDS-CA	10%	20596	3 h 36 m	148	19.03%	11	3
AIDS-CM	20%	433	22 m	111	28.91%	7	4
AIDS-CM	15%	779	32 m	131	27.44%	9	4
AIDS-CM	10%	2054	1 h 10 m	163	24.94%	9	4
AIDS-CM	5%	9943	5 h 02 m	225	20.43%	9	4
UD-PUD-En	10%	164	1 m	162	39.55%	5	2
UD-PUD-En	5%	458	3 m	249	34.45%	5	2
UD-PUD-En	1%	6021	19 m	523	28.14%	7	2
UD-PUD-En	0%	233434	9 h 57 m	773	26.25%	7	2

relationships between words of sentences of multiple corpora in multiple languages. We used the trees corresponding to the English version of the PUD corpus.

Table 1 presents the main characteristics of the three datasets that we use: the number of elementary graphs in the dataset, the total amount of vertices, the total amount of edges, the number of different vertex labels, and the number of different edge labels. Since GRAPHMDL works on a single graph instead of a collection, we aggregate collections into a single graph with multiple connected components when needed. We generate candidate patterns by using a gSpan implementation available on its author's website[6].

4.2 Quantitative Evaluation

Table 2 presents the results of the first experiment. For instance the first line tells that we ran GRAPHMDL on the AIDS-CA dataset, with as candidates the 2194 patterns generated by gSpan for a support threshold of 20%. It took 19 min for our approach to select a CT composed of 115 patterns, yielding a description length that is 24% of the description length obtained by the singleton-only CT_0. Selected patterns have a median of 9 labels and 3 ports.

We observe that the number of patterns of a CT is often significantly smaller than the number of candidates. This is particularly remarkable for experiments ran with small support thresholds, where GRAPHMDL reduces the number of patterns up to 300 times: patterns generated for these support thresholds probably contain a lot of redundancy, that GRAPHMDL avoids.

We also note that the description lengths of the CTs found by GRAPHMDL are between 20% and 40% of the lengths of the baseline code tables CT_0, which shows that our algorithm succeeds in finding regularities in the data. Description

---

[6] https://sites.cs.ucsb.edu/~xyan/software/gSpan.htm.

lengths are smaller when the number of candidates is higher: this may be because with more candidates, there are more chances of finding "good" candidates that allow to better reduce description lengths.

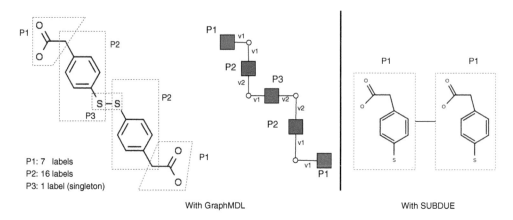

Fig. 7. How GRAPHMDL (left) and SUBDUE (right) encode one of AIDS-CM graphs.

We observe that GRAPHMDL can find patterns of non-trivial size, as shown by the median label count in Table 2. Also, most patterns have few ports, which shows that GRAPHMDL manages to find models in which the original graph is described as a set of components without many connections between them. We think that a human will interpret such a model with more ease, as opposed to a model composed of "entangled" components.

4.3   Qualitative Evaluations

Interpretation of Rewritten Graphs. Figure 7 shows how GRAPHMDL uses patterns selected on the AIDS-CM dataset to encode one of the graphs of the dataset (more results are available in our git repository). It illustrates the key idea behind our approach: find a set of patterns so that each one describes part of the data, and connect their occurrences via ports to describe the whole data.

We observe that GRAPHMDL selects bigger patterns (such as P2), describing big chunks of data, as well as smaller patterns (such as P3, edge singleton), that can form bridges between pattern occurrences. Big patterns increase the description length of the CT, but describe more of the data in a single occurrence, whereas small patterns do the opposite. Following the MDL principle, GRAPHMDL finds a good balance between the two types of patterns.

It is interesting to note that pattern P1 in Fig. 7 corresponds to the carboxylic acid functional group, common in organic chemistry. GRAPHMDL selected this pattern without any prior knowledge of chemistry, solely by using MDL.

Comparison with SUBDUE. On the right of Fig. 7 we can observe the encoding found by SUBDUE on the same graph. The main disadvantage of SUBDUE is information loss: we can see that the data is composed of two occurrences of pattern P1, but not how these two occurrences are connected. Thanks to the notion of ports, GRAPHMDL does not suffer from this problem: the user can exactly know which atoms lie at the boundary of each pattern occurrence.

Table 3. Classification accuracies. Results of methods marked with * are from [8].

Algorithm	AIDS-CA/CI	Mutag	PTC-MR	PTC-FR
Baseline-Largest	50.01 ± 0.03	66.50 ± 0.00	55.80 ± 0.00	65.50 ± 0.00
GRAPHMDL	71.61 ± 0.96	80.79 ± 1.51	57.38 ± 1.68	62.70 ± 1.86
WL*	N/A	87.26 ± 1.42	63.12 ± 1.44	67.64 ± 0.74
P-WL-C*	N/A	90.51 ± 1.34	64.02 ± 0.82	67.15 ± 1.09
RetGK*	N/A	90.30 ± 1.10	62.15 ± 1.60	67.80 ± 1.10

Assessing Patterns Through Classification. We showed in the previous experiments that GRAPHMDL manages to reduce the amount of patterns, and that the introduction of ports allows for a precise analysis of graphs. We now ask ourselves if the extracted patterns are *characteristic* of the data. To evaluate this aspect, we adopt the classification approach used by Krimp [10]. We apply GRAPHMDL independently on each class of a multi-class dataset, and then use the resulting CTs to classify each graph: we encode it with each of the CTs, and classify it in the class whose CT yields the smallest description length $L(D|M)$. Since GRAPHMDL is not designed with the goal of classification in mind, we would expect existing classifiers to outperform GRAPHMDL. In particular, note that patterns are selected on each class independently of other classes. Indeed, GRAPHMDL follows a descriptive approach whereas classifiers generally follow a discriminative approach. Table 3 presents the results of this new experiment. We compare GRAPHMDL with graph classification algorithms found in the literature [8], and a baseline that classifies all graphs as belonging to the largest class. The AIDS-CA/CI dataset is composed of the CA class of the AIDS dataset and a same-size same-labels random sample from the CI class (corresponding to negative examples). The other datasets[7] are from [8]. We performed a 10-fold validation repeated 10 times and report average accuracies and standard deviations.

GRAPHMDL clearly outperforms the baseline on two datasets, AIDS and Mutag, but is only comparable to the baseline for the PTC datasets. On Mutag, GRAPHMDL is less accurate than other classifiers but closer to them than to the baseline. On the PTC datasets, we hypothesize that the learned descriptions are not discriminative w.r.t. the chosen classes, although they are characteristic enough to reduce description length. Nonetheless results are still better than random guessing (accuracy would be 50%). An interesting point of GRAPHMDL

---

[7] For concision, we do not report on PTC-{MM,FM}, they yield similar results.

classification is that it is explainable: the user can look at how the patterns of the two classes encode a graph (similarly to Fig. 7) and understand *why* one class is chosen over another.

5   Conclusion

In this paper, we have proposed GRAPHMDL, an MDL-based pattern mining approach to select a representative set of graph patterns on labeled graphs. We proposed MDL definitions allowing to compute description lengths necessary to apply the MDL principle. The originality of our approach lies in the notion of *ports*, which guarantee that the original graph can be perfectly reconstructed, i.e., without any loss of information. Our experiments show that GRAPHMDL significantly reduces the amount of patterns w.r.t. complete approaches. Further, the selected patterns can have complex shapes with simple connections. The introduction of the notion of ports facilitates interpretation w.r.t. to SUBDUE. We plan to apply our approach to more complex graphs, e.g. knowledge graphs.

References

1. Cook, D.J., Holder, L.B.: Substructure discovery using minimum description length and background knowledge. J. Artif. Intell. Res. **1**, 231–255 (1993)
2. Elias, P.: Universal codeword sets and representations of the integers. IEEE Trans. Inf. Theory **21**(2), 194–203 (1975)
3. Grünwald, P.: Model selection based on minimum description length. J. Math. Psychol. **44**(1), 133–152 (2000)
4. Koopman, A., Siebes, A.: Characteristic relational patterns. In: Proceedings of the 15th ACM SIGKDD International Conference on Knowledge Discovery and Data Mining, KDD 2009, pp. 437–446. ACM (2009)
5. Koutra, D., Kang, U., Vreeken, J., Faloutsos, C.: Summarizing and understanding large graphs. Stat. Anal. Data Mining: ASA Data Sci. J. **8**(3), 183–202 (2015)
6. Lee, T.C.M.: An introduction to coding theory and the two-part minimum description length principle. Int. Stat. Rev. **69**(2), 169–183 (2001)
7. Nijssen, S., Kok, J.N.: The Gaston tool for frequent subgraph mining. Electron. Notes Theor. Comput. Sci. **127**(1), 77–87 (2005)
8. Rieck, B., Bock, C., Borgwardt, K.: A persistent Weisfeiler-Lehman procedure for graph classification. In: Proceedings of the 36th International Conference on Machine Learning, pp. 5448–5458. PMLR (2019)
9. Tatti, N., Vreeken, J.: The long and the short of it: summarising event sequences with serial episodes. In: Proceedings of the International Conference on Knowledge Discovery and Data Mining (KDD 2012), pp. 462–470. ACM (2012)
10. Vreeken, J., van Leeuwen, M., Siebes, A.: KRIMP: mining itemsets that compress. Data Min. Knowl. Discov. **23**(1), 169–214 (2011)
11. Wörlein, M., Meinl, T., Fischer, I., Philippsen, M.: A quantitative comparison of the subgraph miners MoFa, gSpan, FFSM, and Gaston. In: Jorge, A.M., Torgo, L., Brazdil, P., Camacho, R., Gama, J. (eds.) PKDD 2005. LNCS (LNAI), vol. 3721, pp. 392–403. Springer, Heidelberg (2005). https://doi.org/10.1007/11564126_39

12. Yan, X., Han, J.: gSpan: graph-based substructure pattern mining. In: Proceedings of the 2002 IEEE International Conference on Data Mining (ICDM 2002), pp. 721–724. IEEE Computer Society (2002)
13. Yan, X., Han, J.: CloseGraph: mining closed frequent graph patterns. In: ACM SIGKDD International Conference Knowledge Discovery and Data Mining (KDD), pp. 286–295. ACM (2003)
14. Zhu, F., Yan, X., Han, J., Yu, P.S.: gPrune: a constraint pushing framework for graph pattern mining. In: Zhou, Z.-H., Li, H., Yang, Q. (eds.) PAKDD 2007. LNCS (LNAI), vol. 4426, pp. 388–400. Springer, Heidelberg (2007). https://doi.org/10.1007/978-3-540-71701-0_38

16

Gibbs Sampling Subjectively Interesting Tiles

Anes Bendimerad[1]([envelope]), Jefrey Lijffijt[2], Marc Plantevit[3], Céline Robardet[1], and Tijl De Bie[2]

[1] Univ Lyon, INSA, CNRS UMR 5205, 69621 Villeurbanne, France
ahmed-anes.bendimerad@insa-lyon.fr
[2] IDLab, ELIS Department, Ghent University, Ghent, Belgium
[3] Univ Lyon, UCBL, CNRS UMR 5205, 69621 Lyon, France

Abstract. The local pattern mining literature has long struggled with the so-called pattern explosion problem: the size of the set of patterns found exceeds the size of the original data. This causes computational problems (enumerating a large set of patterns will inevitably take a substantial amount of time) as well as problems for interpretation and usability (trawling through a large set of patterns is often impractical).

Two complementary research lines aim to address this problem. The first aims to develop better measures of interestingness, in order to reduce the number of uninteresting patterns that are returned [6,10]. The second aims to avoid an exhaustive enumeration of all 'interesting' patterns (where interestingness is quantified in a more traditional way, e.g. frequency), by directly sampling from this set in a way that more 'interesting' patterns are sampled with higher probability [2].

Unfortunately, the first research line does not reduce computational cost, while the second may miss out on the most interesting patterns. In this paper, we combine the best of both worlds for mining interesting tiles [8] from binary databases. Specifically, we propose a new pattern sampling approach based on Gibbs sampling, where the probability of sampling a pattern is proportional to their subjective interestingness [6]—an interestingness measure reported to better represent true interestingness.

The experimental evaluation confirms the theory, but also reveals an important weakness of the proposed approach which we speculate is shared with any other pattern sampling approach. We thus conclude with a broader discussion of this issue, and a forward look.

Keywords: Pattern mining · Subjective interestingness · Pattern sampling · Gibbs sampling

1 Introduction

Pattern mining methods aim to select elements from a given language that bring to the user "implicit, previously unknown, and potentially useful information from data" [7]. To meet the challenge of selecting the appropriate patterns for a user, several lines of work have been explored: (1) Many constraints on some measures that assess the quality of a pattern using exclusively the data have been designed [4,12,13]; (2) Preference measures have been considered to only retrieve patterns that are non dominated in the dataset; (3) Active learning systems have been proposed that interact with the user to explicit her interest on the patterns and guide the exploration toward those she is interested in; (4) Subjective interestingness measures [6,10] have been introduced that aim to take into account the implicit knowledge of a user by modeling her prior knowledge and retrieving the patterns that are unlikely according to the background model.

The shift from threshold-constraints on objective measures toward the use of subjective measures provides an elegant solution to the so-called pattern explosion problem by considerably reducing the output to only truly interesting patterns. Unfortunately, the discovery of subjectively interesting patterns with exact algorithms remains computationally challenging.

In this paper we explore another strategy that is pattern sampling. The aim is to reduce the computational cost while identifying the most important patterns, and allowing for distributed computations. There are two families of local pattern sampling techniques.

The first family uses Metropolis Hastings [9], a Markov Chain Monte Carlo (MCMC) method. It performs a random walk over a transition graph representing the probability of reaching a pattern given the current one. This can be done with the guarantee that the distribution of the considered quality measure is proportional on the sample set to the one of the whole pattern set [1]. However, each iteration of the random walk is accepted only with a probability equal to the acceptance rate α. This can be very small, which may result in a prohibitively slow convergence rate. Moreover, in each iteration the part of the transition graph representing the probability of reaching patterns given the current one, has to be materialized in both directions, further raising the computational cost. Other approaches [5,11] relax this constraint but lose the guarantee.

Methods in the second family are referred to as direct pattern sampling approaches [2,3]. A notable example is [2], where a two-step procedure is proposed that samples frequent itemsets without simulating stochastic processes. In a first step, it randomly selects a row according to a first distribution, and from this row, draws a subset of items according to another distribution. The combination of both steps follows the desired distribution. Generalizing this approach to other pattern domains and quality measures appeared to be difficult.

In this paper, we propose a new pattern sampling approach based on Gibbs sampling, where the probability of sampling a pattern is proportional to their Subjective Interestingness (SI) [6]. Gibbs sampling – described in Sect. 3 – is a special case of Metropolis Hastings where the acceptance rate α is always equal to 1. In Sect. 4, we show how the random walk can be simulated without materializing any part of the transition graph, except the currently sampled pattern. While we present this approach particularly for mining tiles in rectangular databases, applying it for other pattern languages can be relatively easily achieved. The experimental evaluation (Sect. 5) confirms the theory, but also reveals a weakness of the proposed approach which we speculate is shared by other direct pattern sampling approaches. We thus conclude with a broader discussion of this issue (Sect. 6), and a forward look (Sect. 7).

2 Problem Formulation

2.1 Notation

Input Dataset. A dataset $\mathbf{D}$ is a Boolean matrix with m rows and n columns. For $i \in [\![1, m]\!]$ and $j \in [\![1, n]\!]$, $\mathbf{D}(i, j) \in \{0, 1\}$ denotes the value of the cell corresponding to the i-th row and the j-th column. For a given set of rows $I \subseteq [\![1, m]\!]$, we define the support function $supp_C(I)$ that gives all the columns having a value of 1 in all the rows of I, i.e., $supp_C(I) = \{j \in [\![1, n]\!] \mid \forall i \in I : D(i, j) = 1\}$. Similarly, for a set of columns $J \subseteq [\![1, n]\!]$, we define the function $supp_R(J) = \{i \in [\![1, m]\!] \mid \forall j \in J : D(i, j) = 1\}$. Table 1 shows a toy example of a Boolean matrix, where for $I = \{4, 5, 6\}$ we have that $supp_C(I) = \{2, 3, 4\}$.

Table 1. Example of a binary dataset $\mathbf{D}$.

#	1	2	3	4	5
1	0	1	0	1	0
2	0	1	1	0	0
3	1	0	1	0	1
4	0	1	1	1	0
5	1	1	1	1	1
6	0	1	1	1	0
7	0	1	1	1	1

Pattern Language. This paper is concerned with a particular kind of pattern known as a tile [8], denoted $\tau = (I, J)$ and defined as an ordered pair of a set of rows $I \subseteq \{1, ..., m\}$ and a set of columns $J \subseteq \{1, ...n\}$. A tile τ is said to be contained (or present) in $\mathbf{D}$, denoted as $\tau \in \mathbf{D}$, iff $\mathbf{D}(i, j) = 1$ for all $i \in I$ and $j \in J$. The set of all tiles present in the dataset is denoted as T and is defined as: $T = \{(I, J) \mid I \subseteq \{1, ..., m\} \wedge J \subseteq \{1, ...n\} \wedge (I, J) \in \mathbf{D}\}$. In Table 1, the tile $\tau_1 = (\{4, 5, 6, 7\}, \{2, 3, 4\})$ is present in $\mathbf{D}$ ($\tau_1 \in T$), because each of its cells has a value of 1, but $\tau_2 = (\{1, 2\}, \{2, 3\})$ is not present ($\tau_2 \notin T$) since $\mathbf{D}(1, 3) = 0$.

2.2 The Interestingness of a Tile

In order to assess the quality of a tile τ, we use the framework of subjective interestingness SI proposed in [6]. We briefly recapitulate the definition of this measure for tiles, denoted $\mathrm{SI}(\tau)$ for a tile τ, and refer the reader to [6] for more details. $\mathrm{SI}(\tau)$ measures the quality of a tile τ as the ratio of its subjective information content $\mathrm{IC}(\tau)$ and its description length $\mathrm{DL}(\tau)$:

$$\mathrm{SI}(\tau) = \frac{\mathrm{IC}(\tau)}{\mathrm{DL}(\tau)}.$$

Tiles with large $\mathrm{SI}(\tau)$ thus compress subjective information in a short description. Before introducing IC and DL, we first describe the background model—an important component required to define the subjective information content IC.

Background Model. The SI is subjective in a sense that it accounts for prior knowledge of the current data miner. A tile τ is informative for a particular user if this tile is somehow surprising for her, otherwise, it does not bring new information. The most natural way for formalizing this is to use a background distribution representing the data miner's prior expectations, and to compute the probability $\Pr(\tau \in \mathbf{D})$ of this tile under this distribution. The smaller $\Pr(\tau \in \mathbf{D})$, the more information this pattern contains. Concretely, the background model consists of a value $\Pr(\mathbf{D}(i,j) = 1)$ associated to each cell $\mathbf{D}(i,j)$ of the dataset, and denoted p_{ij}. More precisely, p_{ij} is the probability that $\mathbf{D}(i,j) = 1$ under user prior beliefs. In [6], it is shown how to compute the background model and derive all the values p_{ij} corresponding to a given set of considered user priors. Based on this model, the probability of having a tile $\tau = (I, J)$ in $\mathbf{D}$ is:

$$\Pr(\tau \in \mathbf{D}) = \Pr\left(\bigwedge_{i \in I, j \in J} \mathbf{D}(i,j) = 1\right) = \prod_{i \in I, j \in J} p_{ij}.$$

***Information Content IC*.** This measure aims to quantify the amount of information conveyed to a data miner when she is told about the presence of a tile in the dataset. It is defined for a tile $\tau = (I, J)$ as follows:

$$\mathrm{IC}(\tau) = -\log(\Pr(\tau \in \mathbf{D})) = \sum_{i \in I, j \in J} -\log(p_{ij}).$$

Thus, the smaller $\Pr(\tau \in \mathbf{D})$, the higher $\mathrm{IC}(\tau)$, and the more informative τ. Note that for $\tau_1, \tau_2 \in \mathbf{D} : \mathrm{IC}(\tau_1 \cup \tau_2) = \mathrm{IC}(\tau_1) + \mathrm{IC}(\tau_2) - \mathrm{IC}(\tau_1 \cap \tau_2)$.

***Description Length DL*.** This function should quantify how difficult it is for a user to assimilate the pattern. The description length of a tile $\tau = (I, J)$ should thus depend on how many rows and columns it refers to: the larger are $|I|$ and $|J|$, the larger is the description length. Thus, $\mathrm{DL}(\tau)$ can be defined as:

$$\mathrm{DL}(\tau) = a + b \cdot (|I| + |J|),$$

where a and b are two constants that can be handled to give more or less importance to the contributions of $|I|$ and $|J|$ in the description length.

2.3   Problem Statement

Given a Boolean dataset $\mathbf{D}$, the goal is to sample a tile τ from the set of all the tiles T present in $\mathbf{D}$, with a probability of sampling P_S proportional to $\mathrm{SI}(\tau)$, that is: $P_S(\tau) = \dfrac{\mathrm{SI}(\tau)}{\sum_{\tau' \in T} \mathrm{SI}(\tau')}.$

A naïve approach to sample a tile pattern according to this distribution is to generate the list $\{\tau_1, ..., \tau_N\}$ of all the tiles present in $\mathbf{D}$, sample $x \in [0, 1]$ uniformly at random, and return the tile τ_k with $\dfrac{\sum_{i=1}^{k-1} \mathrm{SI}(\tau_i)}{\sum_i \mathrm{SI}(\tau_i)} \leq x < \dfrac{\sum_{i=1}^{k} \mathrm{SI}(\tau_i)}{\sum_i \mathrm{SI}(\tau_i)}.$

However, the goal behind using sampling approaches is to avoid materializing the pattern space which is generally huge. We want to sample without exhaustively enumerating the set of tiles. In [2], an efficient procedure is proposed to directly sample patterns according to some measures such as the frequency and the area. However, this procedure is limited to only some specific measures. Furthermore, it is proposed for pattern languages defined on only the column dimension, for example, itemset patterns. In such language, the rows related to an itemset pattern $F \subseteq \{1, ..., n\}$ are uniquely identified and they correspond to all the rows containing the itemset, that are $supp_R(F)$. In our work, we are interested in tiles which are defined by both columns and rows indices. In this case, it is not clear how the direct procedure proposed in [2] can be applied.

For more complex pattern languages, a generic procedure based on Metropolis Hasting algorithm has been proposed in [9], and illustrated for subgraph patterns with some quality measures. While this approach is generic and can be extended relatively easily to different mining tasks, a major drawback of using Metropolis Hasting algorithm is that the random walk procedure contains the acceptance test that needs to be processed in each iteration, and the acceptance rate α can be very small, which makes the convergence rate practically extremely slow. Furthermore, Metropolis Hasting can be computationally expensive, as the part of the transition graph representing the probability of reaching patterns given the current one, has to be materialized.

Interestingly, a very useful MCMC technique is Gibbs sampling, which is a special case of Metropolis-Hasting algorithm. A significant benefit of this approach is that the acceptante rate α is always equal to 1, i.e., the proposal of each sampling iteration is always accepted. In this work, we use Gibbs sampling to draw patterns with a probability distribution that converges to P_S. In what follows, we will first generically present the Gibbs sampling approach, and then we show how we efficiently exploit it for our problem. Unlike Metropolis Hasting, the proposed procedure performs a random walk by materializing in each iteration only the currently sampled pattern.

3   Gibbs Sampling

Suppose we have a random variable $X = (X_1, X_2, ..., X_l)$ taking values in some domain Dom. We want to sample a value $x \in Dom$ following the joint distribution $P(X = x)$. Gibbs sampling is suitable when it is hard to sample directly from P but known how to sample just one dimension x_k ($k \in [\![1, l]\!]$) from the conditional probability $P(X_k = x_k \mid X_1 = x_1, ..., X_{k-1} = x_{k-1}, X_{k+1} = x_{k+1}, ..., X_l = x_l)$. The idea of Gibbs sampling is to generate samples by sweeping through each variable (or block of variables) to sample from its conditional distribution with the remaining variables fixed to their current values. Algorithm 1 depicts a generic Gibbs Sampler. At the beginning, x is set to its initial values (often values sampled from a prior distribution q). Then, the algorithm performs a random walk of p iterations. In each iteration, we sample $x_1 \sim P(X_1 = x_1^{(i_1)} \mid X_2 = x_2^{(i_1)}, ..., X_l = x_l^{(i_1)})$ (while fixing the other dimensions), then we follow the same procedure to sample x_2, ..., until x_l.

Algorithm 1: Gibbs sampler

---

1 Initialize $x^{(0)} \sim q(x)$

2 **for** $k \in [\![1, p]\!]$ **do**

3   draw $x_1^{(k)} \sim P\left(X_1 = x_1 \mid X_2 = x_2^{(k-1)}, X_3 = x_3^{(k-1)}, ..., X_l = x_l^{(k-1)}\right)$

4   draw $x_2^{(k)} \sim P\left(X_2 = x_2 \mid X_1 = x_1^{(k)}, X_3 = x_3^{(k-1)}, ..., X_l = x_l^{(k-1)}\right)$

5   ...

6   draw $x_l^{(k)} \sim P\left(X_l = x_l \mid X_1 = x_1^{(k)}, X_2 = x_2^{(k)}, ..., X_{l-1} = x_{l-1}^{(k)}\right)$

7 return $x^{(p)}$

The random walk needs to satisfy some constraints to guarantee that the Gibbs sampling procedure converges to the stationary distribution P. In the case of a finite number of states (a finite space Dom in which X takes values), sufficient conditions for the convergence are irreducibility and aperiodicity:

Irreducibility. A random walk is irreducible if, for any two states $x, y \in Dom$ s.t. $P(x) > 0$ and $P(y) > 0$, we can get from x to y with a probability > 0 in a finite number of steps. I.e. the entire state space is reachable.

Aperiodicity. A random walk is aperiodic if we can return to any state $x \in Dom$ at any time. I.e. revisiting x is not conditioned to some periodicity constraint.

One can also use blocked Gibbs sampling. This consists in growing many variables together and sample from their joint distribution conditioned to the remaining variables, rather than sampling each variable x_i individually. Blocked Gibbs sampling can reduce the problem of slow mixing that can be due to the high number of dimensions used to sample from.

4   Gibbs Sampling of Tiles with Respect to SI

In order to sample a tile $\tau = (I, J)$ with a probability proportional to SI(τ), we propose to use Gibbs sampling. The simplest solution is to consider a tile τ as $m + n$ binary random variables $(x_1, ..., x_m, ..., x_{m+n})$, each of them corresponds to a row or a column, and then apply the procedure described in Algorithm 1. In this case, an iteration of Gibbs sampling requires to sample from each column and row separately while fixing all the remaining rows and columns. The drawback of this approach is the high number of variables $(m + n)$ which may lead to a slow mixing time. In order to reduce the number of variables, we propose to split $\tau = (I, J)$ into only two separated blocks of random variables I and J, we then directly sample from each block while fixing the value of the other block. This means that an iteration of the random walk contains only two sampling operations instead of $m+n$ ones. We will explain in more details how this Blocked Gibbs sampling approach can be applied, and how to compute the distributions used to directly sample a block of rows or columns.

Algorithm 2: Gibbs-SI

---

1 Initialize $(I, J)^{(0)} \sim q(x)$
2 for $k \in [\![1, p]\!]$ **do**
3 $\quad$ draw $I^{(k)} \sim P\left(\mathbf{I} = I \mid \mathbf{J} = J^{(k-1)}\right)$, draw $J^{(k)} \sim P\left(\mathbf{J} = J \mid \mathbf{I} = I^{(k)}\right)$
4 return $(I, J)^{(p)}$

Algorithm 2 depicts the main steps of Blocked Gibbs sampling for tiles. We start by initializing $(I, J)^{(0)}$ with a distribution q proportional to the area $(|I| \times |J|)$ following the approach proposed in [2]. This choice is mainly motivated by its linear time complexity of sampling. Then, we need to efficiently sample from $P(\mathbf{I} = I \mid \mathbf{J} = J)$ and $P(\mathbf{J} = J \mid \mathbf{I} = I)$. In the following, we will explain how to sample I with $P(\mathbf{I} = I | \mathbf{J} = J)$, and since the SI is symmetric w.r.t. rows and columns, the same strategy can be used symmetrically to sample a set of columns with $P(\mathbf{J} = J \mid \mathbf{I} = I)$.

Sampling a Set of Rows I Conditioned to Columns J. For a specific $J \subseteq \{1, ..., n\}$, the number of tiles (I, J) present in the dataset can be huge, and can go up to 2^m. This means that naïvely generating all these candidate tiles and then sampling from them is not a solution. Thus, to sample a set of rows I conditioned to a fixed set of columns J, we propose an iterative algorithm that builds the sampled I by drawing each $i \in I$ separately, while ensuring that the joint distribution of all the drawings is equal to $P(\mathbf{I} = I | \mathbf{J} = J)$. I is built using two variables: $R_1 \subseteq \{1, ..., m\}$ made of rows that belong to I, and $R_2 \subseteq \{1, ..., m\} \setminus R_1$ that contains candidate rows that can possibly be sampled and added to R_1. Initially, we have $R_1 = \emptyset$ and $R_2 = supp_R(J)$. At each step, we take $i \in R_2$, do a random draw to determine whether i is added to R_1 or not, and remove it from R_2. When $R_2 = \emptyset$, the sampled set of rows I is set equal to R_1. To apply this strategy, all we need is to compute $P\left(i \in \mathbf{I} \mid R_1 \subseteq \mathbf{I} \subseteq R_1 \cup R_2 \wedge \mathbf{J} = J\right)$, the probability of sampling i considering the current sets R_1, R_2 and J:

$$P\left(i \in \mathbf{I} \mid R_1 \subseteq \mathbf{I} \subseteq R_1 \cup R_2 \wedge \mathbf{J} = J\right) = \frac{P\left(R_1 \cup \{i\} \subseteq \mathbf{I} \subseteq R_1 \cup R_2 \wedge \mathbf{J} = J\right)}{P\left(R_1 \cup \subseteq \mathbf{I} \subseteq R_1 \cup R_2 \wedge \mathbf{J} = J\right)}$$

$$= \frac{\sum_{F \subseteq R_2 \setminus \{i\}} SI(R_1 \cup \{i\} \cup F, J)}{\sum_{F \subseteq R_2} SI(R_1 \cup F, J)} = \frac{\sum_{F \subseteq R_2 \setminus \{i\}} \frac{IC_{(R_1 \cup \{i\}, J)} + IC_{(F, J)}}{a + b \cdot (|R_1| + |F| + 1 + |J|)}}{\sum_{F \subseteq R_2} \frac{IC_{(R_1, D_i)} + IC_{(F, D_i)}}{a + b \cdot (|R_1| + |F| + |J|)}}$$

$$= \frac{\sum_{k=0}^{|R_2|-1} \frac{1}{a + b \cdot (|R_1| + k + 1 + |J|)} \sum_{\substack{F \subseteq R_2 \setminus \{i\} \\ |F| = k}} (IC(R_1 \cup \{i\}, J) + IC(F, J))}{\sum_{k=0}^{|R_2|} \frac{1}{a + b \cdot (|R_1| + k + |J|)} \sum_{\substack{F \subseteq R_2 \\ |F| = k}} (IC(R_1, J) + IC(F, J))}$$

$$= \frac{\sum_{k=0}^{|R_2|-1} \frac{1}{a + b \cdot (|R_1| + k + 1 + |J|)} \left(\binom{|R_2|-1}{k} \cdot IC(R_1 \cup \{i\}, J) + \binom{|R_2|-2}{k-1} \cdot IC(R_2 \setminus \{i\}, J)\right)}{\sum_{k=0}^{|R_2|} \frac{1}{a + b \cdot (|R_1| + k + |J|)} \left(\binom{|R_2|}{k} \cdot IC(R_1, J) + \binom{|R_2|-1}{k-1} \cdot IC(R_2, J)\right)}$$

$$= \frac{IC(R_1 \cup \{i\}, J) \cdot f(|R_2| - 1, |R_1| + 1) + IC(R_2 \setminus \{i\}, J) \cdot f(|R_2| - 2, |R_1| + 1)}{IC(R_1, J) \cdot f(|R_2|, |R_1|) + IC(R_2, J) \cdot f(|R_2| - 1, |R_1|)},$$

with $f(x, y) = \sum_{k=0}^{x} \frac{\binom{x}{k}}{a + b \cdot (y + k + |J|)}$.

Complexity. Let's compute the complexity of sampling I with a probability $P(\mathbf{I} = I | \mathbf{J} = J)$. Before starting the sampling of rows from R_2, we first compute the value of $\mathrm{IC}(\{i\}, J)$ for each $i \in R_2$ (in $\mathcal{O}(n \cdot m)$). This will allow to compute in $\mathcal{O}(1)$ the values of IC that appear in $P(i \in \mathbf{I} \mid R_1 \subseteq \mathbf{I} \subseteq R_1 \cup R_2 \wedge \mathbf{J} = J)$, based on the relation $\mathrm{IC}(I_1 \cup I_2, J) = \mathrm{IC}(I_1, J) + \mathrm{IC}(I_2, J)$ for $I_1, I_2 \subseteq [\![1, m]\!]$. In addition to that, sampling each element $i \in R_2$ requires to compute the corresponding values of $f(x, y)$. These values are computed once for the first sampled row $i \in R_2$ with a cost of $\mathcal{O}(m)$, and then they can be updated directly when sampling the next rows, using the following relation:

$$f(x - 1, y) = f(x, y) - \frac{1}{a + b \cdot (x + y + |J|)} \cdot f(x - 1, y + 1).$$

This means that the overall cost of sampling the whole set of rows I with a probability $P(\mathbf{I} = I | \mathbf{J} = J)$ is $\mathcal{O}(n \cdot m)$. Following the same approach, sampling J conditionned to I is done in $\mathcal{O}(n \cdot m)$. As we have p sampling iterations, the worst case complexity of the whole Gibbs sampling procedure of a tile τ is $\mathcal{O}(p \cdot n \cdot m)$.

Convergence Guarantee. In order to guarantee the convergence to the stationary distribution proportional to the SI measure, the Gibbs sampling procedure needs to satisfy some constraints. In our case, the sampling space is finite, as the number of tiles is limited to at most 2^{m+n}. Then, the sampling procedure converges if it satisfies the aperiodicity and the irreducibility constraints. The Gibbs sampling for tiles is indeed aperiodic, as in each iteration it is possible to remain in exactly the same state. We only have to verify if the irreducibility property is satisfied. We can show that, in some cases, the random walk is reducible, we will show how to make Gibbs sampling irreducible in those cases.

Theorem 1. *Let us consider the bipartite graph $G = (U, V, E)$ derived from the dataset $\mathbf{D}$, s.t., $U = \{1, .., m\}$, $V = \{1, ..., n\}$, and $E = \{(i, j) \mid i \in [\![1, m]\!] \wedge j \in [\![1, n]\!] \wedge \mathbf{D}(i, j) = 1\}$. A tile $\tau = (I, J)$ present in $\mathbf{D}$ corresponds to a complete bipartite subgraph $G_\tau = (I, J, E_\tau)$ of G. If the bipartite graph G is connected, then the Gibbs sampling procedure on tiles of $\mathbf{D}$ is irreducible.*

Proof. We need to prove that for all pair of tiles $\tau_1 = (I_1, J_1), \tau_2 = (I_2, J_2)$ present in $\mathbf{D}$, the Gibbs sampling procedure can go from τ_1 to τ_2. Let G_{τ_1}, G_{τ_2} be the complete bipartite graphs corresponding to τ_1 and τ_2. As G is connected, there is a path from any vertex of G_{τ_1} to any vertex of G_{τ_2}. The probability that the sampling procedure walks through one of these paths is not 0, as each step of these paths constitutes a tile present in $\mathbf{D}$. After walking on one of these paths, the procedure will find itself on a tile $\tau' \subseteq \tau_2$. Reaching τ_2 from τ' is probable after one iteration by sampling the right rows and then the right columns.

Thus, if the bipartite graph G is connected, the Gibbs sampling procedure converges to a stationary distribution. To make the random walk converge when G is not connected, we can compute the connected components of G, and then apply Gibbs sampling separately in each corresponding subset of the dataset.

Table 2. Dataset characteristics.

Dataset	# rows	# columns	Avg. |row|
mushrooms	8124	120	24
chess	3196	76	38
kdd	843	6159	65.3

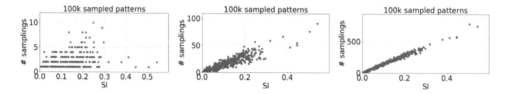

Fig. 1. Distribution of sampled patterns in synthetic data with 10 rows and 10 columns.

5 Experiments

We report our experimental study to evaluate the effectiveness of Gibbs-SI. Java source code is made available[1]. We consider three datasets whose characteristics are given in Table 2. *mushrooms* and *chess* from the UCI repository[2] are commonly used for evaluation purposes. *kdd* contains a set of SIGKDD paper abstracts between 2001 and 2008 downloaded from the ACM website. Each abstract is represented by a row and words correspond to columns, after stop word removal and stemming. For each dataset, the user priors that we represent in the SI background model are the row and column margins. In other terms, we consider that user knows (or, is already informed about) the following statistics: $\sum_j D(i,j)$ for all $i \in I$, and $\sum_i D(i,j)$ for all $j \in J$.

Empirical Sampling Distribution. First, we want to experimentally evaluate how the Gibbs sampling distribution matches with the desired distribution. We need to run Gibbs-SI in small datasets where the size of T is not huge. Then, we take a sufficiently large number of samples so that the sampling distribution can be created. To this aim, we have synthetically generated a dataset containing 10 rows, 10 columns, and 855 tiles. We run Gibbs-SI with three different numbers of iterations p: $1k$, $10k$, and $100k$, for each case, we keep all the visited tiles, and we study their distribution w.r.t. their SI values. Figure 1 reports the results. For $1k$ sampled patterns, the proportionality between the number of sampling and SI is not clearly established yet. For higher numbers of sampled patterns, a linear relation between the two axis is evident, especially for the case of $100k$ sampled patterns, which represents around 100 times the total number of all the tiles in the dataset. The two tiles with the highest SI are sampled the most, and the number of sampling clearly decreases with the SI value.

---

[1] http://tiny.cc/g5zmgz.
[2] https://archive.ics.uci.edu/ml/.

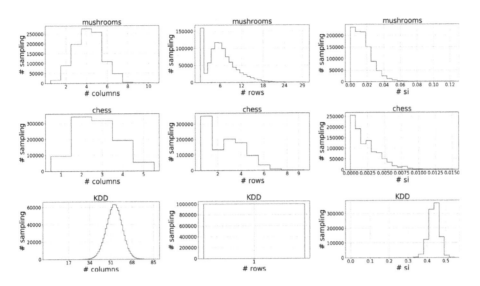

Fig. 2. Distributions of the sampled patterns w.r.t. # rows, # columns and SI.

Characteristics of Sampled Tiles. To investigate which kind of patterns are sampled by Gibbs-SI, we show in Fig. 2 the distribution of sampled tiles w.r.t their number of rows, columns, and their SI, for each of the three datasets given in Table 2. For *mushrooms* and *chess*, Gibbs-SI is able to return patterns with a diverse number of rows and columns. It samples much more patterns with low SI than patterns with high SI values. In fact, even if we are sampling proportionally to SI, the number of tiles in T with poor quality are significantly higher than the ones with high quality values. Thus, the probability of sampling one of low quality patterns is higher than sampling one of the few high quality patterns. For *kdd*, although the number of columns in sampled tiles varies, all the sampled tiles unfortunately cover only one row. In fact, the particularity of this dataset is the existence of some very large transactions (max = 180).

Quality of the Sampled Tiles. In this part of the experiment, we want to study whether the quality of the top sampled tiles is sufficient. As mining exhaustively the best tiles w.r.t. SI is not feasible, we need to find some strategy that identifies high quality tiles. We propose to use LCM [14] to retrieve the closed tiles corresponding to the top 10k frequent closed itemsets. A closed tile $\tau = (I, J)$ is a tile that is present in **D** and whose I and J cannot be extended anymore. Although closed tiles are not necessarily the ones with the highest SI, we make the hypothesis that at least some of them have high SI values as they maximize the value of IC function. For each of the three real world datasets, we compare between the SI of the top closed tiles identified with LCM and the ones identified with Gibbs-SI. In Table 3, we show the SI of the top-1 tile, and the average SI of the top-10 tiles, for each of LCM and Gibbs-SI.

Unfortunately, the scores of tiles retrieved with LCM are substantially larger than the ones of Gibbs-SI, especially for *mushrooms* and *chess*. Importantly,

Table 3. The SI of the top-1 tile, and the average SI of the top-10 tiles, found by LCM and Gibbs-SI in the studied datasets.

	Mushrooms		Chess		KDD	
	Top 1 SI	Avg(top 10 SI)	Top 1 SI	Avg(top 10 SI)	Top 1 SI	Avg(top 10 SI)
Gibbs sampling	0.12	0.11	0.015	0.014	0.54	0.54
LCM	3.89	3.20	0.40	0.40	0.83	0.70

there may exist tiles that are even better than the ones found by LCM. This means that Gibbs-SI fails to identify the top tiles in the dataset. We believe that this is due to the very large number of low quality tiles which trumps the number of high quality tiles. The probability of sampling a high-quality tile is exceedingly small, necessitating a practically too large sample to identify any.

6   Discussion

Our results show that efficiently sampling from the set of tiles with a sampling probability proportional to the tiles' subjective interestingness is possible. Yet, they also show that if the purpose is to identify some of the most interesting patterns, direct pattern sampling may not be a good strategy. The reason is that the number of tiles with low subjective interestingness is vastly larger that those with high subjective interestingness. This imbalance is not sufficiently offset by the relative differences in their interestingness and thus in their sampling probability. As a result, the number of tiles that need to be sampled in order to sample one of the few top interesting ones is of the same order as the total number of tiles.

To mitigate this, one could attempt to sample from alternative distributions that attribute an even higher probability to the most interesting patterns, e.g. with probabilities proportional to the *square* or other high powers of the subjective interestingness. We speculate, however, that the computational cost of sampling from such more highly peaked distributions will also be larger, undoing the benefit of needing to sample fewer of them. This intuition is supported by the fact that direct sampling schemes according to itemset support are computationally cheaper than according to the square of their support [2].

That said, the use of sampled patterns as features for downstream machine learning tasks, even if these samples do not include the most interesting ones, may still be effective as an alternative to exhaustive pattern mining.

7   Conclusions

Pattern sampling has been proposed as a computationally efficient alternative to exhaustive pattern mining. Yet, existing techniques have been limited in terms of which interestingness measures they could handle efficiently.

In this paper, we introduced an approach based on Gibbs sampling, which is capable of sampling from the set of tiles proportional to their subjective interestingness. Although we present this approach for a specific type of pattern language and quality measure, we can relatively easily follow the same scheme to apply Gibbs sampling for other pattern mining settings. The empirical evaluation demonstrates effectiveness, yet, it also reveals a potential weakness inherent to pattern sampling: when the number of interesting patterns is vastly outnumbered by the number of non-interesting ones, a large number of samples may be required, even if the samples are drawn with a probability proportional to the interestingness. Investigating our conjecture that this problem affects all approaches for sampling interesting patterns (for sensible measures of interestingness) seems a fruitful avenue for further research.

Acknowledgements. This work was supported by the ERC under the EU's Seventh Framework Programme (FP7/2007-2013)/ERC Grant Agreement no. 615517, the Flemish Government under the "Onderzoeksprogramma Artificiële Intelligentie (AI) Vlaanderen" programme, the FWO (project no. G091017N, G0F9816N, 3G042220), and the EU's Horizon 2020 research and innovation programme and the FWO under the Marie Sklodowska-Curie Grant Agreement no. 665501, and by the ACADEMICS grant of the IDEXLYON, project of the Université of Lyon, PIA operated by ANR-16-IDEX-0005.

References

1. Boley, M., Gärtner, T., Grosskreutz, H.: Formal concept sampling for counting and threshold-free local pattern mining. In: Proceedings of SDM, pp. 177–188 (2010)
2. Boley, M., Lucchese, C., Paurat, D., Gärtner, T.: Direct local pattern sampling by efficient two-step random procedures. In: Proceedings of KDD, pp. 582–590 (2011)
3. Boley, M., Moens, S., Gärtner, T.: Linear space direct pattern sampling using coupling from the past. In: Proceedings of KDD, pp. 69–77 (2012)
4. Boulicaut, J., Jeudy, B.: Constraint-based data mining. In: Maimon, O., Rokach, L. (eds.) Data Mining and Knowledge Discovery Handbook, pp. 339–354. Springer, Heidelberg (2010). https://doi.org/10.1007/978-0-387-09823-4_17
5. Chaoji, V., Hasan, M.A., Salem, S., Besson, J., Zaki, M.J.: ORIGAMI: a novel and effective approach for mining representative orthogonal graph patterns. SADM 1(2), 67–84 (2008)
6. De Bie, T.: Maximum entropy models and subjective interestingness: an application to tiles in binary databases. DMKD 23(3), 407–446 (2011)
7. Frawley, W.J., Piatetsky-Shapiro, G., Matheus, C.J.: Knowledge discovery in databases: an overview. AI Mag. 13(3), 57–70 (1992)
8. Geerts, F., Goethals, B., Mielikäinen, T.: Tiling databases. In: Suzuki, E., Arikawa, S. (eds.) DS 2004. LNCS (LNAI), vol. 3245, pp. 278–289. Springer, Heidelberg (2004). https://doi.org/10.1007/978-3-540-30214-8_22
9. Hasan, M.A., Zaki, M.J.: Output space sampling for graph patterns. PVLDB 2(1), 730–741 (2009)
10. Kontonasios, K.N., Spyropoulou, E., De Bie, T.: Knowledge discovery interestingness measures based on unexpectedness. Wiley IR: DMKD 2(5), 386–399 (2012)
11. Moens, S., Goethals, B.: Randomly sampling maximal itemsets. In: Proceedings of KDD-IDEA, pp. 79–86 (2013)

12. Pei, J., Han, J., Wang, W.: Constraint-based sequential pattern mining: the pattern-growth methods. JIIS **28**(2), 133–160 (2007)
13. Raedt, L.D., Zimmermann, A.: Constraint-based pattern set mining. In: Proceedings of SDM, pp. 237–248 (2007)
14. Uno, T., Asai, T., Uchida, Y., Arimura, H.: An efficient algorithm for enumerating closed patterns in transaction databases. In: Suzuki, E., Arikawa, S. (eds.) DS 2004. LNCS (LNAI), vol. 3245, pp. 16–31. Springer, Heidelberg (2004). https://doi.org/10.1007/978-3-540-30214-8_2

Evaluation of CNN Performance in Semantically Relevant Latent Spaces

Jeroen van Doorenmalen$^{(\boxtimes)}$ and Vlado Menkovski$^{(\boxtimes)}$

Eindhoven University of Technology, Eindhoven, The Netherlands
`j.v.doorenmalen@student.tue.nl`, `v.menkovski@tue.nl`

Abstract. We examine deep neural network (DNN) performance and behavior using contrasting explanations generated from a semantically relevant latent space. We develop a semantically relevant latent space by training a variational autoencoder (VAE) augmented by a metric learning loss on the latent space. The properties of the VAE provide for a smooth latent space supported by a simple density and the metric learning term organizes the space in a semantically relevant way with respect to the target classes. In this space we can both linearly separate the classes and generate meaningful interpolation of contrasting data points across decision boundaries. This allows us to examine the DNN model beyond its performance on a test set for potential biases and its sensitivity to perturbations of individual factors disentangled in the latent space.

Keywords: Deep learning · VAE · Metric learning · Interpretability · Explanation

1 Introduction

Advances in machine learning and deep learning have had a profound impact on many tasks involving high dimensional data such as object recognition and behavior monitoring. The domain of Computer Vision especially has been witnessing a great growth in bridging the gap between the capabilities of humans and machines. This field tries to enable machines to view the world as humans do, perceive it similar and even use the knowledge for a multitude of tasks such as Image & Video Recognition, Image Analysis and Classification, Media Recreation, recommender systems, etc. And, has since been implemented in high-level domains like COMPAS [8], healthcare [3] and politics [17]. However, as black-box models inner workings are still hardly understood, can lead to dangerous situations [3], such as racial bias [8], gender inequality [1].

The need for confidence, certainty, trust and explanations when using supervised black-box models is substantial in domains with high responsibility. This paper provides an approach towards better understanding of a model's predictions by investigating its behavior on semantically relevant (contrastive) explanations. The build a semantically relevant latent space we need a smooth space that corresponds well with the generating factors of the data (i.e. regions well-supported by the associated density should correspond to realistic data points) and with a distance metric that conveys semantic information about the target task. The vanilla VAE without any extra constraints is insufficient as is does not necessarily deliver a distance metric that corresponds to the semantics of the target class assignment (in our task). Our target is to develop semantically relevant decision boundaries in the latent space, which we can use to examine our target classification model. Therefore, we propose to use a weakly-supervised VAE that uses a combination of metric learning and VAE disentanglement to create a semantically relevant, smooth and well separated space. And, we show that we can use this VAE and semantically relevant latent space can be used for various interpretability/explainability tasks, such as validate predictions made by the CNN, generate (contrastive) explanations when predictions are odd and being able to detect bias. The approach we propose for these tasks is more specifically explained using Fig. 1.

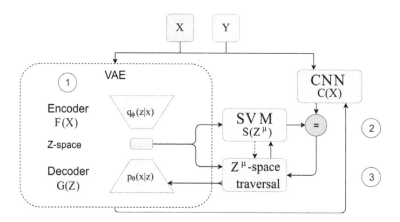

Fig. 1. The diagnostics approach to validate and understand the behavior of the CNN. (1) extra constraints, loss functions are applied during training of the VAE in order to create semantically relevant latent spaces. The generative model captures the essential semantics within the data and is used by (2) A linear Support Vector Machine. The linear SVM is trained on top of the latent space to classify input on semantics rather than the direct mapping from input data X and labels Y. If the SVM and CNN do not agree on a prediction then (3) we traverse the latent space in order to generate and capture semantically relevant synthetic images, tested against the CNN, in order to check what elements have to change in order to change its prediction from a to b, where a and b are different classes.

In this paper, the key contributions are: (1) an approach that can be used in order to validate and check predictions made by a CNN by utilizing a weakly-supervised generative model that is trained to create semantically relevant latent spaces. (2) The semantically relevant latent spaces are then used in order to train a linear support vector machine to capture decision rules that define a class assignment. The SVM is then used to check predictions based on semantics rather than the direct mapping of the CNN. (3) if there is a misalignment in the predictions (i.e. the CNN and SVM do not agree) then we posit the top k best candidates (classes) and for these candidates traverse the latent spaces in order to generate semantically relevant (contrastive) explanations by utilizing the decision boundaries of the SVM.

To conclude, This paper posits a method that allows for the validation of CNN performance by comparing it against the linear classifier that is based on semantics and provides a framework that generates explanations when the classifiers do not agree. The explanations are provided qualitatively to an expert within the field. This explanation encompasses the original image, reconstructed images and the path towards its most probable answers. Additionally, it shows the minimal difference that makes the classifiers change its prediction to one of the most probable answers. The expert can then check these results to make a quick assessment to which class the image actually belongs to. Additionally, the framework provides the ability to further investigate the model mathematically using the linear classifier as a proxy model.

2 Related Work

Interest in interpretability and explainability studies has significantly grown since the inception of "Right to Explanation" [20] and ethicality studies into the behavior of machine learning models [1,3,8,17]. As a result, developers of AI are promoted and required, amongst others, to create algorithms that are transparent, non-discriminatory, robust and safe. Interpretability is most commonly used as an umbrella term and stands for providing insight into the behavior and thought processes behind machine-learning algorithms and many other terms are used for this phenomenon, such as, Interpretable AI, Explainable machine learning, causality, safe AI, computational social science, etc. [5]. We posit our research as an interpretability study, but it does not necessarily mean that other interpretability studies are directly closely related to this work.

There have been many approaches that all work towards the goal of understanding black-box models: Linear Proxy Models: Lime [18] are approaches that locally approximate complex models using linear fits, Decision trees and Rule extraction methods, such as deepred [21] are also considered highly explainable, but quickly become intractable as complexity increases and salience mapping [19] that provide visual information as to which part of an image is most likely used in its prediction, however, it has been demonstrated to be unreliable if not strongly conditioned [10]. Additionally, another approach to interpretability is explaining the role of each part within a black-box models such as the role of a layer or individual neurons [2] or representation vectors within the activation space [9].

Most of the approaches stated above assume that there has to be a tradeoff between model performance and explainability. Additionally, as the current interpretable methods for black-box models are still insufficient and approximated can cause more harm than good when communicated as a method that solves all problems. A lot of the interpretability methods do not take into account the actual needs that stakeholders require [13]. Or, fail to take into account the vast research into explanations or interpretability of the field of psychology [14] and social sciences [15]. The "Explanation in Artificial Intelligence" study by Miller [15] describes the current state of interpretable and explainable algorithms, how most of the techniques currently fail to capture the essence of an explanation and how to improve: an interpretability or explainability method should at least include, but is not limited to, a non-disputable textual- and/or mathematical- and/or visual explanation that is selective, social and depending on the proof, contrastive.

For this reason, our approach focuses on providing selective (contrastive) explanations that combines visual aspects as well as the ability to further investigate the model mathematically using a proxy model that does not impact the CNN directly. Usually, generative models such as the Variational Autoencoders (VAE) [11] and Generative Adversarial Networks (GAN)s are unsupervised and used in order to sample and generate images from a latent space, provided by training the generative network. However, we posit to use a weakly-supervised generative network in order to impose (discriminative) structure in addition to variational inference to the latent space of said model using metric learning [6].

This approach and method is therefore most related to the interpretability area of sub-sampling proxy generative models to answer questions about a discriminative black box model. The two closest studies that attempt similar research is a preprint of CDeepEx [4] by Amir Feghahati et al. and xGEMs [7] by Joshi et al. Both cDeepEx and xGEMS propose the use of a proxy generative model in order to explain the behavior of a black-box model, primarily using generative adversarial networks (GANs). The xGems paper presents a framework to characterize and explaining binary classification models by generating manifold guided examples using a generative model. The behavior of the black box model is summarized by quantitatively perturbing data samples along the manifold. And, xGEMS detects and quantifies bias during model training to understand how bias affects black box models. The xGEMS approach is similar to our approach as in using a generative model in order to explain a black box model. Similarly, the cDeepEx paper posits their work as generating contrastive explanations using a proxy generative model. The generated explanations focus on answering the question "why a and not b?" with GANs, where a is the class of an input example I and b is a chosen class to which to capture the differences.

However, both of these papers do not state that in a multi-class (discriminative) classification problem if the generative models' latent space is not smooth, well separated and semantically relevant then unexpected behavior can happen. For instance, when traversing the latent space it is possible to can pass from a to any number of classes before reaching class b because the space is not well separated and smooth. This will create ineffective explanations, as depending on how they generate explanations will give information on 'why class a and not b using properties of c'. An exact geodesic path along the manifold would require great effort, especially in high dimensions. Also, our approach is different in the fact that we utilize a weakly-supervised generative model as well as an extra linear classifier on top of the latent space to provide us with extra information on the data and the latent space. Some approaches we take, however, are very similar, such as using a generative model as a proxy to explain a black-box model as well as sub-sampling the latent space to probe the behavior of a black-box model and generate explanations using the predictions.

3 Methodology

This paper posits its methodology as a way to explain and validate decisions made by a CNN. The predictions made by the CNN are validated and explained utilizing the properties of a weakly-supervised proxy generative model, more specifically, a triplet-vae. There are three main factors that contribute to the validation and explanation of the CNN. First, a triplet-vae is trained in order to provide a semantically relevant and well separated latent space. Second, this latent space is then used to train an interpretable linear support vector machine and is used to validate decisions by the CNN by comparison. Third, when a CNN decision is misaligned with the decision boundaries in the latent space, we generate explanations through stating the K most probable answers as well as provide a qualitative explanation to validate the top K most probable answers. Each of these factors respectively refer to the number stated in Fig. 1 as well as link to each section: (1) triplet-vae Sect. 3.1, (2) CNN Decision Validation, Sect. 3.2, (3) Generating (contrastive) Explanations, Sect. 3.3.

3.1 Semantically Relevant Latent Space

Typically, a triplet network consists of three instances of a neural network that share parameters. These three instances are separately fed differences types of input: an anchor, positive sample and negative sample. These are then used to learn useful representations by distance comparisons. We propose to incorporate this notion of a triplet network to semantically structure and separate the latent space of the VAE using the available input and labels. A triplet VAE consists of three instances of the encoder with shared parameters that are each fed pre-computed triplets: an anchor, positive sample and negative sample; x_a, x_p and x_n. The anchor x_a and positive sample x_p are of the same class but not the same image, whereas negative sample x_n is from a different class. In each iteration of training, the input triplet is fed to the encoder network to get their mean latent embedding: $\mathcal{F}(x_a)^\mu = z_a^\mu$, $\mathcal{F}(x_p)^\mu = z_p^\mu$, $\mathcal{F}(x_n)^\mu = z_n^\mu$. These are then used to compute a similarity loss function as to induce loss when a negative sample z_n^μ is closer to z_a^μ than z_p^μ distance-wise. i.e. $\delta_{ap}(z_a^\mu, z_p^\mu) = ||z_a^\mu - z_p^\mu||$ and $\delta_{an}(z_a^\mu, z_n^\mu) = ||z_a^\mu - z_n^\mu||$ and, provides us with three possible situations: $\delta_{ap} > \delta_{an}$, $\delta_{ap} < \delta_{an}$ and $\delta_{ap} = \delta_{an}$ [6].

We wish to find an embedding where samples of a certain class lie close to each other in the latent space of the VAE. For this reason, we wish to add loss the algorithm when we arrive in the situation where $\delta_{ap} > \delta_{an}$. In other words,

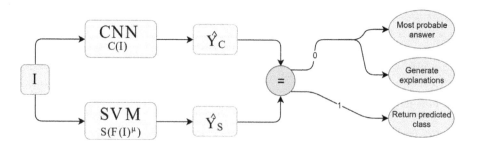

Fig. 2. Given an input image I we check the prediction of the CNN as well as the SVM. If both classifiers predict the same class, we return the predicted class. In contrast, if the classifiers do not predict the same class, we propose to return the top k most probable answers as well as an explanation why those classes are the most probable.

we wish to push x_n further away, such that we ultimately arrive in the situation where $\delta_{ap} < \delta_{an}$ or $\delta_{ap} = \delta_{an}$ with some margin ϕ. As such we arrive at the triplet loss function that we'll use in addition to the KL divergence and reconstruction loss within the VAE: $L(z_a^\mu, z_p^\mu, z_n^\mu) = \alpha * \mathrm{argmax}\{||z_a^\mu - z_p^\mu|| - ||z_a^\mu - z_n^\mu|| + \phi\,, 0\}$. Where ϕ will provide leeway when $\delta_{ap} = \delta_{an}$ and push the negative sample away even when the distances are equal.

We have an already present CNN which we would like to validate, and is trained by input data $X : x_i...x_n$ and labels $Y : y_i...y_n$ where each y_i states the true class of x_i. We then use the same X and Y to train the triplet-VAE. (1) First, we compute triplets of the form $x_a, x_p x_n$ from the input data X and labels Y which are then used to train the triplet VAE. A typical VAE consists of an $\mathcal{F}(x) = Encoder(x) \sim q(z|x)$ which compresses the data into a latent space Z, a $\mathcal{G}(z) = Decoder(z) \sim p(x|z)$ which reconstructs the data given the latent space Z and a prior $p(z)$, in our case a gaussian $\mathcal{N}(0, 1)$, imposed on the model. In order for the VAE to train a latent space similar to its prior and be able to reconstruct images it is trained by minimizing the Evidence Lower Bound (ELBO). $ELBO = -\mathbb{E}_{z \sim Q(z|X)}[\log P(x|z)] + \mathcal{KL}[Q(z|X)||P(z)]$ This can be explained as the reconstruction loss or expected negative loglikelihood: $-\mathbb{E}_{z \sim Q(z|X)}[\log P(x|z)]$ and the KL divergence loss $\mathcal{KL}[Q(z|X)||P(z)]$, to which we add the triplet loss:

$$\mathcal{L}(z_a^\mu, z_p^\mu, z_n^\mu) = \alpha * \mathrm{argmax}\{||z_a^\mu - z_p^\mu|| - ||z_a^\mu - z_n^\mu|| + \phi\,, 0\}$$

This compound loss semi-forces the latent space of the VAE to be well separated due to the triplet loss, disentangled due to the KL divergence loss combined with β scalar, and provides a means of (reasonably) reconstructing images by the reconstruction loss. And, thus results in the following loss function for training the VAE:

$$loss = -\mathbb{E}_{z \sim Q(z|X)}[\log P(x|z)] + \beta * \mathcal{KL}[Q(z|X)||P(z)] + \mathcal{L}(z_a^\mu, z_p^\mu, z_n^\mu).$$

3.2   Decision Validation

Afterwards, given a semantically relevant latent space we can use it for step two and three as indicated in Fig. 1. (2) Second step - CNN Decision Validation, we train an additional classifier on top of the triplet-VAE latent space, specifically z^μ. We train the linear Support Vector Machine using Z^μs as input data and Y as labels where $[Z^\mu, Z^\sigma] = \mathcal{F}(\mathcal{X})$. The goal of the linear support vector machine is two-fold. It provides a means of validating each prediction made by the CNN by using the encoder and the linear classifier. i.e. given an input example I, we have $\mathcal{C}(I) = \hat{y}_{\mathcal{C}(I)}$ and $\mathcal{S}(\mathcal{F}(I)^\mu) = \hat{y}_{\mathcal{S}(I)}$, and compare them against each other $\hat{y}_{\mathcal{C}(I)} = \hat{y}_{\mathcal{S}(I)}$. And, as the linear classifier is a simpler model than the highly complex CNN it will function as the ground-truth base for the predictions that are made. As such, we arrive at two possible cases:

$$\text{Comparison(I)} = \begin{cases} \text{Positive} & \text{if } (\hat{y}_{\mathcal{C}(I)} = \hat{y}_{\mathcal{S}(I)}) \\ \text{Negative} & \text{if } (\hat{y}_{\mathcal{C}(I)} \neq \hat{y}_{\mathcal{S}(I)}) \end{cases} \tag{1}$$

First, If both classifiers agree then we arrive at an optimal state, meaning that the prediction is based on semantics and the direct mapping found by the CNN. In this way, we can say with high confidence that the prediction is correct. In the second case, if the classifiers do not agree, three cases can occur: the SVM is correct and the CNN is incorrect, the SVM is incorrect and the CNN is correct, or both the SVM and the CNN is incorrect. In each of these cases we can suggest a most probable answer as well as a selective (contrastive) explanation indicated as step 3 of the framework as explained in Fig. 2.

3.3   Generating (contrastive) Explanations

An explanation consists of (1) the most probable answers and (2) a qualitative investigation of latent traversal towards the most probable answers The most probable answer is presented by the averaged sum rule [12] over the predicted probabilities per class for both the CNN and SVM and selecting the top K answers, where K can be appropriately selected. Additionally, originally an SVM does not return a probabilistic answer, however, applying Platts [16] method we apply an additional sigmoid function to map the SVM outputs into probabilities. These top k answers are then used in order to present and generate selected contrastive explanations.

The top K predictions or classes will be used in order to traverse and sub-sample the latent space from the initial representation or Z_I^μ location towards another class. We can find a path by finding the closest point within the latent space such that the decision boundary is crossed and the SVM predicts the target class. Alternatively we could use the closest data point in the latent space that adheres to the training set $\arg\min \mathcal{F}(x_i)^\mu - Z_I^\mu$ for every $x_i \in X$. Traversing and sub-sampling the latent space will change the semantics minimally to change the class prediction. We capture the minimal change needed in order to change both the SVM and CNN prediction to the target class. This information is then

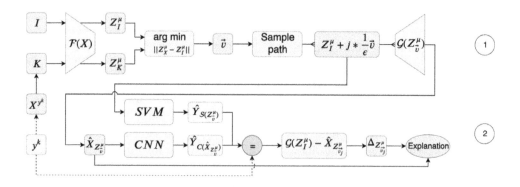

Fig. 3. Generating (contrastive) explanations consist of several steps: First, given an input image I in question and the K top most probable answer. K denotes training data X for class k labeled with $y = k$. We feed both I and K through the encoder $\mathcal{F}(X)$ to receive their respective semantic location in the latent space. We then find the closest training point that belongs to the target class k and find the vector $\boldsymbol{v}$; the direction of that point. Afterwards, uniformly sample ϵ data points along this vector $\boldsymbol{v}$, where j iterates over $0 \cdots j \cdots \epsilon$ and is denoted as Z_v^μ. Z_v^μ is then used to check these against the SVM and use them to generate images $X_{Z_v^\mu}$ using the decoder $\mathcal{G}(Z_v^\mu)$. The generated images are then fed to the CNN to make a prediction and as the images will semantically change along the vector the prediction will change as well. Afterwards, we can compare the predictions from both the CNN and SVM. Subsequently, we use the first moment where both predictions are equal to target class k, denoted as moment l for generating an explanation - minimal semantic difference necessary to be equal to the target class, ΔU_l.

presented to the domain expert for verification and answers the following question: The most probable answer is a because the input image I is semantically closest to the following features, where the features are presented qualitatively. The explanations are generated as follows: see Fig. 3.

The decision boundaries around the clusters within the latent space are fitted by the SVM and can be used to answer questions of the form 'why a and not b?'. If $\hat{y}_{\mathcal{C}(I)}$ and $\hat{y}_{\mathcal{S}(I)}$ do not predict the same class, then, we assume that $\hat{y}_{\mathcal{S}(I)}$ is correct. We then use the find a path, indicated by $\boldsymbol{v}$ from $\hat{y}_{\mathcal{S}(I)}$ to $\hat{y}_{\mathcal{C}(I)}$, Z_I^μ to the target class. This can be done by calculating a vector orthogonal to the hyper-plane fitted by the SVM towards the target class. Alternatively, we can find the closest $z^\mu \in Z^\mu$ that satisfies $\hat{y}_{\mathcal{S}(z^\mu)} = \hat{y}_{\mathcal{C}(z^\mu)}$ that are not the same as the initial prediction $\hat{y}_{\mathcal{C}(I)}$. This means that $\boldsymbol{v}$ is the vector from I to the closest data point of the target class, with respect to Euclidean distance.

We then uniformly sample points along vector $\boldsymbol{v}$ and check them against the SVM as well as the CNN. The sampled points can directly be fed to the SVM to get a prediction $\hat{y}(\int(v_i))$ for every $v_i \in V$. Similarly, we can get predictions of the CNN by transforming the images using the decoder $\mathcal{D}$. The images are then fed to the CNN to get a prediction $\hat{y}(\mathcal{C}(\mathcal{D}(v_i)))$ for every $v_i \in V$. The predictions of both classifiers will change as the images start looking more and more like the target class as generative factors change along the vector. If we capture the changes that make the change happen, we can show the minimal difference required in order to change the prediction of the CNN. In this way we can generate contrastive examples: For the top 'close' class that is not $\hat{y}_I$ we answer the question: 'why $\hat{y}_I$ and not the other semantically close class?'. Hence, we find the answer to the question "why a and not b?", as the answer is the shortest approximate changes between the two classes that make the CNN change its prediction. As a result, we have found a way to validate the inner workings of the CNN. If there are doubts about a prediction it can be investigated and checked.

4 Results

In this paper we show experimental results on MNIST by generating (contrastive) explanations to provide extra information to predictions made by the CNN and evaluate its performance. The creation of these explanations requires a semantically relevant and well separated latent space. Therefore, we first show the difference between the latent space of the vanilla VAE and the triplet-VAE and its effects on training a linear classifier on top of the latent space. The Figs. 4 and 5 show a tSNE visualization of the separation of classes within the latent space. Not surprisingly the triplet-VAE separated the data in a far more semantically relevant way and this is also reflected with respect to the accuracy of training a linear model on the data.

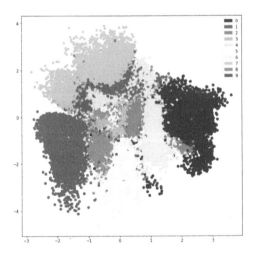

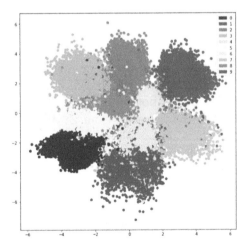

Fig. 4. Visualization of a two-dimensional latent space of a vanilla VAE on MNIST

Fig. 5. Visualization of a two-dimensional latent space of a $\mathcal{T}$-VAE on MNIST

Second, the percentages show as to know how much both classifiers agree by showing the percentage per possible case, as shown in Table 1. Not surprisingly case four happens more often than case three and can mean two things, our latent space is too simple to capture the full complexity of the class assignment and the CNN is not constraint by extra loss functions. However, in three of the four cases where $Y_S \neq Y_C$ we can explain the most probable predictions and provide a generated (contrastive) explanation. The only case we cannot check or know about is case two, where both Y_S and Y_C predict the same class but is wrong. The only way to capture this behavior is by explaining every single decision by generating explanations for everything. Nevertheless, as an example for generating explanations we use an example: 6783 (case 5) as shown in Fig. 6.

Table 1. This table shows the percentages of agreement with respect to all possible cases.

Case	Percentage
(1) $\hat{Y}_S = \hat{Y}_C = Y$	0.9586
(2) $\hat{Y}_S = \hat{Y}_C \neq Y$	0.003
(3) $(\hat{Y}_S = Y) \neq \hat{Y}_C$	0.0086
(4) $\hat{Y}_S \neq (\hat{Y}_C = Y)$	0.0314
(5) $\hat{Y}_S \neq \hat{Y}_C \neq Y$	0.0044

Generating explanations consists of three parts: First, we propose the top K probable answers: for this example the true label is 1, the most probable answers are 6, 8 and then 1 with averaged probabilities 0,512332, 0.3382, 0.1150. Second, Then for those most probable target classes, 6, 8, 1 we traverse the latent space from the initial location Z_I^μ to the closest point of that class, denoted as $v \in$ that is predicted correctly i.e. the SVM and CNN agree. Figure 7 shows the generated images from the uniformly sampled data points along vectors $v_k \in V$ where $k \in K$ stand for 6, 8, 1 in this case.

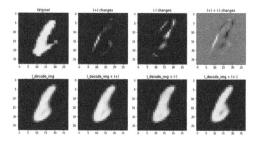

Fig. 6. Once the SVM and the CNN both predict the target class we capture the minimal changes that are necessary to change their predictions

The figures show which changes happen when traversing the latent space and at which points both the SVM and the CNN agree with respect to their decision.

For the traversal from Z_I^μ to class 6 it can be seen that rather quickly both classifiers agree and only minimal changes are required to change the predictions. Third, for such an occurrence we can further zoom in on what is happening and what really makes that the most probable answer. Figure 6 shows these minimal changes required to change its prediction as well as the transformed image on which the classifiers agree. The first row shows the original image, positive changes, negative changes and the changes combined. The second row shows the reconstructed image and the reconstructed images with the positive changes, negative changes and positive and negative changes respectively. In this way, for each probable answer it shows its closest representative and the changes required to be part of that class.

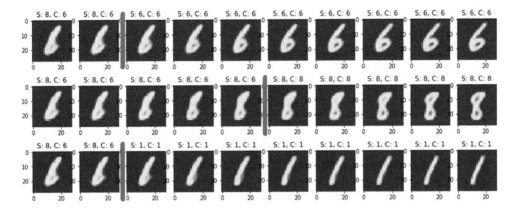

Fig. 7. Per top k probable answers we traverse and sample the latent space to generate images that can be used to test the behavior of the CNN. The red line indicates the moment where both the SVM and the CNN predict the target class (Color figure online)

5   Conclusion

This paper examines deep neural network's behaviour and performance by utilizing a weakly-supervised generative model as a proxy. The weakly-supervised generative model aims to uncover the generative factors underlying the data and separate abstract classes by applying metric learning. The proxy's goal is three-fold: the semantically meaningful space will be the base for a linear support vector machine; The model's generative capabilities will be used to generate images that can be probed against the black box in question; the latent space is traversed and sampled from an anchor I to another class k in order to find the minimal important difference that changes both classifier's predictions. The goal of the framework is to be sure of the predictions made by the black box by better understanding the behaviour of the CNN by simulating questions of the form 'Why a and not b?' where a and b are different classes.

We examine deep neural network (DNN) performance and behaviour using contrasting explanations generated from a semantically relevant latent space. The results show that each of the above goals can be achieved and the framework performs as expected. We develop a semantically relevant latent space by training an variational autoencoder (VAE) augmented by a metric learning loss on the latent space. The properties of the VAE provide for a smooth latent space supported by a simple density and the metric learning term organizes the space in a semantically relevant way with respect to the target classes. In this space we can both linearly separate the classes and generate relevant interpolation of contrasting data points across decision boundaries and find the minimal important difference that changes the classifier's predictions. This allows us to examine the DNN model beyond its performance on a test set for potential biases and its sensitivity to perturbations of individual factors in the latent space.

References

1. Buolamwini, J., Gebru, T.: Gender shades: intersectional accuracy disparities in commercial gender classification. In: Friedler, S.A., Wilson, C. (eds.) Proceedings of the 1st Conference on Fairness, Accountability and Transparency. Proceedings of Machine Learning Research, vol. 81, pp. 77–91. PMLR, New York, February 2018. http://proceedings.mlr.press/v81/buolamwini18a.html

2. Carter, S., Armstrong, Z., Schubert, L., Johnson, I., Olah, C.: Activation atlas. Distill (2019). https://doi.org/10.23915/distill.00015, https://distill.pub/2019/activation-atlas

3. Challen, R., Denny, J., Pitt, M., Gompels, L., Edwards, T., Tsaneva-Atanasova, K.: Artificial intelligence, bias and clinical safety. BMJ Qual. Saf. **28**(3), 231–237 (2019). https://doi.org/10.1136/bmjqs-2018-008370. https://qualitysafety.bmj.com/content/28/3/231

4. Feghahati, A., Shelton, C.R., Pazzani, M.J., Tang, K.: CDeepEx: contrastive deep explanations (2019). https://openreview.net/forum?id=HyNmRiCqtm

5. Gilpin, L.H., Bau, D., Yuan, B.Z., Bajwa, A., Specter, M., Kagal, L.: Explaining explanations: an approach to evaluating interpretability of machine learning. CoRR abs/1806.00069 (2018). http://arxiv.org/abs/1806.00069

6. Ishfaq, H., Hoogi, A., Rubin, D.: TVAE: triplet-based variational autoencoder using metric learning (2018)

7. Joshi, S., Koyejo, O., Kim, B., Ghosh, J.: xGEMs: generating examplars to explain black-box models. CoRR abs/1806.08867 (2018). http://arxiv.org/abs/1806.08867

8. Angwin, J., Larson, J., Mattu, S., Kirchner, L.: Machine bias, May 2016. https://www.propublica.org/article/machine-bias-risk-assessments-in-criminal-sentencing

9. Kim, B., et al.: Interpretability beyond feature attribution: quantitative testing with concept activation vectors (TCAV). In: Dy, J., Krause, A. (eds.) Proceedings of the 35th International Conference on Machine Learning, vol. 80, pp. 2668–2677, July 2018

10. Kindermans, P.J., et al.: The (un)reliability of saliency methods. CoRR abs/1711.00867 (2017). http://dblp.uni-trier.de/db/journals/corr/corr1711.html#abs-1711-00867

11. Kingma, D.P., Welling, M.: An introduction to variational autoencoders. CoRR abs/1906.02691 (2019). http://arxiv.org/abs/1906.02691

12. Kittler, J., Hatef, M., Duin, R.P.W., Matas, J.: On combining classifiers. IEEE Trans. Pattern Anal. Mach. Intell. **20**(3), 226–239 (1998). https://doi.org/10.1109/34.667881

13. Lipton, Z.C.: The doctor just won't accept that! In: NIPS Proceedings 2017, no. 24, pp. 1–3, November 2017. https://arxiv.org/pdf/1711.08037.pdf

14. Lombrozo, T.: Explanation and abductive inference. In: Oxford Handbook of Thinking and Reasoning, pp. 260–276 (2012). https://doi.org/10.1093/oxfordhb/9780199734689.013.0014

15. Miller, T.: Explanation in artificial intelligence: insights from the social sciences. CoRR abs/1706.07269 (2017). http://arxiv.org/abs/1706.07269

16. Platt, J.C.: Probabilistic outputs for support vector machines and comparisons to regularized likelihood methods. In: Advances in Large Margin Classifiers, pp. 61–74. MIT Press (1999)

17. Prakash, A.: Ai-politicians: a revolution in politics, August 2018. https://medium.com/politics-ai/ai-politicians-a-revolution-in-politics-11a7e4ce90b0

18. Ribeiro, M.T., Singh, S., Guestrin, C.: Why should I trust you?: explaining the predictions of any classifier. CoRR abs/1602.04938 (2016). http://arxiv.org/abs/1602.04938
19. Selvaraju, R.R., Das, A., Vedantam, R., Cogswell, M., Parikh, D., Batra, D.: Grad-CAM: why did you say that? Visual explanations from deep networks via gradient-based localization. CoRR abs/1610.02391 (2016). http://arxiv.org/abs/1610.02391
20. European Union: Official journal of the European union: Regulations (2016). https://eur-lex.europa.eu/legal-content/EN/TXT/PDF/?uri=CELEX:32016R0679&from=EN
21. Zilke, J.R., Loza Mencía, E., Janssen, F.: DeepRED – rule extraction from deep neural networks. In: Calders, T., Ceci, M., Malerba, D. (eds.) DS 2016. LNCS (LNAI), vol. 9956, pp. 457–473. Springer, Cham (2016). https://doi.org/10.1007/978-3-319-46307-0_29

Addressing the Resolution Limit and the Field of View Limit in Community Mining

Shiva Zamani Gharaghooshi[1], Osmar R. Zaïane[1(✉)], Christine Largeron[2], Mohammadmahdi Zafarmand[1], and Chang Liu[1]

[1] Alberta Machine Intelligence Institute, University of Alberta, Edmonton, AB, Canada
{zamanigh,zaiane,zafarman,chang6}@ualberta.ca
[2] Laboratoire Hubert Curien, Université de Lyon, Saint-Etienne, France
Christine.Largeron@univ-st-etienne.fr

Abstract. We introduce a novel efficient approach for community detection based on a formal definition of the notion of community. We name the links that run between communities weak links and links being inside communities strong links. We put forward a new objective function, called SIWO (Strong Inside, Weak Outside) which encourages adding strong links to the communities while avoiding weak links. This process allows us to effectively discover communities in social networks without the resolution and field of view limit problems some popular approaches suffer from. The time complexity of this new method is linear in the number of edges. We demonstrate the effectiveness of our approach on various real and artificial datasets with large and small communities.

Keywords: Community detection · Social network analysis

1 Introduction

Community detection is an important task in social network analysis and can be used in different domains where entities and their relations are presented as graphs. It allows us to find linked nodes that we call communities inside graphs. There are community detection methods that partition the graph into subgroups of nodes such as the spectral bisection method [4] or the Kernighan-Lin algorithm [27]. There are also hierarchical methods such as the divisive algorithms based on edge betweenness of Girwan et al. [18] or agglomerative algorithms based on dynamical process such as Walktrap [20], Infomap [24] or Label propagation [22]. We do not detail them and refer the interested reader to [7,10,12], but we come back on another class of hierarchical algorithms that aim at maximizing Q-modularity introduced by Newman et al. [18]. After the greedy agglomerative algorithm initially introduced by Newman [19], Blondel et al. [5] proposed Louvain, one of the fastest algorithms to optimize Q-modularity and to solve the community detection task. However, Fortunato et al. [11] showed that Q-Modularity suffers from the resolution limit which means by optimizing

Q-modularity, communities that are smaller than a scale cannot be resolved. The field of view limit [25] is in contrast to the resolution limit leads to overpartitioning the communities with a large diameter.

To overcome the resolution limit of Q-modularity, several proposals have been made, notably by [2,17,23], who introduced variants of this criterion allowing the detection of community structures at different levels of granularity. However, these revised criteria make the method time-consuming since they require to tune a parameter. Therefore, we retain the greedy approach of Louvain for its efficiency and ability to handle very large networks, but we introduce SIWO because it relies on the notions of strong and weak links defined in Sect. 2.

We consider that a community corresponds to a subgraph sparsely connected to the rest of the graph. Contrary to the majority of methods which do not formally define what is a community and simply consider that it corresponds to a subset of nodes densely connected internally, we define the conditions a subgraph should meet to be considered as a community in Sect. 2. In Sect. 3, we present the generic community detection algorithm. We can apply this general process regardless of the objective function to improve other community detection methods as our experiments show.

Finally, the extensive experiments described in Sects. 4 and 5, confirm that our objective function is less sensitive to the resolution and the field of view limit compared to the objective functions mentioned earlier. Also, our algorithm has consistently good performance regardless of the size of communities in a network and is efficient on large size networks having up to a million edges.

2 Notations and Definitions

2.1 Strong and Weak Links

A community is oftentimes defined as a subgraph in which nodes are densely connected while sparsely connected to the rest of the graph. One way to find such subgraphs is to divide the network into parts so that the number of links lying inside that part is maximized. However, if there is no prior information about the number of communities or their sizes, one can maximize the number of links within communities by putting all the nodes in one community, but the final result will not be the true communities. To avoid this approach, we penalize the missing links within the communities and we introduce the notions of strong and weak links.

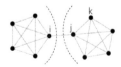

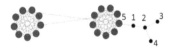

Fig. 1. A network with two communities; each consists of a clique of size 5.

Fig. 2. A network with 2 communities and 4 dangling nodes (1, 2, 3, and 4).

Weak links lie between communities, while strong links are inside them. We develop our criterion so that it encourages adding strong links to the communities while avoiding weak ones instead of penalizing the missing links. As these different types of links play different roles in graph connectivity; removing a weak link may divide the graph into disconnected subgraphs, whereas removing a random link would not. Let us focus on the link between nodes i and j in Fig. 1 and also the link between nodes j and k in this graph. Node j is connected to all the neighbors of node k, whereas node i and j have no common neighbors. As generally, nodes in the same community are more likely to have common neighbors, (i, j) can be considered as a weak link whereas (j, k) as a strong link and it is exactly what we want to capture through weights assigned to the links.

2.2   Edge Strength

Given a graph $G = (V, E)$ where V is the set of nodes and E the set of edges, we propose to assign a weight in the range of $(-1, 1)$ to each edge; such that strong links have larger weights. As nodes in the same community tend to have more common neighbors compared to nodes in different communities, if $S_{xy} > S_{xy'}$ then e_{xy} is more likely to be a strong link compared to $e_{xy'}$ with S_{xy} defined by:

$$S_{xy} = |\{k \in V : (x, k) \in E, (y, k) \in E\}| \tag{1}$$

We can compare two links according to S only if they share a node. Thus, if we consider nodes x and y that have 5 and 20 links incident to them, then S can be in range of $[0, 4]$ and $[0, 19]$ for x and y respectively. Consequently, for comparisons, we have to scale down S values to $(-1, 1)$. If S_{xy} has the maximum value of S_x^{max} ($S_x^{max} = \max_{y:(x,y)\in E} S_{xy}$) for a particular node x. We divide the range $[-1, 1]$ into $S_x^{max} + 1$ equal length segments. Each S value in the range of $[0, S_x^{max}]$ is then mapped to the center of $(n + 1)^{th}$ segment using equation:

$$w_{xy}^x = S_{xy} \frac{2}{S_x^{max} + 1} + \frac{1}{S_x^{max} + 1} - 1 \tag{2}$$

where w_{xy}^x is the scaled value of S_{xy} from the viewpoint of node x (min-max normalization could also work). We can also scale S_{xy} from the viewpoint of node y: $w_{xy}^y = S_{xy} \frac{2}{S_y^{max}+1} + \frac{1}{S_y^{max}+1} - 1$ where $S_y^{max} = \max_{x:(y,x)\in E} S_{xy}$. To decide whether we should trust x or y, we need to look at the importance of each one in the network. Local clustering coefficient (CC) [28], given below, is a measure that reflects the importance of nodes and it can be computed even on large graphs, for instance with Mapreduce [15].

$$CC(x) = \frac{|\{e_{ij} : i, j \in N_x, e_{ij} \in E\}|}{\binom{d_x}{2}} \tag{3}$$

where d_x and N_x are respectively the degree and the set of neighbors of node x. CC is in the range of $[0,1]$ with 1 for nodes whose neighbors form cliques, and 0 for nodes whose neighbors are not connected to each other directly. Here, we scale each edge from the viewpoint of the endpoint that is more likely to be in a dense neighborhood characterized by a large CC:

$$w_{xy} = \begin{cases} w_{xy}^x, & \text{if } CC(x) \geq CC(y) \\ w_{xy}^y, & \text{otherwise} \end{cases} \tag{4}$$

2.3 SIWO Measure

The new measure that we propose encourages adding strong links into the communities while keeping the weak links outside of the communities (**S**trong **I**nside, **W**eak **O**utside). This measure is defined as follows:

$$SIWO = \sum_{i,j \in V} \frac{w_{ij}\delta(c_i, c_j)}{2} \tag{5}$$

where c_i is the community of node i and $\delta(x, y)$ is 1 if $x = y$ and 0 otherwise. SIWO is the sum of weights of the edges that reside in the communities. This objective function provides a way to partition the set of nodes but it does not specify the conditions required by a subset of nodes to be a community. These conditions are defined in the following.

2.4 Community Definition

Following [21] we consider that a subgraph C is a community in a weak sense if the following condition is satisfied:

$$\frac{1}{2} \sum_{v \in C} |N_v^C| > \sum_{v \in C} |N_v - N_v^C| \tag{6}$$

where N_v is the set of the neighbors of node v and N_v^C is the set of the neighbors of node v that are also in community C. This condition means that the collective of the nodes in a community have more neighbors within the community than outside. In this paper, we expand this definition by adding one more condition. Given a partition $p = \{C_1, C_2, ..., C_t\}$ of a network, subgraph C_i is considered as a **qualified community** if it satisfies the following conditions:

1. C_i is a community in a weak sense (Eq. 6).
2. The number of links within C_i exceeds the number of links towards any other subgraph C_j ($j \neq i$) in the partition p taken separately, such that:

$$\frac{1}{2} \sum_{v \in C_i} |N_v^{C_i}| > \sum_{v \in C_i} |N_v^{C_j}|, j \in [1..t], j \neq i \tag{7}$$

3   The SIWO Method

This method has four steps: pre-processing, optimizing SIWO, qualified community identification, and post-processing. They are discussed in detail below.

Step 1. Pre-processing

The first step calculates the edge strength weights (w_{ij}) needed during the SIWO optimization. Moreover, to reduce the computational time, we remove the dangling nodes temporally. Node x is a dangling node if there exists node y such that by removing e_{xy}, the network would be divided into two disconnected parts with $part_x$ (the part containing node x) being a tree. Since $part_x$ has a tree structure, it cannot form a community on its own. So all the nodes in $part_x$ belong to the same community as node y. In Fig. 2, nodes 1, 2, 3 and 4 are dangling nodes and they belong to the same community as node 5, unless we consider them outliers. Even though such tree-structured subgraphs attached to the network are very sparse and cannot be considered as communities, they satisfy Eqs. (6) and (7) defined for qualified communities. So we do not need to consider them during the community detection process. To remove them (and the links incident to them), we need to investigate every node of the network in the first time to identify nodes with degree of 1. However, after the first visit, we only need to check the list of the neighbors of the nodes that are removed in the previous time.

Step 2. Optimizing SIWO

We use Louvain's optimization process to maximize SIWO since it has been proven to be very efficient but we replace the modularity by our criterion. This greedy optimization process has two main phases, iteratively performed until a local maximum of the objective function (SIWO measure) is reached. The first phase starts by placing each node of graph G in its community. Then each node is moved to the neighbor community which results in the maximum gain of the SIWO value. If no gain can be achieved, the node stays in its community. In the second phase, a new weighted graph G' is created in which each node corresponds to a community in G. Two nodes in G' are connected if there exists at least one edge lying between their corresponding communities in G. Finally, we assign each edge e_{xy} in G' a weight equal to the sum of the weights of edges between the communities that match with x and y. These two phases are repeated until no further improvement in the SIWO objective function can be achieved.

Step 3. Qualified Community Identification

This step determines qualified communities complying with Eqs. (6) and (7) for the dense subgraphs discovered in the previous step. However, there may exist communities consisting of one node weakly connected to all of its neighbors ($S_x^{max} = 0$) and that have links with non-positive weight incident to it, we call them Lone communities. Since the decision about the communities of such nodes can not be made on edge strength, we let the majority of their neighbors decide about their communities but, to reduce the computational time, like for dangling nodes, we temporarily remove these nodes in this step and bring them back in the final step. Then, we identify the unqualified communities which do not satisfy Eqs. (6) or (7). We keep merging each unqualified community with one of its neighboring communities (qualified or not) until no more unqualified community exists. For that, first, we assign a weight equal to 1 to each edge. Then, we repeat the two phases of Louvain. In phase 1, we create a new graph G^* in which each node corresponds to a community identified in step 3 for the first iteration of in phase 2 for the next ones and where each edge e_{xy} is assigned a weight equal to the sum of the weights of edges between the communities that correspond to x and y. We also add a self-loop to each node that has a weight equal to the sum of the weights of the edges that reside in its corresponding community. In phase 2, we visit all nodes in G^*. If a node x has a self-loop with a weight that is larger than (1) half of sum of the weights of the edges incident to it and (2) weight of any edge connecting x to another node in G^*, it means the community assigned to x satisfies both the conditions in Eqs. (6) and (7), we let x stay in its community. Otherwise, we move node x to the neighboring community that results in the maximum decrease in the sum of the weights of the edges that lie between communities of G^*.

Step 4. Post-processing
Finally, each lone community that was temporarily removed is sequentially added back to the network and merged with the community in which it has the most neighbors. If two or more communities tie and they have more than one connection to the node, then one is chosen at random. Otherwise, we choose the community of the most important neighbor, based on the largest degree of centrality within its community. Since we add lone nodes one after the other, the community that a former node is assigned to, might not be the best for that node. To resolve this issue, once all lone nodes are added to the network, we repeat moving each one of them to the community of the majority of its neighbors until no further movement can be made. Dangling nodes are also added to the network in the reverse order that they were removed and they are assigned to the community of their unique neighbor.

4   The Resolution Limit of SIWO

Fortunato and Barthélemy [11] used two sample networks, shown in Fig. 3, to demonstrate how Q-modularity is affected by the resolution limit. The first example is a ring of cliques where each clique is connected to its adjacent cliques through a single link. If the number of cliques is larger than about $\sqrt{m}$ with m being the total number of edges in the network, then optimizing Q-modularity results in merging the adjacent cliques into groups of two or more, despite that each clique corresponds to a community. The second example is a network containing 4 cliques: 2 of size k and 2 of size p. If $k >> p$, Q-modularity similarly fails to find the correct communities and the cliques of size p will be merged.

To prove how SIWO resolves the resolution limit of Q-modularity, the exact structure of the network should be known; which is not possible. So, we analyze whether SIWO is affected by the resolution limit on these networks Given the definition of SIWO, let us consider the edge e_{xy} between two adjacent cliques

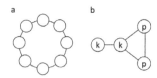

Fig. 3. Schematic examples (a) a ring of cliques; adjacent cliques are connected through a single link (b) a network with 2 cliques of size k and 2 cliques of size p.

in the first network. Since x and y do not have any common neighbors, the edge between them has a non-positive weight. Therefore, by maximizing SIWO measure in our algorithm, the adjacent cliques will not be merged. For the edge e_{xy} between the cliques of size p in the second network, since x and y have at most one common neighbor, the edge between them has a non-positive weight. Therefore, the cliques in the second network will not be merged either.

5   Experimental Results

We compared the performance of our method with the most widely used and efficient algorithms, as pointed out in several recent state of art studies [8,29], on both real and synthetic networks. The algorithms are: 1- Fastgreedy [6]; 2- Infomap; 3- Infomap+ which is Infomap to which we added the third step of our algorithm (to relieve its sensitivity to the field of view limit and demonstrate that our framework can be used to improve other algorithms); 4- Label Propagation [22]; 5- Louvain[1] [5]; 6- Walktrap[2] [20]. It should be noted that Infomap is the only algorithm that suffers from the filed of view limit among these algorithms.

The results are evaluated according to the Adjusted Rand Index (ARI) [14] and Normalized Mutual Information (NMI) [26]. As both ARI and NMI show similar results, we only present ARI results for lack of space. We also compared the results of different methods according to the ratio of the number of detected communities over the true number of communities in the ground-truth to observe how a method is affected by the resolution and the field of view limits.

5.1   Real Networks

We used 5 real networks and the ground-truth communities are available for 4 of them. Table 1 presents the properties of these networks.

We compared SIWO and Louvain on Eurosis network [9] which represents scientific web pages from 12 European countries and the hyperlinks between them without known ground-truth communities. However, since each European country has its own language, web pages in different countries are sparsely connected to each other. Moreover, as reported in [9], some of the countries can be

---

[1] https://github.com/taynaud/python-louvain.
[2] https://www-complexnetworks.lip6.fr/~latapy/PP/walktrap.html.

Table 1. Properties of real networks

Network	#nodes	#edges	#C	Network	#nodes	#edges	#C
Karate [30]	34	78	2	Eurosis [9]	1218	5999	-
Polbooks[a]	105	441	3	Polblogs [1]	1222	16717	2
Football [13]	115	613	12				

[a]http://www.orgnet.com

divided into smaller components e.g. Montenegro network includes three components: 1- Telecom and Engineering, 2- Faculties and 3- High Schools. Louvain detects 13 communities whereas SIWO detects 16 communities in this network. Louvain assigns all nodes in Montenegro network to one giant community. However, SIWO puts Faculties and High Schools in one community and Telecom and Engineering web pages in another community. These two communities are connected to each other with only 7 links. However, Louvain cannot separate them due to its resolution limit.

Table 2. Comparison of 7 algorithms according to ARI and the ratio of the number of detected communities over the true number of communities in the ground-truth on real networks. Tables shows the average results and standard deviation computed on 10 iterations of the algorithms on each network.

		Karate	Polbooks	Football	Polblogs
SIWO	ARI	1 ± 0	$\mathbf{0.67 \pm 0}$	0.79 ± 0	0.77 ± 0
	$\overline{C}/C_r$	1 ± 0	1.3 ± 0	1 ± 0	$\mathbf{1.5 \pm 0}$
Fastgreedy	ARI	0.68 ± 0	0.63 ± 0	0.47 ± 0	0.78 ± 0
	$\overline{C}/C_r$	1.5 ± 0	1.3 ± 0	0.5 ± 0	5 ± 0
Infomap	ARI	0.7 ± 0	0.64 ± 0	0.84 ± 0	0.68 ± 0
	$\overline{C}/C_r$	1.5 ± 0	1.6 ± 0	0.9 ± 0	17.5 ± 0
Infomap+	ARI	0.70 ± 0	0.66 ± 0	$\mathbf{0.84 \pm 0}$	0.76 ± 0
	$\overline{C}/C_r$	1.5 ± 0	1.3 ± 0	0.9 ± 0	1.5 ± 0
Label_prop	ARI	0.66 ± 0.3	0.66 ± 0	0.73 ± 0	$\mathbf{0.8 \pm 0}$
	$\overline{C}/C_r$	1.2 ± 0.35	$\mathbf{1.1 \pm 0.1}$	0.8 ± 0.1	2.1 ± 0
Louvain	ARI	0.46 ± 0	0.55 ± 0	0.8 ± 0	0.77 ± 0
	$\overline{C}/C_r$	2 ± 0	1.3 ± 0	0.8 ± 0	4.5 ± 0
Walktrap	ARI	0.32 ± 0	0.65 ± 0	0.81 ± 0	0.76 ± 0
	$\overline{C}/C_r$	3 ± 0	1.3 ± 0	0.8 ± 0	5.5 ± 0

Table 2 presents the comparison with respect to ARI and $\overline{C}/C_r$, the ratio of the number of detected communities over the true number of communities (both ARI and $\overline{C}/C_r$ should be as close to 1 as possible) in the ground-truth, on real networks with ground-truth communities. It shows that SIWO performs better on Karate and Polbooks based on ARI. It also outperforms the others methods on Karate, Football, and Polblogs networks according to $\overline{C}/C_r$ measure (SIWO could detect the exact communities with respect to the ground-truth on these networks). Infomap detects a considerably larger number of communities in Polblogs network which indicates this algorithm is sensitive to the field of view limit [25]. However, Infomap+ is much less sensitive to this limit which implies the third step of SIWO, added to Infomap+, is effective in resolving the field of view limit. Considering results for all networks, SIWO is the top performer among these algorithms on a variety of networks.

5.2 Synthetic Networks

To analyze the effect of the resolution and field of view limit, it is important to test how community detection algorithms perform on networks with small/large communities. Therefore, in this work we generated two sets of networks using LFR [16] to test the different algorithms: one with large communities and one with small communities. The first set is in favor of algorithms that suffer from resolution limit such as Louvain and the second set is in favor of algorithms with field of view limit such as Infomap. Each set includes networks with a varying number of nodes and mixing parameter. The mixing parameter controls the fraction of edges that lie between communities. We do not generate networks with mixing parameter ≥ 0.5 since beyond this point and including 0.5, the communities in the ground truth no longer satisfy the definition of community. The input parameters used to generate these two sets are presented in Table 3. Figures 4 and 5 present respectively ARI or the ratio of the number of detected communities over the true number of communities ($\overline{C}/C_r$). Panels correspond to networks with a specific number of nodes (1000 to 100000) and they are divided into two parts; the lower (respectively upper) part illustrates the average ARI (or $\overline{C}/C_r$) (respectively standard deviation) computed over 20 graphs (10 small and 10 large communities) as a function of the mixing parameter.

Table 3. Input parameters of LFR benchmark: Set 1 contains networks with large communities and Set 2 contains networks with small communities. For each combination of parameters we generated 10 networks.

	Set 1	Set 2
#nodes (N)	$[1, 10, 50, 100] \times 10^3$	$[1, 10, 50, 100] \times 10^3$
Average and max degrees	20 - $N/10$	20 - $\sqrt{N}$
Mixing parameter	$[1, \ldots, 7] \times 0.1$	$[1, \ldots, 7] \times 0.1$
Min and max community sizes	$N/20$ - $N/10$	Default - by default $\sqrt{N}$

Figure 4 shows the performance of Fastgreedy decreases as the mixing parameter increases. Louvain and Walktrap perform well on the smallest networks in the set; however, its performance drops when we apply it to the networks with sizes 50000 and larger. Label propagation, Infomap and Infomap+ perform well up to when the mixing parameter reaches 0.3. However, a larger mixing parameter causes a rapid decrease in the ARI value when applying these algorithms to the two largest networks in the set. These three algorithms have a large standard deviation and their outputs are not stable on these networks. SIWO correctly detects the communities when the mixing parameter is less than or equal to 0.3 (ARI $\simeq$ 1) regardless of size of the network and has the best performance overall.

Figure 5 clearly shows the resolution limit of Louvain and Fastgreedy as they underestimate the number of communities. SIWO is the best performer in terms of the number of communities and it has a very small standard deviation whereas, Infomap+ and Label propagation have a large standard deviation and fail to find the correct number of communities when the mixing parameter exceeds 0.3.

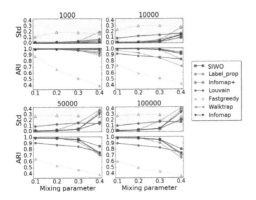 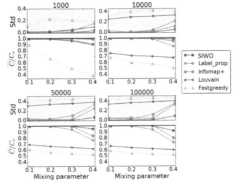

Fig. 4. Evaluation according to ARI on synthetic networks generated with LFR.

Fig. 5. Evaluation of SIWO, Label propagation, Infomap+, Louvain and Fastgreedy according to $\overline{C}/C_r$ on synthetic networks generated with LFR.

6   Scalability

We analyze how the computational cost of SIWO varies with the size of the network. The pre-processing step has two phases: removing dangling nodes which requires a time of the order of n where n is the number of nodes, and calculating the edge strength weights which requires a time of the order of $nd^2 = 2md$ where m is the number of edges and d is the average degree. In many real networks d is much smaller than n and it does not grow with n [10]. The second and third step follows the same greedy process as Louvain does. Louvain is theoretically cubic but was demonstrated experimentally to be quasi-linear [3] and has been applied with success to handle large size networks having several million nodes, and 100 million links. The time complexity of the post-processing step depends on the number of Lone communities and if all the nodes are in Lone communities, it requires a time $O(nd^2)$. Overall, the time complexity of SIWO is $O(n + md)$, which is similar to Louvain due to the fact that d is small and $n = 2m/d$. SIWO can detect communities in a networks with 100000 nodes and 1 million edges, in about 1 min on a commodity i7 and 8GB RAM laptop. The current implementation of SIWO is in Python[3], derived from python-louvain.

7 Conclusion

This paper introduces SIWO, a novel objective function based on edge strength for community detection, and a formal definition of community, that we use to lead the community detection process after optimizing the objective function. This framework can also be applied to other community detection methods to remedy their inability that causes the resolution or the field of view limit. Our extensive experiments using both small and large networks confirm that our algorithm is consistent, effective and scalable for networks with either large or small communities demonstrating less sensitivity to the resolution limit and field of view limit that most community mining algorithms suffer from. As a future direction, we will generalize the proposed algorithm for weighted/directed networks. Notably, SIWO algorithm can be easily generalized to handle weighted graphs. It requires only to adjust the pre-processing step by combining the weights from the input graph and the weights computed by SIWO to evaluate the edge strength.

References

1. Adamic, L.A., Glance, N.: The political blogosphere and the 2004 U.S. election. In: Proceedings of the 3rd International Workshop on Link Discovery, pp. 36–43 (2005)
2. Arenas, A., Fernandez, A., Gomez, S.: Analysis of the structure of complex networks at different resolution levels. New J. Phys. **10**(5), 053039 (2008)
3. Aynaud, T., Blondel, V.D., Guillaume, J.L., Lambiotte, R.: Multilevel Local Optimization of Modularity, pp. 315–345. Wiley, Hoboken (2013)
4. Barnes, E.R.: An algorithm for partitioning the nodes of a graph. SIAM J. Alg. Discr. Meth. **3**(4), 541–550 (1982)
5. Blondel, V.D., Guillaume, J.L., Lambiotte, R., Lefebvre, E.: Fast unfolding of communities in large networks. J. Stat. Mech. Theor. Exp. **2008**(10), P10008 (2008)
6. Clauset, A., Newman, M.E.J., Moore, C.: Finding community structure in very large networks. Phys. Rev. E **70**, 066111 (2004)
7. Coscia, M., Giannotti, F., Pedreschi, D.: A classification for community discovery methods in complex networks. Stat. Anal. Data Min. **4**(5), 512–546 (2013)
8. Emmons, S., Kobourov, S., Gallant, M., Börner, K.: Analysis of network clustering algorithms and cluster quality metrics at scale. PLoS One **11**(7), 1–18 (2016)

---

[3] SIWO Code and datasets available at https://www.dropbox.com/sh/eehjt5qblll0yvg/ AACW2XjHJjHX2Q876Vbk0e4Ya?dl=0 .

9. EUROSIS Final Report: Webmapping of science and society actors in Europe, final report. www.eurosfaire.prd.fr/7pc/documents/1274371553_finalreporteurosis3_1. doc. Accessed 01 June 2018

10. Fortunato, S.: Community detection in graphs. Phy. Rep. **486**(3–5), 75–174 (2010)

11. Fortunato, S., Barthélemy, M.: Resolution limit in community detection. PNAS **104**(1), 36–41 (2007)

12. Fortunato, S., Hric, D.: Community detection in networks: a user guide. Phys. Rep. **659**, 1–44 (2016)

13. Girvan, M., Newman, M.E.J.: Community structure in social and biological networks. PNAS **99**(12), 7821–7826 (2002)

14. Hubert, L., Arabie, P.: Comparing partitions. J. Classif. **2**(1), 193–218 (1985)

15. Kolda, T.G., Pinar, A., Plantenga, T.D., Seshadhri, C., Task, C.: Counting triangles in massive graphs with MapReduce. SIAM J. Sci. Comput. **36**(5), S48–S77 (2014)

16. Lancichinetti, A., Fortunato, S., Radicchi, F.: Benchmark graphs for testing community detection algorithms. Phys. Rev. E **78**(4), 1–5 (2008)

17. Li, Z., Zhang, S., Wang, R.S., Zhang, X.S., Chen, L.: Quantitative function for community detection. Phys. Rev. E **77**(3), 36109 (2008)

18. Newman, M., Girvan, M.: Finding and evaluating community structure in networks. Phys. Rev. E **69**, 026113 (2004)

19. Newman, M.: Fast algorithm for detecting community structure in networks. Phys. Rev. E - Stat. Nonlinear Soft Matter Phys. **69**, 066133 (2004)

20. Pons, P., Latapy, M.: Computing communities in large networks using random walks. In: Yolum, I., Güngör, T., Gürgen, F., Özturan, C. (eds.) ISCIS 2005. LNCS, vol. 3733, pp. 284–293. Springer, Heidelberg (2005). https://doi.org/10.1007/11569596_31

21. Radicchi, F., Castellano, C., Cecconi, F., Loreto, V., Parisi, D.: Defining and identifying communities in networks. PNAS **101**(9), 2658–63 (2004)

22. Raghavan, N., Albert, R., Kumara, S.: Near linear time algorithm to detect community structures in large-scale networks. Phys. Rev. E - Stat. Nonlinear Soft Matter Phys. **76**, 036106 (2007)

23. Reichardt, J., Bornholdt, S.: Statistical mechanics of community detection. Phys. Rev. E **74**, 16110 (2006)

24. Rosvall, M., Bergstrom, C.: Maps of random walks on complex network reveal community structure. PNAS **105**(4), 1118–1123 (2008)

25. Schaub, M.T., Delvenne, J.C., Yaliraki, S.N., Barahona, M.: Markov dynamics as a zooming lens for multiscale community detection: non clique-like communities and the field-of-view limit. PLoS One **7**, e32210 (2012)

26. Strehl, A., Ghosh, J.: Cluster ensembles – a knowledge reuse framework for combining multiple partitions. J. Mach. Learn. Res. **3**, 583–617 (2003)

27. Kernighan, B.W., Lin, S.: An efficient heuristic procedure for partitioning graphs. Bell Syst. Tech. J. **49**(2), 291–307 (1970)

28. Watts, D.J., Strogatz, S.H.: Collective dynamics of 'small-world' networks. Nature **393**(6684), 440–442 (1998)

29. Yang, Z., Algesheimer, R., Tessone, C.J.: A comparative analysis of community detection algorithms on artificial networks. Sci. Rep. **6**, 30750 (2016)

30. Zachary, W.: An information flow model for conflict and fission in small groups. J. Anthropol. Res. **33**, 452–473 (1977)

Overlapping Hierarchical Clustering (OHC)

Ian Jeantet[(⊠)], Zoltán Miklós, and David Gross-Amblard

Univ Rennes, CNRS, IRISA, Rennes, France
{ian.jeantet,zoltan.miklos,
david.gross-amblard}@irisa.fr

Abstract. Agglomerative clustering methods have been widely used by many research communities to cluster their data into hierarchical structures. These structures ease data exploration and are understandable even for non-specialists. But these methods necessarily result in a tree, since, at each agglomeration step, two clusters have to be merged. This may bias the data analysis process if, for example, a cluster is almost equally attracted by two others. In this paper we propose a new method that allows clusters to overlap until a strong cluster attraction is reached, based on a density criterion. The resulting hierarchical structure, called a quasi-dendrogram, is represented as a directed acyclic graph and combines the advantages of hierarchies with the precision of a less arbitrary clustering. We validate our work with extensive experiments on real data sets and compare it with existing tree-based methods, using a new measure of similarity between heterogeneous hierarchical structures.

1 Introduction

Agglomerative hierarchical clustering methods are widely used to analyze large amounts of data. These successful methods construct a dendrogram – a tree structure – that enables a natural exploration of data which is very suitable even for non-expert users. Various tools offer intuitive top-down or bottom-up exploration strategies, zoom-in and zoom-out operations, etc.

Let us consider the following real-life scenario: a social science researcher would like to understand the structure of specific scientific domains based on a large corpus of publications, such as dblp or Wiley. A contemporary approach is to construct a word embedding [23] of the key terms in publications, that is, to map terms into a high-dimensional space such that terms frequently used in the same context appear close together in this space (for the sake of simplicity, we omit interesting issues such as preprocessing, polysemy, etc.). Identifying for example the denser regions in this space directly leads to insights on the key terms of Science. Moreover, building a dendrogram of key terms using an agglomerative method is typically used [9,14] to organize terms into hierarchies. This dendogram (Fig. 1a) eases data exploration and is understandable even for non-specialists of data science.

Despite its usefulness, the dendrogram structure might be limiting. Indeed, any embedding of key terms has a limited precision, and key terms proximity is a debatable question. For example, in Fig. 1a, we can see that the *bioinformatics* key term is almost equally attracted by *biology* and *computing*, meaning that these terms appear frequently together, but in different contexts (e.g. different scientific conferences). Unfortunately, with classical agglomerative clustering, a merging decision has to be made, even if the advantage of one cluster on another is very small. Let us suppose that arbitrarily, *biology* and *bioinformatics* are merged. This may suggest to our analyst (not expert in computer science) that *bioinformatics* is part of *biology*, and its link to *computing* may only appear at the root of the dendrogram. Clearly, an interesting part of information is lost in this process.

In this paper, our goal is to combine the advantages of hierarchies while avoiding early cluster merge. Going back to the previous example, we would like to provide two different clusters showing that *bioinformatics* is closed both to *biology* and *computing*. At a larger level of granularity, these clusters will still collapse, showing that these terms belong to a broader community. This way, we deviate from the strict notion of trees, and produce a directed acyclic graph that we call a quasi-dendrogram (Fig. 1b).

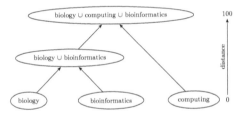
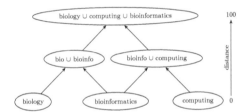

(a) A classical dendrogram, hiding the early relationship between *bioinformatics* and *computing*.

(b) A **quasi-dendrogram**, preserving the relationships of *bioinformatics*.

Fig. 1. Dendrogram and quasi-dendrogram for the structure of Science.

Our contributions are the following:

- We propose an agglomerative clustering method that produces a directed acyclic graph of clusters instead of a tree, called a quasi-dendrogram,
- We define a density-based merging condition to identify these clusters,
- We introduce a new similarity measure to compare our method with other, quasi-dendrogram or tree-based ones,
- We show through extensive experiments on real and synthetic data that we obtain high quality results with respect to classical hierarchical clustering, with reasonable time and space complexity.

The rest of the paper is organized as follows: Sect. 2 describes our proposed overlapping hierarchical clustering framework[1]. Section 3 details our experimen-

---

[1] Source code available at https://gitlab.inria.fr/ijeantet/ohc.

tal evaluation. Section 4 presents the related works, while Sect. 5 concludes the paper.

2   Overlapping Hierarchical Clustering

2.1   Intuition and Basic Definitions

In a nutshell, our method obtains clusters in a gradual agglomerative fashion and in a precise way. At each step, when we increase the neighbourhood of the clusters by including more interconnections, we consider the points that fall in this connected neighbourhood and we take the decision to merge some of them whenever they are connected enough to a cluster using a *density criterion* λ. Taking interconnections into account may lead to overlapping clusters.

More precisely, we consider a set $V = \{X_1, \ldots, X_N\}$ of N points in a n-dimensional space, i.e. $X_i \in V \subset \mathbb{R}^n$ where $n \geq 1$ and $|V| = N$. In order to explore this space in an iterative way, we consider points that are close up to a limit distance $\delta \geq 0$. We define the δ-neighbourhood graph of V as follows:

Definition 1 (δ-neighbourhood graph). *Let $V \subset \mathbb{R}^n$ be a finite set of data points and $E \subset V^2$ a set of pair of elements of V, let d be a metric on $\mathbb{R}^n$ and let $\delta \geq 0$ be a positive number. The δ-neighbourhood graph $G_\delta(V, E)$ is a graph with vertices labelled with the data points in V, and where there is an edge $(X, Y) \in E$ between $X \in V$ and $Y \in V$ if and only if $d(X, Y) \leq \delta$.*

Property 1. If $\delta = 0$ then the δ-neighbourhood graph consists of isolated points while if $\delta = \delta_{max}$, where δ_{max} is the maximum distance between any two nodes in V then $G_\delta(V, E)$ is the complete graph on V.

Varying δ will allow to progressively extend the neighbourhood of the vectors to form bigger and bigger clusters. Clusters will be formed according to the density of a region of the graph.

Definition 2 (Density). *The density [16] $dens(G)$ of a graph $G(V, E)$ is given by the ratio of the number of edges of G to the number of edges of G if it were a complete graph, that is, $dens(G) = \frac{2|E|}{|V|(|V|-1)}$. If $|V| = 1$, $dens(G) = 1$.*

A cluster is simply defined as a subset of the nodes of the graph and its density is defined as the density of the corresponding subgraph.

2.2   Computing Hierarchies with Overlaps

Our algorithm, called OHC, computes a hierarchy of clusters that we can identify in the data. We call the generated structure a quasi-dendrogram and it is defined as follows.

Definition 3 (Quasi-dendrogram). *A quasi-dendrogram is a hierarchical structure, represented as a directed acyclic graph, where the nodes are labelled with a set of data points, the clusters, such as:*

- *The leaves (i.e. the nodes with 0 in-degree) correspond to the singletons, i.e. contain a unique data point. The level of the leaf nodes is 0.*
- *There is only one root node (node with 0 out-degree) that corresponds to the set of all the data points.*
- *Each node (except the root node) has one or more parent nodes. The parent relationship corresponds to inclusion of the corresponding clusters.*
- *The nodes at a level δ represent a set of (potentially overlapping) clusters that is a cover of all the data points. Also, for each pair of points of a given cluster, it exists a path between points of this cluster that have a distance less than δ. In other terms, a node contains a part of a connected subgraph of the δ-neighbourhood graph.*

The OHC method works as presented in Algorithm 1. We first compute the distance matrix of the data points (I3). We chose the cosine distance, widely use in NLP. Then we construct and maintain the δ-neighbourhood graph $G_\delta(V, E)$, starting from $\delta = 0$ (I4).

We also initialize the set of clusters, i.e. the leaves of our quasi-dendrogram, with the individual data points (I4). At each iteration, we increase δ (I6) and consider the new added links to the graph (I8) and the impacted clusters (I9). We extend these clusters by integrating the most linked neighbour vertices if the density does not change more than a given threshold λ (I10–15). We remove all the clusters included in these extended clusters (I16) and add the new set of clusters to the hierarchy as a new level (I18). We stop when all the points are in the same cluster which means that we reached the root of the quasi-dendrogram.

Also to improve the efficiency of this algorithm we use dynamic programming to avoid to recompute information related to the clusters like their density and the list of their neighbour vertices. It lead to significant improvements in the execution time of the algorithm. We will discuss this further in the Sect. 3.3.

Property 2 ($\lambda = 0$). When $\lambda = 0$, each level δ_i of a quasi-dendrogram contains exactly the cliques (complete subgraphs) of the δ_i-neighbourhood graph G_{δ_i}.

Property 3 ($\lambda = 1$). When $\lambda = 1$, each level δ_i of a quasi-dendrogram contains exactly the connected subgraphs of the δ_i-neighbourhood graph G_{δ_i}.

3 Experimental Evaluation

3.1 Experimental Methodology

Tests: The tests we performed were focused on the quality of the hierarchical structures produced by our algorithm. To measure this quality we used the classical hierarchy produced by *SLINK*, an optimal single-linkage clustering algorithm proposed in *Sibson et al.* [28], as a baseline. Our goal was to study the behaviour of the **merging criterion** parameter λ that we introduced, as long as its influence on the **execution time**, to verify if for $\lambda = 1$ we experimentally obtain the same hierarchy as *SLINK* (Property 3) and hence observe the **conservativeness** of our algorithm. We also compared our method to other agglomerative

---

Algorithm 1. Overlapping Hierarchical Clustering (OHC)

1: Input:
　　– $V = \{x_1, \ldots, x_N\}$, N data points.
　　– $\lambda \geq 0$, a merging density threshold.
2: Output: quasi-dendrogram H.
3: Preprocessing: obtain $\Delta = (\delta_1, \ldots, \delta_m)$ the distances between data points in increasing order.
4: Initialization:
　　– Create the graph $G(V, E_0 = \emptyset)$.
　　– Set a list of clusters $C = [\{x_1\}, \ldots, \{x_N\}]$.
　　– Add the list of clusters to the level 0 of H.
5: i=1.
6: **while** $\#C > 1$ and $i \leq m$ **do**
7: 　　**for each** pair $(u, v) \in V^2$ such as $d(u, v) = \delta_i$ **do**
8: 　　　　Add (u, v) to $E_{\delta_{i-1}}$.
9: 　　　　Determine the impacted clusters C_{imp} of C containing either u or v.
10: 　　**for each** impacted cluster $C_{imp_j} \in C_{imp}$ **do**
11: 　　　　Look for the points $\{p_1, \ldots, p_k\}$ that are the most linked to C_{imp_j} in G_{δ_i}.
12: 　　　　Compute the density $dens(S_j)$ of the subgraph $S_j = C_{imp_j} \cup \{p_1, \ldots, p_k\}$.
13: 　　　　**if** $S_j \neq C_{imp_j}$ and $|dens(S_j) - dens(C_{imp_j})| \leq \lambda$ **then**
14: 　　　　　　Continue to add the most linked neighbors to S_j the same way if possible.
15: 　　　　　　When S_j stops growing remove C_{imp_j} from the list of clusters C and add S_j to the list of new clusters C_{new}.
16: 　　Remove all cluster of C included in one of the clusters of C_{new}.
17: 　　Concatenate C_{new} to C.
18: 　　Add the list of clusters to the level δ_i of H.
19: 　　i=i+1.
20: **return** H

---

methods such as the *Ward* variant [29] and *HDBSCAN** [8]. To compare such structures we needed to create a new similarity measure which is described in Sect. 3.2.

Datasets: To partially see the scalability of our algorithm but also to avoid too long running times we had to limit the size of the datasets to few thousand vectors. To be able to compare the results, we run the tests on datasets of same size that we fixed to **1000 vectors**.

- The first dataset is composed of 1000 **randomly** generated 2-dimensional points.
- To test the algorithm on real data and in our motivating scenario, the second dataset was created from the **Wiley** collection via their API[2]. We extracted the titles and abstracts of the scientific papers and trained a word embedding model on the data of a given period of time by using the classical *SGNS* algorithm from *Mikolov et al.* [22] following the recommendation of *Levy et al.* [20]. We set the vocabulary size to only 1000 key words per year even though this dataset allows us to extract up to 50000 of them. This word embedding algorithm created 1000 300-dimensional vectors for each year over 20 years.

Experimental Setting: All our experiments are done on a Intel Xeon 5 Core 1.4 GHz, running MacOS 10.2 on a SSD hard drive. Our code is developed with

---

[2] https://onlinelibrary.wiley.com/library-info/resources/text-and-datamining.

Python 3.5 and the visualization part was done on a Jupyter NoteBook. We used the *SLINK* and Ward implementations from the scikit-learn python package and the *HDBSCAN** implementation of *McInnes et al.* [21].

3.2   A Hierarchy Similarity Measure

As there is no ground truth on the hierarchy of the data we used, we need a similarity measure to compare the hierarchical structures produced by hierarchical clustering algorithms. The goal is not only to compare the topology but also the content of the nodes of the structure. However up to our knowledge there is very little in the literature about hierarchy comparison especially when the structure is similar to a DAG or a quasi-dendrogram. *Fowlkes and Mallows* [19] defined a similarity measure per level and the new similarity function we propose is based on the same principle. First we construct a similarity between two given levels of the hierarchies, and then we extend it to the global structures by exploring all the existing levels.

Level Similarity: Given two hierarchies h_1 and h_2 and a cardinality i, we assume that it is possible to identify a set l_1 (resp. l_2) of i clusters for a given level of hierarchy h_1 (resp. h_2). Then, to measure the similarity between l_1 and l_2, we take the maximal Jaccard similarity among one cluster of l_1 and every clusters of l_2. The average of these similarities, one for each cluster of l_1, will give us the similarity between the two sets. If we consider the similarity matrix of h_1 and h_2 with a cluster of l_1 for each row, a cluster of l_2 for each column and the Jaccard similarity between each pair of clusters at the respective coordinates in the matrix, we can compute the similarity between l_1 and l_2 by taking the average of the maximal value for each row. Hence, the similarity function between two sets of clusters l_1, l_2 is defined as:

$$sim_l(l_1, l_2) = mean\{max\{J(c_1, c_2) \mid c_2 \in l_2\}|c_1 \in l_1\} \qquad (1)$$

where J is the Jaccard similarity function.

However, taking the maximal value of each row shows how the clusters of the first set are represented in the second. If we take the maximal value of each column we will see the opposite, i.e. how the second set is represented in the first set. Hence with this definition the similarity might not be symmetrical so we propose this corrected similarity measure that shows how both sets are represented in the other one:

$$sim_l^*(l_1, l_2) = mean(sim_l(l_1, l_2), sim_l(l_2, l_1)) \qquad (2)$$

Complete Similarity: Now that we can compare two levels of the hierarchical structures, we can simply average the similarity for each corresponding levels of the same size. For classical dendograms, each level has a distinct number of clusters so identification of levels is easy. Conversely, our quasi-dendrograms may have several distinct levels (pseudo-levels) with the same number of clusters. If so, we need to find the best similarity between these pseudo-levels. For a given level (i.e. number of clusters), we want to build a matching M that maps each pseudo-level $l_1^1, l_1^2, \ldots$ of h_1 to at least one pseudo-level $l_2^1, l_2^2, \ldots$ of h_2 and conversely (see Fig. 2). This matching M should maximize the similarity between pseudo-levels while preserving their hierarchical relationship. That is, for a, b, c, d representing the height of pseudo-levels in the hierarchies, if $(l_1^a, l_2^c) \in M$ and $(l_1^b, l_2^d) \in M$, then $(b \geq a \rightarrow d \geq c)$ or $(b < a \rightarrow d < c)$ (no "crossings" in M, such as $((l_1^{231}, l_2^{303})$ with $(l_1^{230}, l_2^{304}))$.

To produce this mapping, our simple algorithm is the following. We initialize M and two pointers with the two highest pseudo-levels $((l_1^{231}, l_2^{304})$, step 1 of Fig. 2). At each step, for each hierarchy, we consider current pointers and their children, and compute all their similarities (step 2). We then add pseudo-levels with maximal similarity to M (here, (l_1^{230}, l_2^{303})). Whenever a child is chosen, the respective pointer advances, and at each step, at least one pointer advances. Once pseudo-levels have been consumed on one side, ending with l, we can finish the process by adding (l^f, l) to M for all remaining pseudo-level l' on the other side (here, $l = l_1^{230}$. On our example, the final matching is $M = \{(l_1^{231}, l_2^{304}), (l_1^{230}, l_2^{303}), (l_1^{230}, l_2^{302}), (l_1^{230}, l_2^{301}), (l_1^{230}, l_2^{300}), (l_1^{230}, l_2^{299})\}$.

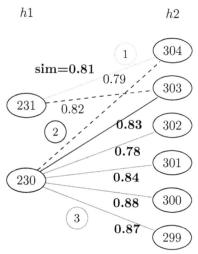

Fig. 2. Computing the similarity between two quasi-dendograms h_1 and h_2 for levels having the same number of clusters.

Finally, from (2) we define the similarity between two hierarchies as

$$sim(h_1, h_2) = mean\{sim_l^*(l_1, l_2) | (l_1, l_2) \in (h_1, h_2) \ \& \ (l_1, l_2) \in M\}. \quad (3)$$

3.3 Experimental Results

Expressiveness: With this small following example we would like to present the expressiveness of our algorithm compared to classical hierarchical clustering algorithms such as *SLINK*. On the hand-built example shown in Fig. 3a we can clearly distinguish two groups of points, $\{A, B, C, D, E\}$ and $\{G, H, I, J, K\}$ and two points that we can consider as noise, F and L. Due to the chaining effect we expect that the *SLINK* algorithm will regroup the 2 sets of points early in the hierarchy while we would like to prevent it by allowing some cluster overlaps.

Figure 3b shows the dendrogram computed by *SLINK* and we can see as expected that when F merges with the cluster formed by $\{A, B, C, D, E\}$ the next step is to merge this new cluster with $\{G, H, I, J, K\}$.

On the contrary in Fig. 4 that presents the hierarchy built with our method for a specific merging criterion, we can see an example of diamond shape that

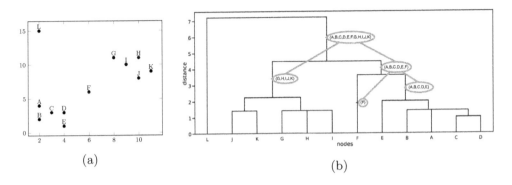

Fig. 3. A hand-built example (a) and its *SLINK* dendrogram (b).

is specific to our quasi-dendrogram. For simplicity the view here slightly differs from the quasi-dendrogram definition as we used dashed arrows to represent the provenance of some elements of a cluster instead of going further down in hierarchy to have a perfect inclusion and respect the lattice-like structure. The merge between the clusters $\{A, B, C, D, E\}$ and $\{G, H, I, J, K\}$ is delayed to the very last moment and the point F will belong to these 2 clusters instead of forcing them to merge. Also depending on the merging criterion we obtain different hierarchical structures by merging earlier of later some clusters.

Merging Criterion: As we can see in Fig. 5b when the merging criterion increases we obtain a hierarchy more and more similar to the one produced by the classical *SLINK* algorithm until we obtain exactly the same for a merging criterion of 1. Knowing this fact it is also normal to have a similarity between OHC and *Ward* (resp. *HDBSCAN**) hierarchies converging to the similarity between *SLINK* and *Ward* (resp. *HDBSCAN**) hierarchies. However we can notice that the OHC and *Ward* hierarchies are the most similar for a merging criterion smaller than 1.

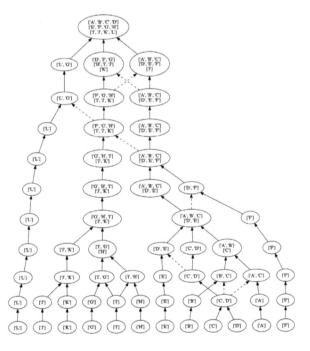

Fig. 4. *OHC* quasi-dendrogram obtained from the hand-built example in Fig. 3a for $\lambda = 0.2$.

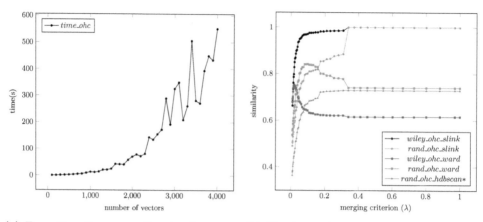

(a) Execution time according to the number of vectors.

(b) Similarity between hierarchical structures according to the merging criterion.

Fig. 5. Study of the merging criterion.

Execution Time: We observe that when the merging criterion increases the execution time decreases. It is due to the fact that when the merging criterion increases we are more likely to completely merge clusters so we reach faster the top of the hierarchy. It means less levels and less overlapping clusters so less computation. However in this case we have the same drawback of chaining effect as the single-linkage clustering that we wanted to avoid. Even if it was not the objective of this work we set $\lambda = 0.1$, as it is an interesting value according to the study of the merging criterion (Fig. 5a), to observe the evolution of the execution time (Fig. 5a). The trend gives a function in $O(n^{2.45})$ so to speed up the process and scale up our algorithm is it possible to precompute a set of possibly overlapping clusters over a given δ-neighbourhood graph with a classical method, for instance CLIQUE, and build the OHC hierarchy on top of that.

4   Related Work

Our goal is to group together data points represented as vectors in $\mathbb{R}^n$. For our motivating application domain of understanding the structure of scientific fields, it is important to construct structures (i) that are hierarchical, (ii) that allow overlaps between the identified groups of vectors and (iii) which groups (clusters) are related to dense areas of the data. There are a number of other application domains where obtaining a structure with these properties is important. In the following, we relate our work to relevant literature.

Hierarchical Clustering: There exist two kinds of hierarchical clustering. Divisive methods follow a top-down strategy while agglomerative techniques compute the hierarchy in a bottom-up fashion. It produces the well known dendrogram structure [1]. One of the oldest methods is the single-linkage clustering that first appeared in the work of *Florek et al.* [18]. It had many improvements over the years until an optimal algorithm named *SLINK* proposed by *Sibson* [28]. However the commonly cited drawback of the single-linkage clustering is that it is not robust to noise and suffers from chaining effects (spurious points merging clusters prematurely). It led to the invention of many variants with their advantages and disadvantages. In the NLP world we have for instance the *Brown clustering* [7] and its generalized version [13]. The drawback of choosing the number of clusters beforehand present in the original Brown clustering is corrected in the generalized version. Researchers also tried to address directly the chaining effect problem with approaches through defining new objective functions such as the *Robust Hierarchical Clustering* [4,11]. However these variants do not allow any overlaps in the clusters. Other variants tried to allow this fuzzy clustering in the hierarchy such as *SOHC* [10], a hierarchical clustering based on a spatial overlapping metric but with a fixed number of clusters, or *HCOSM* [26], that use an overlap similarity measure to merge clusters and then compute a hierarchy from an already determined set of clusters. Generalization of dendrogram to more complex structures like *Pyramidal Clustering* [15] and *Weak Hierarchies* [5] were also proposed. We can find examples to prove that our method produces even more general hierarchical structures that include the weak hierarchies.

Density-Based Clustering: Another important class of work is the density-based clustering. Here, clusters are defined as regions in the data that have a higher density. The data points in the sparse areas that are required to separate clusters are considered as noise or border points. One of the most widely-used algorithms of this category is *DBSCAN* defined by *Ester et al.* [17]. This method connects data points that satisfy a specific density-based criterion: the minimum number of other data points within a given radius must be above a predefined threshold. The main advantage of this method is that it allows detecting clusters of arbitrary shapes. More recently improved versions of *DBSCAN* were proposed such as *HDBSCAN** [8]. This new variant not only improved notions from *DBSCAN* and *OPTICS* [3] but also proposed a procedure to extract a simplified cluster tree from the reachability relation which allows determining a hierarchy of the clusters but again with no overlapping.

Overlapping Clustering: Fuzzy clustering methods [6] allow that certain data points belong to multiple clusters with a different level of confidence. In this way, the boundary of clusters is fuzzy and we can talk about overlaps of these clusters. In our definition it is a different notion, a data point either does or does not belong to a specific cluster and might also belong to multiple clusters. While *HDBSCAN* is closely related to connected components of certain level sets, the clusters do not overlap (since overlap would imply the connectivity).

Community Detection in Networks: A number of algorithmic methods have been proposed to identify communities. The first kind of methods produces a partition where a vertex can belong to one and only one community. Following the *modularity* function of *Newman and Girvan* [24], numerous quality functions have been proposed to evaluate the goodness of a partition with a fundamental drawback, the now proved existence of a resolution limit. The second kind of methods, such as *CLIQUE* [2], *k-clique* [25], *DBLC* [31] or *NMF* [30], aims at finding sets of vertices that respect an edge density criterion which allows overlaps but can lead to incomplete cover of the network. Similarly to *HCOSM*, the method *EAGLE* [27] builds a dendrogram over the set of predetermined clusters, here the maximal cliques of the network so overlaps appear only at the leaf level. Coscia et al. [12] have proposed an algorithm to reconstruct a hierarchical and overlapping community structure of a network, by hierarchically merging local ego neighbourhoods.

5   Conclusion and Future Work

We propose an overlapping hierarchical clustering framework. We construct a quasi-dendrogram hierarchical structure to represent the clusters that is however not necessarily a tree (of specific shape) but a directed acyclic graph. In this way, at each level, we represent a set of possibly overlapping clusters. We experimentally evaluated our method using several datasets and also our new similarity measure that hence proved its usefulness. If the clusters present in the data show no overlaps, the obtained clusters are identical to the clusters we can compute using agglomerative clustering methods. In case of overlapping and nested clusters, however, our method results in a richer representation that can contain relevant information about the structure of the clusters of the underlying dataset. As a future work we plan to identify interesting clusters on the basis of the concept of stability. Such methods give promising results in the context of hierarchical density-based clustering [21], but the presences of overlaps in the clusters requires specific considerations.

References

1. Achtert, E.: Hierarchical subspace clustering. Ph.D. thesis, LMU (2007)
2. Agrawal, R., Gehrke, J., Gunopulos, D., Raghavan, P.: Automatic subspace clustering of high dimensional data. Data Min. Knowl. Disc. **11**(1), 5–33 (2005)
3. Ankerst, M., Breunig, M.M., Kriegel, H.P., Sander, J.: OPTICS: ordering points to identify the clustering structure. In: ACM SIGMOD Record, vol. 28, pp. 49–60. ACM (1999)
4. Balcan, M.F., Liang, Y., Gupta, P.: Robust hierarchical clustering. J. Mach. Learn. Res. **15**(1), 3831–3871 (2014)
5. Bandelt, H.J., Dress, A.W.: Weak hierarchies associated with similarity measures- an additive clustering technique. Bull. Math. Biol. **51**(1), 133–166 (1989). https://doi.org/10.1007/BF02458841
6. Bezdek, James C.: Pattern Recognition with Fuzzy Objective Function Algorithms. Springer, Boston (1981)

7. Brown, P.F., Desouza, P.V., Mercer, R.L., Pietra, V.J.D., Lai, J.C.: Class-based n-gram models of natural language. Comput. Linguist. **18**(4), 467–479 (1992)
8. Campello, R.J., Moulavi, D., Zimek, A., Sander, J.: Hierarchical density estimates for data clustering, visualization, and outlier detection. ACM Trans. Knowl. Discov. Data (TKDD) **10**(1), 5 (2015)
9. Chavalarias, D., Cointet, J.P.: Phylomemetic patterns in science evolution - the rise and fall of scientific fields. PloS One **8**(2), e54847 (2013)
10. Chen, H., Guo, G., Huang, Y., Huang, T.: A spatial overlapping based similarity measure applied to hierarchical clustering. In: Fuzzy Systems and Knowledge Discovery (FSKD 2008), vol. 2, pp. 371–375. IEEE (2008)
11. Cohen-Addad, V., Kanade, V., Mallmann-Trenn, F., Mathieu, C.: Hierarchical clustering: objective functions and algorithms. In: Proceedings of the 29th Annual ACM-SIAM Symposium on Discrete Algorithms, pp. 378–397. SIAM (2018)
12. Coscia, M., Rossetti, G., Giannotti, F., Pedreschi, D.: Uncovering hierarchical and overlapping communities with a local-first approach. ACM Trans. Knowl. Discov. Data **9**(1), 6:1–6:27 (2014)
13. Derczynski, L., Chester, S.: Generalised brown clustering and roll-up feature generation. In: AAAI, pp. 1533–1539 (2016)
14. Dias, L., Gerlach, M., Scharloth, J., Altmann, E.G.: Using text analysis to quantify the similarity and evolution of scientific disciplines. R. Soc. Open Sci. **5**(1), 171545 (2018)
15. Diday, E.: Une représentation visuelle des classes empiétantes: les pyramides (1984)
16. Diestel, R.: Graph Theory. Graduate Texts in Mathematics, vol. 101 (2005)
17. Ester, M., Kriegel, H.P., Sander, J., Xu, X., et al.: A density-based algorithm for discovering clusters in large spatial databases with noise. In: KDD, vol. 96, pp. 226–231 (1996)
18. Florek, K., Łukaszewicz, J., Perkal, J., Steinhaus, H., Zubrzycki, S.: Sur la liaison et la division des points d'un ensemble fini. In: Colloquium Mathematicae, vol. 2, p. 282 (1951)
19. Fowlkes, E.B., Mallows, C.L.: A method for comparing two hierarchical clusterings. J. Am. Stat. Assoc. **78**(383), 553–569 (1983)
20. Levy, O., Goldberg, Y., Dagan, I.: Improving distributional similarity with lessons learned from word embeddings. Trans. Assoc. Comput. Linguist. **3**, 211–225 (2015)
21. McInnes, L., Healy, J.: Accelerated hierarchical density based clustering. In: 2017 IEEE International Conference on Data Mining Workshops (ICDMW), pp. 33–42. IEEE (2017)
22. Mikolov, T., Chen, K., Corrado, G., Dean, J.: Efficient estimation of word representations in vector space. arXiv preprint arXiv:1301.3781 (2013)
23. Mikolov, T., Sutskever, I., Chen, K., Corrado, G.S., Dean, J.: Distributed representations of words and phrases and their compositionality. In: Advances in Neural Information Processing Systems, pp. 3111–3119 (2013)
24. Newman, M.E., Girvan, M.: Finding and evaluating community structure in networks. Phys. Rev. E **69**(2), 026113 (2004)
25. Palla, G., Derényi, I., Farkas, I., Vicsek, T.: Uncovering the overlapping community structure of complex networks in nature and society. Nature **435**(7043), 814 (2005)
26. Qu, J., Jiang, Q., Weng, F., Hong, Z.: A hierarchical clustering based on overlap similarity measure. In: Eighth ACIS International Conference on Software Engineering, Artificial Intelligence, Networking, and Parallel/Distributed Computing (SNPD 2007), vol. 3, pp. 905–910. IEEE (2007)
27. Shen, H., Cheng, X., Cai, K., Hu, M.B.: Detect overlapping and hierarchical community structure in networks. Phys. A: Stat. Mech. Appl. **388**(8), 1706–1712 (2009)

28. Sibson, R.: SLINK: an optimally efficient algorithm for the single-link cluster method. Comput. J. **16**(1), 30–34 (1973)
29. Ward Jr., J.H.: Hierarchical grouping to optimize an objective function. J. Am. Stat. Assoc. **58**(301), 236–244 (1963)
30. Yang, J., Leskovec, J.: Overlapping community detection at scale: a nonnegative matrix factorization approach. In: Proceedings of the Sixth ACM International Conference on Web Search and Data Mining, pp. 587–596. ACM (2013)
31. Zhou, X., Liu, Y., Wang, J., Li, C.: A density based link clustering algorithm for overlapping community detection in networks. Phys. A: Stat. Mech. Appl. **486**, 65–78 (2017)

Permissions

List of Contributors

Micky Faas and Matthijs van Leeuwen
LIACS, Leiden University, Leiden, The Netherlands

Laura Isabel Galindez Olascoaga, Nimish Shah and Marian Verhelst
Electrical Engineering Department, KU Leuven, Leuven, Belgium

Wannes Meert
Computer Science Department, KU Leuven, Leuven, Belgium

Guy Van den Broeck
Computer Science Department, University of California, Los Angeles, USA

Clément Gautrais
Department of Computer Science, KU Leuven, Leuven, Belgium

Peggy Cellier and Alexandre Termier
Univ Rennes, Inria, INSA, CNRS, IRISA, Rennes, France

Biraja Ghoshal and Allan Tucker
Brunel University London, Uxbridge UB8 3PH, UK

Cecilia Lindskog
Department of Immunology, Genetics and Pathology, Rudbeck Laboratory, Uppsala University, 75185 Uppsala, Sweden

Jisu Kim
Scuola Normale Superiore, Pisa, Italy

Alina Sîrbu
University of Pisa, Pisa, Italy

Fosca Giannotti and Lorenzo Gabrielli
Istituto di Scienza e Tecnologie dell'Informazione, National Research Council of Italy, Pisa, Italy

Chang Liu, Osmar R. Zaïane and Shiva Zamani Gharaghooshi
Alberta Machine Intelligence Institute, University of Alberta, Edmonton, Canada

Christine Largeron
Laboratoire Hubert Curien, Université de Lyon, Saint-Etienne, France

Alexandre Millot and Jean-François Boulicaut
Univ de Lyon, CNRS, INSA Lyon, LIRIS, UMR5205, 69621 Villeurbanne, France

Romain Mathonat
Univ de Lyon, CNRS, INSA Lyon, LIRIS, UMR5205, 69621 Villeurbanne, France
Atos, 69100 Villeurbanne, France

Rémy Cazabet
Univ de Lyon, CNRS, Université Lyon 1, LIRIS, UMR5205, 69622 Villeurbanne, France

Dimitar Ninevski and Paul O'Leary
University of Leoben, 8700 Leoben, Austria

Mohammad Hossein Shaker and Eyke Hüllermeier
Heinz Nixdorf Institute and Department of Computer Science, Paderborn University, Paderborn, Germany

Maximilian Stubbemann and Gerd Stumme
L3S Research Center, Leibniz University of Hannover, Hannover, Germany
Knowledge and Data Engineering Group, University of Kassel, Kassel, Germany

Tom Hanika
Knowledge and Data Engineering Group, University of Kassel, Kassel, Germany

Tom Julian Viering and Alexander Mey
Delft University of Technology, Delft, The Netherlands

Marco Loog
Delft University of Technology, Delft, The Netherlands
University of Copenhagen, Copenhagen, Denmark

Ayman Alazizi
Univ. Lyon, Univ. St-Etienne, UMR CNRS 5516, Laboratoire Hubert-Curien, 42000 Saint-Etienne, France
Worldline, 95870 Bezons, France

Amaury Habrard and François Jacquenet
Univ. Lyon, Univ. St-Etienne, UMR CNRS 5516, Laboratoire Hubert-Curien, 42000 Saint-Etienne, France

Liyun He-Guelton and Frédéric Oblé
Worldline, 95870 Bezons, France

Tien-Dung Nguyen, Tomasz Maszczyk, Katarzyna Musial and Bogdan Gabrys
University of Technology Sydney, Sydney, Australia

Marc-André Zöller
USU Software AG, Karlsruhe, Germany

Abdullah Al Safi, Christian Beyer, Vishnu Unnikrishnan and Myra Spiliopoulou
Fakultät für Informatik, Otto-von-Guericke-Universität, Postfach 4120, 39106 Magdeburg, Germany

Francesco Bariatti, Peggy Cellier and Sébastien Ferré
Univ Rennes, INSA, CNRS, IRISA, Campus de Beaulieu, Rennes, France

Anes Bendimerad and Céline Robardet
Univ Lyon, INSA, CNRS UMR 5205, 69621 Villeurbanne, France

Jefrey Lijffijt and Tijl De Bie
IDLab, ELIS Department, Ghent University, Ghent, Belgium

Marc Plantevit
Univ Lyon, UCBL, CNRS UMR 5205, 69621 Lyon, France

Jeroen van Doorenmalen and Vlado Menkovski
Eindhoven University of Technology, Eindhoven, The Netherlands

Shiva Zamani Gharaghooshi, Osmar R. Zaïane, Mohammadmahdi Zafarmand and Chang Liu
Alberta Machine Intelligence Institute, University of Alberta, Edmonton, AB, Canada

Ian Jeantet, Zoltán Miklós and David Gross-Amblard
Univ Rennes, CNRS, IRISA, Rennes, France

Index

A

Anomaly Detection, 141-142, 144, 149-150, 152-153
Antibody-based Proteomics, 40-41, 51
Arithmetic Circuits, 14, 26
Attributed Networks, 65-67, 76-77

B

Bayesian Network, 15, 17, 25
Beam Search, 27-28, 33, 38
Big Data, 52-54, 63
Binary Attributes, 66, 68-69, 73, 76, 157
Boolean Data, 1, 3

C

Cell Type Prediction, 40
Code Length Analysis, 36-37
Community Detection, 65-67, 69, 71, 73-77, 218-219, 222, 226, 228-229, 239, 242
Community Structure, 65, 69, 77, 228-229, 240-241
Cutset Networks, 14

D

Data Analysis, 77, 91, 230
Data Collection, 54-55, 60
Data Mining, 1, 12-13, 27, 79, 89, 116, 124, 153, 166, 190-191, 203, 241-242
Decision Diagrams, 14, 16, 25-26
Decision Node, 16-17, 19
Deep Learning Models, 42, 168
Discontinuity Detection, 91, 102
Discriminative Bias, 14, 17, 19-22, 24

E

Early Fusion, 65
Encoded Length, 29-31, 33
Encoding, 6-7, 17, 21, 24, 27, 29-33, 36-37, 148-149, 152, 169-170, 181, 183-185, 189

F

Fault-tolerant Patterns, 2, 12

Feature Variables, 14-15, 17-20
Fraud Detection, 141-143, 145, 149, 151-152
Free-knot Splines, 91

G

Geometric Matrices, 1, 12
Geometric Pattern, 1-3, 7, 12
Greedy Algorithm, 7, 33

H

Heuristic Approach, 7
Human Protein Atlas, 40, 46-47

I

Instance Matrix, 5, 7-9
Instantiation Matrix, 5-6, 8
Intelligent Data, 77
International Migration, 52-53, 63-64

L

Late-fusion, 65-68, 70-76
Late-fusion Approach, 65-68, 74, 76
Learning Curve, 129-131, 133, 137-139
Learning Models, 14, 42, 129, 168, 207
Learning Tasks, 14, 202
Learning Theory, 129, 140
Lexicographical Order, 5, 8, 10
Local Structure, 1-2
Logarithms, 7, 9, 31
Logistic Regression, 20-21, 25, 124-126

M

Machine Learning, 14, 21, 25, 48, 51, 79, 85, 103-106, 114-117, 128-129, 140-142, 152, 154, 159, 166, 168, 178, 190, 202, 205, 207, 216
Median Thresholding, 68, 73
Metric Spaces, 116-117, 119-122, 126
Minimum Description Length, 1-2, 13, 27-30, 38-39, 179-180, 190
Model Selection, 2, 6, 28-30, 38-39, 129, 131, 133, 139-140, 190
Monotonicity, 129-132, 135-140

Multi-label Classification, 40-43, 46-48, 50-51

N
Naive Algorithm, 33, 36-37, 186
Naive Bayes, 17, 21-22, 25
Node Connections, 65, 67, 76
Numeric Attributes, 67, 69, 72, 76, 157-158, 161

O
Original Matrix, 4
Orometric Methods, 116

P
Pattern Lengths, 9
Pattern Mining, 1-3, 7, 12, 29-30, 33, 39, 81, 89, 179, 181, 190-192, 202-204
Postprocessing Model, 74, 76
Probabilistic Models, 14, 21, 25, 67
Probabilistic Sentential, 14, 16, 25-26
Probabilistic Sentential Decision, 14, 16, 25-26
Proteomics, 40-41, 51

R
Random Forest, 104, 110-111, 115
Raster-based Data, 1, 3, 12
Root Decision, 17, 19

S
Sequential Data, 141, 146, 150-151

Signal-to-noise Ratio, 10-11
Signature Discovery, 27
Signature Patterns, 27-28, 38
Statistical Analysis, 12, 178
Subgroup Discovery, 78-83, 85-86, 88-90
Sum-product Networks, 14, 25-26
Symposium, 51, 77, 178, 241
Synthetic Data, 3, 12, 93, 99, 200, 231
Synthetic Networks, 65, 69-70, 224, 226-227
Synthetic Patterns, 10

T
Tractable Inference, 14
Traditional Data, 27, 52-53
Tree Augmented Naive Bayes, 17, 21

U
Uncertainty Estimation, 40, 46, 51, 115

V
Variational Autoencoder, 141, 144, 147, 149, 205, 215-216
Virtuous Circle, 78, 81, 83, 88-89
Vouw Algorithm, 7, 11

W
Wikidata, 116, 118, 122-123, 126-128

Printed in the USA
CPSIA information can be obtained
at www.ICGtesting.com
JSHW051409221024
72173JS00006B/1326